THE EMOTIONS OF PROTEST

THE EMOTIONS OF PROTEST

JAMES M. JASPER

The University of Chicago Press
Chicago and London

The University of Chicago Press, Chicago 60637
The University of Chicago Press, Ltd., London
© 2018 by The University of Chicago
Published 2018
Printed and bound by CPI Group (UK) Ltd,
Croydon, CR0 4YY

27 26 25 24 23 22 21 20 19 18   1 2 3 4 5

ISBN-13: 978-0-226-56164-6 (cloth)
ISBN-13: 978-0-226-56178-3 (paper)
ISBN-13: 978-0-226-56181-3 (e-book)
DOI: https://doi.org/10.7208/chicago/9780226561813.001.0001

Library of Congress Cataloging-in-Publication Data

Names: Jasper, James M., 1957– author.
Title: The emotions of protest / James M. Jasper.
Description: Chicago ; London : The University of Chicago
Press, 2018. | Includes bibliographical references and index.
Identifiers: LCCN 2017054084 | ISBN 9780226561646
(cloth : alk. paper) | ISBN 9780226561783 (pbk. : alk. paper) |
ISBN 9780226561813 (e-book)
Subjects: LCSH: Emotional intelligence. | Emotions—Political
aspects. | Political psychology.
Classification: LCC BF576 .J387 2018 | DDC 152.4—dc23
LC record available at https://lccn.loc.gov/2017054084

For
Naomi Gerstel
Robert Zussman
Mary Clare Lennon
Ian Roxborough
Judy Gerson

*No one ever had a simple sensation by itself. Conscious-
ness, from our natal day, is of a teeming multiplicity of
objects and relations, and what we call simply sensations are results of discriminative attention, pushed
often to a very high degree.*

WILLIAM JAMES

CONTENTS

CONTENTS

PREFACE

My first political protest was against apartheid, which in 1978 was emerging as the favorite cause on college campuses. None of my friends were involved, but after devouring Marxist and anti-imperialist books for a couple years I had come to see this struggle as a fundamental moral issue. I went to my first march, a picket line around the building where the university trustees were meeting, after seeing a poster in my dormitory.

It was fun to shout in unison and march to chants such as "Two, four, six, eight: don't support the racist state," a classic cadence adapted to a new cause. It felt good in a deeper way as well, a satisfaction that persisted—even increased—as the line thinned out and I felt mostly alone shouting at occasional scholarly passersby, who looked confused and embarrassed. The disagreeable feelings of vulnerability and rudeness somehow intensified the deep moral satisfaction, which included a tinge of self-righteousness (I was twenty years old). But it was also a relief when we regrouped into a tighter crowd to hear a speech. I probably went to a dozen such events in my final three semesters of college. Shy, I rarely talked to other participants and made no friends among the increasingly familiar faces. (And contrary to some theories of recruitment, I was not hoping to meet a girl, although I did have a crush on the group's brilliant leader Gay Seidman.)

I suppose we thought we would win—eventually. But in the year or two after the Soweto uprising and Steve Biko's murder, the end of apartheid seemed a long way off. As indeed it was. But a tinge of frustration merely strengthened my angry indignation. Instead of divesting, Harvard gave a degree to Bishop Desmond Tutu and a fellowship to the exiled anti-apartheid journalist Donald Woods. Getting to know Woods bolstered my knowledge about South Africa but had little effect either way on my already-high enthusiasm for protest.

Today there are many theories of why protest happens but few theories of why and how protest *feels good*. To the contrary, most scholars still assume that it feels bad, a cost to be paid to achieve some other end. It *is* often costly or painful, just as it is often exciting and pleasurable. Sometimes it is both at once, or in quick succession, along with a dozen other things that protest makes us feel. To understand these processes, we need to untangle the complex feelings that are central to all human action. A generation of scholars detailed the economic and political structures that constrain human endeavor, but they paid less attention to the players who act within those structures. When people did appear, it was frequently as calculating maximizers of self-interest. A new generation of scholars is developing better theories of political action, and emotions are part of such theories. It is an exciting time for theories of protest.

In my previous work on protest and politics, I have tried to bring common sense and straightforward language to scholarly models that sometimes lack them. Scholars once worked hard to ignore the emotions that pervade social and political life. I have countered with a number of concepts for understanding emotions, especially in *The Art of Moral Protest*, published in 1997, which contributed to a wave of research on emotions and protest. Today I think we still need a book that sums up what we know, offers some fruitful distinctions, points us in some new directions, and links the emotions of protest and politics with those of action more generally.

Scholars love to call for this or that—"bringing X back in"—without doing the hard work to show what X is, or why it matters. Twenty years ago this was the status of emotions, which appeared occasionally in critiques of other theories of action, especially of rational choice theories. Today it is still true, some claim, of the body. Maurice Merleau-Ponty said sixty years ago that we are embodied, but we still don't know much about what that means or how we should view action differently because we are embodied. Others point to "affect" as a mysterious force but have not broken it down into manageable mechanisms for us to observe. Scholars of social movements have acknowledged emotions by pairing the word with familiar terms—emotional communities, emotional habitus, emotional liberation, emotional resources—but we need to push further by specifying the concrete emotions at work in all these.

Psychologists have showed how emotions help us operate in the world, help us think and orient ourselves, and prepare us for action. At the very least, most contribute to a form of "fast thinking." This book asks what this new image of feelings means for our understanding of protest and politics. Some political action requires quick decisions, guided by intuition and emotion. But a lot of politics requires slow thinking, unfolding through long meetings but also sustaining years of hard work at a cause. Here, too, it turns out, emotions guide us. Some feelings are forms of slow thinking, related to long-run solidarities, moral convictions, and our cognitive maps of the world and its challenges.

We know a lot about specific emotions, but attempts to make general statements about them—although plentiful—have largely failed. Whenever I read a statement beginning "emotions are . . ." or "What emotions do . . . ," I immediately think of exceptions. This book tries to find a middle path between treating dozens or hundreds of emotions separately and, on the other hand, seeking statements that apply to all of them. I offer what I hope is a useful classification of types that feel similar, so that we can move beyond crude talk about "emotions" and instead discuss reflex emotions, urges, moods, affective solidarities, and moral emotions.

Protestors are often described—explicitly by their opponents but implicitly by investigators who should know better—as "bleeding hearts." The contemptuous image is of involuntary and ineffectual activity, unaided by hard thinking. I hope to show that our feelings are mostly ways of processing information, orienting ourselves to the world, signaling to others, and preparing ourselves for purposive action. I use the awkward neologism *feeling-thinking processes* to try to break us out of an old habit of *contrasting* feeling and thinking, which our mind falls into whenever we use the two words separately. Feeling-thinking processes consist of dozens of bodily processes and mental constructs: biochemistry, memories, muscle contractions, facial expressions, sensory input, verbal labels for our emotions. These permeate our action and awareness. (I have declined Eviatar Zerubavel's enthusiastic suggestion that I call them "finkings" or "theelings," which I fear would just not catch on.)

For two thousand years scholars have dismissed protestors as irrational by focusing on two emotions above all, fear and anger. This encouraged a *panic model* of emotions, the dark flip side of the exaggerated *calculating-brain model* of thought and rationality. As we come to appreciate the full range of emotions, we will see how distorted these exemplars are, because fear and anger, a subset of reflex emotions, are the emotions most likely to lead to regret and disruption, compared to the dozens of other relevant emotions. They are a misleading paradigm for understanding the impact of emotions on politics (just as the calculating brain is a poor model of how we think, precisely because it excludes our feelings).

A number of people have given me suggestions, sometimes without knowing it, for improvements to the articles and chapters in which I have thought out many of the ideas in this book. The participants in the 1999 conference on emotions that led to the publication of *Passionate Politics* greatly advanced my understanding of emotions, including several whose work did not appear in the final volume, such as Patricia Clough, Helena Flam, Chuck Tilly, and Guobin Yang. I also thank Yohan Ariffin, Jack Barbalet, Colin Barker, Louis Esparza, Geir Flikke, John Hall, David Heise, Hank Johnston, Farhad Khosrokhavar, John Krinsky, Charlie Kurzman,

Ned Lebow, Bleuwenn Lechaux, Roger Masters, Nonna Mayer, Emma Naughton, Erik Neveu, Frances Fox Piven, Geoffrey Pleyers, Sarah Rosenfield, Steven Scanlan, Tom Scheff, Johanna Siméant, Verta Taylor, Alain Touraine, Christophe Traïni, and dozens of participants in audiences where I have given talks in the past decade. I have learned the most from collaborations with Jeff Goodwin and Francesca Polletta, who coauthored some of the previous articles; I have shamelessly borrowed their ideas and no doubt some of their phrases. I've also learned a lot from kind critics such as Debbie Gould, Cristina Flesher Fominaya, and Isabelle Sommier. Marisa Tramontano and Kevin Moran were tireless research assistants. Johanna Siméant, Isabelle Sommier, Christophe Traïni, Carissa Véliz, and Robert Zussman (twice!) gave me marvelous comments on earlier drafts, as did two spirited reviewers for the press. I began this book at the Netherlands Institute for Advanced Study (NIAS) in Wassenaar and finished the final edits at the Scuola Normale Superiore in Florence, and I thank NIAS, Donatella della Porta, and Lorenzo Bosi for hosting me. The Politics and Protest Workshop, as usual, pointed out more failings than I have been able to fix, always in a gentle, witty, but assertive way. The Graduate Center of the City University of New York has proved a fruitful intellectual home since 2007. Doug Mitchell has been persevering, serene, exasperated, hungry, cajoling, loyal, proud, anxious, and relieved across the many years this book took, and I love him for all those feelings.

When I met my wife, Sarah, in 1992, her dowry included five friends who soon became my own good friends as well. I dedicate this book to Naomi Gerstel, Robert Zussman, Mary Clare Lennon, Ian Roxborough, and Judy Gerson. They have surprised me (reflex emotions), provided me with food and drink (urges), put me in good moods, and imparted moral advice and inspiration. Above all, they have defined for me the solidarities of friendship.

Palazzo Strozzi, May 2017

INTRODUCTION: THINKING HEARTS

The heart has its reasons which reason does not understand.

PASCAL

Only a passion can triumph over a passion.

HELVÉTIUS

In the usual view, emotions well up from within us, take control over our actions, and interrupt whatever we have been doing; they lead us to do things that we later regret and disrupt the ways in which we are cooperating and coordinating with others. They are irrational, or lead us to be irrational. Western thinkers since Plato have elaborated on this image, and even today reporters and politicians contrast emotions and thought in their coverage and arguments. Some version of this distinction has done enormous work throughout the history of politics and philosophy.

Since the 1980s, psychologists, neurologists, and other social scientists have developed a different view of emotions, which portrays them as helpful rather than harmful; as ways of processing information about the world more rapidly than our conscious brains could; as means of communicating with others and of judging how things are unfolding for us at any given moment. Emotions can be helpful, functional, sometimes even wise. They include long-term orientations to the world, which tell us what we care about, as well as short-run reactions that carry some potential for regret.

Although the balance of evidence favors the new view, there is some truth to both images. In addition to their information and communications functions, we sometimes manage our emotions in order to take advantage of their immediacy, their urgency, and their apparent irrationality. We use them to motivate ourselves. We place ourselves in situations that we know or hope will make us angry or joyful, in order to feel that we have been taken over by passion. And we use these feelings to convince others that we care deeply. But this is not simply acting: we really do feel strongly, we really do feel as if our emotions have a logic of their own outside our control. Because they do. These episodes of passion have a place in our most cognitive, considered lines of action.

In this book I ask what this image of emotions—stage-managed and planned, but also dangerous and out of control—means for protest and political action. A wave of research into protest and emotions has already shown us a great deal about the advantages of emotions, reflecting the new psychology, but the reaction against the old view of emotions as irrational may have gone too far. Emotions are part of all action, good and bad, successful and unsuccessful. They are a normal part of action, and we no longer have to assume a normative stance—against or for—emotions when we analyze them.

Social movements and other collective efforts have long been a kind of laboratory for working out theories of social action, human goals and agency, the constraints of structure or culture, and other basic theoretical issues. Emotions are no exception: the world of protest is proving a real-world testing ground for all sorts of feelings that have been observed in the labs of behavioral economists and the surveys of social psychologists. This book ambitiously aims for a dialogue between two vast literatures, one on emotions, the other on social movements and protest. At stake, ultimately, is nothing less than a theory of action.

My starting assumption is that politics, like all strategic action, is full of trade-offs and dilemmas, so that any path of action carries with it a bundle of potential risks, costs, and benefits. There will be bad results as well as good, unforeseen consequences as well as anticipated ones, complex combinations of gains and losses at the same time.[1] This is as true of emotions as it is of resources or laws. There will be dozens of unpleasant feelings as well as pleasant ones. Some will help get us what we want, while others lead us astray. I will describe two main categories of emotional trade-offs, in which what feels good at the moment may lead to later regret, and in which what feels good for an individual is not necessarily good—and perhaps disruptive—for a collectivity. I dub these *regretful* and *disruptive* emotional dynamics.

Even more centrally, I try to show how short-run, medium-run, and long-run emotions interact with each other. Social movements articulate our moral visions and group allegiances through our feelings as well as thoughts, and especially by moving back and forth across distinct types of emotions. We have many stable convictions—about places, people, ideas, and what is better and worse morally—that form the background to emotional reactions, urges, and moods. And those temporary feelings are elaborated, amplified, and stabilized through symbols, artifacts, and ideologies that are the main product of movements. They are still feelings, but a different kind of feeling from momentary anger or shock.

*　*　*

Research into emotions, although flourishing in recent years, leads a kind of schizoid existence. Traditions that rely on natural-science models of inquiry have crafted precise operational definitions of variables, elaborated techniques for measuring brain and body activity, and developed formal models of relationships and effects. With a few exceptions, they have also restricted themselves to narrow corners of human reality. So a parallel tradition has emerged that uses emotion terms more loosely, deploys fuzzier techniques such as introspection and observation, and grandly recognizes that emotions color all social life. One tradition focuses on physiology, the other on cultural labels. Natural scientists seem solidly in one camp and humanities scholars in the other, while social scientists are split between the two. I hope to add a bit of the rigor of the former to the humanistic ambition of the latter. People's subjectivity is central, even though we must link it to physiological processes inside each individual and to our social settings and interactions with others.

Emotions are everywhere. They influence our goals, even as—or especially as—the goals shift in response to circumstances. Emotions also affect our choices about means to pursue those goals, since means are never neutral choices about efficiency but have emotional reverberations themselves. (In other words, we have tastes in tactics). Emotional dynamics can also show us how accomplishments in one round of interaction become the means deployed in the next round, bending our usual means–ends logic. In the form of moods, emotions influence how attentive to or distracted from politics we are, how much energy we bring to it, and how much we enjoy it. We additionally divide the world into those we love, like, hate, trust, respect, and so on, according to an emotional logic. Finally, morality influences us, when it does, through our feelings of shame, pride, compassion, and more.

Even this brief list indicates the diverse feelings, provocations, and engagements that fall under the general rubric of *emotions*. Encouraged by its broad and vague usage in English (at least), many analysts have applied this single word in far too many areas. This *homogenization of the general term "emotion"* is one of confusions I hope to address in this book. Perhaps ironically, the best way to demonstrate the wide influence of emotions is to distinguish among them. So one of my goals will be to develop a variegated vocabulary, to do some conceptual splitting to counter the bold lumping that remains common because it attracts attention and advances careers. I can stick close to accepted lay usage, because our cultural labels

SIDEBAR 1. FIVE TYPES OF FEELINGS

Reflex Emotions: fairly quick, automatic responses to events and information, often taken as the paradigm for all emotions: anger, fear, disgust, surprise, shock, disappointment, and joy

Urges: urgent bodily needs that crowd out other feelings and attention until they are satisfied: lust, hunger, substance addictions, the need to urinate or defecate, exhaustion or pain

Moods: energizing or de-energizing feelings that persist across settings and do not normally take direct objects; they can be changed by reflex emotions, as during interactions

Affective Commitments: relatively stable feelings, positive or negative, about others or about objects, such as love and hate, liking and disliking, trust or mistrust, respect or contempt

Moral Emotions: feelings of approval or disapproval (including of our own selves and actions) based on moral intuitions or principles, such as shame, guilt, pride, indignation, outrage, and compassion

for emotions actually shape what we feel—constituting perhaps the most influential feeling-thinking process.

I begin this task with a simple typology, summarized in sidebar 1, that structures the book's chapters. *Reflex emotions* are reactions to our immediate physical and social environment, usually quick to appear and to subside, and normally accompanied by a package of facial expressions and bodily changes. Two reflex emotions, fear and anger, have been used as the exemplars for most theories of emotions in politics, selected to exaggerate the suddenness and disruptive power of emotions. But they are a small subset of our emotions.

Urges are strong bodily impulses, hard to ignore, such as lust, substance addiction, or the need to sleep or defecate. Their impact on politics is often to interfere with promised coordinated action, so that organizers try to control them (just as torturers use them to break players down). Not everyone would call them emotions (Jon Elster prefers "strong feelings"), but they are certainly feeling-thinking processes that inform us about the current state of our bodies.

Moods last longer, so that we can carry a mood from one setting to another; they differ from other emotions in lacking a direct object. Mostly good or bad, they are summaries of our feeling-thinking processes, often dubbed simply "affect." Moods both condition our reflex emotions and are changed by them. Their primary political impact is on the energy level we bring to political activity. They are medium-term feelings. Drawing on the French sociologist Émile Durkheim, Randall Collins has done the most to explain moods, especially the joys of crowds and other intense interactions, in which bodily copresence and shared foci of attention excite participants.

My last two categories are emotions that usually last a long time and become tightly entwined with cognitive elaboration and rationalization. They are basic orientations to the world around us. They are part of the broad cultural background out of which social movements emerge, but activists in turn try to reinforce, reinterpret, and redirect these convictions.

Affective commitments are relatively long-term attachments or aversions: love, respect, trust, admiration, as well as their negative counterparts. They are less tied to short-term assessments of how we are doing in the world and more to cognitive appraisals of others (although the objects need not be humans; we are also attached to ideas, objects, and places). Affective loyalties can change, even sometimes suddenly as through the shock of betrayal, but for the most part they provide basic collective identities and goals of action.

Finally, *moral emotions* involve approval and disapproval of our own and others' actions. They include the satisfactions that we feel when we do the right thing, a kind of deontological pride, but also when we feel the right thing, such as compassion for the unfortunate or indignation over injustice. Even more powerful are the emotions of *dis*approval, which are frequent spurs to action. From Immanuel Kant to Lawrence Kohlberg, a calculating-brain model portrayed morality as the application of basic principles without any emotional involvement such as loyalties to our group. Instead, if we wish to incorporate morality into social science as a set of motivations for action, we must acknowledge the emotions involved: it feels good to do the right thing.

Much of this book is about how these five types of feelings interact with one another. The immediate feelings are prolonged and crystalized into longer commitments, but the latter also get embodied in short-run emotions. We also have emotions about our own emotions, partly as we interact with enemies, authorities, loved ones, and bystanders. They react to our emotions, and we to theirs: this is the core of political engagement. The combinations and sequences of feeling-thinking processes are hard to disentangle, but we cannot give up. This is our only hope for unraveling the mystery of social action.[2]

*   *   *

If the term *emotion* is usually too broad to be useful, so are many individual emotion terms. Words such as *fear* or *anger* are imprecise, and each can refer to several distinct states of arousal rather than a single one. Here we see a second confusion, a problematic *homogenization of individual emotion terms.* The shame we feel when we have violated our own moral standards is different from the cringing shame we feel when a bully humiliates us on the playground. The anger we feel at the dog for pooping indoors is not the same anger we feel at Donald Trump for his stereotypes of Latino immigrants. We can avoid this second confusion by adopting some typology like mine: reflex fears are not the same as fearful moods or long-run fears about immigrants, even though we use the same word for all these.

Most emotions are cultural labels that correspond imperfectly to the many feeling-thinking processes going on, such as adrenaline and other chemicals, blood flow and pulse rates, a furrowed brow and other expressions, a loss of fine motor skills, memory associations, body clocks, and dozens or even hundreds of other small changes in our bodies. Once we become aware of having an emotion, once we label it, those labels in turn reshape many of these underlying processes—one reason that we can still talk about these emotions. Just as we label bundles of feeling-thinking processes as emotions, so we formulate other thoughts. Both emotions and thoughts take their place among the other feeling-thinking processes that occur. Some are displays and utterances that can be observed and interpreted by others, some are only for us to interpret, and most do not even reach our conscious awareness. Who stops to think, I've just had a surge in oxytocin? As Kristen Lindquist expresses current psychological thinking, "Neither bodily changes nor interpretation are thought to 'turn on' in a given context, but instead are ever-present processes that are continually interacting with one another in a conscious brain."[3]

In this book I will use the term *feeling-thinking processes,* or the shorthand, *feelings.* I will also use the word *emotions,* as recognized, labeled bundles of these feelings. Emotion labels matter, since they are how we react to feeling-thinking processes, they are how political players amplify and stabilize our feelings for future uses, and they are themselves a crucial feeling-thinking process. Emotions are familiar entities to normal people, even if they do not make all the distinctions I do. "You *need* an emotion concept in order to experience or perceive the associated emotion," says Lisa Barrett in strong language. "It's a requirement."[4]

What kinds of things do emotions do? Although nit-picking scholars would never admit it, some consensus has emerged that most emotions are a rough-and-ready appraisal of how we are doing in the world, on a number of dimensions. According to the philosopher Martha Nussbaum, "emotions always involve thought of an object combined with thought of the object's salience or importance; in that sense, they always involve appraisal or evaluation." They are, furthermore, salient or important "to the person's own flourishing."[5] She steers between the treacherous images of emotions as automatic bodily disturbances or as an overly calculating, reflexive awareness. Neurologist Antonio Damasio similarly comments, "Emotions provide a natural means for the brain and mind to evaluate the environment within and around the organism, and respond accordingly and adaptively."[6] This appraisal, he suggests, need not be conscious.

Emotions tell us how we are doing in several worlds at once, from immediate physical surroundings and our own bodies all the way up through broad group attachments and abstract moral systems. Except for moods, each of the types of feelings reflects information about a particular "world." We can see how anger at the dog is a different feeling from anger at Russia or at aliens from outer space. They operate in different registers, are elaborated to different degrees, and shape different kinds of actions. This distinction should help us resolve the second confusion. We may use the same word—*anger*—but we quickly recognize that our feelings differ across these cases.

*   *   *

Most feeling is a form of thinking, or rather feeling-thinking. This is the opposite of an old view, still the target for most books on emotions, that emotions derail rationality. This *dualistic outlook*, a third common confusion, has a gut-level plausibility as well as two thousand years of Western philosophy behind it, but it exaggerates *both* the disruptive potential of most emotions *and* the mathematical, calculating nature of rationality (the "rationalist delusion," as Jonathan Haidt puts it).[7] It's a view that is out of favor among scholars and scientists but alive and well in the media.

Politically, the traditional dualism became a contrast between incompetent (emotional) masses and masterful (rational, calculating) elites. In Plato's day it was slaves who had to be ridiculed as driven by appetites and incapable of reason. In the nineteenth century the emerging working class was similarly maligned. For centuries it went without saying that women are too emotional to make competent decisions. In the twentieth century the study of protest and the study of voting went separate but parallel ways, with sociology absorbing the former and political science the latter, but the central debate in both fields remained the rationality or irrationality of normal people engaged in politics (appendix 1 traces this view).[8] Could they be trusted to make good decisions?

As part of the antidemocratic agenda, an unrealistic image of human thought emerged—promoted by philosophers who would be kings—as dispassionate calculation aimed at some already-defined end. On the one hand, this long dualistic tradition reduced emotions to unthinking physical impulses that interfere with thought, and which even—especially in Sigmund Freud's version—have little to do with events in the world around us. On the other hand, the tradition adopted an idealist approach to reason, detaching it from our own bodies or even, with Hegel, from human beings altogether. The ends might come from a utilitarian summation of the public good or, as David Hume suggested, from the basest passions, but once the ends are given, then decisions and action simply follow with almost mathematical derivations. Morality too, at least for Kant, was the emotionless, Olympian calculation of the proper action. Inspiring to generations of powerful men, the dualistic imagery culminated in the cognitive revolution of the latter half of the twentieth century, which adopted the computer as its model of rationality: the brain was a calculator.

The obverse side of the calculating-brain model was the panic model of emotions, in which fairly arbitrary triggers launch us into preprogrammed packages of behaviors. Fight, flight, and other reactions were built into our mammalian DNA before we were humans, in this view, and they still lurk there in the "primitive" parts of our brain, the amygdala and the imagined "limbic system."

Recent theory and research help us develop more reasonable portraits of both emotions *and* rationality, corresponding to increasingly universal participation in politics. It is time to abandon the family of metaphors portraying the brain as a computer. Our nervous systems are more like an array of sensitive devices that register changes in the world around us. But they are also active in their responses, which complicates the metaphors. Damasio suggests "the feeling brain." (A certain line of feminists would embrace the similar trope of a feminine brain.)[9]

Emotions help us gather and process information about the world, more rapidly than the "conscious" part of our brains could proceed; our intuitions can be both useful and surprisingly accurate. (Computers, in contrast, receive only the spare data that humans feed into them.) Emotions also help us begin to formulate paths of action in response to what we are learning. Through emotions, too, we begin to communicate our intentions to others, with whom we may need to coordinate or from whom we desire some reaction. Like information processing, most of this work of launching action takes place without our being aware of it. These are all ways that we "feel our way" through the world. (Robots do feel their way about, but only in the physical sense.)

These quick reactions do not exhaust the realm of emotions, which also help us keep long-run track of what we want from the world. Our goals, conscious or not, are closely tied to how we feel about entities in the world—ourselves, other individuals, groups, places, ideas, technologies, and whatever else is out there—and about moral principles and visions. Many psychologists have modified the feeling/thinking dichotomy into fast thinking / slow thinking, but our love of our nation or hatred of inequality is anything but fast. There are feeling-thinking processes behind both fast thinking and slow. (Fast/slow thinking is a catchy metaphor, not a careful analytic distinction.)

As emotions come to appear more reasonable, cognition seems less calculatingly rational. We see that "more emotional" and "more cognitive" processes belong to the same general category of tricks that we use to go about our lives, connect with others, and move toward our goals. Most of our cognition takes place outside our conscious awareness, as we process information about our positions in time and space, as we move and act in ways that do not require conscious thought. Innumerable bits of preconscious information go into every turn of our head or keystroke at the computer. Even solving mathematical puzzles, in some ways the traditional paradigm of cognition, depends heavily on preconscious routines. As psychology experiments have shown, when we become aware of those routines, that very awareness slows us down.[10] Transparent, logical deductions are rare and unusual forms of thought, not the norm, and perhaps not even the ideal.

If the recent attention to emotions changes our image of thinking, it must also change our model of action. Most obviously, acting and thinking are not as distinct as once believed. They are inextricably tied together. To deny this connection is to portray thought as an abstract exercise in calculation, and action as either an automatic instinct or the calculated implementation of our thoughts. As for action, there are forms that feel automatic because they do not engage our conscious awareness, but they are based on goals nonetheless and involve some processing of information. We jump when we are startled; our chests expand when we hear the national anthem. And yet these actions are not simply a matter of carrying out our conscious desires, either. As for abstract thought, anyone who remembers how she felt when doing and then—quite different—when she solved a challenging mathematical problem will reject the emotionless portrait. Only computers "think" without feeling.

Because emotions do so many different things for us, there can be conflicts among their many functions. We may feel the pull of different types of groups, whose interests and goals conflict, or we may feel a group loyalty that violates a moral intuition. A mood can undermine our ability to pursue an urge or to follow through on our moral vision. Some of the conflicts are across my five types of feelings, but some of them are within the same type. A recurrent task of movement organizers is to reconcile these feelings, or to redirect them into those that are most helpful to the collective effort. This is not always the best thing for individual participants.[11]

* * *

Once we acknowledge the broad impact of emotions, the implications go far beyond political action, which after all is not defined so much by being a special kind of action as much as by appearing in certain kinds of arenas. For starters, most political action is a kind of strategic action, in which groups or individuals are trying to have an impact on others to accomplish their own goals. As I argued in *Getting Your Way*, strategic action is a broader category than political action. Many of the same strategic moves and dilemmas that we find in political engagement we also see in other institutional settings: crime, the family, organizational life, combat, markets, and more. Emotions infuse each of the three basic families of strategic means: persuasion, coercion, and payment. None are emotionally neutral for subject or object.

Nor are emotional dynamics restricted to strategic action, either: they saturate all human activity, even the most mundane and routine. We take comfort in our little habits, or we feel some anxiety every time we watch our children head off to school. We have a complicated array of emotions when we look at a loved one (or a hated one). Once we start looking for emotions, we see them everywhere. We see human life differently. So even though this is a book about protest, I try to point the way toward broader paths of inquiry that could transform the way social scientists picture social life and action. Through emotions we are embedded in a variety of environmental, bodily, social, moral, and temporal contexts, or worlds, as we feel our way both consciously and unconsciously toward some things and away from others. Politics and collective action have always been a kind of laboratory for working out models of human action more generally, and emotions are no exception.

As Merleau-Ponty argued, our bodies are the place where both acting and thinking (itself a kind of action) take place. Many of our intentions occur through our bodies, and much of what our bodies do is in pursuit of our projects. Feeling-thinking processes consist of constant interactions, a set of mutual adjustments among various internal states and between internal states and the external world. There are extreme cases in which we formulate goals and then decide on the best ways to attain them, but these are rare. They occur less often in *simple players* (individuals) than in *compound players* (groups and teams), when we must persuade others through speech acts.[12]

Sociologists, especially, have slogged for decades toward a theory of action that recognizes human intention without reifying it. The best they have done is to talk about "context," about the "relational" nature of humans, about interaction. They can easily show that individuals are shaped by their interactions with others, by their culture, by the messages they receive from parents and peers and the media. This is not enough. Emotions show us the many ways that a person is embedded in a variety of contexts and how her action emerges from those contexts. But this does not make the person an automatic effect of her contexts, partly because those contexts include our own bodies and our own minds. Individuals are social creations, who carry traces of past interactions in their biographies, but they are never reducible to their social settings, past or present.[13]

Emotions might have salvaged a clever recent attempt at a general social theory, to take one example. John Levi Martin usefully argues that we must base our explanations on first-person accounts rather than on the kind of objective third-person descriptions, provided by analysts, that dominate sociology (in the study of social movements this is a straw target, as first-person accounts are already our central source of data). Less convincingly he turns to field theory as the solution, inspired by affective "valences," which are "something that pulls one toward or pushes one away." These have both direction and intensity, forming "vectors." Although Martin uses the verb *feel* many times, and even cites Randall Collins on emotional energy, he misses the opportunity to use emotions, instead insisting that these valences are somehow in the field rather than admitting that emotions are in the individual but connect her to her surroundings. If emotions could make sense of field theory, they could save any number of theories of social action.[14]

Political action is more conscious and explicit than action in many other realms, as we must articulate our goals and defend our means for others when we hope to persuade them. We often make decisions about what emotions to display, and how. But again, scholars need to avoid overly sharp dualisms between politics and other realms or between external displays and internal feelings. Much political meaning is only implied, and we are never aware of everything that we want. And outside the political realm, we are also involved in persuading and demonstrating things to others. The emotions we feel inside us and the emotions we display to others can sometimes be distinguished, but not often. And if there is a gap between the two, it is not unique to politics.

Many sociologists are keen to insist that they are only talking about emotional displays, claiming agnosticism about actual human feelings. This position, which presents itself as extreme constructionism, seems more like an old form of behaviorism in that they restrict themselves to observable billiard-ball interactions without reference to minds. For many purposes, it does not matter what the researchers' ontological beliefs are: their descriptions can be understood to be about emotions *or* about their display equally. But I see no reason to pretend that emotions do not exist, even if most of our methods allow us to see only their displays. In fact, the existence of emotions is more firmly established, thanks to neurological and psychological research, than almost anything else that social scientists study. (Compare them to opportunity structures, social structures, the state, even social movements!)[15]

* * *

Emotions are causal mechanisms that help explain how one action leads to another in politics and social life generally. They allow us to build up from small interactions to big processes rather than deducing or assuming small things from first principles. A bottom-up emotional approach, or at least an approach that acknowledges emotions along with other meanings and institutional contexts, promises to advance scholarship along several fronts.

As I have already suggested, we can move beyond ancient but sterile debates over the rationality of voters and protestors (and politicians, although their rationality is rarely challenged in scholarly research). True rationality or irrationality would be hard to define, much less find in the real world. Instead, we can examine the many ways that humans, across all institutional settings, strive to recognize and attain what they want from life—even when what they want is simply to guard against change and threats. Debates over rationality, especially in anthropology and political science, have rarely been useful efforts to understand why people do what they do. Most of the time, they have been normative stances disguised as analysis.[16]

Explanations of politics and protest have frequently taken a structural form that concentrates on changes in institutions. This research, best exemplified in the work of Charles Tilly, often takes a long historical perspective, observing major shifts in the opportunities open to individuals and groups, who (eventually) adjust their actions accordingly. Largely missing from these accounts are humans and their actions: how they make decisions, form groups and alliances, try to transform the structures, and modify their goals and means. Emotions can help us develop a rich theory of action that structural perspectives lack. Often we want to know how people change institutions, not how they adapt to them.

A robust emotional-mechanisms approach has grown out of rational choice theory, even though it is limited by the latter's traditional emphasis on how humans *should* act at the cost of empirical research into how they *do* act. Tellingly, the preeminent theorist in this tradition, Jon Elster, is a philosopher, not an empirical social scientist. And although he has postulated a number of emotional mechanisms that take humans away from the ideal of perfect rationality, he still works within a framework that begins with an exaggerated ideal of what perfect rationality is. We will see more mechanisms if we abandon the normative rationalist agenda. Emotions are among the most powerful causal mechanisms.[17]

Cultural approaches have been offered as a corrective to both structural and rationalist models. How people understand the world around them—including other players, arenas, and even themselves—is central to any theory of action that aspires to go beyond the simplistic, self-interested individuals of rational choice theory. There is an objective world outside our interpretations of it, but it only affects how we act when it is filtered through those interpretations. Meaning is unavoidable.

Yet, in a version of idealism, cultural theories too often reduce human meaning to dry cognitive schemas, narratives, ideologies, and frames: thoughts rather than thinking, the product rather than the process. This reduction aids analysis: one can always find frames or scripts to interpret. But there remains a gap between action and cultural product that only emotions can fill. I may see the world in a certain way, but what gives me the motivation to act on the basis of that vision? I interpret the world not only by applying scripts and schemas but also by feeling my way around in it.[18]

But by emphasizing meaning, cultural approaches seem the most promising path for understanding emotions. The *capacity* to feel-think—to produce hormones, to hear sounds, to move our muscles—is mostly biological, but almost everything else (how we *use* those capacities) has a cultural basis. Our expectations, our understandings of situations, and other things that trigger emotions are all cultural. The emotion labels that we use to make sense of—and to organize—our feeling-thinking processes are cultural. And our displays of emotions are cultural.

After a generation of development, cultural theories have told us a lot about frames, narratives, collective memory, boundaries, and identities, but they have yet to tell us why one frame or symbol resonates with audiences and another does not. They have not quite cracked the nut of "meaning," central though that is to cultural theories. Something has meaning to us, it grabs us, resonates in our bodies, when it stimulates our emotions. If it does not trigger feeling-thinking processes, it falls flat. It cannot move us to action.

Structural, cultural, and rationalist theories, or even a combination of all three, go a long way toward certain types of explanation. But they will never yield a commonsense theory of action or outcomes until they make room for emotional dynamics.

* * *

Chapter 1 tries to show that most feeling-thinking processes are ways of understanding our situation in the world and what to do about it. This approach allows me to redescribe emotions, not as irrational but nonetheless as containing some potential for mistakes, just as all thinking does. There is no reason to think we make more mistakes because of emotions than because of bad information or poor logic, but we still need to recognize the potential for regret and for disruption. Chapters 2 through 6 lay out the basic categories of emotions and demonstrate how they weave in and out of protest activities.

I wrote the afterword to address the fascinating phenomenon of Donald Trump, whose triumph in 2016 seems to challenge my claim that emotions do not make us irrational. Appendix 1 reviews some of ways that political scholars have misrepresented emotions, thought, and action for political purposes. Some cases reflect cognitive limitations, but in most the real trouble is a form of moral cheerleading meant to promote some players and demean others. Appendix 2 briefly reviews the research techniques that can be and have been used to better understand the role of emotions in politics.

Pascal was right that the heart has its reasons; he was wrong to *contrast* them with rationality and its reasons. Hearts and minds, bodies and souls are not so separate. They rely on the same feelings racing through our central and peripheral nervous systems. Our hearts rarely bleed: they pump blood—and the pace at which they do so is one feeling-thinking process that helps us feel our way through life. Protestors have emotions, like everyone else, but theirs are "thinking hearts," not bleeding hearts. Brains can feel, and hearts can think.

I: BEYOND THE
CALCULATING BRAIN

*Because we don't understand the brain very well we're constantly
tempted to use the latest technology as a model for trying to understand it. In my childhood we were always assured that the brain
was a telephone switchboard. (What else could it be?) And I was
amused to see that Sherrington, the great British neuroscientist,
thought that the brain worked like a telegraph system. Freud often
compared the brain to hydraulic and electromagnetic systems.
Leibniz compared it to a mill, and now, obviously,
the metaphor is the digital computer.*

JOHN R. SEARLE

Among the supreme moral heroes of the twentieth century are those who
stood up to the paramount evil of the century, the Holocaust. Many men
and women risked their lives to save those, especially Jews, whom the Nazis were hunting down for extermination. Kristen Monroe, an expert on
these admirable people, was surprised that none of those she interviewed
expressed any sense of choice in their arduous rescue activities. "Normally,
you don't teach a mother how to love her baby," commented one rescuer.
"She has that naturally.... So your instinct that you develop in yourself is to
react in that way. And so it was a quite natural development. Not, 'Should I
do it or not?'" Even at this fateful moment, and despite the risk to their own
lives, the rescuers were thinking and acting through their feelings. They
knew what they had to do without any calculations, based on the characters
they had become over their lives, on their empathy for beings whom they
viewed as fellow humans: "Character counted more than the influences
traditionally said to provide the impetus behind moral action, and emotions and feelings trumped the cool and impartial calculus of reason."[1] If
we feel our way through momentous actions like these, then we probably
do so through most of the rest of life. Our brains—or rather, our nervous
systems—do more than calculate.

THINKING THROUGH EMOTIONS

If we stop thinking of emotions as sudden disruptions, we can ask what they do *for* us as well as *to* us. There are not many things we can say about emotions as a whole, but we can usefully analyze most of them as forms of feeling-thinking. Or rather, we can think of feeling-thinking processes as the ingredients in emotion episodes. There are all sorts of processes going on in our bodies and nervous systems at any time. We are accustomed to calling some of these processes "thoughts" and others "feelings" or "emotions," depending on what triggers them and (if we are neurologists) on what parts of the brains are activated and what chemicals released. We also look for different bodily changes with thoughts and with emotions. This approach is less dependable, since some thoughts trigger visible bodily changes (the excited "ah-ha" expression when we grasp an idea), while most emotions do not. Our main clues come from our knowledge about the situation we are in.[2]

According to dictionaries, *thinking* consists of mental processes that integrate new information into what we already know, allowing us to model the world and to deal with it according to our plans and desires. Once we stop thinking of "mental" as some ethereal, unemotional activity—an echo of the traditional Christian idea of an immaterial soul—then we can see that emotions fit the same definition, leading psychologists to speak of "the wisdom of feeling."[3]

Psychologists have gone wild in recent years over the many feeling-thinking processes that allow us to process information without even being conscious of it, especially in the notion of fast thinking. At one extreme, Gerd Gigerenzer believes that the intuitive heuristics we deploy are typically *better* than the calculations we make when we stop to think things through consciously. In familiar situations, we usually arrive at the best response first, but when we are given time to think up other possibilities, we begin to imagine less worthy ones, partly because we begin to rely on irrelevant bits of information. Gigerenzer believes that our brains' evolution has left us with a number of forms of fast thinking that pick out the information most relevant to our choices. He criticizes the view of the brain which "assumes that minds function like calculating machines and ignores our evolved capacities, including cognitive abilities and social instincts." He prefers to view the mind "as an adaptive toolbox with genetically, culturally, and individually created and transmitted rules of thumb."[4]

Others remain skeptical, pointing to the large number of cognitive illusions people have. Daniel Kahneman and Amos Tversky created prospect theory out of hundreds of experiments (now thousands) showing the decision-making biases that people tend to employ unless carefully trained to avoid them.[5] Often, the examples of useful fast thinking involve catching a fly ball or reaching for something in our peripheral vision—physical reactions that are poor exemplars for political decisions. Most psychologists prefer to see two distinct ways of thinking, fast inferences and slower calculations; in many cases we make snap judgments but then correct them as we gather more information. Kahneman observes, "Jumping to conclusions is efficient if the conclusions are likely to be correct and the costs of an occasional mistake acceptable, and if the jump saves much time and effort. Jumping to conclusions is risky when the situation is unfamiliar, the stakes are high, and there is no time to collect more information."[6] (Of course if there is no time to collect more information, as in some strategic interactions, jumping to conclusions based on feelings is inevitable.) For other psychologists, this sounds too much like the age-old effort to exclude people from decision making on the basis of their emotions, leaving policies such as nuclear energy to slow-thinking experts. But it turns out that experts, too, have emotions.[7]

There is a vast continuum from the least conscious to the most conscious feeling-thinking, another from the fewest to the greatest bodily changes that accompany the feeling-thinking. Working my pencil through a crossword puzzle may not be very different from jumping when I am startled by a loud noise or a sudden movement in the shadows. The two activities both activate many different parts of our bodies, especially but not exclusively in our brains. In what passes for cognition as well as what passes for emotion, we are perceiving the world around us, processing that information, and working up an appropriate response, based on many feeling-thinking processes. Thinking is an engagement with our physical and social contexts, whether the suitable action is to sit and look over the finished puzzle or to jump up and run. Moving my pencil from square to square and forming letters is every bit as preconscious—and speedy—as my jumping when startled.

We can expand this image of feeling as thinking into feeling as communicating with ourselves—or signaling, as Sigmund Freud said. Emotions are rough-and-ready evaluations of what is happening, alerting us to what is important. First, what is happening inside our own bodies through urges: when we are hungry, tired, excited. Second, as in the case of startle and other reflex emotions, what is happening in our immediate physical environment.

Feeling-thinking also tells us about our social environment: my emotional displays tell others what is going on with me, and my feelings tell me what seems to be going on with them. According to neurologist Antonio Damasio, feelings "serve as internal guides, and they help us communicate to others signals that can also guide them. And feelings are neither intangible nor elusive. Contrary to traditional scientific opinion, feelings are just as cognitive as other percepts."[8] If emotions were elusive rather than predictable, they could hardly play this communicative role. Social life would be impossible.

Reflex emotions in particular are easily read by others, allowing them to prepare their own responses. They may get out of our way, come to our aid, or scan the environment to see what has startled us. Emotional displays allow humans to coordinate what they do, whether for cooperation or competition with each other. Body language and facial expressions are ways we communicate with others, who understand this somatic vocabulary without necessarily becoming conscious of it. *Prosody* is all the variations in intonation or melody, the pauses and stresses, the intensity or timbre of our speech—all of which is also crucial in displaying emotions intelligibly to others.

Finally, emotions tell us about the moral and (for some) spiritual worlds, about our connections to the very meaning of life. Robert Solomon, an existentialist philosopher, argues that emotions give life whatever meaning it has, since "they are ways of seeing and engaging in the world, our ways of 'being tuned' into the world, in Heidegger's delightful metaphor." According to Solomon, "An emotion is a basic judgment about our Selves and our place in our world, the projection of the values and ideals, structures and morphologies, according to which we live and through which we experience our lives."[9] Feelings tell us about the state of our gut *and* our place in the world.

An extremely sociological philosopher, Martha Nussbaum, has elaborated a sensible framework for understanding emotions that recognizes their close connection to thought, in a number of books but chiefly *Upheavals of Thought: The Intelligence of Emotions*. There have been the inevitable scholarly quibbles over her portrait, but the main outlines have stood up well, particularly as a starting point for social scientists.[10]

Emotions, Nussbaum begins, "involve judgments about the salience for our well-being of uncontrolled external objects." To understand emotions, we must examine human attachments in all their diversity: to our own bodies, to the physical world, to concrete and abstract others, taken singly and collectively, to ideas and moral principles, to places and things, and to our own self-images. But emotions are not just a catalog of what we value, they tell us how we are doing in relation to what we value. They "are not just the fuel that powers the psychological mechanism of a reasoning creature, they are parts, highly complex and messy parts, of this creature's reasoning self."[11]

Her view contains three central components: "the idea of a cognitive appraisal or evaluation; the idea of one's own flourishing or one's important goals and projects; and the idea of the salience of external objects as elements in one's own scheme of goals."[12] She stresses the role of imagination and active interpretation in our emotional experience, which "contains rich and dense perceptions of the object, which are highly concrete and replete with detail."[13] Our imagination brings alive the object of our emotion (moods, lacking objects, are an exception; and with urges our own bodies are the relevant objects).

Among our feeling-thinking processes, the imagination is central in politics, as it helps us react to mediated events as well as to face-to-face interactions. Symbols and words that are remote from our present situation can still arouse various feelings, and they are rhetorically crafted for that very purpose. It is our emotional reactions that keep us reading a novel or watching a political speech on television. These reactions depend especially on our ongoing emotional commitments. Plus, imagination is central to the empathy that allows us to communicate and coordinate with others.

Nussbaum distinguishes usefully between background and "situational" emotions. Her background emotions correspond to what I call affective and moral commitments. "One loves one's parent, children, spouse, friends, continuously over time, even when no specific incident gives rise to an awareness of the love."[14] She also mentions fear of death and anger over a persisting wrong: these seem to be reflex emotions but in fact become ongoing concerns or (in the case of anger) moral judgments. By placing two major categories of feelings in the "background," Nussbaum avoids confronting exceptions to her view of emotions as judgments about how well we are doing in the world at a given moment.

Although we can have emotions about goals that are not well articulated or not even conscious, the focus on goals and appraisal is especially apt for approaching the emotions involved in politics. Although it includes many murky motivations as well, politics frequently calls on us to articulate our goals when we try to persuade others. Affective and moral commitments are crucial references.

Whether we exclude nonconscious goals or not, we must include a variety of nonconscious feeling-thinking processes, such as biochemical changes. In fact, this helps us see how emotions, our verbal labels, are only one component of feeling-thinking. There may be dozens of feeling-thinking dynamics at work before I realize I am "afraid," and that emotion label does not put an end to them. But it does transform some of them, as feeling-thinking processes interact. However, nonconscious does not mean unpredictable, irregular, or even complicated. Nonconscious feeling-thinking processes (which are the vast majority) are still subject to analysis.

We might better understand feeling-thinking processes by reflecting on the amazing sensitivity of many dogs, which pick up all sorts of cues

in—obviously—a nonverbal way, and perhaps nonconscious, too. We don't
hesitate to recognize these sensitivities in canine companions, but we are
reluctant to acknowledge the same feeling-thinking mechanisms in ourselves. As pack animals, dogs need to be aware of what other creatures
around them are doing, much as humans need to. We can think of this as
what William James described as a stream of consciousness. (By the way,
in humans this flow has been estimated, to borrow at least once from computer analogs, to reach the astounding volume of eleven million bits of
information per second.)[15] It's a fair guess that other mammals use all the
feeling-thinking processes that we do except for one, verbal labels, and a
few apes have learned even those when forced to interact with humans.[16]

Except for moods, emotions are *about* something, and they are closely
tied to our beliefs about that thing. Emotions can be inappropriate, unjus-
tified, or unreasonable (when they are based on false beliefs), so that new
information creates, modifies, and (quickly or slowly) extinguishes them.[17]
Emotions are also more or less intense depending on how central to our
lives their objects are. And in a good example of their intelligence, our
feeling-thinking processes occasionally surprise our conscious selves—for
instance, leading us to realize that we care more about something or someone than we had realized.

Nussbaum's cognitive-evaluative approach challenges the contrast between body and cognition. "Human emotions are all bodily processes,"
since we are always embodied, but bodily sensations alone are not sufficient
to define an emotion. For that we also need cognitive activity. A person's
own experience is central to labeling an emotion. If a person says she is sad
but a brain image does not show the activity neurologists associate with
sadness, we would probably agree with her and not with them. Given the
complexity of the human nervous system, individuals have diverse ways of
experiencing emotions, and "what has constancy across subjects is a pattern of thought, which is of course a type of experience."[18] Circumstances
also affect how we feel emotions; for example, when we are distracted or
trying hard to suppress them. We follow a number of cultural feeling rules,
but we also have idiosyncratic ways of doing so.

If we keep in mind the flow of feeling-thinking processes, it is easier
to view emotions as processes instead of states, as adverbs more than as
nouns, as episodes and sequences. Our emotion labels tend to stabilize
and reify complex processes, sometimes distorting them but more often
reorganizing them or even creating them. In many cases we identify combinations of emotions—anger with fear, rather than anger with outrage—that
get at these nuances.[19]

And yet, even though the categories and concepts we use in our emotional life are just one type of feeling-thinking process, they are singularly

important because they don't just help us make sense of our perceptions and experiences: they help create them. According to Barrett, "categorization constructs *every* perception, thought, memory, and other mental event that you experience, so *of course* you construct instances of emotion in the same manner." We can have concepts for emotions without having the words for them, as preverbal infants do, thanks to all the other feeling-thinking processes. "Emotions are not reactions *to* the world; they are your constructions *of* the world," Barrett argues. Although words are not necessary for this construction, they are uniquely efficient ways to summarize and to convey our feelings to others.[20]

Armed with images of feeling-thinking, or the feeling brain and the thinking body, we can overcome traditional dualistic extremes of mind and body and recognize the many forms of feeling-thinking on the continuum linking them. Feeling our way through the world involves many processes. Even the most abstract thinking is a way of engaging the world, of monitoring it and reacting to it, and even the most gut-level reactions are ways of coping with our environments, of forming responses to what happens. Cognition and feeling are parts of the same universe, not opposites.[21] Both reflect a constant flow of signals flowing through our bodies. We can see some convergence on this point between two approaches usually seen as unrelated: phenomenology and neurology.[22]

THE PHENOMENOLOGICAL BODY

All thoughts and actions take place in and through our bodies. This is the often rediscovered insight of Maurice Merleau-Ponty's version of phenomenology. He was navigating between two unpalatable views: René Descartes's notion that mind and body are entirely separate (raising the obvious question, where exactly *is* our mind or spirit located?) and a reductionist materialism that has no place for mind at all beyond the mechanical movement of molecules (a view once associated with neurology but also more generally with the calculating-brain model).

Our subjectivity is always embodied, implying that we always encounter the world from a specific physical location and that we carry intentions, goals, and emotions with us which give that world meaning.[23] Our bodies are the way in which we are in the world, not observing it objectively but acting in it to carry out our projects and desires. We "come to grips" with our body—and the physical world of which it is part—without having to think consciously about it.[24] For Merleau-Ponty, this directed activity is somewhere between blind mechanism and fully conscious calculation, a realm in which feelings are central. Now that we better understand feeling-thinking processes, we can add flesh to Merleau-Ponty's theory.

Sexual love seems to be Merleau-Ponty's favorite—and very French—exemplar, as it captures how fully connected we are to the world around us. The social and the physical aspects are tightly entwined: "The importance we attach to the body and the contradictions of love are, therefore, related to a more general drama which arises from the metaphysical structure of my body, which is both an object for others and a subject for myself."[25] We build up a personal history through bodily habits that are learned over time and not entirely under our control—an idea that sociologist Pierre Bourdieu exploited to advantage.[26] We have some control over the bodily habits we learn, given enough training, such as the disciplines imposed on soldiers, factory workers, and crowds in recent centuries.[27] Love is also a paradigm of how we must often work to discover our own emotions, not just through introspection but through engagement with others. Emotions such as love pull us toward others.[28]

For Merleau-Ponty, thoughts are thoroughly embodied, not only by operating through complex neurology but also by occurring in organisms in action, with projects and a particular place and trajectory in the world. Once we place cognition in its proper social and bodily context, it no longer looks so different from feelings. Bodies and minds partake of the same systems, with chemical and electrical impulses flying around them at all times. The window is open for us to see all sorts of ways for people to feel their way through the world.

Something like the calculating-brain model was Merleau-Ponty's central target. Although it went under many names, since Plato philosophers have seen humans' connection to the world primarily as a form of thinking, of explicit propositions and formulations about the world. Merleau-Ponty's career was devoted to perception, to the many ways we learn, engage, and know about the world that fall short of verbal formulation and mathematical calculation. We care about the world, and have intentions toward it—just as emotions are usually *about* something. (The French word *sens* means what the English *sense* means, but it also means "direction" or "way," neatly capturing Merleau-Ponty's intentionality.) As one commentator puts it, "perception is not a *mental* phenomenon, if by 'mental' we mean something in contrast to material or physical. Rather, perception is a *bodily* phenomenon, which is to say that we experience our own sensory states not as mere states of *mind*, but as states of our bodies."[29]

I cannot do justice to the many intellectual strands that Merleau-Ponty inspired, but one stands out as a profound contribution to the sociology of emotions. In *How Emotions Work*, Jack Katz reestablishes the power of a phenomenological approach to emotions, especially reflex emotions.[30] For instance, to examine road rage in Los Angeles, Katz sent undergraduates off to gather accounts, mostly from older drivers, of an episode of anger while driving, from which he teases several strands of theory. One has especially to do with driving, when the car is an engaged extension of your body, so that being cut off in traffic is a deeply visceral experience (Katz notes that passengers, who are just as much at risk, don't respond with road rage).

Other observations generalize to other kinds of anger. We not only demonize the other drivers, but—since we don't know much about them—expatiate about them as a "type": BMW owners are . . . ; women drivers are . . . ; and so on (we draw on culturally plentiful stereotypes and our own affective commitments). We find ways to portray ourselves as victims who must get revenge, thus restoring our own sense of agency as we transform ourselves into heroes. Our opponent is either a villain or an inept clown. We invoke a broader moral community to condemn those who have offended us and to assert our superiority over them—even if we must wait for the dinner table later to do so. We reshape reflex emotions into moral emotions. These are rhetorical strategies found in a wide range of settings, even in the absence of anger.

Katz examines two episodes of crying. In one, a preschooler whines constantly and annoyingly: a willful act of assertion, "at times a protest and at times a kind of song she sings to herself."[31] Like many emotions, her mild crying is an alternative to speaking, to language, and to the depersonalization they bring. Crying keeps attention on her body and allows her to remain inside herself rather than (or also) engaging with her toys and with other kids. Most emotional displays are intelligible to others; they are modes of interaction.

The other episode of crying occurs at key moments in the interrogation of a murder suspect. When police introduce new evidence that undermines the story he has been fabricating, the suspect reacts to the crisis with tears. He also, according to Katz, uses gestures and other body language to conjure up the image that he is falling. The account is fascinating for the struggle over the suspect and his body that unfolds between him and the interrogators. We observe a sudden "fall" from his habitual identity, with its embodied supports, to a less stable one, accompanied by emotional displays, a kind of moral shock to an immoral man.

In all these cases, Katz examines how our bodies create and display emotions. "The body," he says, "is an endless emotional resource because it transcends all the situations a person moves through." He also notices the strategic dimension of many emotions, whether consciously deployed or not. He "examines both the situation-specific and the situation-transcending projects that people pursue through their conduct." Emotions arise through social interactions. Katz demonstrates how emotions can lubricate those interactions, carefully orchestrated to attain a variety of ends. Laughter, for example, "is governed by a sensitive monitoring of gaze, pause, and sequential behavior, all conducted with an eye to the consequences for shaping interaction (usually conversations) with other people."[32]

Even when words fail us, we are capable of thinking about our situation and even communicating it to others through feeling-thinking processes. Whether we see laughing and crying as feeling-thinking or as forms of interaction, we can see how bodies have their own forms of working through what is happening to us, of doing things for us. We are not passive victims of our bodies, although we sometimes give ourselves over to our emotions. Protestors are often aware of the inadequacy of the old mind–body contrast, especially with humor. As a member of the Grupo de Teatro 15 de Mayo put it, "When you stay at the rational level you suddenly disconnect from your body and your emotions, it's as if they separate from each other and that's a mistake because they also have things to say. They are like levels that have to be together because they are part of you. So I think that humor finds an easy way to arrive at this connection."[33]

And yet we must be cautious in talking about "the body" as though it were distinct from the mind. "Embodied" action should not be contrasted with "mental" activity. One extreme form of bodily "knowledge" occurs when we train our muscles, so that we can play the piano briskly, purse our lips in the way necessary to pronounce proper French, or create fast-twitch muscles to sprint rapidly. We have made our bodies into more adept physical resources—not quite the same as our bodies' having *knowledge*. Another way to put it is that knowledge consists of the feeling-thinking processes that help us do things by engaging many parts of our nervous systems.

Beyond muscle training, other forms of "embodied knowledge" are in our central and peripheral nervous systems. Even the "ways of the hand" that pianist-sociologist David Sudnow discusses are really ways that feeling-thinking processes coordinate brain and body. In his effort to overcome mentalist images of action, he ends up alienating his hands when, "from an upright position I look down at my hands on the piano keyboard during play . . . I sing with my fingers, so to speak, and only so to speak, for there is a new 'I' that the speaking I gestures toward with a pointing at the music that says: It is a singing body and this I (here, too, so to speak) sings."[34] Having two *I*s is exactly the dualism we are trying to overcome—and an unnatural feeling.

The "I" is a construct we make from the same raw materials—memories, chemistry, muscle twitches, perceptions, and so on—out of which we build other feeling-thinking processes. They are all in the body, all working constantly as we feel our way about. Such images from phenomenology begin to converge with research from the natural sciences.

EVIDENCE FROM NEUROLOGY

In the brain-as-computer analogy, it once appeared as if different parts of the human brain performed discrete functions. In the 1990s neurologists expected to map the brain circuitry of each emotion thanks to such new scanning equipment as functional MRIs and positron-emission tomography (PET) scans. Paul MacLean posited a "triune brain" consisting of parts added through evolution: a reptilian brain, a paleomammalian brain, and a neomammalian brain (for language and thought).[35] If each emotion had its characteristic package of feelings and behaviors, as Paul Ekman suggested in identifying the distinctive facial expressions of anger, fear, joy, sadness, surprise, and disgust, it followed that we should be able to distinguish each of these as it works its way through its distinctive path in the central nervous system. Finally, we would know what "anger" really is, for example. And if an emotion could not be so clearly traced, it follows that it must be a "secondary emotion" built out of the "primary emotions" observable in the brain. There was also a vaguer promise that specific parts of the brain could be linked to each emotion.

The new imaging at first gave a boost to the hardware side of things, which now seemed prior to the culture side of things. Brain scanning is in its infancy, and perhaps someday it will yield results of interest to *social* scientists who study emotions. But with a hundred billion nerve cells and a million billion connections in the brain alone—not to mention the entire nervous system—this will take some time. Whenever a tiny piece of the puzzle is discovered, each hormone or gene, the news media jump on it as though it explained an emotion. But emotions depend on dozens of processes spread across many parts of the brain, not on just one.

As evidence accumulated, it became apparent that emotions are not so simple. The better the scans, the more parts of the brain were seen to be involved in any given feeling. Just as emotions are causal mechanisms that can be put together to help explain political actions and outcomes, they themselves are complex compositions of many smaller feeling-thinking mechanisms. Neurologist Antonio Damasio speaks of a "multi-tiered neural mechanism for the production of emotions. After the processing of an emotionally competent stimulus, cortical sites initiate the actual emoting by triggering activity in other sites, largely subcortical, from where the execution of the emotion ultimately can be carried out."[36] Numerous parts of our bodies are already interacting with each other, each changing the other in rapid succession. (Feelings are going on constantly, even while we sleep.) Well into this interaction, our minds may begin to formulate a "feeling," Damasio's word for an emotional label that is familiar to us. (Most authors follow standard English usage and reverse this, making *feeling* closer to the bodily symptoms and *emotion* closer to the label—usage I follow in this book.)

Innumerable nerve firings and chemical releases are involved in a single emotion, following multiple pathways through multiple parts of the brain and back out to other parts of the body. Far from the old dream of linking each emotion to a distinct part of the brain or a functional pathway, emotions are the result of complex interactions involving many parts of the central nervous system—and the rest of the body (these include communications among various parts of the brain). We take in sensory cues from our external environment along a number of pathways leading to the brain. Other information has to do with our own bodily state: blood flows, contractions of smooth muscles, heart rate, glucose levels, oxygen and carbon dioxide levels, chemicals signaling injury, and so on. At the same time, neurotransmitters such as dopamine and neuromodulators such as oxytocin are produced and affect our bodies; one hundred neurotransmitters have been discovered to date, with more coming all the time.[37] Eventually, facial expressions, bodily postures, vocalizations, changes in hair follicles, and other behaviors appear. Only occasionally do these "multiple volleys of neural and chemical responses" make their way into our consciousness.[38] They are working hard for us and on us even when they do not rise to awareness.

As (or if) we become aware of some of the results of this activity, additional processes kick in. We may notice a sensation, such as "butterflies" in our stomach or a surge of adrenalin. We begin to search our memory for similar patterns in the past, and we begin to grope for a verbal label for the combination of feelings. As we do this work, which may still not be fully conscious, it feeds back and affects the other processes, perhaps calming or exacerbating some of them according to what we think is happening. Whether we are interpreting what our bodies are feeling or whether we are reacting to an external object, our brain is constantly creating its own images of what is happening based on all the bits of information flowing to it.[39] Emotions are *compilations* of many tiny feeling-thinking processes that occur throughout our bodies, to which we can sometimes attach a label. Even the human brain is more adaptable than once assumed. Whereas neurologists had once thought that damage to one part wiped out the functions associated with that part, they now see that other parts of the brain can sometimes take over new functions after injuries.[40]

As Clore and Ortony put it, "Increasingly, it is apparent that behavior-relevant processing in the brain is highly recursive. Incoming sensory information is progressively refined in an iterative process. The kinds of subcortical processes that LeDoux and colleagues' work has highlighted presumably serve as early signals that something should be processed further, so that its significance can be determined."[41] We can experience cascades or spirals of feeling-thinking processes, since they include feelings about the significance of what is happening.

Psychologists have coined the term "meta-emotions" to describe the emotions we have about our emotions, as the interactions among feelings continue even after we arrive at an emotion label. We may realize that we enjoy feeling a certain way or instead that we are embarrassed to feel that way. This kind of reflexivity most of the time involves labeling an emotion, with some rearrangement of our other feeling-thinking processes into a familiar package. Meta-emotions sometimes exacerbate what we are feeling, like embarrassment over a blush that only intensifies the blush.[42]

It is tempting to contrast feelings we have about our own body with feelings we have about the world outside it, but even the latter come to us through our bodies in complex ways. The phenomenological point that we are embodied means, according to philosopher Matthew Ratcliffe, that "we do not perceive our bodies in complete isolation from how we perceive everything else, and then link the two kinds of perception together by means of some subsequent mental process. Consider, for example, the sense of balance. Losing one's balance or feeling disoriented is not just a perception of one's body or of the world outside one's body. It is a perception of the relationship between one's body and its surroundings."[43] Feeling-thinking processes, too, represent a constant interaction and situating of ourselves in various contexts.

Although Damasio insists that there is a rigid pattern to the activities associated with each feeling or emotion, others find it hard to see clear packages that correspond neatly to the words we use for emotions. The supposedly objective indicators of emotion do not line up especially well with our subjective experiences of emotion—for example, in distinguishing among anger, fear, and other emotions. At the least, the labels we apply, derived from our culture and biography, play a role in the patterning. The mind and the body cannot plausibly be *contrasted* with each other in our emotional compilings.

In the face of the difficulties that scientists have had in pinpointing emotions as opposed to the finer feeling-thinking mechanisms that comprise them (and in making their definitions line up with our everyday experience of emotions), psychologist Lisa Barrett suggests that emotions are acts of categorization, efforts to make sense of those various bodily processes. "People experience emotion," she says, "in the same way that they see color or the way that they perceive behaviors in others: People use knowledge to parse and conceptualize the bottom-up information that is sensorially given." She rejects the "basic emotion" approach in which events lead to emotions that in turn produce facial expressions and other bodily symptoms, including behavior. Rather than fixed programs triggered by the same events, emotions emerge in ways that reflect nuanced differences in our situations, and in our understandings of those situations.[44]

It is difficult to specify behavioral packages that necessarily accompany a given emotion. "Behaviors are specific, context-bound attempts to deal with a situation," Barrett argues. "Functional demands vary with situations, making it likely that a range of behaviors will occur with instances of the same emotion category."[45] We can also display different facial expressions with the same emotion. Instead of a bottom-up process, top-down processing is also necessary for having an emotion: our linguistic labels, which we have learned from experience and culture, inevitably influence our emotions. Barrett's "conceptual act" model reminds us not to give up on the phenomenology of emotions. Humans' subjective perspectives and interpretations are part of how emotions happen, comprising key mechanisms alongside all the others.

With our emotion labels we carve out aspects of a vague "core affect" which is merely "the constant stream of transient alterations in an organism's neurophysiological state that represents its immediate relationship to the flow of changing events." (This is more or less a mood, which reflects a kind of summary of feelings divided largely into positive or negative.) We then interpret that core affect through conceptual knowledge that is "tailored to the immediate situation, represented in sensorimotor cortex, acquired from prior experience and supported by language."[46] Barrett does not assume that all emotions are hardwired into us from evolution but instead recognizes that epigenetic forces are also at work after birth, including culture and language.

Neurology's recent findings tell us how Merleau-Ponty's general claims about embodiment actually operate. "Mind" and "body" are crude, misleading labels covering up more specific processes that link various parts of our nervous systems as well as the rest of our bodies, in a constant, rich flow of signals. "Mind" could not possibly do anything emotional by itself. Nor could "body." Rather than closing the door to culture, neurology has opened it wider. Because our labels and understandings go into the complex mix of mechanisms guiding us through various feelings, my typology should allow us to distinguish cases of shame, fear, and so on based on the sources and interpretations associated with them. Our labels matter, which means that political persuasion, manipulation, repetition, and demonstration are all part of our emotional life.

REGRET AND DISRUPTION POTENTIAL

Once we appreciate the full range of human emotions and feeling-thinking processes, we can dismiss the stark mind–body contrasts that thinkers have imagined for thousands of years. In almost all cases, emotions were viewed as a kind of panic in which primitive parts of our body and brain (for instance, our "reptilian" brain) take over from our conscious or evolved brains, launching us into action that may be inappropriate for the situation and uncontrollable by our will. The contrast between rational and irrational brains inevitably and dangerously became a contrast between rational and irrational groups, as philosophers, anthropologists, economists, and others have thought they had special access to rationality and the truth.[47]

At the same time that they denigrated emotions, these dualisms typically made rationality into a lofty, mathematical calculation, the ideal being a computer with a narrow range of inputs and outputs and otherwise divorced from any social or physical context. But thinking and feeling are forms of engagement with the world, not disengagement from it. Models of feeling organisms help us understand how they deal with the world. If there is such a thing as irrationality, it probably consists of making the same mistakes over and over, due to an inability to learn from those mistakes. Such traps are probably rare, and there is no reason to blame them especially on emotions.

Many of the misguided debates over rationality, especially in anthropology, were resolved by what I call the *common-humanity test:* Are social scientists treating the people they study as being like them in fundamental ways? Do they have goals we could imagine adopting, the same kinds of affective commitments to other people, the same range of emotions? Are we willing to give them the benefit of the doubt when they make the same kind of dumb mistakes that we do? If we treat them with the same sympathy that we would demand for ourselves, we are unlikely to dismiss them as irrational.[48]

Scholars of protest occasionally fail the common-humanity test when they write about movements of the far right. Instead of a movement grappling with strategic dilemmas, trying to invent effective frames, and mobilizing needed resources, participants are dealing with unacknowledged shame, trapped in primitive belief systems, and abused by tyrannical leaders. Negative emotional dynamics come to the fore.

Instead of far-fetched questions about rationality, we can simply define a good strategic move as one that advances a player's means or ends, a bad one as undermining them. Players make bad moves all the time, at least as often because of limited thinking or incorrect information as because of emotions. In many cases they are caught on the horns of a dilemma and must accept some losses in order to make other gains. Because these trade-offs often involve emotions—all action does—they can help us understand why it sometimes appears as if emotions are part of bad moves. (Of course they are: they are a part of *all* moves.) In other cases players are taking a risk, consciously or not, that does not succeed.

I see two situations in which emotions especially contribute to actions that we or others later wish we had not taken. I will refer to the *regret potential* of an emotion when we ourselves are likely to regret our action later, but I call it *disruption potential* when other people—those depending on us—are disappointed because our action disrupts some effort that requires our support and coordination.

Regret is a matter of what feels good at the moment but will later on—usually in another arena—prove to have been a bad move. The angry violence of the mob is the paradigm: it may feel good at the time, but it can undermine your cause if caught on camera and used to characterize your group as essentially dangerous. Police also have regret potential: momentary violence can get them in trouble later. But on both sides, violence is not always regretted: it works well for many police, and it is intentional on the part of some protest groups. (Remember, too, that there are emotions on both sides of the short run / long run trade-off: the joy of acting in the moment versus the pride of acting in ways that uphold the core values of your group.)

In many cases, individuals do *not* regret giving in to short-run impulses, even when they face long-run costs as a result. Sometimes that Guinness is worth leaving the march for. More troubling are the cases when we regret something *even when we are doing it*, such as taking drugs instead of fulfilling a work commitment. We are aware of the trade-off even while we opt for the short-run pleasure. We are ambivalent, with one part of our mind desiring something of which another part disapproves. Long-run shame may be the price we pay for short-run satisfactions in the form of satisfying our urges and reflex emotions.

In many of these cases, the person's companions may come to regret what she did: there is no cost to her, but there is disruption to the group. Whatever she feels about her drug habit, we suffer when it causes her to break a commitment she has made to help us. If enough people leave the march for the pub, the march collapses. This is the disruption potential of actions and their associated emotions: an individual defects from group projects. Just as the immediate term can crowd out longer-term goals, so personal goals can crowd out group goals. The protestor (or the soldier) who panics when attacked; the doctor who believes in abortion rights but stops performing the procedure when threatened; the sheriff who loses his temper in front of cameras: they have let down their team for their own purposes.

In the case of the defector, the group will try to discipline her or, failing that, expel her. Some groups are better able than others to do so, if they have control over their boundaries. Protest groups have less influence over who shows up at the public events they sponsor than police forces have over who works within them. (Only in recent years, and only in some countries, do police managers try to rid themselves of individuals who get angry easily or violently.)[49] Discipline also varies by activity: a protest group has more control over who speaks to reporters in its name than over who joins a public protest.

There has been a historical shift in the advanced industrial world away from the public expression (and perhaps private expression, too) of violent anger. Those who organize rallies and marches work hard to discipline participants. A primary reason is the omnipresence of the media. Seventeenth-century mobs could intimidate their targets directly, without fear that third parties would intervene. They had little concern for "national" public opinion, which did not exist. Today, what is reported on the news or shown online matters enormously. We must be especially wary of using anger as the paradigm for political emotion if anger itself—or at least the way it is expressed—varies over time.

Some disruptions occur because a person feels that an action is an end in itself, regardless of practical consequences—what Max Weber called the ethic of "ultimate ends." Nonviolence or participatory democracy may not always advance a protest group's stated goals, but each is a strongly felt taste in tactics—in other words, a kind of goal in itself. Commitments like these can disrupt other flows of action, as when an individual blocks an action out of her own, possibly idiosyncratic, moral commitment. (More often, she shares such commitments with her group, otherwise she is likely to look for another group.)

The emotional rewards of familiar tactics might include pride in doing the right thing (Weber's ultimate ends), pride in doing it well (in being technically competent, which can itself become an ultimate end), a sense of solidarity with our companions, or a kind of aesthetic thrill as we anticipate what will happen. New tactics have their own thrills, having more to do with risks as to whether we can pull them off and suspense as to how others will react. These are visceral rewards of the present as opposed to the long run.

If emotions lend various intrinsic rewards to many actions, this can confound means and ends, making it impossible to select the "best" means to attain a given goal. You attend a protest because it is fun, but your goal of having pleasure is also a means for you (or for organizers) to press their case with bystanders or the media. Constructing a proud collective identity is a great satisfaction to group members, but it also energizes them to pursue further group goals. The ends are also means. This is a serious challenge for simple models of decision making such as those of game theory, which require clear, rankable payoffs of choices among which the calculating brain can choose. But it is less of a problem for our feeling-brain model, which allows constant feedback about how satisfying various paths of action are. Life is a constant flow of pleasurable and painful feelings; when we select paths of action, we anticipate a long series of feelings rather than a single clear end point. Few political projects have definitive end points, when

TABLE 1. Typical Regret and Disruption Potential of Five Types

Type of Feelings	Regret Potential	Disruption Potential
Reflex Emotions:		
anger, fear	High	High
disgust	Medium	Medium
surprise, disappointment, joy	Low	Low
Urges (except addiction)	Variable, but mostly low	Medium (except pain: high)
Moods	Medium	Medium (except depression: high)
Affective Commitments	Low	Medium
Moral Emotions	Very Low	Low to Medium

players add up their rewards and go home.[50] This blurring of means and ends is a challenge to some definitions of rationality, but not all.

I reject the irrationality hypothesis but acknowledge some of the derailing power of emotions by looking at their regret and disruptive potentials. Different types of feelings have different forms and capacities for each. I hope these two concepts capture much of the anxiety that drove the rationality debates. Regret is what we see with mistakes and the immediate term. Disruption is the problematic effect of individual defection. When actions become ends, that is a different issue.

In my view, only two of the reflex emotions (and, among urges, pain and addiction) are high in both regret and disruption potential: fear and anger, just those emotions taken as "typical" of protestors. Most of the other reflex emotions are pretty low on both, except that disgust can send a strong and unintended signal to others that might prevent later alliances. Among the other types of emotions, most are fairly low on both, although a depressed mood can be extremely disruptive. Table 1 suggests the regret and disruption potential of the five types of feelings I defined in the introduction.

Because there is considerable variation within each type of emotion as well as across the types, we would ideally replace this table with one listing individual emotions. But single words, such as *fear*, come in multiple forms that would also challenge a table like this one. I have tried to take a middle path, sticking to the five basic categories except for breaking reflex emotions into three groupings that seem to operate with different degrees of regret and disruption potential.

Questions persist about the capacity of emotions to make us do things we later regret. Why don't these questions arise with other aspects of protest? No one asks if resources are good or bad, whether political opportunities lead us to make mistakes. The reason is that resources and opportunities are not inherently part of action, whereas emotions are. Resources do not do anything until we put them to use; opportunities can simply be ignored. When it comes to action, there are all sorts of ways it can go poorly or well. Other action-oriented concepts have the same quality: decisions can be right or wrong, strategic dilemmas can trip us up when we face them. Our anxiety over their rationality demonstrates that emotions take us to the heart of human action.

Political activities contain many processes to slow down our thinking to try to avoid both regret and disruption. We go to meetings at which we have to defend our impulses, articulate our underlying commitments, and hear challenges to our perspectives. Some of these interactions are excruciatingly slow. It takes longer to coordinate our actions with other people, and some of our reflex emotions, urges, even moods may subside during that period—although others appear. Our disruptive actions may trigger responses that others will regret, such as angry exchanges that escalate, leading to both disruption and regret all around.

*   *   *

The rest of this book is structured by the typology of feelings I presented in the introduction. In many ways it is similar to other typologies, but I have modified them somewhat to reflect our experiences in political action.[51] I hope to clear up a number of confusions with the typology. For example, the philosopher David Hume distinguished calm and violent passions, arguing that the apparent conflict between reason and passion is actually a conflict between calm and violent passions. This perspective led to his famous remark, "Reason is and ought only to be the slave of the passions, and can never pretend to any other office than to serve and obey them." Calm passions can be strong, even if they are not as histrionic as the violent passions. Hume is here distinguishing between reflex emotions, usually visible and often turbulent, and ongoing moral and affective commitments that guide our longer-term projects. The mistake, he says, is to see the latter as reason rather than as emotion. When we include these commitments or convictions as emotions, it becomes harder to see emotions as generally irrational.[52]

These five categories seem useful for comparing emotions or feeling labels. Emotions are distinct assemblages of underlying feeling-thinking processes, pulled together and given coherence by our cultural training—although I leave it to neurologists to describe those smaller mechanisms. To explain political action and outcomes, emotions and urges are mechanistic enough. The five next chapters work through the five categories. I begin with reflex emotions, because these have so often been taken as the paradigm of all emotions in politics, a stance designed to associate emotions with regret and disruption.

2: REFLEX EMOTIONS

Anger, if not restrained, is frequently more hurtful
to us than the injury that provokes it.

SENECA

I had intended to begin this chapter with a story about a dictator's panicked flight in the face of a revolutionary mob. Such decisions set the course of history, and perhaps, I thought, I could find examples of fear that had led to deep regret. I scanned books about such cases, especially King Louis XVI of France and Czar Nicholas II of Russia, popular subjects. What I found were careful calculations, unfolding over days and weeks, lots of planning and preparation, and mistakes made from miscalculation or misinformation rather than from reflex emotions: strategic moves instead of the heat of the moment. There were emotions, of course, such as frustration, anger, fears, feelings of betrayal, and more. But I did not find, even in the reflex emotions most likely to create them, mistakes made primarily because of unthinking feelings.

More than any other feelings, anger and fear are taken to be the typical emotions of politics leading to abrupt, unthinking behaviors that cause disruption and regret. But these are just one type of emotion, what philosopher Paul Griffiths calls "reflex emotions."[1] These are usually quick to appear and quick to subside. Anger, fear, joy, sadness, disgust, and surprise are often described as "primary emotions," or "programs" that are universal and hardwired into us. They include the stereotyped "fight or flight" responses. Their powerful bodily components mean they cannot be sustained for very long. How long could you walk around with a surprised or angry look on your face? When we take reflex emotions as the paradigm for all emotions, we inevitably exaggerate their regret and disruption potentials.

Among types of feelings, reflex emotions are most clearly reactions to external events. Typically, we respond to something that happens in our immediate physical environment (although new information can have a similar effect). We often think that our physical welfare is at stake. The emotion may launch us in the direction of action, as we clench our fists in anger or gag in disgust. Reflex emotions grab our attention to the exclusion of almost everything else, and they help us process information about the nature of what is happening. In many cases they subside rapidly because we realize that the event was not what we had thought. The snake in the grass turns out to be a stick; our leader is asleep, not dead. In other cases our reaction runs its course: we flee, vomit, or simply are no longer surprised.

Our natural language for emotions is confusing here, as elsewhere, applying the same word to different clusters of feelings. The reflex emotion normally called sadness is better understood as a variety of disappointment. Other versions of sadness, such as grief, can last a long time and become a kind of ongoing mood. Fear and anger, too, can take more permanent, less acute forms. I flinch at a sudden movement at the periphery of my vision, but this differs from the fear I felt for eight years over George W. Bush's policies. And my anger at the invasion of Iraq in 2003 was moral indignation—different from the anger I express when I stub my toe on the rug. We will return to these more cognitive, moral forms of anger and fear in chapter 6.

More than the other types, reflex emotions depend on our expectations about the world. We are more afraid of a snake than of a ceiling fan, given our cultural knowledge about each. Although surprise is its own feeling, the other reflex emotions have some element of surprise mixed in. The joy of unexpected good news differs from more permanent contentment. This element of surprise is part of the suddenness of reflex emotions, in which the surprise of the unexpected probably intensifies what we feel. Reflex emotions are part of "fast time," according to Lynn Owens, as opposed to the "slow time" of moral and affective commitments.[2]

The reflex emotions relevant to politics usually occur within longer sequences of actions: at a march we stir up our anger by chanting and shouting; interactions with police become more stubborn and sullen; the sound of a plate glass window shattering thrills or sickens us (or both); a smile or a joke breaks the tension into a kind of joy. Rioting and rage reinforce each other over several hours, as a group of protestors egg each other on. They play cat and mouse with the police, so that both sides are ready for physical confrontation when it finally comes. Such emotions are reactions to what others do, whether our side or the other side. The reactions of bystanders can also influence our reflex emotions.

We will see that even among reflex emotions, fear and anger have greater regret and disruption potential than do joy, sadness, and surprise, with disgust in between. And even fear and anger do not usually play the role of irrational spoilers as they are depicted by crowd theories (see appendix 1), partly because they are sometimes not short-run reactions at all but rather long-run anxieties and other affective commitments. What's more, they are not the dominant emotions guiding political action that they are sometimes made out to be.

EKMAN'S FACES

Paul Ekman's "affect program" theory, perhaps the most influential treatment of emotions in the 1970s and 1980s, is especially suited to reflex emotions.[3] He uses the term *program* for the neurally encoded responses that he says constitute emotions, including facial expressions, vocal changes, body movements such as flinching, shifts in the endocrine system and subsequent hormonal changes, and other modifications of the nervous system. Such packages, he insists, are automatic, coordinated, complex, and common across cultures. To his original six—anger, disgust, fear, joy, sadness, and surprise—he later added contempt, a modification that already raises doubts about whether these programs are as obvious as he claimed.[4]

The main evidence for affect program theory comes from photographs of the human face. If you take photos in one culture of people expressing these basic emotional reactions, people of other cultures can identify the emotions expressed. A Ugandan will supposedly have no trouble identifying the emotion in a photo of a Frenchman displaying anger. What's more, people from different cultures display the same, socially appropriate emotions when shown a film of humans interacting in normal ways. They are surprised or disgusted at the same moments. One apparent exception was that Japanese students did not express the expected negative emotions despite the proper stimuli. Then it was discovered that, when authority figures were not present, they displayed the same expressions as people from other cultures. What is more, when videotapes were slowed down, very brief expressions could be detected even when the authority figures were present, covered immediately by a bland smile.[5] It turns out there are thousands of facial expressions based on discrete movements (or "action units") of the lips, eyes, cheeks, jaws, eyebrows, and nostrils, but despite these complexities, hundreds of experiments have supported the main lines of Ekman's arguments.[6]

Ekman's interest in grounding emotions in biology led him to insist that humans can read one another's facial expressions regardless of context—hence the use of photos and videos without any other information.[7] Critics have pointed out how implausible and unnatural this is. At any given moment in social life, we usually already have a number of expectations, are already sending signals to those around us, are already interacting, by the time we see someone's expression. The faces of others help us continue to coordinate our actions; they rarely if ever initiate actions from scratch. Like the feeling-thinking processes that get compiled into emotional bundles, these other bodily reactions are also parts of a complex interaction that lead us to feel happy, angry, sad, or fearful.

Psychologists who believe, as I do, that concepts and labels are usually key parts of feeling an emotion have found flaws in Ekman's methods. The six reflex expressions were not taken from any empirical study but from the nineteenth-century natural scientist Charles Darwin's hypotheses, and the images shown to subjects were those of actors asked to express those emotions. Subjects were given a list of English words for the six emotions and asked which emotion the photo seemed to express. In distant cultural contexts, research subjects had to be trained to recognize these particular expressions, and when they were given free rein, they mentioned a range of other emotions or cited behaviors such as smiling rather than emotions such as happiness. Without considerable priming, research subjects simply did not recognize the supposedly six (or maybe seven) universal emotions. Even reflex emotions do not come with automatic programs free from culture.[8]

We may roughly distinguish the situational and bodily triggers for a set of feelings, the feelings themselves, and the visible displays that are one part of those feelings. The triggers and displays, even Ekman admits, are heavily influenced by cultural norms. The question remains of the "feeling itself." Ekman sees a biologically based, unchanging package. But if there are many components to any emotion, *including our conscious labels*, then our expectations can rearrange all these elements to some extent. There is an opening for cultural influence in what we feel, not only in the triggers and displays. Theories of "meta-emotions"—how we feel about our emotions when we reflect on them—suggest that they can transform and reorder the original feelings.[9] The capacities for feelings—nerves, chemicals, eyes and ears, and so on—may be given by biology, but not what we do with those capacities. (Even those capacities are probably not entirely given at birth, as the new field of epigenetics has taught us.)

Ekman concentrated on faces, but posture, gestures, and voices also convey emotional tones. With humans, in contrast to other primates, voices are the preeminent tool we use to coordinate action—and often to correct mistakes made on the basis of facial expression alone. The nonverbal aspects of speech often convey the most emotional information, through loudness, breathing patterns, and pitch.[10] Rather than conveying specific emotions, however, voice would seem primarily to signal urgency and importance. Like facial expressions, it is typically a call to attention and action. Most of the time voices are also conveying words, and it is hard to disentangle the rhetorical impact of the words and of the voice. We saw some exceptions in the last chapter—namely, such behaviors as laughter or weeping—that entail vocalization without words.

In Darwin's evolutionary approach, emotions are quick to appear and subside, and dramatic enough to signal to others. They are useful for coordinating face-to-face interaction in the immediate term, not for organizing a protest movement or running a political party. They are reactions to our immediate environment, especially our physical environment, which—for our distant ancestors—held considerable risks.

Reflex emotions seem to fit this description best, especially since we "read" others' facial expressions very, very quickly. As we move to other kinds of emotions, through which we relate to other worlds, facial expressions become less urgent and less apparent. A mood of calm, a fondness for my companions, mild anxiety about tomorrow's speech: these feelings lack such visible bodily expressions. (Ekman dislikes the term *expression*, which implies that our bodily actions are the result of inner emotions, rather than an integral part of them.) Reflex emotions tend to arise from our monitoring of the physical world for bodily threats; even they are a way for humans to feel their way around the world successfully.

When we look at specific reflex emotions, we will see the distinct but ultimately modest role they play in politics. They may be woven into paths of interaction such as humiliation or violence, and they may be elaborated into affective commitments such as hate. Their immediate impacts include some regret and disruption potential, but also the joyful thrill of participation.

FEAR

"The thing I fear most," said Michel de Montaigne, "is fear." (A sign of Franklin Roosevelt's wisdom is that he stole lines from the greats.) Along with anger, fear is often singled out as the emotion that can do the most to undermine political rationality. These are also the two emotions most often used to build theories of all emotions, even in such sophisticated accounts as Antonio Damasio's.[11] Montaigne's reasoning was that fear "exceeds all other disorders in intensity" (although the same charge is leveled against anger). The usual claim is that fear causes people to act in haste—to panic—rather than to weigh their actions carefully, as in the hotly debated concept of "moral panics." Through much of human history, masculinity has demanded a reckless contempt for fear, reinforcing the fear of fear.

Let's start with the Greeks. Thucydides' *History of the Peloponnesian War* is partly a "meditation on fear," according to classicist William Desmond and the long tradition of political "realists" who claim Thucydides as their inspiration.[12] On the one hand, fear is the cause of domestic and international conflicts, due to ignorance and suspicion of others' motives. But Thucydides also implies that a certain level of fear, in the form of self-doubt, is healthy—a fear mostly lacking in hubristic Athens as it prepared for war with Sparta and its allies.

Thucydides uses three different words, rather inconsistently. Following Desmond, I shall call these *panic*, *fear*, and *anxiety*. Panic, or terror, is the most vehement, implying paralysis, being outside oneself. This type of fear is closer to a mood, in that ""sheer terror . . . is not a localized emotion but an all-encompassing way of being. The terror is not felt in a situation; it is the situation."[13] The second is fear of something immediately present: the usual reflex emotion. Third is anxiety about more general threats: "the anticipation or suspicion of evil."[14] Anxiety is a more elaborated, long-term commitment, along with love or hate, respect or mistrust, of the type that we will examine in chapter 5. Panic can only interfere with reasonable action, according to Thucydides, but anxiety can (sometimes) lead to prudence.

Anxieties and phobias form the background to reflex emotions. My general fear and disgust for snakes are background conditions, with me always, but a more startled fear erupts when I actually encounter a snake (or used to, before I moved to snake-free Manhattan). My suspicions about hazardous waste might also shape how I react to green water coming from my well. Here we have moved away from reflex emotions and toward a permanent anxiety or unease. With my fear of Republicans, say, this is even clearer. I would not jump if one walked into the room, the way I would react to a snake. The term *anxieties* underlines their persistence.

Because terror can paralyze, political players try to provoke it in their opponents. The purpose of state repression is to discourage open dissent through fear, although—following the calculating brain model—certain perspectives have defined the response as a cool calculation of the likelihood of injury. We will see in the next chapter how governments can use our bodily urges in this process. Puzzlement about the diverse effects of state violence—sometimes it decreases protest as the calculating brain predicts, but sometimes it increases it—can best be resolved through examination of the emotional dynamics. Even though the violent repression arouses reflex fear and the urge to avoid pain, it also triggers affective and moral commitments that may outweigh the reflexes and urges. Participants look to each other for signals from feeling-thinking processes as they juggle outrage, fear, and anticipation of what will happen next. The police may chase away protestors today, but they may return tomorrow, after some hours to reflect on their moral positions and to talk with friends and family.

Protest organizers try hard to control reflex fear and prevent a mood of panic on their own team in the short and medium run.[15] Jeff Goodwin and Steven Pfaff sketch a number of techniques for this, what they call "encouragement mechanisms," which they derived from research on the US and the East German civil rights movements: intimate social ties and support; emotional mass meetings; identification with the movement; faith in their ultimate victory; shaming of defectors; training in civil disobedience; and media coverage. Two additional mechanisms in the American movement were the possession of firearms and faith in divine protection (a very American combination).[16] Organizers try to prevent reflex fears from developing into an encompassing mood of panic, and perhaps even to reduce them to background anxieties. These techniques include strengthening affective and moral commitments—especially to one's affinity group or its equivalent: it would be more shameful to abandon one's training in front of them than in front of strangers.

In contrast to paralyzing panic, some anxiety is useful, perhaps necessary, for mobilizing protest. Without it, few would vote, protest, or engage in other political activities. A map of a society's anxieties is a map of its politics. Moral panics and other forms of mobilization are based on that map. As David Altheide, a symbolic interactionist, puts it, "Every era promotes fear. The nature of fear and the methods of its promotion simply differ. The promotion of fear and attendant 'solutions' have been a staple of social control efforts throughout history."[17] He seems to be describing long-term anxieties, but discussions of moral panics are always confused because different kinds of fears are lumped together: people do not actually panic in moral panics but instead act on their moral and affective commitments. A sustained effort at mobilizing people and resources to solve a claimed social problem—an effort that can persist over months or years—is hardly a panic, except metaphorically. I would prefer to describe it as a mobilization of anxieties rather than lump it with reflex fears.

Political scientist George Marcus and his colleagues find that anxiety causes voters to seek more information about candidates and to set aside their normal routines by which they mostly follow partisan leads and other deeply engrained habits. (They also find that enthusiasm makes people more likely to volunteer to help candidates, but enthusiasm is more of a mood, and so I discuss it in chapter 4.) Marcus attributes this attention to a "surveillance system": feeling-thinking processes are constantly scanning our environments, bringing to our attention any unexpected information, interrupting or redirecting our flow of action. As we accumulate information through these feelings, we may develop a full-blown reflex emotion. But once our attention is aroused through anxiety, it can persist for a long time—through an electoral campaign—and so is more of a mood.[18]

The news media help construct our underlying anxieties but also arouse reflexes based on them as we watch or read the news. Some observers, such as Barry Glassner in *The Culture of Fear*, place great weight on the media's ability to distort the facts to make them seem scarier, in an effort to sell the news.[19] Others, such as Anthony Giddens, point to factors in modern life, such as large technological systems and impersonal bureaucracies, that are unsettling.[20] The media amplify anxieties that are already there: "The media's preoccupation with risk," insists Frank Furedi, "is a symptom of the problem and not its cause. It is unlikely that an otherwise placid and content public is influenced into a permanent state of panic through media manipulation."[21] A "permanent state of panic" is impossible; what is possible is that the media shape and stoke our anxieties. One round of mobilization leaves anxieties and symbols that surface in the next round, even years later, as grounds for appeal.[22] A reflex fear, stirred by a news report, may leave a mark on our abiding anxieties about the world. Reflex and background emotions shape each other.

Anxieties seem to be part of broader shifts in our feeling-thinking mechanisms, especially as we desire control and certainty. Thus, when we are afraid, we become more interested in order, less tolerant of ambiguity, more decisive and predictable, and more closed-minded. Although anxiety can increase our search for relevant information, it can also shut it down.[23]

What are we afraid of? It would be wonderful to have a general theory of threats. Affect control theory is partly an effort in this direction, as a theory of our emotional reactions to people and their actions in the world around us. Its three basic dimensions of roles and actions—namely, good/bad, strong/weak, and active/passive (evaluation, potency, and activity, or "EPA space")—are compatible with an evolutionary framework: creatures that were malevolent, strong, and active were more threatening to our ancestors.[24] Even today, when we are more worried about muggers than mammoths, we orient ourselves to the world partly around these dimensions, still on the lookout for malevolent, strong, and active opponents.

Klaus Scherer posits that we undertake a largely unconscious series of "stimulus evaluation checks" that generate emotions as we appraise stimuli around us. We first check for novelty and for intrinsic unpleasantness, followed by a check to see if an event is relevant and urgent to our goals, then a "coping potential check" of our own resources, options, and capacities for reacting, and last, a "norm-self compatibility check" that registers the fit with our moral commitments.[25] At each stage, there is the possibility that we will be reassured, our reflex fear will subside, and our attention will move elsewhere. Scherer's model suggests the steps by which reflex emotions arise and subside through a variety of underlying feelings. Political activists must address each of these checks for their issues and frames to resonate with their audiences.

What does fear feel like? Linguists have identified the kinds of metaphors used to express fear. Zoltán Kövecses lists the following in English:

fear is fluid in a container ("filled with fear"), a hidden enemy (fear "preys on" you or "creeps up" on you), a tormentor ("tormented by fear"), a supernatural being ("haunted by" fear), an illness ("sick with" fear), insanity ("insane with" fear), a force that divides the self (you are "beside yourself" with fear), an opponent in a struggle (fear "grabs you"), a burden (fear "weighs on you"), a natural force ("engulfed by" it), and a social superior (it "dictates" your actions).[26] Political rhetoric uses such tropes to express, arouse, and sustain fear.

The list, it turns out, contains many traits popularly attributed to emotions in general: their physical nature, their ability to work against your "will," the sense that they are somehow outside you, that they overwhelm you. We will see in a moment that the list for anger is almost identical. It is not easy to describe feelings in words, and some of these metaphors are rather fanciful, but people try hard to label what they are feeling. "Fear" says it all. Fear also says too much, by not distinguishing reflexes, moods, and permanent anxieties.

So what does fear mean for politics? Moods of terror, the most paralyzing form of fear, derive from elaborate programs of suppression, usually imposed over months or years. True reflex fears affect action in more immediate ways, typically in face-to-face engagements with the police. Both types of fear have considerable regret and disruption potential. But our long-run anxieties are background emotions: more a part of how we understand the world, supported through symbols and justifications, to which political organizers must appeal to get us to become involved. The primary impact of reflex fear may be its influence on those affective commitments.

ANGER

Anger is generally thought to be a mobilizing bundle of feelings, normally aimed outward, in contrast to fear, which pushes inward on us. With the right cultural work, anger becomes indignation, the essence of protest; it may also encourage people to conduct more modest activities such as voting.[27] The central distinction among forms of anger is between reflex anger and the moral commitment of indignation.

There are probably even more types of anger than of fear, and we can again turn to the Greeks for help. Martha Nussbaum observes that there are more words for anger in ancient Greek than in Latin, and she marvelously lists those that the Roman Stoics described from Greek texts: incipient anger, swollen anger, anger that breaks out suddenly (reflex anger in its pure form), anger that awaits the right time for vengeance, longing for things to go badly for someone with eager intensity, longing for things to go badly for someone for his own sake, or that same longing when it "bides its time and does bad things."[28] The first three seem reflex versions, the others long-term commitments of hate or (in one case) perhaps love. There are nuanced ways of experiencing every emotion, but anger has received the most attention.

Although the Stoics did not include indignation as a form of anger, Plato did. He distinguished between a kind of reflex anger that is similar to the appetites, in that it disturbs our bodies much as it does to infants and other species, and an anger tied to judgment about injustice and revenge (including shame, when our anger is directed against ourselves). We can often curtail or correct our anger by thinking about it. The distinction allowed Plato to define reflex anger as a vicious aspect of rhetoric capable of turning a crowd into an irrational mob (see appendix 1).

Anger has always raised fear in others. On its borders, it shades into several unsavory states and actions. If it is too intense, it becomes a kind of madness, or rage, like that of the stereotypical mob. (This is parallel to the panic form of fear, and equally rare.) It encourages action, leading not only to aggression in the short run but vengeance and hate in the long run. Although it is sometimes seen as reinforcing social order by righting a wrong, as Aristotle insisted (moral indignation), it is also seen as upsetting the social order in its aggression (the reflex form).[29]

Reflexes of the moment may lead us to overreact, not only righting a wrong but going so far as to create another wrong when we do. This is a likely source of regret. Nussbaum cites a story about Plato when he thought it necessary to punish one of his slaves. Instead of doing it himself, he assigned the task to someone else: "I am angry: I shall do more than is appropriate, I shall do it with pleasure. Let this slave not be in the power of someone who is not in his own."[30] To the man who helped create the calculating-brain and panic models, regret was of special concern.

Anger over an injustice, in contrast, rarely leads to regrets. Indignation and outrage are usually lofty human feelings, reflecting stable moral intuitions and principles. There is a twist here, however. Our anger can also lead us to hate others, another long-term emotional commitment. In that case, we are no longer passionate about justice but about harm and vengeance. Our strategic attention shifts from obtaining the rewards of an arena to punishing other players in that arena (a version of the strategic dilemma I call Players or Prizes).[31] This kind of affective commitment may lead to violence and disregard, although it is primarily outside observers who condemn it as mistaken or irrational. It can be extremely satisfying. Vengeance is a widespread human motivation, often overlooked by contemporary social scientists; we will revisit it in chapter 6.

Just as anger so often becomes the paradigm for all emotions, so a single form of anger is the paradigm for all forms of anger. "In all ages the quintessential scene of anger," comments classicist William Harris, "because it is so full of unpredictability and drama, is a display of titanic rage, which no one can continue for long."[32] The most intense, aggressive, reflex form of anger as a kind of tantrum dominates our view of it, and especially its role in politics.

The frustration-aggression model of the 1930s, in which all frustration leads to aggression and all aggression arises from frustration, was intended to explain this kind of angry antagonism. In the years since, it has been improved in two ways. Foremost, not *all* frustration is thought to cause aggression, and not all aggression is traced to frustration. In addition, anger is thought to mediate between frustration and aggression when the link does occur, and anger leads to aggression only when "there are appropriate cues or releasers."[33] Frustration itself might be a reflex emotion because it is a reaction to specific events, but it might just as easily be seen as a form of anger.

Randall Collins also distinguishes reflex and moral forms of anger. He regards the former as "the capacity to mobilize energy to overcome a barrier to one's ongoing efforts." But if frustration is too great, or one's power and emotional energy too low, the barriers arouse fear instead of anger. Reflex anger leads to aggression; Collins even defines high emotional energy as "aggressiveness," in the sense of taking the initiative or dominating others. But there is also righteous anger, which he defines as an "emotional outburst, shared by a group (perhaps led by particular persons who act as its agents) against persons who violate its sacred symbols. It is group anger against a heretic or scapegoat."[34] In his Durkheimian commitment to face-to-face interactions, Collins focuses on the outburst and ignores the underlying indignation, as well as insisting on the existence of a group and outsiders: righteous anger is only possible when one group faces another. But this cannot be right: indignation, like the moral intuitions underlying it, has a variety of sources.

Kövecses again offers a list of English-language metaphors: anger is a hot fluid in a container, a fire, insanity, an opponent in a struggle, a captive animal, a burden, aggressive animal behavior, trespassing, physical annoyance, a natural force, a functioning machine (that really "got him going"), and a social superior. Overall, the increased heat, pressure, and agitation are thought to impair normal functioning.[35] The overlap with the list for fear shows that much of the imagery has to do with emotions as generally perceived, as a force pushing us (from outside or inside) in a certain direction despite our conscious intentions: the panic model. These folk images are the raw materials of much political argument.

We also have visual means of expressing anger, which can be important rhetoric in posters, caricatures, and other media. Charles Forceville has cataloged expressions of anger in the French Asterix album, *La Zizanie*. He calls these "pictorial runes," the visual equivalent of linguistic metaphors. The most common are hands and arms either kept tightly next to the body (controlling anger) or thrust outward (expressing it); eyes that are either shut or bulging (again controlling or expressing anger); a tight or a wide-open mouth; and a red face. These images correspond to some of the expressions and gestures we imagine in real people, not just cartoon characters. In addition are expressions peculiar to the cartoon form: dialogue in boldface, jagged lines emanating from the angry character, and a spiraling way of portraying the head.[36]

As with fear, it would be useful to have a catalog of what makes people angry. One source, relevant to politics, is a perception of injustice in social interactions. Although sociologists have studied unfairness primarily in intimate family relationships, even there we see the influence of moral emotions such as indignation and outrage, and explicit processes of blame.[37] In such cases, background emotions prime us to respond in a certain way, through a history of prior interactions. (As any spouse knows, a relationship builds up a store of triggers, often seemingly trivial things.) Elaborated forms of anger, such as that over Angela Merkel's economic austerity policies, will be even more tightly associated with our moral commitments.

Triggers for anger differ across cultures, particularly perhaps in its moral forms. The ancient Greeks, living in an honor culture, expressed anger especially as a reaction to personal slights to one's status rather than to infractions against interpersonal justice. The latter form of anger is better developed in the modern world.[38] Behavioral economists have shown that people are willing to pay significant amounts to avenge what they perceive as unfair actions by one third party against another.

If most anger is oriented toward action, it may discourage information gathering or reflection, especially compared to more cautious emotions such as fear and anxiety. This may be true not only for immediate reflex anger but also for moral forms. Three political scientists who examined American reactions to 9/11 and the invasion of Iraq found that anger "leads to a reduced perception of the war's risks and promotes support for military intervention," while "anxiety heightens perceived risk and reduces support for the war." Angry respondents were no less informed than others, but they seem to have "put less effort into thinking about the war."[39] If angry people devote less time to thought when they have months to do it, how much less do they think when they have only seconds or minutes? Such is the stuff of regret. But when they do have more time, they sustain anger by transforming it into indignation or vengeful hate. It can't remain reflex anger.

We usually regret our reflex anger when it results in aggressive actions: when we lash out, when one group attacks another, when rioters break windows. The long tradition of fearing crowds has portrayed them not only as having strong emotions but also as acting on them. Anger supposedly encourages us to choose the "naughty" option in the naughty-or-nice strategic dilemma, when we must choose between aggressive, rule-breaking tactics and those that obey the norms and rules.[40] And to nod further to crowd theories, it is possible that certain people—young men—gravitate toward aggressive activities for amusement. Young men's aggressive tendencies are not linked only to testosterone, as many would have it. Stronger, larger, and quicker, they may simply have less to fear from violent encounters than others do. Another bit of truth from crowd theory is that, just as groups' fears and anger can be calmed, they can be stoked: shouting and gesturing can make people angrier, even when it does not necessarily lead to aggression.

Because of anger's disruptive potential, formal organizations usually try to control its displays. If they are able to control who is a member, they frequently purge those prone to anger. Most protest groups teach techniques to all members to help them remain "cool" when taunted or harassed by opponents or the police. Training in nonviolence has become a regular part of preparation for demonstrations and blockades to which the police are expected to respond forcefully, in order to prevent angry outbursts that might exacerbate the repression or discredit the organizing group via media coverage. Not just leaders but protestors themselves take steps to prevent regret; in the 1980s many Amsterdam squatters "brought cameras to actions not just to document the event, but also to keep their hands full so that they would not be compelled to start throwing rocks."[41]

Short of action, mere displays of anger can change others' impressions of us. Many groups struggle to be able to express their anger, such as the women's movement, while others try hard to suppress these displays, such as the US civil rights movement. The displays are an important part of public relations, as they help define a group's character. In affect-control terms, anger makes us appear stronger but also more malevolent and more active. This may not be the collective identity a group wants to cultivate. Both feminist and African American activists have had to fight against cultural expectations: of women as too passive, of militant Blacks as too aggressive. It is difficult to negotiate the naughty-or-nice dilemma. Most protestors aim for controlled outrage, not uncontrolled rage. Displays of anger—or their absence—are crucial to impression management.[42]

Despite its potential for regret and disruption, despite the possibility of sending the wrong message about one's group, anger is a crucial motivation for protest. Without outrage over an injustice, without a villain to blame, there simply is no cause. Protest groups flourish when they take advantage of reflex anger to build up outrage, but also when they can tap that outrage to help participants display anger at rallies and marches. Negative emotions such as fear and anger are powerful motivators, even though we can never draw a direct line (as crowd theorists did) from personal reflex anger to the goals of a social movement.[43]

DISGUST

Disgust appears to be a primitive reaction to something that our body tells us it does not want inside us, with vomiting as the extreme reaction if we ingest it. We are typically disgusted by substances that are slimy, smelly, or decaying, and which we feel might contaminate us if they get on or in us. They pollute everything they touch. Animal products, including human excretions, are the main source of disgust. Although disgust may have evolved to protect us from poisons, it has a strong cognitive and cultural basis. The same odor disgusts us if we are told it is feces but not if we are told it is cheese.[44]

Because cultural interpretation is possible, we can learn to be disgusted by other humans and to reject them as "polluting." Bodily segregation is the ultimate form of hierarchy. Separate seats or pathways for different castes or races, and of course distinct water sources and cooking utensils, are all meant to prevent even a drop of sweat or saliva from a member of the rejected group from polluting the upper caste or race. This is an extreme way to dehumanize an oppressed group, defining them as less than fully human, in a process that Erik Erikson called "pseudo-speciation." We deploy disgusting metaphors of rot and disease to describe them, and sometimes we literally believe they are dirty and smelly. Philosopher David Smith has examined the ways in which we dehumanize others by labeling them as parasites, vermin, cockroaches, rats, donkeys, monkeys, vultures, and virtually every other (nonhuman) species.[45]

In these cases, disgust develops from a reflex emotion into a long-term affective commitment closely connected to hate and contempt and highly elaborated through cognitive means. Disgust also takes a moral form. "Jews, women, homosexuals, untouchables, lower-class people—all these are imagined as tainted by the dirt of the body," Nussbaum observes. Some of the imagery is highly metaphorical: "the Jew is a maggot in a festering abscess," according to the Nazis, "hidden away inside the apparently clean and healthy body of the nation." Added to this moral disgust was reflex disgust, as the Nazis felt "that Jews' bodies were actually different, in crucial ways, from the bodies of 'normal people.'"[46] So moral disgust was part of the background shaping reflex disgust, the kind of ongoing conviction that political organizers try to activate.

Even in societies without formal caste systems, disgust may play a role in politics. It can be deployed rhetorically to taint a person or group, as in the 2010 New York Republican primary, when Carl Paladino mailed out thousands of flyers that smelled like rotting garbage. "Something stinks in Albany," they said, showing pictures of Paladino's opponent and other state politicians embroiled in scandals. Paladino's pitch played on affective commitments, such as a moral disgust or dislike of disgraced former governor Eliot Spitzer (caught with a prostitute), but it was also meant to arouse reflex disgust. Experiments have shown that if people can be made to feel or even think about disgusting things, they tend to be more moralistic and more conservative.[47] (This tendency did not sufficiently help Paladino, who received only 34 percent of the vote.)

Paladino's efforts were mild compared to the flyer that Hindu activists circulated in India in 1917 to stimulate attacks on Muslims: anyone who did not copy out and forward the chain letter, it said, "will mount on his daughter, drink his wife's urine and his sister's milk, and marry his mother to a Musulman. We are not afraid."[48] Disgusted, perhaps, but not afraid.

Physical disgust is so deep-rooted that individuals can rarely modify it, meaning that its regret potential is limited. But individuals also have trouble hiding it, meaning that there is some regret potential when it interferes with alliances and other political programs. Its strategic advantage lies in its ability to make certain group boundaries into species-like absolutes, but doing so also prevents alliances with those groups.

You can say that you are "disgusted with yourself," but this is a figurative use of the term. We rarely gag when we think of something we have done or who we are. Used loosely like this, self-disgust usually means shame. Like fear and anger, the reflex form of disgust has less bearing on politics than its moral forms, elaborated in cooperation with others. The same is true of shame.

SHAME, SHAMING, HUMILIATION

Shame is a painful feeling of being unworthy. It applies to the whole person, in contrast to guilt over a particular action. A central feeling is that others are looking at you, so the impulse is to try to shrink or hide. Because shame is generated by failure to live up to some ideal, there are many sources of shame that vary across cultures. Pride is the opposite of shame, a powerful feeling of worth, of belonging to a group, of living up to one's ideals. Shame and pride, like fear, anger, and disgust, come in both reflex and moral forms. They can be reflex emotions easily read from a person's face and body, a primordial recognition of one's place in the pecking order. This kind of shame may be a form of submission and acknowledgment of a lower place in a hierarchy, having little to do with morality. Humans can feel ashamed even if they have not done anything "shameful." Powerful players can humiliate you even if you have not internalized their moral standards, simply because they can attack your basic human dignity.[49]

The evidence for reflex shame and pride can be seen in nonhuman primates.[50] The body language of power and victory is similar in gorillas and Olympic medalists: a puffed-up chest, head thrown back, arms in the air. Defeat brings a narrowed chest, bowed head, and slumped shoulders. For apes, this behavior acknowledges and reinforces the pecking order, and it is dangerous for them to act inappropriately for their position. The shame posture expresses an unwillingness to fight, and so it may protect against further assault. Psychologists have observed these bodily expressions in athletes blind from birth, suggesting that the expressions are not entirely learned through one's culture.[51] These gestures and postures related to hierarchies seem more salient in boys and men than in girls and women.[52]

Moral shame, to which we'll return in chapter 6, is not based on physical intimidation but on shared moral values. We know when we have broken the rules, even when we are alone without an audience. We have disappointed ourselves as well as others, and our deepest selfhood is polluted. Moral shame is thus crucial to social life. "It goads us onward," says Nussbaum, "with regard to many different types of goals and ideals, some of them valuable."[53]

The action that triggers shame can be something that *we* do, or it can be something that *others* do to cow us (physically) or humiliate us (morally). The immediate physical signs are similar for self- and other-initiated shame. Thomas Scheff offers an extensive catalog: hiding behavior, a hand covering the face, gaze aversion, lowered or averted eyes, blushing, control, turning in, biting, or licking the lips, biting the tongue, wrinkled forehead, false smiling, and other masking behaviors. Among verbal markers, Scheff lists words such as *alienated, confused, ridiculous, inadequate, uncomfortable,* and *hurt.* He also identifies paralinguistic markers: hiding, disorganization of thought, hesitation, irregular rhythms, self-interruption (censorship), stammering, mumbling, and so on (see appendix 2 for his full list).[54]

Humiliation and shame interact and combine. The petty humiliations that the Israeli Defense Force inflicts on Palestinians is backed up by the threat of physical force, especially against those who do not display proper deference, but it is meant much more as a status reducer. The Palestinians are ashamed of their inability to be true "men," to protect their families. They are perceived as weak. As we'll see later, whether or not the victims of moral shame internalize it depends on whether they share the values of their oppressors: Do they blame themselves, or the system? Are they blameless victims, or somehow implicated? The challenge for many movements is to shift that blame, to externalize it.

There may be a third form of shame and pride, neither a reflex nor an explicitly moral dimension, but one which arises simply from belonging to a group. At the extreme, moral worth is permanently or almost permanently assigned to individuals based on ascriptive traits such as skin color or—the ultimate form—caste. Suffice it to say, people vary in how thoroughly they internalize such machineries of moral worth, and challenges and rejections are possible. In status systems, shame and pride are built into the groups themselves. To be a member of a lower caste is to embody shame, to be a polluted person. Here, too, vigorous efforts are required to throw off a status hierarchy beaten into one from birth.

Status is often beaten into one literally, with the three sources of shame reinforcing each other: one belongs to a shamed group; one is forced to perform shameful acts; resistance is met with physical intimidation and coercion. In contrast, children from high-status groups are taught to hold their heads high, to walk proudly, and to display other kinds of habitus to mark their status.

Shame has a tendency to become permanent, like a stigma. Erving Goffman distinguished three types of stigma: "First there are abominations of the body—the various physical deformities. Next there are blemishes of individual character perceived as weak will, domineering or unnatural passions, treacherous and rigid beliefs, and dishonesty, these being inferred from a known record of, for example, mental disorder, imprisonment, addiction, alcoholism, homosexuality, unemployment, suicidal attempts, and radical political behavior. Finally there are the tribal stigma of race, nation, and religion, these being stigma that can be transmitted through lineages and equally contaminate all members of a family."[55] Although the second type arises from an individual's actions, often perceived as freely chosen, it joins the other two types in eventually becoming an ascribed, permanent trait, a sign of moral character.

Social movements frequently arise to defend those thus shamed or humiliated, as we'll see in chapter 6. They reverse the pseudo-speciation of shame and disgust with a language of universal human rights.

THRILLS

So far I have mostly described negative reflex emotions, but there are positive ones as well. On Ekman's list we see joy and we see surprise, which can be positive as well as negative. In fact, joy depends on surprise, before it settles into a happy mood. John Lofland celebrated the joy of crowds, although I prefer the term *thrill*, which is more immediately tied to interactions.[56]

Randall Collins' interaction ritual chains begin with thrills, as "human bodies moving into the same place starts off the ritual process. There is a buzz, an excitement, or at least a wariness when human bodies are near each other."[57] That excitement can have negative undertones, a sense of danger, as well as positive ones, and the two are often mixed together. Bodies become alert and attuned to each other, mostly beneath our conscious awareness.

Erika Summers Effler, a student of Collins, describes the thrills experienced by a Catholic Workers' community. They were due largely to the contrast with the more constant "stress and strain, the stress of financial uncertainty—and the fear of failure, suffering, and pain that accompanied this uncertainty," all of which "left the Workers open to moments of joyous serendipity." Being religious, they experienced such moments as miracles: "An unexpected check from an unknown parish felt like a miracle when the group was down to its last dollar."[58] Groups that are never down to their last dollar presumably miss out on this joy.

The word *thrill* links the final outcome, joy, back to the processes that produced it—namely, an uncertainty about what that outcome might be. This is what I call a *moral battery*, a compelling combination of positive and negative feelings that attract us to one pole and repel us from the other. "When risks were *successfully* resolved," Summers Effler explains, "the release of tension was accompanied by a flood of complementary positive emotions. Victory filled the void created by vigilant fear. Joy filled the void created by vigilant grief."[59] Moments like these can put participants in a good mood that lasts until unpleasant experiences erode it.

With thrills and joy we begin to see that reflex emotions matter as part of interactive sequences, often by surprising our expectations. Another crucial sequence has to do with how reflex emotions spread in interactions.

CONTAGION

One of the claims with which observers discredited crowds for hundreds of years was that emotions spread by means of an automatic contagion, like a virus, avoiding participants' calculating brains. This is why people in crowds might do things they would otherwise never consider, and why their emotions are often extreme, as they feed off each other's feelings. There is some truth to the contagion theory, as we do tend to mirror each other's facial expressions, in turn feeling what our expressions suggest we should be feeling. But there is no reason to think this form of feeling-thinking is always a bad thing.

Elaine Hatfield, John Cacioppo, and Richard Rapson wrote a book detailing the mechanisms by which emotional contagion operates. For one, we may consciously imagine another's experience, a kind of sympathy. There may also be automatic reactions, such as we feel when we hear someone's shrill, hysterical tone of voice expressing that she is upset. Finally, there are mechanisms of direct mimicry, which occurs in two waves of feeling-thinking processes: "In conversation, people tend automatically and continuously to mimic and synchronize their movements with the facial expressions, voices, postures, movements, and instrumental behaviors of others." These behaviors in turn affect our emotions, as we feel what is appropriate to our behaviors.[60]

Individuals differ considerably in their capacity to affect others' emotions and in their ability to be affected by others' displays. The latter capacity revisits one strand of crowd theory, which suggested that certain kinds of people were more likely to be absorbed into crowds. Psychologists tell us that some people respond strongly to "situational cues," and hence are more susceptible to contagion, than those who respond more to "self-produced cues."[61] Gustave Le Bon's opinion that crowds are feminine in their susceptibility presages recent findings that women are indeed more sensitive to emotional cues. "Females of all ages gaze more, show greater facility at remembering faces and discriminating various affective expressions, and respond more emphatically (as measured by matching expression) than do their male counterparts."[62] Today, we can see emotional contagion in a positive light, as useful communication rather than a blockage of thinking.

Even more interesting is the suggestion that some people are especially talented at influencing others' emotions: this is the essence of a good orator. Personality matters, and Hatfield and her colleagues suggest that extroverts may better express strong emotions. They also revisit the extensive research on facial expressions, pointing out that individuals differ in the location and form of facial muscles. Half of all humans, strikingly, do not even have the risorius muscle that helps produce certain expressions.[63] It also seems that effective expressers are themselves insensitive to the feelings of others, when those others are displaying feelings incompatible with their own. They are not easily distracted. (Rhetorical theory suggests that good orators need to be sensitive in certain ways, able to gauge how an audience is responding, but not so easily distracted that they lose their train of thought.) There are leads here for understanding the tricky concept of charisma, still a mystery to social scientists.

If contagion operates through facial expressions, then only a handful of emotions are subject to it. Reflex emotions are the most obvious ones, often detectable through people's faces. Moods are also sometimes visible, in a pleased, calm smile or in a scowl or faraway resignation. Other types are not easily perceived. You cannot readily tell, standing next to me in a crowd, that I love my hometown, despise Silvio Berlusconi, disapprove of torture, or am extremely hungry (although some bodily urges may be detected, such as fatigue or the need to urinate, and there may be a slight contagion effect). To get at most of my affective loyalties and moral sentiments, you will probably have to engage me verbally (unless I have conveniently put them on a T-shirt, button, or tattoo for you to read).

Disgust can be contagious, as CIA recruiters learned when they visited the University of Colorado at Boulder in 2005. A group of student protestors, purportedly hoping to be interviewed for jobs, took the emetic ipecac to induce vomiting. The sight but even more the smell of this action cleared the building—one of the most unusual deployments of reflex emotions that I know of.[64] This is a unique form of contagion. The sight, sound, and especially smell of vomiting are disgusting to most people, in turn triggering additional rounds of vomiting or—as a form of avoidance—immediate retreat.

VIOLENCE

Scholars have been obsessed with fear and anger because, under some circumstances, they can contribute to aggression, another important interactive sequence. Even if scholars of the past exaggerated the irrationality of emotions, all emotions, there are intense emotional states when individuals are "out of control." Sometimes we can usefully view this condition as a privileging of the short over the long term, as I described in chapter 1, but sometimes our emotions take over in a way that precludes any kind of comparison of present and future. We might even do things that we regret at the time we do them. In his microsociological theory of violence, Collins calls these episodes "forward panics." Drawing on Durkheim's crowd theory, he suggests an explanatory path from interactions to emotions to—in rare cases—violence.

Collins begins with moments of confrontation, filled with tension and fear of direct bodily harm. When a crowd of shouting protestors is face-to-face with a line of riot police or soldiers, both sides are charged with adrenaline and fears about what might happen. Prolonged tensions of this kind can become unbearable. When a chance arises to shift from relatively passive to more active engagement, releasing that tension, there can be a rush of action, "carrying [participants] on to actions that they would not normally approve of in calm, reflective moments. . . . Once they get into a high level of arousal, they can no longer control themselves." Although Collins is describing soldiers in war zones who massacre civilians and police who savagely beat suspects such as Rodney King, the same confrontational tensions and fears can lead to violent protests—with the violence usually arising from the "forces of order."[65]

Collins also explains why it is more often the police who turn violent. It is hard for most people to inflict physical harm on another human, and groups tend to do it when they vastly outnumber or have much greater force than their victims. In violent encounters, people must overcome a strong impulse—from years of socialization and probably evolutionary selection—to feel solidarity with others, "to get into a common rhythm and common cognitive universe."[66] They must resist a number of feeling-thinking processes. Human tendencies toward sympathy can be put aside in strategic interaction, so that instead each side focuses on the hostility and anger of the other, as each opponent arouses the other. People can goad themselves into reflex anger. That hostility is all the easier when suspicion and hate have been built over long periods into affective commitments, forming a background amenable to angry engagement. Protestors stereotype the police, who in turn have misinformed impressions of what protestors are like.

The unusual combination of fear, anger, and exhilaration—perhaps best identified as rage—that comprises a forward panic is a reflex emotion that leaves behind a mood: "it is a hot emotion, a situation of being highly aroused, steamed up. It comes on in a rush, explosively; and it takes time to calm down."[67] A mood of elation, often marked by hysterical laughter, can outlive the situation. Predictable sequences of interaction, and not simply some mysterious surge of adrenalin, bring on the rage, but it has physiological components.

Anne Nassauer has painstakingly pieced together video footage from dozens of German and American protests that turned violent. It takes several hours for this to occur, as the moods of police and protestors gradually sour. They come to misunderstand and mistrust each other's actions and motives. Typically, the police lose contact with headquarters (radio batteries go dead, for instance), feel abandoned, are hungry and tired. Frustration builds. These emotions, Nassauer argues, are more important to the violent outcome than anyone's initial plans and intentions.[68]

Collective violence requires several components. Preexisting affective commitments, especially hatred for another group, prepare the way. Then there needs to be a series of triggers: rumors (often encouraged by the hatred or fear), followed by assembling. Once a crowd has gathered, a variety of emotional processes may occur, especially incitement by leaders, shouting, and other behaviors that increase anger. During these steps, in addition, the forces of order are either absent or, more frequently, starting the violence. As Nassauer shows, the process is an interaction, often characterized by confusion, frustration, and bad moods on both sides.

The moments when our reflex emotions are truly out of control are rare and brief. Even in these cases of violence, participants are monitoring their own emotions during most of the episode. They put themselves into situations that they know might lead to violence; they step back when they do not wish to take that risk (although sometimes it is too late, especially when their opponents are aggressive). As with many other feelings, we manage the situations that then influence our reflex emotions: sometimes we want to lose control. We also want to manage other people's feelings.

GOADING AND COWING OTHERS

Protestors are aware of forward panics, because they sometimes try to goad the police into them. When it comes to reflex emotions, we strive to elicit adverse reflexes in opponents as well as to manage our own team's feelings. Brave protestors may hope to enrage a police officer so that he lashes out in front of cameras, taking advantage of the disruption potential of this emotion. The officer may or may not come to regret his anger, perhaps not even his violent action, but the rest of his team may regret them. This depends on how that action is portrayed and used. It may arouse fear in the protestors, as the officer intends, thus decreasing their activity. But, observed by other audiences, especially through the media, it may elicit sympathy and action from other political players. It may arouse regret as well as disruption.

Forces of order may try to paralyze protestors through fear. This is the definition of state terror and authoritarian regimes. Although I described terror as a mood earlier, we can also see an interesting way in which reflex emotions can be extended into affective commitments. With enough instances of state violence, the population comes to expect it. Fear and related emotions such as mistrust and hate become part of the way citizens think about their government. These background commitments then shape expectations during specific interactions. Under these conditions, the population develops feelings much like those of the tortured: a sense of vulnerability, alertness, a feeling of powerlessness, and distorted perceptions of what is real and possible as opposed to imaginary.[69] Indeed, cases of torture—examined in the next chapter—are a primary mode of instilling this form of fear, along with a sadly long repertoire including arbitrary arrests, disappearances, and house searches.

Fear often puts a person in the role of a passive victim, who arouses different reactions from different players. Distanced observers may be sympathetic, especially if the victims are otherwise benevolent. But opponents may respond with even greater fury. Hence Collins' observation that violence between groups occurs most often when there is strategic inequality between them: "It is when the strong attack the weak that most violence is successful."[70] As with many emotional dynamics, there is a trade-off between short-run and long-run effects. Remaining nonviolent may increase the violence of the other side, but in the long run it may gain compassion from other audiences. (Scholars of nonviolence tend to paper over this kind of trade-off—reflecting their own version of the calculating-brain faith that there will be one right answer to any problem.)

If we turn our lens around, we can see that protestors can also sometimes intimidate those in power. Louis XVI may not have fled in his carriage on the spur of the moment, but he and his advisors saw no advantage to remaining in the Tuileries amid the crowds of Paris. Frances Fox Piven and Richard Cloward famously insisted that poor people get concessions only when they bring production or other valued activities to a halt, scaring elites a bit. Because elites fear crowds, riots are especially effective ways to get attention (whether that leads to concessions or to repression).[71]

*   *   *

Western cultures may be especially likely to see emotions as something to resist. More generally, the messages that our emotions are sending to us may feel—to our most conscious brain—as though they are coming from outside us. And they are: these are responses, often strong, to our bodies and to the world. We are surprised by our own ability to process information about the world so rapidly.

The kernel of truth to Ekman's affect program theory is that there are recognizable bundles of feeling-thinking processes that, once triggered, sometimes interrupt whatever the person had been doing. Surprise renders us speechless; anger makes us incapable of hearing other voices. So the disruption potential of some reflex emotions (anger and fear) is high. Since they sometimes disrupt our own intended paths of action, the regret potential is also high. We listen to ourselves losing our temper, saying things we know we will regret. It is no surprise that the elite observers, examined in appendix 1, who have castigated emotions as irrational for so long, pretend that reflex emotions are the only emotions in politics.

Because reflex emotions occur primarily in face-to-face interactions, the characteristic mistakes they can lead us into have to do with their suddenness. They relate us to our immediate environment, both social and physical, especially when those emotions demand quick action. That action may be the wrong one, or at least one that has unforeseen drawbacks as well as advantages. Reflex emotions are the paradigm of the immediate term, focusing our attention on short-run goals. They allow little time for reflection, consultation, or information gathering. Nonetheless, they reflect our background commitments and are subject to training. They are anything but arbitrary eruptions, even when they lead to regret or disruption.

Reflex emotions play a number of roles in politics, although their limited duration means that their effects are often on other emotions. Reflexes develop into moral emotions: fear into anxiety, anger into indignation, humiliation into moral shame. They get elaborated and sustained through cognitive processes, or they subside. Even though anger and fear are often taken as the paradigm of all emotions, their moral forms will prove to be more central to politics. Our reflex emotions are not simply automatic programs: they also stay in our memories, as patterns we use to work ourselves up into desired emotions. We use them the way method actors do, as triggers for the emotions we want to feel and express. They are like rhetorical commonplaces that we can pull out as needed.

As we examine other types of feelings, we will see how small a role reflex emotions play in politics. We turn now to urges, which, like reflexes, unfold in the short term. Reflexes arise suddenly and subside almost as quickly. Urges may arise gradually but typically disappear as soon as they are satisfied. Most urges are not primarily social, having more to do with our relationship to our own bodies. Reflexes and urges have intricate networks connecting them to our pasts and futures—sources and reverberations—but they themselves usually live and die in the current situation.

3: URGES

A hungry man is not a free man.

ADLAI STEVENSON

The quenching of thirst is so exquisite a pleasure that it is a scandal that no amount of ingenuity can prolong it.

IRIS MURDOCH

The least pain in our little finger gives us more concern and uneasiness than the destruction of millions of our fellow-beings.

WILLIAM HAZLITT

In 1964 Saul Alinsky needed to shame Chicago's mayor Richard J. Daley into keeping commitments he had made to Alinsky's community organizing group, the Temporary Woodlawn Organization. He knew that O'Hare airport was Daley's pride and joy, so that any problems there would embarrass and infuriate the mayor. He decided to pressure Daley by disrupting air travelers' urges, threatening the world's first "shit-in." A couple thousand activists could occupy all the airport's toilets and create long lines at its urinals, forcing arriving passengers to relieve themselves wherever they could. The mere hint of such a tactic brought Daley around in the negotiations.[1]

Certain impulses well up from our bodies with such force that they can overpower our conscious intentions, propelling us to act. As a portrait of reflex emotions, this would be mostly an exaggerated view. It works better as a picture of urges, which can crowd out other goals, focusing our attention exclusively on satisfying the urge before we do anything else. These are clearly bodily *feelings*, although few scholars include them as "emotions." Nothing depends on whether or not we call them emotions, as long as we are clear about them. Urges usually end as soon as they are satisfied, but they can be fast or slow to develop. Urges channel and constrain what human bodies can do, yet they are rarely acknowledged in political analysis.

I call these feelings *urges* to emphasize the sense of urgency they often carry (both words come from the Latin *urgere*, "to press, drive, compel"). Most urges are information about the state of our own bodies, as opposed to other types of emotions that are primarily about the physical and social worlds around us. Only a few of them, like lust, arise out of interactions with other people. Like emotions, urges consist of complex bundles of bodily processes and cognitive interpretations. All feeling-thinking signals come through our bodies, but with urges the signals are also mostly *about* the state of our bodies.

Not all urges are overpowering. Like emotions proper, they come in varying intensities. Although I concentrate on strong urges, with their ability to obliterate other motivations, in moderate forms they are mere distractions rather than bodily failures. A mild urge to urinate, able to distract, will eventually become a strong urge; but discomfort with the cold may or may not become an overpowering need to warm up. There are other distractions, such as fiddling with a cell phone, that take you out of one flow of action by putting you—partly—in another. Mild urges may affect the costs and benefits of political participation on the margins, while strong urges can crowd out most other costs and benefits. Some are unexpected, like the quaking or "weak legs" that prevent us from moving forward toward the police line. But good organizers expect all these urges and arrange to prevent, redirect, or satisfy them to avoid disruption.

At one border, urges shade into what the ancients called "appetites" and even "luxuries." Early philosophers like Socrates, Seneca, and the Christian theologians worried that a taste for luxury would, by multiplying basic "needs," lead to aggression against neighbors. This was a basic theme in Plato's *Republic*, grounded in the unsustainable contrast between healthy, natural needs and luxurious, unnatural needs. And this contrast, in turn, reduces to that between the rational, enlightened part of the soul and the base, appetitive part. Suspiciously, in Plato, educated citizens are driven by rationality whereas slaves, women, and the mob are driven by the appetites—the prototype for the rationality-versus-emotion dualism.

Urges join reflexes at the short-term end of the spectrum of feelings. Reflexes usually come on suddenly, whereas urges may develop slowly, but both diminish rapidly compared to our other categories. Antonio Damasio, too, distinguishes simple appetites such as hunger and thirst from more complex emotions such as fear and anger: in my terms, urges versus reflex emotions. For hunger and thirst, the triggers are mostly internal, "a diminution in the availability of something vital for survival, namely energy from food and water. But the ensuing behaviors are aimed at the environment and involve the search for the missing something."[2] What triggers fear and anger, in contrast, is more likely to be external ("even when," Damasio points out, "they are conjured up from memory and imagination in our brains they tend to stand for external objects").[3] Whereas addiction fits his model well, lust tends to be triggered by external opportunities—although it leads to internal changes.

Damasio also points to interactions between urges and other classes of emotions. The point is sharpest with reflex emotions. Fear, sadness, and disgust inhibit hunger and lust, while happiness promotes them. The satisfaction of urges leads to happiness, while the thwarting of them can cause anger or sadness. Moods also interact with urges, in much the same way but over a longer time horizon. A sequence of satisfied urges can put us in good moods, blockages put us in bad ones.[4]

Some forms of crying and laughing seem similar to other urges, in that they can overpower us unexpectedly. As Goffman put it, a person *floods out* if she can no longer keep up the definition of the situation, as when she "can no longer 'keep a straight face' and bursts out laughing."[5] As behaviors, laughing and crying make few lists of emotions. But since they normally occur in interaction with other people rather than reflecting our bodily states, they share some traits with reflex emotions. In these cases, Jack Katz shows, they aid interaction: someone comforts you when you cry; a group feels solidarity by laughing together.[6] That we can see them as either urges or reflex emotions shows that they are complex and variable bundles, not unitary feelings.

We can think of urges as temporary disabilities that erode our capacity to carry on many of the projects we pursue as normal adults. Sickness is a similar form of bodily failure that can incapacitate us in the same way that urges do. No one is going to march anywhere (in an army or a protest rally) when severe diarrhea strikes. Mild forms of incapacity include sneezing or coughing fits. A facial tic or a recurrent sniffling can distract others. As Odysseus complained, "There's no way to hide the belly's hungers—what a curse, what mischief it brews in all our lives."[7]

We might learn something from more permanent disabilities as well. Interesting debates over the political capacities of those who are permanently disabled have pitted liberal visions, in which autonomous individuals engage in politics via agreements and mutual advantage, versus "care ethics" in which humans' affective bonds to others are a basic part of who they are. When people are ill or depend on others' care, they may be too far removed from the assumptions of the contract model for it to apply to them. An empathic ethics of care recognizes that there are beings whom the rest of us must take into account and for whom we do politics. When urges become permanent, as with addictions, perhaps we need to give up expectations of autonomous players.[8]

At the extreme, our bodies can fail even our own intentions. They are thinking for us. These are not quite urges, but bodily failures. Or rather, our bodies resist what we are consciously asking them to do. Contemplating courage in combat, William Ian Miller notes, "Weak legs figure in soldiers' accounts as an insistent motif, seeming to serve as the emblem for the many kinds of fracturing that battle works on the unity of sense and sensibility, but mostly the split between mind and body. The body goes its own way and the soldier looks on in dismay. This is the body that befouls the soldier's pants during shelling or in the midst of a charge; this is the body that sheds tears, sweats, faints, and even instinctively feints." Speaking of a helicopter pilot in the Vietnam War whose legs collapsed after seventeen grueling hours in combat, the man's legs "reveal to us, but even more clearly to him, the physical and psychic costs of what he had done. If he did not know until then, it was only because he needed his legs to tell him."[9] Combat is extreme, but politics has its milder echoes, as protestors who face armed riot police know.

Urges have disruption as well as regret potential, but urges vary on both scores. When we see an urge as potentially controllable—lust, for example—we may come later to regret following it; but not if we see it as an unavoidable force that can't be blamed on us. I may not like being in pain or having to leave a march to find a place to defecate, but regret is not my salient feeling. I do not see any alternative. (I am more likely to be ashamed of my bodily failure.) After a bout of addiction, however, I may well feel regret, if I see addiction as a choice. With addiction, I may even regret it while I am shooting up—a state of mind at war with itself that combines positive and negative (anticipated) emotions.

Their regret potentials vary considerably, but all urges have disruptive potential. I am taken out of broader coordinated activities in order to satisfy more personal needs. The desire for the substance can always lead someone to privilege the very short run over the long—and the coordinated activities that require long-run planning.

The word *urge* offers an example of how one term can be used to cover different feelings. We also use the word to mean an impulse or desire (I have an urge to call my sister), which is not the same as the chemical imbalances I have been describing as signals from our own bodies. In the broader usage, any motivation is an urge. For our own analytic purposes in explaining action, we need to distinguish the two, and I will follow the narrower definition.

ELSTER'S "STRONG FEELINGS"

Philosopher Jon Elster, referring to urges as "strong feelings," includes chemical addictions as well as "hunger, thirst, and sexual desire; urges to urinate, defecate, or sleep; as well as organic disturbances such as pain, fatigue, vertigo, and nausea."[10] Hunger, thirst, lust, and addictions are what Plato called the "appetites," that part of the human "soul" that draws us toward things. Plato, for whom the clearest appetites are hunger and thirst, comments, "the soul of the thirsty, in so far as it thirsts, wishes nothing else than to drink."[11] The others are bodily failures that are less poetic but still powerful. Some of these pressing urges are relatively independent of culture and cognition, while others are satisfied differently across cultures and across individuals.

Elster distinguishes strong feelings from emotions, which are more closely linked to culture and cognition. But he admits that only some urges have this largely visceral inevitability, mentioning thirst, the need to urinate, and fatigue. These are bodily states, but they are based on packages of neurological and chemical signals just as emotions are. In fact, Elster offers three links between urges and culture. An urge may be triggered by a belief about the external world, for one thing. It can be shaped by our belief about what kind of urge it is, for another; I may act differently if I come to identify myself as a drug addict, rather than someone simply craving or taking a drug. Third, many urges move us toward objects, and our beliefs about those objects matter. I would have to be much hungrier to eat a squiggling insect than a piece of tarte tatin. True emotions, Elster says, normally entail all three sorts of beliefs (moods, I'll argue, are an exception). Urges need not. Once we see emotions as labels for complicated packages of feeling-thinking signals, however, the distinction between emotions and urges blurs.

Urges interest Elster, whose specialty as a philosopher is rationality and deviations from it, because some urges challenge traditional rational choice images of careful decision makers maximizing a menu of goals: "Intense pain, intense shame, intense sexual arousal, and intense craving for cocaine have in common a capacity to derail the agent from his normal mode of functioning and to induce behaviors that go against what external observers and the agent himself, before and after the visceral experience, would deem to be in his best interest."[12] Although Elster, with his calculating-brain model, sees this as a form of irrationality, we can instead view these urges as a strong short-term focus that discounts the future, potentially leading to regrets and disruptions.

Urges can trigger other types of emotions, even complex moral emotions. Elster highlights the shame we may feel about an addiction, reflecting a moral desire to rid ourselves of the addiction alongside the urge to satisfy it. We may also feel guilty, embarrassed, or ashamed of falling asleep at the opera, urinating in public, or having sex with someone we are not supposed to. Such moral emotions, when strong enough, may even help addicts control their habits. At the same time, the shame often associated with addictions may drive the person to further substance abuse as a way to avoid dealing with the stigma, preferring a short-run dulling of the stigma's pain. We can begin to recognize complex interactions among types of feelings.

No one would entrust a crucial political task to an addict, whose extreme cravings might easily disrupt things. But even here, it partly depends on the specific effects of the substance; some addicts function perfectly well as long as they are not yet in need of a fix. I might trust a cocaine addict to get something done, but not a heroin addict. And possibly not a pothead: I've seen too many posters for pro-marijuana demonstrations that omitted crucial information such as the date or place. In all these cases, the cravings might interfere with coordinated action. But the use of the substance itself might or might not be debilitating. As the police know, through their use of snitches, you can get addicts to do many things for you if you control their supply.[13]

Addictive urges may be visceral, but there is a complex social construction surrounding the cultural images and practices of satisfying such cravings. It is the latter that can trigger not only moral emotions but political action. Urges and cravings can be the object of policy and protest. Sociologist Harry Levine attributes the invention of the modern concept of addiction to the physician Benjamin Rush at the end of the eighteenth century. Before that, the same patterns of drinking were understood differently. "In colonial society there may have been isolated individuals who felt 'overwhelmed' by their desires for drink, but there was no socially legitimate vocabulary for organizing the experience and for talking about it; it remained an inchoate and extremely private experience."[14] In the contemporary United States, overflowing with twelve-step and similar self-help programs, addiction is private no more. It is a recognized pattern that reorders the associated bundles of feelings.[15]

Moral panics can target a group's food, drink, lusts, and drugs as easily as its music or ideas. "Dope, hair, beads, easy sex," observes Todd Gitlin of the 1960s: "all that might have started as symbols of teenage *difference* or *deviance*, were fast transformed into signs of cultural *dissidence* (or what both protagonists and critics considered dissidence, which amounted to the same thing)."[16] Because urges involve some degree of cultural shaping and choice, they can become symbols of collective identity and subjects of controversy.

LUST

Is lust like other urges? Norman Mailer, an authority of sorts on male lust, linked it to drugs. "Lust exhibits all the attributes of junk. It dominates the mind and other habits, it appropriates loyalties, generalizes character, leaches character out, rides on the fuel of almost any emotional gas—whether hatred, affection, curiosity, even the pressures of boredom—yet it is never definable because it can alter to love or be as suddenly sealed from love."[17] Mailer makes lust sound more complex than it usually is, but he makes several good points about the appetitive urges, especially their ability to affect and be affected by other emotions.

Some urges, especially addiction but also lust and pain, are amenable to elaborate planning and are capable of permeating a personality. Mailer himself was a "lustful" fellow, obsessed with conquests in a repulsive way not unusual for men of his generation. (He calls lust "an epic work for any man"!) If lust can color a person's temperament, then substance addiction can absorb it entirely—the point of Mailer's comparison. We can sometimes "manage" addictions, but they continue to absorb a person enough to disrupt other collective projects—with even more disruption potential than regret potential.

Mailer also suggests that emotions feed off each other, weaving together in unexpected ways. A relatively simple urge becomes complicated by riding the fuel of other feelings. This is Elster's observation that even simple bodily urges can have broader emotional and cognitive meanings: are we good, are we happy, normal?

Lust and sex are themes woven throughout Gitlin's account of the movements of the 1960s, a moment that combined overt sexism with sexual excitement and a faith that sex might be a revolutionary force. "Sex was less a motive than a cement," he says of early Students for a Democratic Society (SDS), as "the circle was made of triangles, consummated and not, constantly forming, collapsing, reforming, overlapping." The movement "was a sexy place to mix. . . . Meetings were sites for eyeplay and byplay and bedplay." Lusts helped draw people to the movement, but jealousies and resentments also mounted. Women disliked being treated as conquests, and their unequal distribution was one more mechanism creating egomaniacal male "stars."[18] In chapter 5 we'll examine the band of brothers dilemma: efforts to develop affective loyalties to the larger group—such as a protest movement—often end up attaching themselves to one or a small number of close comrades instead. When lust is the cement for these bands, they are probably smaller than when bound by trust, affection, and less urgent feelings.

Lust can develop into love, a process with which we are all familiar. The most immediate urges and their satisfactions can leave residues in our feelings, memories, and habits. In this case, a lasting affective commitment can develop—quickly or slowly—from our urges. But stable love—one of the affective commitments discussed in chapter 5—is more predictably disruptive than lust. It can disrupt through permanent defections, on top of the temporary withdrawals that lust brings.

Philippe Braud comments that seduction is the heart of politics.[19] If he means nothing more than persuasion, the remark is trivial, but Braud does imply something more. Seduction is more than words. It is the use of the body, through gestures, glances, postures, breathing, and so on. The corporeal aspects of political seduction are in some ways metaphorical and in some ways literal. Good orators understand our urges. There are various ways to satisfy an urge, but lust especially requires advance planning in most cases (although the preparation may be aimed at constructing a situation in which lust both emerges and is satisfied). Seduction reminds us how our flow of feelings is entwined with the bodily presence of others and our interactions with them.

Inspired by Michel Foucault and by modern feminism, the field of queer studies has shown how our lusts are culturally constructed. We are taught as children that certain desires are normal because they occur "naturally" in our bodies. Just as anthropologists once delighted in the variability of tastes in food and drink, and sociologists in the construction of what it is to be an addict, so queer scholars demonstrate the cultural work behind sexual desire. In *The Invention of Heterosexuality*, Jonathan Ned Katz concludes that "human beings make their own different arrangements of reproduction and production, of sex differences and eroticism, their own history of pleasure and happiness. But they do not make that history just as they please."[20] All our urges are subject to similar resistances and pressures to "normalization." The biochemical signals of urges are just one set of feeling-thinking processes, among many others, most of them influenced by our social settings and definitions.

PAIN

Unfortunately for humanity, our bodily urges can play a role in politics by being used against us. Torturers manipulate a number of urges to concentrate our desire for release. They can deprive us of normal sleep, not only heightening our urge to sleep but sometimes generating paranoia, anxiety, even hallucinations. Thirst and hunger are unpleasant in themselves, but at extremes can generate nausea and fatigue. Our need to defecate or urinate can be manipulated through the deprivation of proper facilities (or the forced feeding of diarrheic oils), adding humiliation to our sense of urgency. Our usual goals, of dignity, loyalty to comrades, even protection of our family, fade in priority in the face of the immediate satisfaction of our urges. The urge to end pain can be overwhelming.[21]

Historically, torturers have focused on one bodily sensation above others: pain. One reason is that torture is not always intended to extract information or action from its victims; often it is meant as a display for others. As a spectacle aimed at an audience, torture requires nothing more than suffering from its victims. The behavioral compliance falls on others, who are thought more likely to obey rules as a result. Until the nineteenth century, most criminal punishment was public, in stocks, public whippings and beatings, and parading criminals through the streets. The modern state emerged partly by waging war on its own subjects.[22]

The ability to inflict pain is proof of one's godlike power, as Michel Foucault argued when he famously opened *Surveiller et Punir* with a 1757 case of a regicide condemned to an extended series of tortures in Paris's central public space in front of Notre Dame—unthinkably cruel in today's world but even more prolonged than intended because the horses could not rip the man apart at the appointed time.[23] The pain of others makes a good spectacle because it is so apparent, even more than most urges or most emotions. (Even when pain is intended as a spectacle, however, there can be a strategic desire that the prisoner act in a certain way, with dignity or with admittance of guilt.)

Pain's other main purpose during torture is to gain information or statements from its unfortunate objects. The creativity devoted to inflicting pain over the centuries is depressing for anyone with any hopes for humanity. Bodies have been beaten, stretched, crushed, burned, boiled, exposed to severe cold or animal attack, cut, stabbed and pierced, and electrocuted. In *strappado*, the victims are suspended by their wrists behind their backs, causing intense pain and shoulder dislocation. Some parts of the body are more tender than others, such as the genitals or fingernails (everything from wooden splinters to red-hot needles have been jammed under them). Most of these excruciating techniques are not blatant enough for public audiences, compared for example to quartering, but they concentrate the attention of the victim.

The effects of pain have been much discussed, thanks to our fascination and (in the modern world, at least) horror, but they are simply at the end of a continuum that includes release from other urges. A literary theorist, Elaine Scarry, argues that pain "unmakes" the world, largely because of the difficulty we have in describing it in words. "Physical pain does not simply resist language but actively destroys it, bringing about an immediate reversion to a state anterior to language, to the sounds and cries a human being makes before language is learned."[24] Scarry seems wrong to suggest that we normally lay aside nonverbal communication in favor of language, as Katz shows that emotions often express what we cannot articulate in words.

But Scarry seems right to point to the unraveling of our normal world, and our sense of a self within it, in the face of intense bodily distractions. Pain obliterates "the contents of consciousness. Pain annihilates not only the objects of complex thought and emotion but also the objects of the most elemental acts of perception." Our world collapses in on us. But this does not disconnect us from others, those who are watching. We may not be able to see them, but they can see and hear us. They can read our pain, just as they can read many of our other feelings. Scarry's solipsistic view of pain, like certain old views of emotions as intensely private, does not hold up in the light of recent research on the communicative purposes of feeling displays.[25]

Jacobo Timerman excrutiatingly captures the collapse of the world under torture. "Of all the dramatic situations I witnessed in clandestine prisons, nothing can compare to those family groups who were tortured, often together, sometimes separately but in view of one another, or in different cells, while one was aware of the other being tortured. The entire affective world, constructed over the years with utmost difficulty, collapses with a kick in the father's genitals, a smack on the mother's face, an obscene insult to the sister, or the sexual violation of a daughter. Suddenly an entire culture based on familial love, devotion, the capacity for mutual sacrifice collapses. Nothing is possible in such a universe, and that is precisely what the torturers know."[26] Affective and moral commitments are crowded out.

To a shocking degree, torture has always been central to political power. "Torture began as a legal practice," observes historian Edward Peters, "and has always had as its essence its public character." He documents a range of ancient political systems that introduced torture and other physical ordeals as part of a policy, ironically, to make the law more systematic.[27] Torture remains a tool of the modern state, even if the emphasis has shifted from an exclusive focus on pain to the manipulation of other bodily urges to extract information and concessions. Under President George W. Bush, CIA agents doused their victims with icy water to keep them awake in the face of exhaustion, prevented them from defecating or urinating normally (keeping them in diapers and forcing them to soil themselves), and used waterboarding to simulate drowning.[28] When US federal forces were trying to draw the Branch Davidian cult out of their Waco, Texas, compound in 1993, they blasted Mitch Miller's sing-along recordings at it. Painful enough.

One way to think about the immediate effects of pain and torture is that the pain, deprivation, and disorientation displace long-term goals with short-terms goals. Bodily urges crowd out everything else. Another way to think about torture is that it renders us incapable of pursuing any of our goals: it destroys our means rather than changing our ends. We cannot keep the secret we want to; we cannot think straight after days of isolation or sleep deprivation. Our bodies fail us. We are *no longer fully functioning players.* The two points of view converge on the same result. We can see the effects of all strong urges in the same dual way.

I have concentrated on the somatic effects of torture, but the symbolic effects are also important. Torture is meant to send signals to diverse audiences (to those who will soon be tortured, to families, to a broader public, even to the torturers themselves, who are asserting something about their own identities). Torture is an elaborate social setting. "It is the totality of the torture *situation,*" observes Marnia Lazreg, "that needs to be grasped in order to understand that torture is not definable in terms of bodily harm or psychological torment alone. . . . It is a structured environment with a texture of its own, a configuration of meanings, a logic and rationale without which physical, let alone psychic pain is incomprehensible and ineffective."[29] The feeling-thinking components of urges are never exclusively physical.

Pain can crowd out cooperation in other settings, too. Several scholars in the "Southern California School" of conversation and interaction analysis have analyzed the panic of emergency callers to 911. In describing the condition as "hysteria," the call takers point to "a kind of situational incompetence—namely the inability to cooperate appropriately in the work of the call," which is to provide information and follow instructions.[30] Instead of clear words in an understandable order, callers curse, sob, scream, wail, and express frustration and annoyance. Their urgency and pain overwhelm them. These emotional displays, the authors point out, are similar to what Goffman called *pain cries:* "a solitary experiencing of intense pain . . . in a sort of dialogic form . . . implying that our current, inner, actually painful state is the business everyone should be hanging on." Whalen and Zimmerman comment, "Their pain cries can be heard as demonstrating the urgency and seriousness of their situation, and therefore legitimating their need and the call for help."[31] Pain highlights the immediate term, but it does not necessarily remove us from social interaction.

Like pain and other urges, extreme hunger can disrupt cooperative projects. In the prison camps that the Confederacy used to slowly kill Union soldiers during the American Civil War, the first stage was desperate self-interest, the second listless apathy. "Raiders" would steal food from their fellow prisoners, and, as one diarist wrote, "everyone was for himself regardless of [moral] consequences."[32] Victims and perpetrators, both suffering from starvation but with different strength levels remaining, became something less than fully human. "Whoever waits for his neighbor to die in order to take his piece of bread is, albeit guiltless, further from the model of thinking man than the most primitive pigmy or the most vicious sadist," Nazi concentration camp survivor Primo Levi commented about Auschwitz.[33] "In the space of a few weeks or months the deprivation to which they were subjected led them to a condition of pure survival, a daily struggle against hunger, cold, fatigue, and blows in which the room for choices (especially moral choices) was reduced to zero."[34] This was extreme disruptive power, with the luxury of regret going only—if at all—to those who survived.

When famines occur in the context of existing social structures and norms, the apathy is there, but criminal behavior is usually absent (except for the well-fed elites who steal relief aid, mismanage distribution, or engineer many famines in the first place). In famines, "time allocated to anything but food-related activities soon approaches zero."[35] This does not mean, as it was once supposed, that social life breaks down, people fight each other for food, revolutions occur, or trust disappears.[36] Rather, exhaustion and lethargy reduce the levels of most activities.[37] The *political* responses to mass hunger come typically from those who are not hungry: humanitarian organizations and governments. For them, suffering becomes a rhetorical trope in appeals for aid. This is one possible impact of urges, when they are carefully documented, but it also takes us into the realm of compassion and other moral emotions, the topic of chapter 6.

DISCIPLINE

Because of the strong disruptive potential of urges, those charged with coordinating collective action must accommodate our bodily needs and frailties. Bathrooms along march routes allow participants to keep going rather than wandering off the route in search of facilities. Heat or cold can also be a problem. In subtropical Taiwan, an anticorruption movement staged a sit-in along Ketagalan Boulevard in front of the president's office in the capital city of Taipei. To avoid heat exhaustion, participants took three-hour turns at particular spots, arranged in advance on the Internet.[38]

Staying comfortable and focused requires that we manage a number of mild bodily urges as well as strong ones. When it rains during a rally, a number of participants will feel an urge to run for cover, the number depending on how hard the rain is. Bitter cold will also drive people indoors or drive them away. These milder urges are less capable of crowding out all other goals, but they can be hard to ignore. Every event organizer prays for good weather.

All sorts of urges must be curtailed or redirected. Parade organizers have to keep their participants sober, or at least sober enough to march to the destination. They must keep them fed and hydrated, awake, and at least minimally healthy. When an individual leaves to satisfy an urge, perhaps never to return, it is a defection for a personal agenda. It is one part of the notorious collective action challenge. People are not necessarily free riding; sometimes they just have to poop.

Sobriety is part of the discipline of a contemporary protest, but drinking was a central pull of many earlier crowds. From the Wilkes agitation of the 1760s, when the modern social movement was born, historian George Rudé reports the arrest of "one Matthew Christian, a 'gentleman of character and fortune,' late of Antigua, who was alleged to have spent £6 or £7 on filling the rioters with beer in a number of ale houses."[39] Alcohol provides enthusiasm, but it is harder for organizers to control and direct a drunken (or stoned) crowd, or even to keep it marching. Nineteenth-century crowd theories that emphasized unruly violence are a poor explanatory model for today's well-disciplined gatherings. But crowds used to be different.

Francesca Polletta captures the disruptive potential of drugs in describing a 1965 meeting of SDS at which a younger cohort—more interested in lifestyle innovation—challenged the sober existing leadership: "Discussions went off on tangents, position papers were ignored, people stood up and made outrageous statements and then wandered out of the room." What was disruption to the older group, still formally in charge, reflected the alternative goals of many newcomers: "Some participants seemed more interested in drugs than in discussion and more interested in action for its own sake than in political effectiveness."[40] Drugs and action for its own sake are both immediate-term priorities, but there is little reason to think that this faction ever came to feel sorry about its choices. Here was disruption, not regret.

Fatigue can have similar effects, diminishing our energy and attention to current tasks. In her work on violence, Anne Nassauer found that police often make mistakes and turn to violence when they are tired, when they have been on duty for hours without a break, when they are thirsty or hungry or need to urinate. Many of these unsatisfied urges leave them confused and angry—at their own superiors. They feel abandoned. Their interactions (or lack thereof) with their bosses leave them in a bad mood for engaging protestors.[41]

If protest requires that participants satisfy or hold many urges in check, protestors can also use the control of their urges in several ways. "Ascetics and mystics," theologian Ariel Glucklich tells us, have effective techniques "for unmaking their own profane selves: First is a rigid diet, then isolation, sleepless nights (vigils), ongoing prayer or chanting, hard physical work, and other psychotropic techniques." Pain, too, "has been voluntarily pursued because its devastating effects in one cultural context are highly meaningful and desirable in others."[42] Many religious virtuosi turn the techniques of the torturer against themselves in an effort to escape from this world into what they perceive as a more important world.[43] In a parallel, those who systematically cut themselves find that the immediate physical pain crowds out other emotional sources of suffering.[44]

Voluntary pain can glue together participants in collective action—even though this fits poorly with scholars' usual exemplars of modern protest, in which participants try to persuade others of their moral worth or engage in deliberations meant to honor democracy. Religious movements and pilgrimages often center on pain to heighten participants' attention, much as any ritual focuses the mind. The Christian flagellants who wandered Europe in the medieval period (and later) were defined by their eponymous practice. A participant in one Hindu pilgrimage—a barefoot, forty-mile trek over gravelly terrain—reports: "With time, pain stops having a causative agency, and ego is obscured or snuffed out because it has nothing to contrast itself with or stand against. . . . There is a 'feeling' of pain, of course, but it is a sensation that has no agent, no tense, and no comparative. . . . Pain is the only sensation belonging to the eternal present."[45] Although other urges and feelings have some of the same effect of obliterating what is not immediately present, the point is that one can merge with the group through the intensity of these shared feelings. Shared suffering, typically of a milder form, certainly binds the members of protest groups together even today.

HUNGER ARTISTS

Pain is not the only urge that can be manipulated for an external audience or deployed for one's own project. It is possible to hold one's own body hostage, as happens in hunger strikes or anorexia. Maud Ellmann links these two, in that fanciful way literary critics have. "Self-starvation is above all a performance," she says. "To hold the body up for ransom, to make mortality into a bargaining chip, hunger strikers must declare the reasons for their abstinence."[46] Self-starvation is a reasonable strategy when someone else is responsible for your body, typically a jailer, but also when your martyrdom would display your moral commitment. Mohandas K. Gandhi went on several hunger strikes, mostly when the British were (albeit loosely) still responsible for his fate, but at least one even after India's independence, designed to get the nation's attention to end religious riots. César Chávez later modeled his own three hunger strikes on Gandhi's. For those devoted to nonviolence, turning violence inward in this way is an aggressive act. Hunger strikers use their deep indignation and desperation to arouse sympathy and corresponding indignation on the part of some third party. Control over one's deepest urges can be a virtuoso political performance, especially as hunger strikes unfold over several weeks during which publicity and negotiation occur (there is risk of brain damage after thirty to forty days and death after sixty). Strikers can increase the urgency dramatically by refusing liquids.[47]

Hunger strikes have deep historical roots as weapons of the weak in caste societies. In ancient India, members of lower castes who had lent money to someone from a higher caste—and so had limited means to force repayment—would simply plant themselves at the latter's door. In pre-Christian Ireland, too, young people often engaged in hunger strikes to protest inequality and injustice. The modern hunger strike became popular in the early twentieth century, when British suffragists and Irish nationalists protested against their British jailers. The former were quickly released after starting a hunger strike; the latter were not, and at least twenty died. Their jailers, responsible for the prisoners' bodies, were blamed for the deaths, as the strikers overcame their own bodily urges.

According to one study, more than two thirds of twentieth-century hunger strikes occurred in prisons—the ultimate setting in which someone else is responsible for your well-being, but also an intense arena of struggle between jailers and jailed. For prisoners and detainees, strategic options are limited. Even their ability to craft rhetoric to appeal to supporters and bystanders is curtailed, but a hunger strike, and the death it risks, must usually be reported to audiences outside the prison. The hunger strike is used as a means of communication with the outside. The announcement of a hunger strike is often sufficient to arouse a reaction. The same study concludes that hunger strikes are typically brief and successful, gaining concessions in three quarters of cases.[48]

After Gandhi, the most renowned hunger strikers were the Republicans in Northern Ireland, the most celebrated of whom was Bobby Sands. In 1976 the British government revoked the political-prisoner status of Irish prisoners, insisting that they were common criminals who had to work and wear prison uniforms. The policy challenged the prisoners' image of themselves as soldiers fighting a war of liberation. Especially galling, prisoners who had been sentenced before March 1976 were still treated as prisoners of war; those sentenced later felt the marked difference. The battle was over dignity, simply seen as an extension of the broader conflict. Outsiders "don't know what it means to be observed, humiliated, made to feel inferior, day-by-day in your own country," as Sands put it, "That's a word: dignity. They can't take that from me either. Naked as I am, treated worse than an animal, I am what I am. They can't and won't change that."[49] His body was Sands's final battleground. He died from starvation in 1981.

Oriana Fallaci, quoting Alexandros Panagoulis, who was tortured by the Greek military regime, shows that control over one's body is often the final strategic choice left: "All those hunger strikes weakened me. You'll say but why also inflict those hunger strikes on yourself? Because during the interrogations a hunger strike is a means of keeping your head. You show them, I mean, that they can't take everything away from you since you have the courage to reject everything. I'll try to explain. If you refuse to eat and you attack them, they get nervous and the fact of being nervous doesn't allow them to apply a systematic form of interrogation. During torture, for instance, if the man being tortured keeps up a provocatory and aggressive attitude, systematic interrogation is transformed into a personal struggle by the tortured man himself. Understand? I mean that with hunger strikes, the body is weakened and this won't allow the interrogation to be continued, since it's useless to interrogate or torture someone who loses consciousness. These conditions are realized after three or four days without food or water, especially if you lose blood because of the wounds inflicted by the tortures. So they're forced to transfer you to the hospital."[50]

Hunger strikes are not the only way to use your body as a weapon when others are responsible for disciplining it. The 1981 Irish strike had been preceded by the refusal to wear prison clothes: four and a half years during which protestors wore only blankets and, if removed from their cells, were entirely naked. Eighteen months into this protest, during which warders reacted by beating and jeering at the naked prisoners on their way to mass or the toilets, the prisoners responded with the "dirty protest." They refused to use the toilets, instead smearing feces on their walls and emptying their chamber pots under their cell doors (soon boarded up). Urine and excrement became resources, almost the only resources prisoners had.

With a controversial definition of *resistance*, some feminists have also seen those with eating disorders as engaged in a struggle using their bodies as weapons. In proanorexia websites, sociologists Abigail Richardson and Elizabeth Cherry see challenges to cultural ideals of beauty and to medical efforts to control female bodies. Rejecting an identity as victims of a disease, anorexics try to demedicalize themselves by emphasizing their habits as a lifestyle choice. They share tips about not only how to fool parents and doctors but also how to remain healthy despite low body weights. Participants seem to have learned something from feminists and Foucault.[51] Kevin McDonald sees anorexia as a struggle for subjectivity: "Losing weight is interpreted as a form of self-mastery, a capacity to reshape and reinvent the self."[52]

For both hunger strikers and anorexics, "their suicide is murder by proxy," according to Ellman. "The spectacle of hunger overrides the bounds of subjectivity. It forces us to feel each other's feelings, think each other's thoughts, and inhabit one another's tortured flesh."[53] More clearly for hunger strikers, they aim to change the actions of their jailers or other responsible authorities by arousing sympathy from some bystander public. The authorities are tarred with a sense of failure and perhaps even shame in the latter's eyes. Suicide becomes murder.

In hunger strikes we see a character battle: who is the victim, who the villain? Character types like these help us allocate blame to those who initiated an interaction. In this case, there is a struggle to claim blamelessness, one dimension of victimhood. If the jailers did something to provoke the hunger strike, the strikers are the victims and the result is, potentially, murder. If the prison system and the government behind it are innocent, with the strikers taking the initiative in some way, then the potential result is instead suicide. As Siméant observes, hunger strikers "create a scene of the lone individual fighting against the blind machine . . . victims fighting for recognition of their social standing and their rights."[54] In a recent twist, more than a thousand prisoners in Kyrgyzstan took the additional—and painful—symbolic step of sewing their mouths shut to dramatize their hunger strike.[55] If they are willing to go this far, it proves how deep their grievance must be. Self-immolation is a similar, more extreme statement about the life-or-death urgency of one's cause.[56]

ALBIE SACHS'S BODY

Urges remind us of the many ways that we struggle—and often struggle against others—to control our bodies. Scholars fashionably mention that our actions are "embodied" but rarely describe the feelings that flesh out this idea. Maurice Merleau-Ponty imagined the example of an amputated limb to describe the integration of mind and body (we feel it even after it is gone), but we have a cruel case from real life in Albie Sachs. A Jewish lawyer and a leader of the African National Congress, in 1988 Sachs lost his right arm and the sight in one eye to a car bomb planted by apartheid's security forces. He writes about the challenges of defecating, getting in and out of a bathtub, learning to write again. His body has become literally unbalanced, as he discovers when he takes his first bath and slides too far into the water. "There are some things," he says, "so intimately involved with your body that you cannot escape them, they are there inside you, part of you, aspects of your innermost existence where your body, mind and personality meet and interact without subterfuge or strategy."[57]

Sachs's very existence became a kind of triumph after the attempt on his life ("all I have to do is get better"), and he uses it as permission to treat himself to some modest pleasures from which he had previously abstained. He could now indulge without feeling immoral. "We spend half our lives trying to build habits of purity and self-denial, in which every tiny action is moralized, and then dedicate the other half to trying to de-moralize ourselves again."[58] Sachs needed to heal in innumerable small ways before he

could be a normal human and, once again, a freedom fighter (after liberation, he became a justice on the Constitutional Court of South Africa). An
assault, like other forms of deprivation we have seen, dehumanizes. If the
victims are lucky, like Sachs, they can slowly and eventually rebuild their
humanity.

Sachs also describes how injury and deprivation alter moods: "I know
that the attempt on my life was totally impersonal, probably undertaken by
someone who had never met me and who almost certainly had no feelings
about me or animus towards me as a person, yet I feel as though a terrible
hatred exists in the world against me, and in spite of the sense of triumph
at having survived, I have an overwhelming and primitive need to be reassured of my worth as a person. I want to be cradled and fondled and
loved, not hear how brave I have been or receive speeches however warm
and comradely."[59] We might see this as a deep, existential version of the
challenges to one's sense of self described by identity control theory, which
would predict a vast need for reassurance after such a challenge.[60]

Part of this process of regaining his sense of human dignity consisted of
rejecting a feeling of victimhood. Sachs focuses not on strength or activity,
but on moral goodness: "I feel intuitively that all bad is attached to those
who tried to kill me, and all good to my doctors, my nurses, the security
team, my comrades, my friends, my family, Lucia and, of course, myself."[61]
Although the reader is surprised that Sachs had felt ambiguities after decades of fighting apartheid, the sharpened contrast between good and evil
reflates his emotional energy. He would not admit to feeling like a hero, but
he does. And he is one.

Sachs observes that one form of oppression is to take away our opportunities for intimate emotional expression: "Ever since I was seventeen
and became politically active, I have lived with the notion that there are
others accompanying every move I make, listening to every word I say.
How can you have an argument, express physical passion, write an intimate letter if you know that others might be listening in or looking on?"[62]
Every orator knows how difficult it is to give a speech if you don't know who
your audience is, whether your performance is verbal or somatic. Those
under intense surveillance can never know for sure who their audiences
are. They must be aware of every emotional display, robbing them of what
we pretend is the essence of emotions, authenticity and spontaneity. Such
surveillance is another form of bodily control.

*   *   *

At one time, most emotions were viewed on the model of urges, as "passions" that propel us without any thought or resistance, as bodily events

that "happen to" us in contrast to willed choice and action. But overpowering urges are a small subset of human feelings. Plus, even urges and reflex emotions are not the simple instinctual programs we once thought.

What is more, such urges come in two forms. One kind, centered on deprivation, focus our attention in such an immediate way that they rarely influence political action—except to suggest how deprivation can crowd out political concerns. Survival needs usually—but not always—impede other motivations.[63] The other kind of urges can be satisfied in multiple ways, or via multiple pathways. Like Scarlett O'Hara in *Gone with the Wind*, we work to avoid the pain of hunger or fatigue. Immediate lust or addiction may crowd out other concerns, but I may take elaborate steps to get to those final moments of pleasure. Indeed, impressing potential lovers is a central human motivation. I may control some urges in order to satisfy others. And of course I frequently use others' urges to seduce, persuade, and coerce them: creating situations in which predictable feelings are likely to arise.

Urges matter in part because they are often entwined with other types of feeling. They can drive or block our reflex emotions. They affect our moods. They can relate us to others, even generating collective loyalties. And they have implications for our moral pride and shame, how we feel about ourselves and others. Short-run emotions shape our long-run emotions, just as they are conditioned by them.

Urges can get us into trouble, often by making us something other than a fully functioning adult. Some of them are simply bodily failures to carry on a path of action rather than attend to immediate needs. We are rarely blamed for these failures. The regret potential is limited for most urges: no one condemns you for fatigue; indeed, there is often sympathy. The exception is addiction, which is sometimes seen as a blameworthy choice and other times seen as an externally imposed infliction. But the disruption potential is always considerable for urges.

The remaining categories of feelings unfold over longer time frames than either reflex emotions or urges. As we move to more abiding emotions, we move further from any image of feelings as sudden disruptions of our planned actions. We turn next to moods, which we often carry with us from one setting to another. Moods may last for hours or even days, and like some urges, they can occasionally be woven into our personalities. They influence political action largely by affecting our levels of energy and enthusiasm for what we are doing.

4: MOODS

Happiness is not a goal; it is a by-product.

ELEANOR ROOSEVELT

You only have power over people as long as you don't take every-thing away from them. But when you've robbed a man of every-thing, he's no longer in your power—he's free again.

ALEXANDER SOLZHENITSYN

No one expected Egypt's uprising in January 2011. There had been out-rage and frustration over President Hosni Mubarak's cronyist regime for decades, and efforts to mobilize around two grisly killings by Alexandrian police in 2010 had failed despite the use of Facebook. People were shocked but remained cynical. Then in Tunisia, Mohamed Bouazizi set himself on fire in protest, and a month later—January 14, 2011—Tunisian dictator Ben Ali panicked and fled the country. Suddenly, there was hope in Egypt.

A rally in Cairo against police brutality, held on National Police Day, Jan-uary 25, drew tens of thousands of protestors, who managed to coordinate their marches partly via cell phones and social media. They demanded term limits on the president, not his resignation. The next day, the gov-ernment shut down Internet access for most Egyptians. But that did not slow the momentum. The twenty-eighth was a Friday, when mosques were filled with the faithful. Buoyed by the feeling of solidarity that Durkheim said religious rituals provide, by the feeling that Allah was on their side, hundreds of thousands took to the streets after prayers. Two tense weeks followed: some concessions from Mubarak, attacks by armed thugs, and the army's crucial decision not to intervene.

The protestors' giant tent camp in Cairo's Tahrir Square grew steadily. Despite the risks, people were on holiday, hopeful of big changes and thus in a good mood. Each victory, small or large, cranked up the emotional energy of that mood. And with that exhilaration as background, each attack—verbal or physical—by Mubarak's thugs and spokespersons created more indignation than fear. Or rather, indignation turned the reflex fear into a useful moral feeling of outrage. Tahrir Square became a carnival, a moment of madness. The outrage peaked on February 10, when Mubarak went on television and—instead of the expected resignation—gave a meandering but defiant refusal. The next day, another Friday, the crowds expanded enormously. Mubarak resigned that evening.[1]

Everyone knows what it is like to be in a good mood or bad, even though we don't always recognize our mood until we begin to interact with others or go about our daily tasks. I may have a strong reflex emotion that surprises me and signals what mood I am in, such as being inappropriately angry. In some cases, being aware of a mood, and tracing its sources, can temper it—as with many feeling-thinking sequences. Because we are often unaware of our moods, those stage-managing our settings can sometimes manipulate them for their own purposes, whether political ads, protest rituals, or candles for a romantic dinner (what Christophe Traïni calls "sensitizing devices").[2]

If other emotions give our actions direction, moods usually affect their pace. They give us more energy and eagerness for tasks, or they deflate that energy. Emotions such as enthusiasm, happiness, and confidence are inflating moods; depression, resignation, and sadness are deflating moods. Verta Taylor calls them "vitalizing" and "devitalizing."[3] Moods filter our intentions and actions, strengthening or dissolving them, changing their tone or seriousness. These energy levels affect our ability to continue collective projects such as politics.

Moods typically last longer than reflex emotions but not as long as affective or moral commitments. We usually carry moods with us from one social setting to another, due to the persisting neurochemical states associated with them. A subcategory of neurotransmitters, called neuromodulators, remain floating around without being reabsorbed immediately; these include histamine, serotonin, dopamine, and noradrenaline. Drugs, legal and illegal, can affect the chemistry directly, too.

Moods differ from other emotional types in not having direct objects but in being a general feeling, along two dimensions: pleasant versus unpleasant, and low versus high arousal. Pleasant moods include elation (high arousal) and serenity (low arousal); unpleasant moods include distress (high arousal) and depression (low arousal). Psychologist William Morris describes them as "frames of mind," suggesting something broader than reflexes and urges.[4] Moods are more diffuse than other emotions or urges. They used to be considered less intense as well, but this idea came from an exaggerated contrast with reflex emotions. Today, we can recognize that some moods are extremely intense, especially depression, while many other moods are mild. Both types affect our availability for collective action.

The obvious contrast is between positive and negative moods. Other states that we sometimes *call* moods—one is in a "silly mood" or a "pensive mood"—either are subcategories (silly moods are generally good moods, pensive are probably negative) or refer to recurrent behaviors. According to the American Psychiatric Association's *Diagnostic and Statistical Manual of Mental Disorders*, only depression and bipolarism (manic depression) are mood disorders: mania being a very good mood and depression a very bad one. But debates rage over the boundary between a normal mood and a mood "disorder." Most of the literature distinguishes moods that result from events in the environment, such as the loss of a loved one, from endogenous moods that recur, arise without external causes, and respond to drug therapy.[5]

Morris paints a similar picture of moods consonant with Martha Nussbaum's cognitive appraisal approach. He sees them as cues in self-appraisal. Good moods indicate that we are generally doing well, bad moods signal some deficit, as in social support or bodily strength. Morris's "continuity hypothesis" is that "all mood states, disordered or not, are the result of an integrated set of psychological and biological processes. Such processes may be triggered by changes in the environment or in the person, and the initiating circumstance may be psychological or biological."[6] Political activists try to create events and environments favorable to pleasant, aroused moods, but they can also hope to take advantage of people's manic moments when these moods occur from other causes.

In everyday English, moods often have negative connotations, as in the adjective *moody*, a term of praise for landscapes but never humans. This condemnation depends on the more general idea that all feelings derail us from reality and rationality. In fact, we are always in some kind of mood—good, bad, or indifferent—as part of being human. Our levels of serotonin, oxytocin, and other neurotransmitters are always exerting some influence, whether they are high, low, or medium.

Moods interact with other types of emotion. They affect our propensity to feel and exhibit other emotions, as in the case of a depressed person inclined to sadness or irritation. Conversely, events and reflex emotions can increase or decrease our energy or enthusiasm because they alter our moods. After feeling anger or disgust, we may remain in a bad mood for some time. We take an echo of the joys of the crowd with us when we go home. We may be in a calm, pleasant mood after the satisfaction of an urge or in a bad mood when it has been thwarted or delayed. If we feel positively toward a particular person, group, or object, this is more of an affective commitment than a mood, but being with or thinking about them may improve our mood.

Scholars of protest have done a poor job of understanding moods, often collapsing them into reflex emotions such as joy or affective attachments to groups. They are indeed hard to distinguish from other emotions, with which they interact constantly. Bert Klandermans and his collaborators Anouk van Leeuwen and Jacquelien van Stekelenburg have perhaps come closest in discussing the "atmosphere" of demonstrations, contrasting those that have gone well from those that have unfolded poorly.[7] Moods can indeed disappear, hardening into more permanent states such as resignation, a kind of affective orientation to other players and arenas. Moods are about energy, and nothing is more central to voluntary action than energy levels.

WHAT TRIGGERS MOODS?

Relatively minor things can affect our moods. A fleeting compliment, a piece of good news, a pleasant aroma, or even a pacemaker regulating a heartbeat can provide energy and improve a person's mood. Economists claim that stock markets do better on sunny days, and Norbert Schwarz and Gerald Clore used good or bad weather as part of their experimental setup, telephoning different groups of subjects on sunny or on gray days.[8] Even seasons, with their varying amounts of light, can shift people's moods for several months at a time. Note the difference between a mood and a reflex emotion: I may feel sad when it rains, but that is different from feeling sad *about* the rain (although this is also possible, if I feel disappointed about having to cancel a rally). And as part of the thinking body, even our intestinal flora may have some impact on our moods.[9]

Events and conscious information also affect moods, primarily via other kinds of emotions. Events leave biochemical traces that affect our moods: when our affective attachments are triggered—if we see a loved one, pet a dog, or join a warm crowd, for instance—our oxytocin levels rise. Reflex emotions, primarily, put us in good or bad moods. Of the reflex emotions, joy and disappointment are closely connected to the moods they leave behind. The other reflex emotions can have varying effects on moods, depending on circumstances and interpretation. They may even affect our moral emotions, which in turn affect our moods: if we are proud or ashamed of our reflex emotions, this in turn will affect our moods. I will be in a bad mood if I am ashamed of having gotten angry with my slow-moving mother but in a good mood if I am proud of my anger at the mistreatment of a passing carriage horse (a self-righteous satisfaction that helped launch animal protection societies in the nineteenth century).

Deborah Gould, in her study of the radicalization of lesbian and gay rights movements, suggests how action puts us in good moods. "Expression of anger and defiance was just the thing [we] needed." After chanting "Civil rights or civil war!" for a while, one participant commented, "This morning I was feeling really depressed, now I feel great. We really needed this. We need to show we're not gonna take it. We're gonna fight back, and hard."[10] We know what will put us in good moods, assuming we are in a sufficiently good mood to have the energy to do it.

Like other emotions, moods arise most often out of interactions with other people. Sociologist Long Doan examines why some reflex emotions are spun out into moods while others are not. The intensity of the emotion and our capacity to reflect on it both seem to increase the chance of its persisting as a mood. These in turn, according to Doan, depend on whether we are interacting with someone with a higher status than ours, whether we feel that the other person is responsible for the interaction, and whether we can attribute the interaction to an organization rather than an individual (we attribute more legitimacy to organizations): these conditions make us more likely to reflect on the interaction and so remain in the relevant mood.[11] Politicized people and groups typically aim to sustain this kind of reflection, presumably creating moods and even background emotions out of reflex emotions.

Like reflex emotions, and partly because of them, moods play out against a backdrop of expectations. If we expect success, a failure is disappointing and deflating. An unexpected success, in contrast, boosts our energy.

Situations, events, and reflex emotions are not the only explanation of moods. Individuals differ in their biochemistry, and so they are prone to different moods. Moods can sometimes be almost permanent, something like aspects of temperament. Or rather, one aspect of personality is that we are prone to certain kinds of moods. Some people are prone to be happy or cheerful, others are depressive. This tendency results in part from variations in brain chemistry, itself the result of developmental influences as well as ongoing ones. Recent developments in epigenetics have demonstrated that our capacities for generating and receiving neurotransmitters develop early, as the result of how we are treated in infancy. The archaic term *humor* linked personality and mood more tightly than we do today, thanks to an ancient theory of both personality and mood as based on the balance of blood, phlegm, and black and yellow bile in our bodies. The French *humeur* still covers both temperament and mood.

Psychologist David Lykken, best known for his studies of twins, concluded that our genes explain half of our levels of happiness, which I'll argue shortly can be a kind of mood. He proposed that each of us has a "set point" of how happy we are. Events can make us more or less happy for a while, but we tend over time to return to our set point (although in the case of losing a job or a spouse, it can take years.)[12] Happiness seems to be related to two personality traits, neurosis and extroversion. Neurotics, especially given to anger, anxiety, and guilt, tend to be in worse moods. One possible reason is that they have fewer affective bonds, a big potential source of happiness and other good moods. For the same reason, extroverts tend to be in better moods and more happy.[13]

It is possible that our set points can change, especially as a result of trauma. Prolonged state terror cows its subjects, leaving them in permanent fear and humiliation—which would have to affect one's mood. Scholars have described this condition as combining a sense of personal weakness or vulnerability, a permanent state of jumpy alertness, feelings of helplessness and powerlessness, and even distorted views of reality.[14] Trauma may produce extreme bad moods, with listless and deflated victims, but some of these traits can be found in less extreme versions as well.

But nothing influences our moods more predictably than our interactions with others.

COLLINS ON EMOTIONAL ENERGY

Randall Collins has developed a sweeping theory of emotional energy. Combining Durkheim and Goffman, Collins argues that face-to-face interactions— ritualized to varying degrees and in various ways—generate emotional energy that gives participants confidence and a sense of agency. They carry this energy to their next encounters, along chains of interactions, with each interaction raising or (if unsuccessful) lowering emotional energy. Although some of this emotional energy involves an affective bond with other participants, most of it consists of a positive (or negative) mood.

For starters, this is a theory of motivation, as humans seek the excitement of emotional energy, or good moods. Collins contrasts his model with rational choice images of calculation and maximization: "Humans are not very good at calculating costs and benefits, but they feel their way toward goals because they can judge everything subconsciously by its contribution to a fundamental motive: seeking maximal emotional energy in interaction rituals." It is not just "a fundamental motive" among others, but "the master motive across all institutional arenas."[15] I am skeptical of any claim about a master motive, but emotional energy is a more plausible candidate than self-interest or normative conformity, those classic tropes of economics and sociology, respectively.

How do interaction rituals work? "The central mechanism," Collins says, "is that occasions that combine a high degree of mutual focus of attention, that is, a high degree of intersubjectivity, together with a high degree of emotional entrainment—through bodily synchronization, mutual stimulation/arousal of participants' nervous systems—result in feelings of membership that are attached to cognitive symbols; and result also in the emotional energy of individual participants, giving them feelings of confidence, enthusiasm, and desire for action in what they consider a morally proper path." Successful ritual interactions generate both positive moods and affective commitments. Physical copresence is important, as the sights, sounds, smells, and physical contact combine for an overwhelming sense of connection with one another. Speakers and audiences unconsciously fall into rhythm with each other. People feel "an energy" or "an electricity" in the room. Moods, like reflex emotions, are contagious.[16] The mood created during the ritual gradually "ebbs away in longer periods of minutes, hours, and days."[17]

Here is a useful way to understand the emotional dynamics of protest events and other meetings. Successful interaction rituals generate moral solidarity, which encompasses both collective identity and trust in others—making collective action more satisfying and hence easier to accomplish. Because moods fade, protest groups usually try to have overlapping cycles of interactions—for example, weekly meetings of a small group along with occasional protests encompassing much larger groupings. In my own work on the emotions of protest rituals, I likened these to regular church services alongside less frequent pilgrimages to sacred sites.[18]

Historian William McNeill, recalling his basic training in the US Army in 1941, describes the coordination of bodies—marching, dancing, chanting, singing, shouting—that creates powerful moods. The constant drilling he experienced, useless for moving troops in a mechanized age, left him with "a sense of pervasive well-being . . . more specifically, a strange sense of personal enlargement; a sort of swelling out, becoming bigger than life, thanks to participation in a collective ritual." This is a mood of euphoria: "a state of generalized emotional exaltation whose warmth was indubitable, without, however, having any definite external meaning or attachment."[19]

Interaction rituals can fail. Little groups talk among themselves; audience members watch passersby instead of listening to the speech; participants begin to leave. If individuals attend because of a sense of obligation, they are unlikely to feel much enthusiasm (one reason that formal rituals often feel empty and unexciting). Sheer numbers also matter: energy dissipates when fewer people show up than expected or when they leave too soon. Expectations are important here, as they are for most emotions. We compare what we expected to what then happens. As a result, people feel less attached to a cause or a group, or they feel that the movement is in decline. They leave in a bad mood.

Collins contrasts emotional energy as a mood with dramatic, disruptive emotions such as "fear, terror, anger, embarrassment, joy, and so forth."

Microsociologists such as Goffman and Harold Garfinkel, he says, have been more interested in the production of feelings of normalcy or "ordinariness," stressing "solidarity, feelings of membership, and in Goffman's case, feelings about one's self."[20] The dramatic emotions, mostly what I have called reflex emotions, affect our longer-term moods. Most obviously, joy and disappointment translate into high or low levels of emotional energy, good or bad moods. Successful interaction rituals use shared reflex emotions to create a common mood.

Part of Collins' theory, indebted to Theodore Kemper's emphasis on power and status hierarchies as producing emotions, addresses inequalities in the emotional energy generated among participants. Some interactions are designed for some people to give orders to others—Collins calls these "power rituals"—and the unsurprising result is that those giving orders are charged up while those who are told what to do lose emotional energy. Other interactions, "status rituals" in Collins' terms, are meant to reinforce the solidarity of a group, but they too provide more energy to those at the center of the ritual, the center of attention, than to those on the periphery. Needless to say, those who can organize and place themselves at the center of interactions are more enthusiastic about them. There are often conflicts over who will lead an interaction and thus grab more emotional energy. These struggles, often dismissed merely as uncomfortable moments, "break the focus of ritual microcoordination and prevent the circular buildup of anticipations on both sides."[21]

Collins links his theory to Thomas Scheff's research on pride and shame. "Pride is the social attunement emotion," Collins says, "the feeling that one's self fits naturally into the flow of interaction, indeed that one's personal sense epitomizes the leading mood of the group." At the extreme, such "energy stars" are recognized as charismatic leaders or heroes. Shame, a form of low emotional energy, is an acknowledgement of low status or attention in a group; its first recognition is often accompanied by reflex anger but it settles into something like a mood of depression.[22]

Collins overreaches somewhat, presenting his interaction rituals as a theory of all emotions. As I see it, he begins with a theory of reflex emotions, then adds a theory of how reflex emotions can affect our moods and even our affective and moral commitments. It is an ambitious and largely successful theory, which works best for explaining the impact of reflex emotions on moods.

Most marches and rallies generate a good mood, but I would expect the effect to be stronger on newcomers to protest, often young people. The reason has to do with expectations: the novelty of the experience for them yields reflex feelings of joy, which can put a participant in an especially good mood, compared to someone who has been to many such events and for whom they may feel routine. (Plus, as we age, our engrained habits of participation or nonparticipation probably influence our participation more than the moods we anticipate.) People don't forget their first protests, just as I have not forgotten mine way back in 1978.[23]

THE EFFECTS OF MOODS

We react to events and process information differently depending on what mood we are in. In a good mood, we react more positively to what happens around us. The stronger the mood, I suspect, the greater the effect. Research in psychology is inevitably conducted on mild moods of the kind that can be induced in laboratories, not the kind of euphoria generated in protests. It seems likely that the latter effects will be similar but stronger. Feats of heroism become possible when people feel exhilarated and aroused, including the kind of bravery that can make a revolution succeed despite the odds.[24]

Positive moods give people optimism and a sense of their own efficacy. Negative moods increase pessimism and lead people to perceive greater risks in their environments. Mood also affects cognitive processes, with positive moods apparently increasing people's ability to make creative associations and negative ones limiting people to rule-based thinking. A good mood also seems to help us face unpleasant information and tasks that are nevertheless beneficial.[25] Protest may depend on just that ability to challenge an unpleasant situation.

Psychologists disagree somewhat about the effects of mild moods, especially positive ones. For more than thirty years, Norbert Schwarz, Gerald Clore, and their collaborators have traced the impact of moods on judgments: good moods lead us to make positive judgments, bad moods to make negative judgments—unless we are reminded of the source of our mood, in which case we compensate and the effect disappears. The focus of this tradition has been on the errors in judgment that moods lead us to make.[26] Political mobilization, often due to leaders who put us in good moods, might just be an error of this sort, in the calculating-brain view.

Fortunately, Alice Isen has worked instead to show that mild positive moods *improve* cognitive functioning and decision making. "The majority of existing data," she summarizes, "suggest that mild positive affect enables cognitive flexibility and thus fosters improved consideration of situations and problems, and improved performance on a wide range of tasks, as long as there is reason for the person to engage the task. People who are feeling mildly happy are better able to think about multiple aspects of situations and to see situations and stimuli in multiple ways, seemingly simultaneously."[27] Good moods, according to Isen, also encourage people to be kind, generous, helpful, friendly, and socially responsible, all impulses that might encourage political participation.[28]

In addition to prosocial action, good moods seem to affect our assessments of future outcomes. This is a central mechanism for political mobilization, as people are more likely to turn out if they think they can win (although, in contrast to rational choice and political opportunity theories, I do not think this calculation of winning is either a necessary or a sufficient condition for participation). In part, good moods may encourage people to think of a wider range of possible outcomes. In part, people in a good mood may discount risks.[29]

Good moods also have a halo effect on our feelings for others: the feeling of merging with the group and our positive feelings for that group that result from successful interaction rituals. If we arrive in a good mood, perhaps from anticipation, it is easier for interaction rituals to sustain it. Our companions take on a glow as, buoyed by oxytocin, we associate them with our own good feelings. If we are in a bad mood, especially a depressed mood, we are less likely to even show up.

Bad moods tend to break down the reciprocal love that fosters collective identity, suggesting their disruption potential. Erika Summers Effler recounts her own deteriorating mood at a poorly organized picket against the death penalty—clearly a failed interaction ritual. "I wasn't sure where to go . . . I wasn't sure where to look." Hostile passersby yelled at her. She describes her feelings as anxiety and frustration, although it is possible also to detect some shaming. Each of her reflex emotions contributed to her emerging bad mood: "I was becoming more and more tense as the negative reactions seemed to heap one upon the other, each one happening before the effects of the previous one had worn off. The few positive responses did little to counter my mounting desire to flee." At the end, she says, "Emotionally worn out, I walked to the bus stop feeling humiliated and frustrated."[30] More typical participants, not writing PhD dissertations as Summers Effler was, would not return.

Events that have nothing to do with politics—such as the death of a loved one—also affect our moods, which in turn shape our ability to function in the political sphere. That is the point of a mood: it colors everything we do, far beyond the realm where it might have been generated. The "normal sadness" that accompanies the loss of someone or something valued usually depresses our activity in all areas. We feel a kind of pain that, like physical pain and the other urges considered in chapter 3, absorbs our attention and crowds out other goals. Gradually, the pain subsides, and our energy returns, sometimes after very long periods of grieving. (Psychologists distinguish *irrelevant affect*, caused by something else, from *relevant affect*, caused by what we are doing, such as the interaction ritual that puts us in a good mood.)

Anger, also a common element of grieving, opens other possibilities for action. The anger of grieving is often directed inward ("if only I could have done more to protect her"), and sometimes outward toward the deceased ("how could she leave me?"). But sometimes it can be directed at others, through complex processes of blame. In these cases, our mood can change to an action orientation, involving moral indignation. This is an unusual case in which a bad mood, supplemented with anger, can encourage action. As Gould's activist from the AIDS Coalition to Unleash Power (ACT UP) suggested, action itself can change a bad mood into a good one.

I have used the term *moral shock* to suggest mechanisms by which extremely bad moods—of paralysis, disappointment, grief, and more—can trigger action to try to set things right again. The shock originates in reflex emotions that arise when we discover that the world is not as it seemed, and we are startled, stunned, sad, angry, disgusted, and/or disappointed. We enter a disoriented mood, which may eventuate in our rethinking or reasserting our basic moral commitments, in action to set things right, or alternatively in depressed withdrawal. Mothers Against Drunk Driving (MADD) was founded and sustained by mothers, stunned by their grief over losing a child, who were able to find satisfying pathways into action.[31]

DEEP MOODS

Not all moods change so easily. Moods differ in how deeply we feel them. I may feel a bit sad because it is raining; I felt much sadder when Donald Trump was elected in 2016; but neither mood reached the depths of clinical depression, perhaps the ultimate bad mood. Philosopher Matthew Ratcliffe insists that "deep moods" such as depression are not simply more intense, nor do they necessarily last longer than other moods (think of panic). Drawing on Martin Heidegger, he describes a category of existential moods that we would say we are *in* rather than something that we *have*. While most moods simply color our experience, deep moods *make possible* that experience, including a range of emotions that go with it.

A deep mood, according to Ratcliffe, is a kind of "pre-intentional state," because "it contributes to the structure of intentionally directed emotion, determining the range of emotions that one is capable of experiencing. For example, in the extreme case of a mood where the world appears utterly bereft of practical significance, *worrying* about whether a project will succeed and *hoping* that it will succeed would not be possible."[32] Deep moods are not the only kind of background emotion that structures the other emotions that we experience: our affective and moral commitments do the same thing. But we are less likely to be aware of our deep moods—one reason, according to Ratcliffe, that they have not been well analyzed.

"Moods constitute the various ways in which we are able to experience things as *mattering*," Ratcliffe says. Reflex emotions depend on things already mattering: they presuppose deep moods. "In order to be afraid, one must already find oneself in the world in such a way that being *in danger* or *under threat* are possibilities. Some being, perhaps oneself, has to matter in a certain kind of way for fear to be possible."[33]

Depression is now a familiar deep mood, thanks to a generation of memoir writers.[34] The authors report similar feelings, amounting to a kind of disconnect from the physical and social worlds. It is impossible to take pleasure in anything. One cannot feel joy. Nothing matters. It is like being dead or numb, under a cloud of darkness. There is nothing to do to fix it, either. If most bad moods sap energy for action, depression does so more than any other.

The novelist David Foster Wallace, whose own depression led him to hang himself in 2008 at the age of forty-six, described it as "the Great White Shark of pain." It is "a level of psychic pain wholly incompatible with human life as we know it . . . a double bind in which any/all of the alternatives we associate with human agency—sitting or standing, doing or resting, speaking or keeping silent, living or dying—are not just unpleasant but literally horrible. . . . Everything is part of the problem, and there is no solution." Most other emotions are impossible: no affective attachments, moral commitments, reflex emotions, urges, or even other moods.[35]

Depression is an extreme case, remarkable in its paralysis. Panic, which we identified in chapter 2, is a similar kind of all-encompassing feeling deeper than the specific emotions we have while panicking. Nostalgia is also a deep mood, with certain kinds of emotions and attachments that it allows or disallows. Resignation, a common influence on politics, is a deep mood that operates as a mild form of depression. Deep moods are deep in the sense of being the background for other emotions, not in the sense of necessarily being intensely felt. (In this way, depression may be a misleading exemplar.)

At the positive end of the spectrum, revolutionary moments of madness such as that at Tahrir Square may be a deep mood, nurturing other moods and cultivating a range of emotions in its bright light. The euphoric mood in which everything is possible is the opposite of a dark depression in which nothing is possible. It becomes worthwhile to imagine those futures and how to craft them.

In the end it is difficult to distinguish moods from deep moods, as all moods are part of our emotional background coloring our short-run actions and feelings. Deep moods are a good heuristic because they dramatically highlight the shaping constraints of moods in general. Political organizers must take deep moods for granted, and appeal to them when possible, but they can do little to transform them. Only after they have initially succeeded in drawing people to their meetings and marches can they influence participants' more normal moods. Nonetheless, deep moods constrain actions, with disruption and (when someone shifts into another mood) regret potential.

HAPPINESS

If depression is the ultimate debilitating bad mood, happiness is—in some forms—an inflatingly good mood. A new field of happiness studies has flourished in the twenty-first century, yielding two distinct ways of measuring happiness, or rather, ways of measuring two related but separate feelings. One approach is to ask people a general question about how satisfied they are with their lives. This question seems to elicit some kind of abstract appraisal, as respondents think about how else their lives might have been. Their expectations matter, and they no doubt compare their lives to those of friends, family, role models, or people in other nations. A strong moral component seems inevitable: "I've been a good spouse, mother, and member of my church. I am satisfied with that." This pride in one's life differs from the superficial-sounding "pleasure" that was the heart of utilitarian theory. (John Stuart Mill keenly pointed out the difference in 1863.)[36]

The "unit" in this case is one's lifetime so far, and a kind of "moral pride" (or shame) is being observed. According to Martin Seligman, the basic components of life satisfaction include having not only positive emotions (presumably including frequent good moods) but also engagement in tasks (what others have called "flow"), a variety of strong affective bonds, a sense of meaning, and recognized accomplishments.[37]

The other approach, and the reason I am addressing happiness in this chapter, is to ask people how they feel or felt at particular moments during the day. Here the time frame is more immediate. Labeled "experience sampling," this approach captures subjects' moods during a variety of activities. As Daniel Kahneman cleverly puts it, this method is about "living," whereas the first method is about "thinking about living."[38] One is a mood, the other a moral judgment. The best way to capture someone's mood at any moment is to call or text her and ask. A less expensive but less accurate version is to ask her the following morning about the previous day's moods and activities—but the tricks of memory already intrude. (Interestingly, for the "lifetime" method, these transitory moods are seen as an interference, not part of happiness.) Contrary to Eleanor Roosevelt, happiness may be a goal *and* a byproduct.

Having children is an example of how moral happiness and mood happiness can diverge: parents tend to be proud of their lives as a whole but less likely to be in a good mood at any given moment.[39] (The good moods mostly return once the children have left home.) Going to lots of protests may be an activity that contributes to happy moods at the time *and* makes one proud of one's life.[40]

Happiness may come in a third form as well: a reflex emotion that we have when something happens that pleases us, and which shows in our face as "joy," a kind of pleasant surprise. With its characteristic short-term facial expressions, this is one of the reflex emotions that Paul Ekman originally claimed to find.

Economists and psychologists have shown that people are not very good at predicting what actions will make them happy—a challenge to economic formulations of expected utility as the basis of decision making. Participating in collective activities is less subject to disappointment than buying more stuff. Those who volunteer seem more satisfied with their lives.[41] Experience sampling also finds that social interactions put us in better moods than solitary activities—in line with Collins' theory of emotional energy. The satisfaction of participation may also be one of the reasons that religious observance is correlated with life satisfaction.[42] A sense of our own collective agency puts us in a good mood, and good moods also enhance our sense of agency.

The three forms of happiness suggest corresponding satisfactions from political activity: the joy we experience while doing something, the good mood this leaves us in, and the broader contribution that the activity makes to our moral sense of our lives. (Good moods also lead us into political action.) We may get so wrapped up in an activity—attaining a sense of "flow"—that we do not have time to ask ourselves whether we are happy. But we feel good. Afterward, we continue to feel good for some time. Much later, after the mood has faded, we are proud of ourselves for having done something admirable, and so it contributes to our sense of a satisfactory life. Presumably, these forms can diverge, as when an activity feels great at the time, but in retrospect we think it was mistaken and we are disappointed with ourselves. The difference is that between reflex joy and moods, on the one hand, and moral emotions, on the other. Presumably, crowd theorists would deploy this contrast to describe the supposed regrets of crowds.

Robert Putnam claims (unsurprisingly, given his commitment to civic groups) that attending group meetings once a month increases life satisfaction.[43] I find it hard to believe that these meetings are always fun, so I suspect the effect is due primarily to moral pride. But some groups *are* fun, giving participants joy *and* allowing them to leave meetings in a good mood *and* feel proud of themselves for going. Another possibility is a kind of cognitive dissonance: because the meetings are dull, participants assure themselves that they are morally important. I have engaged in that internal conversation with myself more than once.

Joy, happy moods, and life pride are all facilitated by our political context, especially the potential openings for collective action and control. Derek Bok sums up this research. Foremost, he says, "Living in a democracy with guarantees of freedom is particularly important.... Other significant correlates include observance of the rule of law, efficient government agencies, a low level of violence and corruption, a high degree of trust in public officials (especially the police), and responsive encounters by citizens with public agencies and officials."[44] These are mostly capacities that help us act (or opportunities, structuralists would say).

When political protections like these are absent or violated, they become grievances. Often, the original complaint fades in comparison with the new outrage over government silence, inaction, even repression. Sometimes state repression frightens protestors into silence, but at other times it increases indignation and activity. The only way to understand the divergence is to map the feeling-thinking mechanisms at work, as participants interact with each other to articulate their outrage, express their fears, and anticipate what will happen next (they may also interact with family members who feel especially the fears). With sufficient indignation, what begins as protest against economic conditions can spiral into support for political revolution.[45]

When you fight for your basic political rights, this is almost always a source of life happiness, a moral pride associated with dignity. Any sense of purpose or meaning in your life contributes to life happiness in this way. This is why positive moral emotions have the lowest regret potential: they help us define what is most important in life. The same political activity may or may not put you in a good mood.

The flip side of life satisfaction is *regret*, when we think about how things might have gone differently, and especially choices we made that now seem to have been wrong. This "life regret" need not be unpleasant, as it may contain fanciful reveries about what might have been, a kind of daydreaming, or a poignant mix of pride and regret. There is a second form of regret, disappointment, a reflex emotion that is opposite to joy: when we first learn that something we did has gone badly. To retain the parallel with forms of happiness, a third kind of regret can put us in a bad mood (although these negative moods, lacking direct objects, are probably not themselves forms of regret, since regret is always *about* something).[46]

HOPE AND CONFIDENCE

Good moods provide energy to commence or continue an activity; they especially provide confidence, which I have argued elsewhere is a big advantage in any kind of strategic engagement.[47] You think your victory is inevitable, and you deploy your forces with that in mind. You develop a sense of agency, control, even of luck. You develop a better image of yourself and your team. Although calculating-brain psychologists tend to speak of confident moods as illusions, they have nonetheless documented their many positive effects on action.

A sense that we can control what happens around us is partly based on personality but also is influenced by situation and hence by mood. In classic work on the subject, Albert Bandura suggested four sources of information about our efficacy: past accomplishments, vicarious experience, verbal persuasion, and physiological states (moods); self-efficacy in turn affects our willingness to initiate coping behavior and to stay at it longer and more energetically.[48] Ellen Langer observed that activities based on skill—especially the presence of options, personal involvement, familiarity with the stimulus, and the exertion of effort—enhance the illusion of our control and so increase enthusiasm for an activity. The titillating but unfortunate language of "illusion" suggests that people normally have an accurate sense of their impact on the world; a more cultural view would try to explain people's views without judging them.[49]

Elizabeth Williamson gets at the role of hope with what she calls "the magic of multiple emotions," showing how courage, confusion, fear, and hope interact with each other to increase the odds that people recruited to one event will return to future events. What I have described as a moral battery combining positive and negative emotions, she stretches out over time into sequences of positive and negative. She argues that the swings from one extreme to another intensify the emotions and that organizers plan the intended sequences carefully.[50] Her data suggest the ultimate need for a hopeful mood: the transformation of fear into hope has a positive effect. Confusion may also be transformed into hope, and sadness may aid the transition from shame or anger to hope. Many of the dynamics here have to do with the creation of emotional intensity, as good moods emerge from bad.

Successful rituals and hopeful understandings of events can create a special confidence in collective action, Ari Zolberg's "moments of madness" when participants feel that anything is possible. Many scholars today mistrust this term, since it sounds like the image of the irrational crowd. But Zolberg is not saying that people become irrational or even that they do things they will regret. To reject the term is to accept the old dualism that strong emotions make people irrational. When we specify the feeling-thinking components of those exuberant moments we can save the concept. It plays a useful role in our tool kit.

The exhilaration that Zolberg captures is actually an extremely good mood. In 1848, 1871, 1936, and 1968, Paris became a joyful, utopian festival. "Nothing puts man in a better mood," said Bertrand de Jouvenal, "than to escape the boredom of his routine and the laziness of his obligations. He laughs, he walks around, and you think that he is naturally good. . . . The 'sit-down strike' is a protracted picnic." In Henri Lefèbvre's Marxist version of the same idea, the proletariat "transforms itself in one leap into a community, a communion, in whose midst work, joy, pleasure, the achievement of needs—and first of all social needs and the need for sociability—will never be separated." According to Zolberg, hatreds disappear in the good mood of solidarity, as "human beings feel that they are in direct touch with one another as well as with their inner selves. The streets of the city, its objects, and even the weather take on harmonious qualities. Falsehood, ugliness, and evil give way to beauty, goodness, and truth." Even urges such as hunger fade.[51]

In a hopeful mood, people's sense of the possible expands; the costs of action seem to decrease, and the possible benefits soar. Nancy Whittier and Helena Flam have (independently) used the inevitable term *emotional liberation* to get at a similar package of emotions that are useful to protest movements.[52] Full emotional liberation would contain changes in all my five types of feelings: some collective control over urges and reflex emotions; a hopeful, exhilarating mood; shifting affective loyalties; and outrage and indignation around the new grievance. The complete package is probably rare. But separate changes in any of these can independently aid a protest movement.

Other evidence for moments of madness comes from another neglected tradition, collective behavior studies of natural disaster. Even in the absence of authorities and preexisting networks, people during and after disasters go to great lengths to take care of each other, organize basic services, find out what has happened, and search for survivors. Communities of survivors emerge, with a strong solidarity and their own ways of getting things done. Their improvised experiments are often then adopted by official authorities. Crime rates tend to fall in the face of this carnival atmosphere.[53]

Participants in political carnivals sometimes describe a sense of "making history" that seems part of their exhilaration, a strong sense of their own agency. A closely related mood comes from the excitement of watching history being made, of being present at the birth of something, at the kind of moment people will talk about in years to come, or which will make the evening news. It seems a blend of excitement and curiosity. Both are hopeful moods. Tahrir Square is a good example. Organizers stoke these feelings through grand narratives of history that give a special place to the current movement, sometimes by linking it to prominent movements of the past.

Judgments of "collective efficacy" have often been posited as a contributor to protest. "In my opinion, the [blank] movement will make the government modify its policy concerning [blank]" is the usual survey wording.[54] Surveys can also ask about impacts on third parties, on the movement itself, even on the satisfaction of individual participants in expressing their values. These opinions are treated as though they were a calculated cognitive prediction about potential outcomes, but it seems more likely that they reflect a positive or negative mood: confidence or the lack of it.

Drawing on individual self-efficacy, scholars have described a sense of collective efficacy that is crucial to collective action. Although Bert Klandermans posits the need for a "collective action frame," consisting of collective identity, a sense of injustice, and collective efficacy, the term *frame* makes it sound purely cognitive.[55] All three parts harbor strong emotional components: a collective identity is an affective conviction, a sense of injustice a moral commitment, and collective efficacy a mood. A sense of efficacy has been shown to be central to many movements pursuing many goals.[56] Doug McAdam's concept of "cognitive liberation" is this sense that a group or movement can change the world, especially when we upgrade it into emotional liberation.[57]

Parallels have been discovered in patterns of voting. David Darmofal has recently shown that individuals with a high sense of self-efficacy are more likely to vote, since they feel that their vote is more likely to matter.[58] Although his work does not examine moods explicitly, in both voting and protest it seems that moods which increase confidence should increase participation.

Researchers who were protestors in the 1960s—perhaps stung by their elders' criticism that they were simply passing through a phase—have been keen to demonstrate that the exhilarations of that period have left a lasting mark, a disposition for activism. Drawing on Bourdieu, Erik Neveu describes the social and political confidence that this generation retained as a kind of "militant capital" consisting of practical know-how, political knowledge and analysis, and social networks. The activists among French baby boomers lived in a world of material security, and they also tended to come from the top strata of the French educational system, reinforcing their feeling of efficacy. There is a social structure to hope, based on hierarchies of power and status.[59]

The hopeful exhilaration that feeds collective energy is known as "morale" or "esprit de corps" in military theory, acknowledged as central to success (in fact probably unduly worshipped, much as "leadership" is, in the interests of idolizing the leaders who can create morale). Hope and confidence are the moods that participants can carry from one battlefield (or political arena) to the next. They are one of the key ways that what happens in one strategic arena can affect what happens in another.[60]

LETHARGY

If hope provides emotional energy for a variety of collective and individual projects, participants can also be dejected and withdraw into a state of listlessness. We can either label lethargy as a mood itself or say that it is reduced action associated with a disheartened mood. Resignation, too, can be interpreted as either a mood or an action level.

One of the most striking examples of paralyzing dejection in today's world concerns global warming. Around the globe, most people, including the most affluent and educated, are "living in denial," as sociologist Kari Marie Norgaard puts it. Under the calculating brain model, rational choice theorists would insist that it is natural not to do anything, the option most people select most of the time. After all, there are costs to action, and we need a well-defined payoff to entice us to participate rather than to free ride. Norgaard shows instead that we work hard on our emotions to accomplish denial and inaction.

She studied a Norwegian town that depends on skiing for much of its livelihood, conducting fieldwork and interviews during an extremely warm— and economically devastating—winter. Acknowledging global warming, and by extension other social problems, would entail unpleasant emotions that most people try to avoid: a feeling of helplessness; guilt over their own role in global warming; fear that their physical surroundings are no longer safe and dependable; and an unsettling threat to their own individual and collective identities. The citizens of Bygdaby preferred to use irony, teasing humor, and more than a little cynicism to deflect these emotions, steering conversations to safer, more mundane topics.[61]

If these dynamics help explain why collective action does not arise in the first place, they can also help account for the decline or collapse of mobilization. Scholars of protest rarely study deflating moods, since there is rarely collective action as a result. We prefer to study the positive cases, when inflating moods are one factor propelling action. But we do sometimes study the decline of collective action, a disheartening topic but one that cannot be ignored.

Lynn Owens describes the emotional trajectory of the Amsterdam squatters' movement in its final stages. External pressures helped pull the movement apart along the lines of tactical tastes: "increasing evictions, a more determined and fierce government response, and a public that was running out of patience and understanding." Caught in the naughty-or-nice dilemma, those who wished to confront the state with violence and those who saw such confrontation as disastrous (a predictably gendered rift) began to blame one another for the setbacks. A mood of sadness, anger, and despair led to mutual recriminations. The mood also exacerbated several kinds of fear, and the split arose around these: existential fear, fear of violence, and fear of isolation. (These are, respectively, a mood, a reflex emotion, and a concern for affective commitments.) The naughty camp tried to address existential and violence fears through radical action; the nice camp fell back on the internal solidarities of the group and tried to withdraw from public confrontation.[62]

Lethargy is not fatally permanent. Richard Solomon has described how Mao dealt with the fatalism and cynicism that discourage political activity by the oppressed. In the case of the Chinese peasants he was trying to mobilize, "Avoidance of landlord and governmental authority was a time-honored technique by which the agricultural population sought to mitigate the harshness of power in the countryside." Instead, Mao famously used simple slogans to channel anxiety and bitterness that were otherwise repressed, transforming them into anger. He described an angry child shouting "Down with Imperialism!" at another. These were effective frames because they applied to daily life. "When somebody who looks like one of the gentry," Mao recounted, "encounters a peasant and stands on his dignity, refusing to make way along a pathway, the peasant will say angrily, 'Hey, you local tyrant, don't you know the Three People's Principles?'" Communists organized meetings to encourage peasants to "vomit the bitter water," in order to "work up all the rage and resentment that by tradition was 'put in the stomach.'" A neat metaphor for the switch from internalizing to externalizing feelings, directing anger outward toward the local and international villains rather than inward into resignation.[63]

NOTHING LEFT TO LOSE

Not all bad moods sap energy for political action. One deep mood is sometimes implicated in protest: a kind of desperation, or what I call the *nothing-left-to-lose effect*. I see at least two paths to this kind of mood. In one, a loved one has been killed, and in grief one feels that things cannot get any worse. In another, people have been forced into a strategic dead end, with few options left. Like the case of hunger strikers, dying with dignity may be the best option left. Personal projects and needs fade; vengeance on perpetrators sometimes gets mixed in with the concern for justice. Desperation must lead to anger instead of to fear.[64]

Deborah Gould gets at the grief path in her discussion of ACT UP in the United States. The explosion of AIDS in urban gay communities meant that "gay men in particular were suffering extreme and multiple losses as close friends, lovers, ex-lovers, acquaintances, neighbors, and co-workers died painful and early deaths; by this point, some gay men had lost their entire social circle to AIDS." In addition, many faced the prospect that they, too, would soon die. It was difficult to carry on the routines of daily life, or to feel constrained any longer by the polite norms of respectable politics.[65]

Even so, it took a moral shock—the *Hardwick* Supreme Court decision upholding state antisodomy laws—to generate radical direct action out of this desperate mood by adding moral emotions. Gay men (and lesbians) flooded into ACT UP when they concluded that their own government was against them and complicit in all the deaths. With a new attribution of blame, AIDS was no longer an epidemic but a genocide. "If you believed that AIDS was a holocaust, then 'business as usual' in the political realm, which by then was clearly ineffective, was not much of a response."[66] Fear and grief developed into anger and outrage. Moral emotions came to the fore.

The most famous movement to emerge from desperate grief—also by adding moral outrage to their despairing mood—is the Madres de Plaza de Mayo in Buenos Aires, formed in 1976 by fourteen mothers whose children had been "disappeared" by the repressive junta that had seized power in March of that year. The group met while searching for evidence about what had happened to their children, mostly students and activists; the mothers were frustrated by the silence of every agency they approached. They would meet weekly in the plaza for thirty years, long after the military had left power, demanding information and some accounting. For most of the founders, this was their first political activity, and their moral shock was perhaps greater for that reason. Several of them disappeared themselves, but the symbolism of mothers in a patriarchal and Catholic context gave them some protection.[67]

One of the Mothers describes the frustration, indignation, and desperation they felt, deepened by their outrageous treatment by the Ministry of the Interior, where they went daily to wait in lines to make inquiries. "They always said there was no news and they asked a lot of questions, like what were our children like, who were their friends, who was their girlfriend or boyfriend. They took information from us. They didn't give us any. Out of desperation we began to shout, 'What have you done with our children?' We began to lose our tempers and this anger helped to make us stronger."[68] As one analyst of the movement comments, "To retain one's humanity in the face of what the Mothers and their children endured and in the throes of a system that continues to threaten them physically and psychologically is a form of defiance."[69] The questions, implying that their children were perhaps to blame for their fates, transformed grief into indignation.

After a democratic government replaced the military in 1983, the Mothers began to stage-manage their grief to keep pressure on the new government to investigate the disappearances. They refused to accept the remains of their children, which would have allowed grief and closure. "Let there be no healing of wounds," they wrote. "Let them remain open. Because if the wounds still bleed, there will be no forgetting and our strength will continue to grow." As Paul Hoggett comments, "In the face of the actuality of the loss that they had experienced, it seems that terror lost its power—the military had lost its capacity to intimidate them"—a neat summary of the nothing-left-to-lose mood. He attributes it to the Mothers' "deep identification with their children." The Mothers' case shows, he says, "how powerful collective emotions such as grief can take possession of people and yet, at times, be open to use in a more reflexive and strategic way." A mood of grief colors and allows other reflex reactions and displays.[70]

Strategic dead ends can also create desperate moods, especially for those who try normal political channels and are rebuffed. Structural theories of protest dismissed so-called frustration models for their implied emphasis on emotions. The older theories may not have adequately formulated the processes of frustration, but anyone who has been frustrated can attest to the emotional energy that frustration can generate. Frustration seems to operate through anger, which we discussed in chapter 2, but we still need to acknowledge frustration as a desperate mood that begins in reaction to events but then takes on a life of its own.

The hunger strikes we examined in the last chapter seem to be a case of the nothing-left-to-lose mood. Imprisonment drastically limits strategic options, often with a taunting humiliation over that very fact. Prisoners' bodies are the last thing they control, their last remaining arena for political action. Humiliation can create that same sense of desperation in other settings; Doron Shultziner has attributed the Montgomery bus boycott in 1955, so central to the US civil rights movement and the rise of Martin Luther King Jr., to the increasing humiliations that white drivers imposed on Black riders, such as forcing them to pay in front but then exit the bus to reenter through the back door, and asking them to give up their seats in the middle of the bus for white riders (as Rosa Parks was famously told to do). This fits with a broader rethinking of the civil rights movement as an emotional response to increasing repression around 1954 instead of a rational response to increased opportunities.[71]

Short of incarceration, the occupation of your neighborhood or nation by an alien power has a similar effect, creating a frustrated mood of humiliation and desperation. Robert Brym and Bader Araj found that a majority of the Palestinian suicide bombers between 2000 and 2005 were motivated by a desire for revenge and retaliation. Such motives are not necessarily at odds with strategic and political goals, but they are at odds—Brym and Araj imply—with the calculating-brain image of the tallying of material costs and benefits. What is left to lose when your fiancé and much of your family has been killed? When you, and the remaining members of your family, have been so humiliated that you feel you have no honor left?[72] Revenge is not necessarily a means to some other goal; it is satisfying in and of itself. When there is nothing left to lose, it may be the only goal that remains.

Interestingly, group commitments may give us something to lose, even when there is little else. When we identify with a group, we care about its reputation and we work to preserve and advance it. The Madres had no group when they started, and few suicide bombers are active in the resistance groups that recruit them. Our mood of desperation can apparently dominate our choices more when it is not balanced by the kind of affective and moral commitments that we'll examine in the next two chapters.[73]

* * *

Like other types of emotions, moods convey information about how well things are going for us in some general way. They also adumbrate how well things will likely go in the near future. In a good mood, we expect good things to happen ("predict" is too calculating); with bad moods, bad outcomes. Moods shape what actions we are willing to attempt, even our capacities for carrying them out. This is not any careful adding up of costs and benefits, although it would shape those calculations, too. Every political organizer knows how to encourage these moods and to elaborate them into hopeful ideologies and stories. Many processes of feeling-thinking also suggest what possibilities for action are available. Moods reflect a general assessment about whether we have many options or few. The desperation of extremely narrowed options can launch us into action, but ongoing participation usually requires an optimism that we have many options.

Politics involves complex interactions among individual emotions and among different types of emotions. Hortencia Jimenez, Laura Barberena, and Michael Young use the image of telescoping to get at some of these processes.[74] As Doan suggests, reflection and intensity enhance the impact of reflex emotions on moods.[75] In the background are the affective and moral commitments that shape our moods, which in turn shape our reflex emotions during events. The lens can turn the other way, as the event leaves certain moods behind and, in the longer term, may have changed our affective and moral loyalties. At moments of emotional intensity, all the types of emotions are engaged at once.

Psychologists have used the term *poignancy* for certain kinds of mixed emotions, a more existentially sad version of the combination that I call *moral batteries*. (I am more interested in combinations like anger and hope that motivate action.) I get a reflex pleasure in visiting my aging father, but it puts me in a sad mood since I know this might be the last time. Protest groups, movements, and campaigns may also be subject to this poignant realization that they are coming to an end, although they may also relish a grand mood of making history.[76]

Reflex emotions both shape moods and are shaped by them. Moods last longer than reflex emotions, normally, and often grow out of them. Yet both of these categories take as background two other types of emotions—namely, affective loyalties and moral emotions. These are long-term commitments, developing slowly as individuals mature and usually with extensive cognitive elaboration, although they can also switch abruptly under dramatic circumstances. Just as these convictions form some of the background for reflex emotions and moods (and urges, too, in some ways), so all of these shorter-run feelings can shape the long-term ones. We turn first to affective commitments, our likes and dislikes, loves and hates, patterns of trust and respect, of security and anxiety. They are closely connected to our life goals.

5: AFFECTIVE COMMITMENTS

Old hatreds are endlessly retrievable.

KIRAN DESAI

One of the founders of subaltern theory, Gyanendra Pandey, has shown how expedient it was for the British to construct a history of India as a primordial, incessant conflict between Hindu and Muslim communities. The colonial rulers compiled lists of communal riots going back hundreds of years, inspired by a form of crowd theory in which primal religious affiliation played the leading emotional role in driving normal people to do awful things. The epidictic message was clear: this vast nation would fall apart without a strong, paternalistic British presence.[1]

An 1809 disturbance in the holy Hindu city of Benares (Varanasi) becomes an emblem of colonial historiography for Pandey, who lists many accounts that eventually contributed to this 1907 summary of the event: "The city experienced one of those convulsions which had so frequently occurred in the past owing to the religious antagonism of the Hindu and Musalman sections of the population."[2] Every problem is attributed to primeval, irrational affiliations that were partly held in check once the British brought "civilization" to the subcontinent. In a replay of the dualisms that pit calculating brains against irrational emotions, the British were rational, with their sense of fair play, while the Indians were childlike and emotional in their primitive faiths and proclivity to turn into lethal mobs.

Pandey traces one hundred years of distortions that led to the 1907 report, which was almost an exact contemporary of Émile Durkheim's formulation of collective effervescence. Even the number of dead increased from twenty in an early account to "hundreds" by 1907 (the exact numbers no longer even matter!). Groups are stereotyped, such as "fighting castes" like Rajputs and Muslims. The mobs are seen as manipulated by local elites. The origin of every street fight is assumed to lie in religion, even though there is no evidence for that in the Benares case. In a primitive religious ritual, the excitement is seen as naturally, inevitably, leading to rioting, criminality, and "a helpless, instinctive violence" between groups who have always and will always detest each other.[3] No other explanations are needed, or searched for. This is the way India has always been and will always be.

Pandey leaves out one thing: since 1947, indigenous groups have stepped into the storytelling role, but they continue to have an interest in the construction of India as convulsed by religious conflict.[4] In almost any political arena—electoral or colonial—a player can gain advantage by portraying opponents as an emotional mob.

In this chapter and the next we turn to emotions that are normally stable parts of our identity and activity as humans, and which form the core of protest and politics. It is difficult to portray these commitments as irrational, disruptive outbursts—although they may contribute to them. Most of the time, their regret and disruption potentials are low or moderate. In this chapter we examine how humans map the world into people, places, and things that are dangerous, good, liked and loved, hated or feared. These convictions shape their most basic goals and identities.

People live in groups; our social attachments are fundamental to our humanity. We become attuned to our mothers' bodies and voices even in the womb. The attachments of our early years define us—and our capacities for future bonds—for life. We unconsciously register innumerable signals from the gestures, smells, expressions, and sounds of others. The more scientists learn about the brain, the more it looks like a collection of systems set up for social interaction and less like a calculator for deriving outputs from inputs. All of our emotions register our relationships to various contexts, but our ongoing connections to other humans are by far the most important to our flourishing.

Affective commitments are more stable, more elaborated, and more tied to cognition than the types of emotions we have seen so far. This makes them, in Desai's term, more retrievable. They are often little more than positive or negative clusters of feelings, mere attraction or repulsion. Love and hate are the obvious ones, but trust, respect, resentment, and some abiding kinds of fear are also examples. In contrast to reflex emotions or passing moods, affective loyalties are relatively enduring orientations to the social and physical worlds. An affective commitment "hardens" over time, says Tomas Sedlacek, "and after repeated mutual confirmations of experiences becomes somewhat an automatic part of our lives. It hardens to a rational form that we simply count on." We hardly need to engage debates over rationality to acknowledge this hardening into a commitment that we simply count on.[5]

Affective orientations provide something close to basic values and goals. Solidarity with various collectives—a nation, an organization, one's family, and so on—consists of positive feelings reinforced by extensive symbols and interpretation. Trust, for instance, arises out of the interaction between expectations and experience with groups and individuals. These positive loyalties—along with negative ones toward outsiders, enemies, and other threats—motivate or allow much political action. For example the nationalist banner under which so many Europeans marched off to war, for decades until 1945, was a complex cluster of positive and negative feelings about groups, especially "us" and "them" as defined by nations.

These affective convictions are not easily changed. We may fall in or out of love with someone, become disenchanted with our team (or with its current leaders), or come to revise our hatred and suspicion of foreigners. On rare occasions we change our affective loyalties through a moral shock that forces us to reinterpret—or "re-feel"—our experiences. The betrayals, seductions, and shocks that reverberate and transform our commitments are usually strong reflex emotions.

Affective and moral commitments are not exactly appraisals of how well I am doing in the world, since they are not usually reactions to events or changes. Their relative permanence typically makes them into backgrounds for more immediate reflex emotions, moods, and (in the case of lust) urges. My patriotism sets me up for shame when my government is humiliated; love for my protest group sets me up for sadness when it fights or disbands.

Because of their stability, affective commitments do not constantly register as flows of feeling-thinking processes. We feel a surge of feeling about a spouse, our nation, an opponent, and so on—but only when we think about them. What happens when we stop thinking about them? Do we stop hating our enemies? No, our loyalties remain in the background, ready to be reactivated when we again pay attention to them. These commitments attach us to the world and make it meaningful to us. They restore some of its magic. When I think about a favorite place or about belonging to a loved group, my mood improves. When I think about things I hate, that triggers anger or contempt.

This is the biggest step away from the panic model of emotions, heavily dependent on reflex examples in portraying emotions as sudden, arbitrary eruptions. If we know something about a person's background commitments, we can make predictions about that person's patterns of disgust, anger, joy, shock, and fear. In the old view of protestors, it hardly mattered what the issue was, as long as it gave participants a feeling of belonging. But the issues do matter, because our long-term emotional commitments are not willy-nilly. Most of the time we are well aware of them, thanks to movements and intellectuals and other symbol makers (including even those who write greeting cards).

Some approaches would make it seem as though emotions are created or re-created anew through each interaction, but there are plenty of emotional attachments that we bring to interactions. Yes, they can be created, changed, or reinforced during those contacts, but they survive most engagements intact. When we confuse these commitments with the reflex emotions that follow from them, we exaggerate the intensity, suddenness, and disruptive capacity of emotions. For instance, the term *moral panic* implies disruptive reflex fears, but moral panics in fact tap into deeper, abiding anxieties.

These patterns of love, hate, and disgust have often been viewed as the heart of politics, an idea articulated most famously by Carl Schmitt, who insisted that we tend to divide the world into friends and foes: "The political is the most intense and extreme antagonism, and every concrete antagonism becomes that much more political the closer it approaches the most extreme point, that of the friend-enemy grouping."[6] Social movements and other political groupings are not based on reflex emotions; they are built *upon affective and moral convictions*.

LOVE AND BELONGING

Positive feelings for others come in many forms. We looked at lust as an immediate urge in chapter 3, but at the opposite end of the time spectrum we find solidarity with a group. In between we find romantic, sexual love, longer lasting and more complex than lust yet including some of lust's physical compulsion. Romantic love is understudied in politics, since it attaches one individual to another rather than to a group. Finally, and most studied, is the love for a group that is the core of collective identity.

Like lust, romantic love can pull people into or out of political participation. We looked at the former process with lust, but Jeff Goodwin has examined some of the latter processes, in which dyads withdraw from larger groups. During their long period of living in the forest, away from their families (1946-1954), the revolutionary Huks in the Philippines constantly had to redirect followers' emotional attention toward the cause and away from spouses and children left behind. It allowed some of them to take "forest wives," at least if they informed their main wives, and they used these ceremonies to remind the partners of their duties to the revolutionary movement as well as to each other. The Huks tried to channel lust in order to avoid the disruptions of love, and to sustain love for the movement alongside that for sexual partners.[7]

Romantic love and group love draw on some of the same energy, else they would not pose trade-offs like these. Psychological attachment theory, developed by John Bowlby, Mary Ainsworth, and others starting in the 1950s, suggests a fundamental need in the human infant for a secure, stable attachment to a primary caregiver. How we learn to make additional attachments in childhood affects how we develop affective loyalties later in life. Recent research in genetics and epigenetics suggests that our earliest experiences create pathways for neurotransmitters, especially oxytocin, that govern our later affective bonds. Oxytocin is present when mothers and infants gaze at each other, but it is also stimulated in humans when their pet dogs stare at them. Even a brief touch, such as a high five in a sports competition, releases oxytocin.[8] Oxytocin simply feels good, but it may also reduce the stress hormone cortisol.

The mere presence of a dog in small groups helps them feel more like a team and work together cooperatively, presumably because of the oxytocin aroused by a species bred over ten thousand years to interact sympathetically with humans. Members of these groups cooperate, show solidarity, trust one another, and respect one another's opinions more than do people in groups without dogs.[9] To my knowledge, no one has examined whether symbols of animals—group mascots, or Durkheim's group totems—have similar effects, but they are often thought to have sacred powers (a hope exploited by sports teams worldwide via their choice of animal mascots). Small-group rituals of solidarity have many ways of arousing oxytocin and its binding powers, including human touch and shared laughter.

A sense of "groupness" can form around the most trivial or arbitrary boundaries, but in politics most of these boundaries cut deep.[10] Libraries have been written about collective identities and politics, ranging from nationalism to American identity politics since the 1960s to the emergence of lesbian, gay, bisexual, transgender, and questioning/queer (LGBTQ) movements since the 1990s.[11] Once viewed primarily as an exercise in constructing collective memory or the drawing of cognitive boundaries, recent work on collective identity has examined the affective loyalties involved, especially love of the group and hatred for outsiders.[12] These identities maintain member enthusiasm, but they are inevitably an aspiration more than an accomplishment.[13] No group is ever entirely, mystically, united.

All groups face the same challenge: the individuals who compose them may share some tastes, feelings, and goals, but never all. A collective identity is created for specific purposes, not to guide an entire life; *it is a necessary fiction.* I call this the extension dilemma: a larger group has many advantages in resources, knowledge, and network contacts, but the larger it gets, the less coherent it is likely to be. It is always in danger of fragmenting.

Leaders strive for that sense of unity, and they pretend that it exists. But collective identity is largely a *claim* to unity and relevance, whether of a nation-state, a social movement, or some demographic category. I analyzed culture in *The Art of Moral Protest* as consisting of cognitive, emotional, and moral strands inseparably woven together. Henri Tajfel's classic work on the psychology of group identities, out of which grew social identity theory, suggests the same. Our feelings about our group memberships are particularly salient, as these feelings yield self-esteem.[14] Perceived external threats naturally increase identification with the group, whether or not it is the group itself that is directly threatened. Hate paired with love, or fear with security, form powerful moral batteries.[15]

A feeling of "groupness" provides many advantages, documented in rich historical research and in the wave of "social-capital" research inspired by Robert Putnam. A sense of power or efficacy is one, the satisfaction of expecting an impact on the world. This sense of efficacy can lead to hope, a mood we analyzed in the last chapter. Social movements are famous for creating this confidence, a sense that history is on your side. In fact, the claim to *being* a social movement is typically a rhetorical construct meant to reassure participants that they are part of something important. (Social movements often lack networks that link local groups, and so consist *mostly* of this shared claim to a collective label.) "Collective efficacy" theorists argue that "the prevalence and density of kinship, friendship, and acquaintanceship networks and the level of participation in community based organizations fosters the emergence of collective *efficacy,* or solidarity and mutual *trust* (social cohesion) among community residents combined with shared expectations for social-control related action."[16]

A feeling of collective identity also motivates collective action through awareness of group-based injustices. Moral emotions seem to become more salient when attached to groups: we may believe in human rights, but we go into the streets to protest when a group (especially our own group) is deprived of them. When we feel we have been humiliated because of individual failings, we are unlikely to protest, but if the reason is our group membership, then we are more apt to become indignant.[17]

Devotion to a group shapes how an individual interprets events in her life, even traumatic ones. Pain and torture, we saw, can be less devastating if their victim believes she is part of a collective struggle. Post-traumatic stress disorder may be moderated by one's group memberships as well. Instead of seeing "an interaction between an individual and a specific event," we can envision "an individual operating within a specific social context and attempting (or not attempting) to reintegrate into that social context subsequent to the traumatizing event." Group membership can affect the likelihood of experiencing trauma in the first place, the appraisal of that trauma, and its psychological impact.[18] When trauma is inflicted to discourage political participation, this kind of deflection of blame is necessary for the individual to return to action.

This identification with a group goes beyond Lofland's reflex crowd joys, providing affective commitments that tend to persist. Group loyalties expand an individual's list of goals to include benefits for the group, even beyond any benefits the individual receives as a member of that group. Such goals are not quite self-interest and not quite altruism—or they are both at the same time.[19]

Strong group identities allow members to feel a number of intense emotions through the imagination, often across great distances, showing the power of what Benedict Anderson famously called "imagined communities." In his extensive interviews with members of al-Qaeda in prison in France, sociologist Farhad Khosrokhavar finds an interaction between the different types of shame based on imagined communities. Few of the young men had felt personally humiliated, except in prison, but they readily imagined the bodily humiliations of Palestinians searched at Israeli checkpoints or of Chechens whose homes were destroyed by Russian troops: "solidarity at a distance," as he puts it. They felt a vivid proxy shame through their identification with these other Muslims, in other nations, because they saw world history as a struggle between Christianity and Islam. Their entire faith was being humiliated by the West. One way to overcome the pain of this humiliation, which was closely tied to their sense of virility, was to become martyrs in the cause. In addition, the prospect of making the West afraid, along with faith in Islam's ultimate triumph, created a precious mood of confidence for the radical Islamists.[20]

Outlets for affective commitments have shifted in the modern world, with the nation becoming a new object of allegiance. As Anderson put it, nations managed to become "emotionally plausible" as objects of loyalty, thanks to market ties, imperial administrative units, and printed languages that could overcome the diversity of dialects. They are imagined communities because we feel positively toward community members we could never meet.[21] Romanticism, a fusion of intellectual and political movements, proposed that each "people" has its own inherent genius, a notion that had its fiery epitome in Fascism, which added the wretched idea that this collective identity could be captured by a single great leader.[22] Like many social movements, nationalism was driven by elites, who needed to mobilize citizens for war and who crafted monuments, folk traditions, rituals, and so on in order to imagine new entities.

Our love for a group is never innate; it must be constructed over time, usually through the efforts of what we might call *identity workers*. Andreas Wimmer lays out various strategies of ethnic boundary making, but they are a useful catalog for most groups, including nations, neighborhoods, protest groups, and any other compound player. Identity workers can *shift the boundaries*, making them more inclusive or more exclusive. They can incorporate new groups into an existing identity or amalgamate two or more identities to form a new one; both processes were used to create modern nation-states. In contrast, they can also exclude a group, in a process of disidentification, as feminists did to lesbian activists in the 1960s.[23]

In addition to moving the boundary, identity workers can also *transform the content* of the identity. Wimmer offers three strategies here: the blurring of the boundary in favor of other divisions or of universalism; repositioning the group in a hierarchy, either through individuals who can assimilate or reposition themselves or (more rarely) through a group's collective efforts; and finally, a change in the moral valuation of the group, either through equalization or through an inversion of the ranking. What we need to add to Wimmer are the emotions that accompany these processes. The blurring of boundaries requires a shift in patterns of love, hate, and trust—on both sides of the boundary. Moral valuations are based on pride and shame, and the grounds for these valuations must shift for the group definitions to change. Love of one's group strengthens love of oneself—a source of pride.

Individual and collective reputations are among the most common human motives: a concern for due honor, pride, recognition of one's basic humanity.[24] Many movements that appear instrumentally interested in power or material benefits are motivated at least as much by a concern for the human dignity that political rights imply.[25] Pride in one's identity is not a goal restricted to the mislabeled "new social movements" of the advanced industrial world. We'll come back to the importance of pride in the next chapter.

PLACE LOYALTIES

People form loyalties to places as well as to other people. These are probably strongest when they combine the two, as in nationalism, a loyalty to a place as well as to the people who live there or who are from there. Other places command loyalty because we see them as special in some way, like the lovely stretch of California coastline that aroused protestors against the Diablo Canyon nuclear plant being built there.[26] Place loyalty tends to arise around one's sense of home, neighborhood, and community, informing our reactions to any perceived threats to them (the essence of what has pejoratively been termed "NIMBYism"—NIMBY standing for "not in my back yard"). As several political psychologists conclude, "participation aimed at defending community is likely to occur when individuals experience both high levels of place attachment and threatening events."[27] Affective commitments to places are part of the background that shapes reflexes such as anger, fear, and shock.

Other authors have grappled with the feeling of being at home. We don't have a good label for it, but it seems to include familiarity, a relaxed feeling of being backstage rather than playing roles in public, a setting for intimate family relations, and a place to express one's style and identity. Sociologist Jan Willem Duyvendak adds that we can feel at home in public places as well, where we share histories with others, where we can express ourselves politically, and where we are part of a "people." Collective identities are bolstered by an association with place. He says that the feeling of home has not been well studied, perhaps because it does not directly lead to action. Affective commitments do not by themselves lead to action, but they usually inform action when there are triggering threats.[28]

So threats to "home" cut especially deep. In a book ominously titled *Domicide*, J. Douglas Porteous and Sandra Smith examine cases in which governments have literally seized people's dwellings in order to construct the kind of large concrete and blacktop projects associated with modernity. They also include cases of ethnic cleansing, mass bombings, hydroelectric dams, and more. The strong affective loyalties associated with home are pitted against the harsh threat (and actuality) of displacement, a frequent moral battery for political action. The deep psychosocial attachments most people have to home, as a source of ontological security, include carriers of childhood memories, a sense of security and control, a refuge from the outside world, a place to bond with family and friends, symbols of permanence and continuity, the capacity to modify and act on our surroundings, and a reflection of our values and ideas. The last four could apply to the places associated with any group.[29]

Under world capitalism, multinational corporations buy and exploit land and the resources it contains, especially oil, gold, and other minerals. The destruction that results often transforms desolate mountain ranges and other underpopulated areas into symbols of a nation's heritage, even its very soul. In some cases, locals are content to make money from the exploitation while city dwellers feel a more abstract attachment to the land that is threatened, frequently based on environmentalist values. Foreign corporations make for good villains: outsiders, making a profit for other outsiders, with little concern for us or our nation. We feel sudden attachments to places that are threatened, speedily linking them to our national histories.[30]

If we use places to strengthen our attachments to each other, Collins would say that it is the ritual interactions that do the real work while the places where they occur play a subsidiary role. In examining Argentina's famous Madres de Plaza de Mayo, Fernando Bosco finds exactly this: even a group entirely associated with the square where it has demonstrated for forty years has an open sense of place that features the social networks which flow across the places more than the plaza itself.[31] On the other hand, we can fill places with resonant symbolic props that aid and enhance our interactions. Places, identities, and interactions animate each other.

SYMBOLIC POLITICS

In addition to people and places, cognitive psychologists have also looked at attachments to *ideas* that we are unwilling or unable to modify. These ideas used to be analyzed as ideologies, coherent packages of assumptions and concepts that were held more or less consciously, but recently the tendency has been to observe our feelings about particular words and symbols. These feelings may not fit together into a neat whole, and they are often not especially conscious. These allegiances are the core of the theory of symbolic politics, as we attach positive and negative feelings to the words and images used to persuade in politics, whether the symbols represent groups, places, ideas, technologies, or anything else.

Tightly interwoven with our cognitions, our affective loyalties influence how we process information—for instance, about political leaders. Most obviously, we remember positive information about (and associate positive character traits with) those leaders whom we like, negative ones about those we dislike. Negative information tends in general to be noticed and remembered more than positive information, however, so that we have to work harder to maintain positive sentiment.[32] Negative information especially affects short-term mobilization, but its influence fades over time. Because so much politics is about group solidarities, affective orientations are crucial motivations.

Drawing on such scholars as Joseph Gusfield and Murray Edelman, David Sears elaborated the term *symbolic politics* in the 1980s. Early in life, he posits, people develop feelings toward images and words, which shape their reactions to political events ever after. These symbolic predispositions include party identification, party ideology, and group attitudes. The symbols, which can be rather abstract and remote from people's daily lives, arouse positive or negative feelings through rapid, automatic, feeling-thinking processes. Some are unusually stable over time, with considerable influence over related attitudes. In many cases, symbolic predispositions have more influence on attitudes and voting than economic self-interest does.[33]

If negative symbols concerning government resonate with Americans, symbols of race do so even more, leading Sears to speak of "symbolic racism." People adopt racial prejudices early in life and cling to them. These symbols influence a variety of opinions about controversial policies around schools and housing. In work with Jack Citrin, Sears used his theory to understand the surprising success of the movement to limit property taxes in California, culminating in "Prop 13," which still wreaks havoc with the state's budgets by limiting property taxes to 1 percent of values. Sears and Citrin examined people's feelings toward a variety of policies. Those seen as "wasteful" government spending were those on behalf of poor people, which in turn was a racialized category, so that the campaign tapped into symbolic racism. "The influence of symbolic racism on support for the tax rebellion among whites in California is still greater than that of either of the more usual partisan predispositions, party identification and liberal-conservative ideology."[34]

As the case of race indicates, groups are frequent primary symbols with deep emotional resonances. A person's attitudes toward policies for a group reflect her evaluations of that group, unsurprisingly. Sears insists, more interestingly, that our symbolic evaluations of particular groups are independent of one another, rather than necessarily placed in an us/them framework: white attitudes toward policies to help Blacks depend on evaluations of Blacks but not on evaluations of their own white group.[35] Symbols need not be comparative. On the other hand, terms like "we" and "ours" tend to elicit positive feelings, while "they" and "theirs" arouse negative feelings, suggesting that people do make affective commitments based on us/them boundaries.[36]

In response to the emotional turn in social science, Sears has articulated more clearly the emotional dimensions of symbolic politics. He now insists that we deploy "automatic processing" in dealing with strong symbols, which "can occur without conscious goals, control, attention, or awareness, and so it places minimal demands on processing capacity."[37] This "continuum," in which more emotional reactions tend to be more automatic while more cognitive ones tend to be slower, is an updated version of the old mind–body dualism, with emotions coming out as less rational. It misses the complexity of feeling-thinking, with a constant flow of information and feedback from more conscious to less conscious processes, and between short- and long-run emotional bundles. Even the most automatic processing depends on some *prior* cognitive appraisal and cultural influence, even if it occurred in childhood or early adulthood.[38] But long-run feelings, with greater cognitive input, can be more open to reflection and adjustment, through the kinds of ideologies and discussions in which social movements specialize.

To return to our earlier discussion, group boundaries are the most salient form of symbolic politics, since they involve trust, love, respect, and preferences for interaction. Donald Kinder and Cindy Kam define *ethnocentrism* as a mental habit, involving several kinds of affective convictions: "Members of in-groups (until they prove otherwise) are assumed to be virtuous: friendly, cooperative, trustworthy, safe, and more. Members of out-groups (until they prove otherwise) are assumed to be the opposite: unfriendly, uncooperative, unworthy of trust, dangerous, and more. Symbols and practices become objects of attachment and pride when they belong to the in-group and objects of condescension, disdain, and (in extreme cases) hatred when they belong to out-groups."[39] Kinder and Kam group feeling-thinking processes into those that lead to stereotypes about groups and those that contribute to warm or cold sentiments about groups. Positive feeling-thinking about one's own group, they find, is not always connected to negative feeling-thinking about other groups.

Not always, but often. Because our affective loyalties and our reflex emotions constantly shape each other, there *is* a tendency for in-group love and out-group hate to accompany each other. Donald Green, Bradley Palmquist, and Eric Schickler have examined what it means to identify strongly with a political party. They notice a great deal of cognitive elaboration that goes into such identification: "To characterize party identification as an emotional attachment perhaps goes too far in downplaying the role that cognition plays in shaping self-categorization. . . . Citizens do seem to respond to information that changes the way that they perceive the social character of the parties."[40] The contrast between information and emotion seems to suggest—wrongly, in my opinion—that affective commitments can never change. What they say elsewhere in the same book is that these group affiliations have their own logic not reducible to political or economic logics: "The analogy between partisan and religious identification has an implication that many political scientists find disconcerting: Partisan change among adults often has little to do with unfolding political and economic events."[41]

Green, Palmquist, and Schickler, whose evidence is based on Democrats' and Republicans' reactions to the Supreme Court decision handing George W. Bush the 2000 election, use the concept of a *rivalry* to show how positive loyalties to one's own group and negative feelings about opponents can reinforce each other: "Those who root for and empathize with a partisan group feel the emotions of someone who is personally locked in competition with a long-standing and often ungracious rival."[42] Sharp conflict imposes a logic of group identification, as well as the appropriate reflex emotions.

Hostility toward outsiders and love for insiders go together, especially when the boundary between two groups operates by contrasting them. This is one of the most important moral batteries, with most good feelings on one side and most bad ones on the other. Psychologists have described a "need for cognitive closure" that encourages stark oppositions, with rigid opinions preferred over ambiguity and complexity.[43] In combination, hostility and the need for closure lead to negative expectations about the other group, and through that sometimes to aggression.[44] Cognitive closure would seem to require emotional closure: strong positive feelings toward one's own group and negative feelings toward opponents.

Although symbolic politics has been studied primarily through national samples, local boundaries arise as well. Francesca Polletta shows how, in

a number of protest groups, disagreement over strategic dilemmas transformed decision-making processes into emotional symbols that could be
deployed as rhetorical weapons. In the Student Nonviolent Coordinating
Committee (SNCC), "participatory democracy" came to symbolize white
participants, in a symbolic process the ancient Greeks called *metonymy*.
In other cases, it was simply a term for demonizing other individuals
with whom one disagreed: "Groups were paralyzed as members charged
unrestrained egotism and power mongering in every exercise of initiative, manipulation in every programmatic suggestion, and a betrayal of
democracy in every effort to get something done."[45] Every word or idea
can become a deep emotional symbol, but especially when it is attached
to a group.

TRUST

I can hardly do justice to the volumes that have been written recently about
trust, an affective commitment correlated with love and respect. Trust is
important to politics, as it determines with whom we align, for whom we
vote, and how we act in a number of institutional settings. My subjective
approach views trust as a confidence that others will act as we expect or
as norms say they should, whereas a structural orientation examines situations that are assumed to reflect subjective trust, when we must rely on
others' good intentions. But we try to avoid interactions with those we do
not trust, and—if we can't avoid them—we feel anxiety instead of confidence. With trust we have confidence not only in others' actions but in our
own ability to judge whether they are trustworthy.[46]

Game theory and behavioral economics have examined the settings
that encourage trusting behavior. In a game designed to test people's levels of trust, unimaginatively dubbed the "trust game," subjects are given
a small amount of money, some or all of which they can give to a trustee
(other research subjects, or a computer program), who will then receive
three or four times the amount entrusted. The trustee can keep all of that
for herself or return some to the "investor": the trustee gets no monetary
reward for being generous. How much the investors are willing to give
to a stranger is thought to be a measure of their willingness to trust, just
as the trustee's generosity (or trustworthiness) is captured by what she
gives back.[47]

Most investors place around half their money in the hands of the trustee,
and most trustees return virtually all the money invested (although pock-
eting most of the multiples of the returns). There are variations across
groups, suggesting cultural differences.[48] Subjects can be manipulated to
see what makes them more trusting. Individuals seem to be more trusting

than groups, which tend to be influenced by their most suspicious members.[49] Unsurprisingly, when they know that the trustees have acted generously in the past, they invest much more: reputations matter.[50] For this reason, trust can be built up over time when the same players interact again and again in successive rounds of the same game. Colin Camerer suggests that group identity, with its accompanying sense of solidarity, may help explain this tendency to trust anonymous strangers whom one will never meet again.[51] Affective commitments can be abstract and impersonal, as the idea of an imagined community suggests.

Exchange-oriented theorists in sociology define trust as the expectation of cooperation from others, and it is often a kind of calculation about uncertainties.[52] Predictability leads to trust. Edward Lawler, Shane Thye, and Jeongkoo Yoon have laid out the emotional basis of this kind of co-operation, demonstrating that affective bonds emerge from interaction and then sustain further interaction. Examining basic mechanisms that have been thought to explain the Hobbesian problem of order—how so-cial order emerges—they argue that recurrent interpersonal interactions lead to norms, trust, and collective identity (the three main mechanisms that in turn lead to order), but only through the intervening variable of emotions. They apply their theory to national loyalties, which they claim "are built on structural interdependencies among a population, but then enhanced by the equalizing definitions of citizenship that overlay social inequalities, perceptions of direct, unmediated ties between the self and the state, and dense network ties within relative to outside the nation-state unit. . . . Under these conditions, people attribute individual feelings, ex-perienced locally, in part to the larger national unit." Even the broadest imagined identities are reinforced by face-to-face interactions and how we interpret them.[53]

In one of his last books, *Trust and Rule*, structuralist Charles Tilly went further and *defined* trust in terms of interactions and relationships rather than individual dispositions. When "people set valued, consequential, long-term resources and enterprises at risk to the malfeasance, mistakes, or failures, of others," this is trust. Throughout his long career, Tilly derided dispositional accounts that explain action through "orientations just before the point of action." In an essentially behaviorist rejection of any refer-ence to internal mental states, Tilly's relational approach acknowledged the communication involved in feeling-thinking, but it gave him no access to *what* was communicated, what was left in people's body/brains for their next interactions. Nor could he trace how orientations change *during* en-gagements.[54]

But even Tilly's polemics cannot avoid emotions, and affective attach-ments turn out to be crucial to trust in his model. He uses the case of the

Waldensians of early modern Europe, driven into the Alps when they were persecuted as heretics. They were a trust network because they "put major, long-term collective enterprises at risk" to each other.[55] But they only did so because they had already drawn a spirited boundary between Waldensians and everyone else, in part because everyone else was trying to burn them alive. Individuals trust categories of others, not merely individual others. As Lawler and his coauthors find, affective loyalties and choices about risk reinforce each other: emotional commitments lead to interactions, which in turn reinforce the feelings.[56] It makes little sense to contrast and compare the interactional and the dispositional models, since each provides part of the picture.

I usually try to see competing theories as cases of "both ... and" rather than "either ... or." Typically, each theory focuses on a single causal mechanism, but most often all the causal mechanisms are possible, and they are sometimes all at work at once. On the grounds that mechanisms are preferable to theories, I would suggest we look for sources of trust in individual dispositions, in institutional arrangements, *and* in social networks.

Harold H. Kelly and John W. Thibaut showed long ago that the subjective and objective processes interact. They studied long-term relationships, finding that partners engage in trust-building exercises by taking risks, with each signaling her good intentions and expectations of the other. As trust builds, the partners feel they are taking less risk when they expose their vulnerabilities. Trust and trusting actions bolster each other.[57] Each interaction reinforces the affective commitments.

Robert Wuthnow comes closest to establishing trust as a long-standing affective commitment. He offers an image of trust as neither an action, a calculation, nor a fuzzy feeling but rather "an aspect of the normative system that makes up the social structure in which we live."[58] It is not simply a calculation between two players, as rational choice traditions would have it. People "do give reasons for trusting someone," but these reasons reflect the local, relevant norms. Some of the warrants that Wuthnow lists have to do with the perceived intentions of the other player: sincerity, empathy, affinity, altruism, congeniality, and fairness. Others reflect an assessment of the other player's capacity for action: accessibility, effectiveness, competence, and reliability. We can link these two categories to the "evaluation" and the "potency" dimensions of affect-control theory's EPA space, the two main things players look for in a strategic alliance. The first dimension is largely a list of our expectations about the other player's own affective and moral commitments, which become an input as we map our worlds according to our own affective commitments.

The calculating-brain model would imply that we size someone up carefully, gathering relevant information, before we decide whether to trust that person. The feeling-brain model instead suggests that we process a large number of signals, including emotional ones below the level of consciousness. Indeed, some studies suggest that we make judgments within a tenth of a second of meeting someone—not only about people's trustworthiness but also about their likability, competence, and potential for aggression.[59] Even after we assess people and situations with extraordinary speed, we tend to cling to those judgments, adding new layers to these loyalties.

Moods build trust as well as other affective commitments. Oxytocin levels rise in people whom others trust, and high levels seem to generate generosity in experiments. In one trust game, some subjects received massages and others did not, then both groups played the trust game. Massaged subjects, flush with oxytocin, proved more trusting.[60] The "feel" of dealing with someone we trust differs from that of interacting with those we mistrust: a good versus a bad mood, calmness or anxiety, optimism or pessimism.

All our affective commitments can be challenged, but trust can actually be falsified, since it generates specific predictions about how others will act. So there is some regret potential. (There is less regret potential in mistrust, as regrets would arise primarily from opportunity costs of not engaging with someone.) The disruption costs are hidden. Trust makes coordination easier; mistrust makes it harder. The latter is a mild form of disruption.

Trust in social movements has not been well studied.[61] But we can make a few observations. Social networks are sustained by trust, helping people join and participate because they trust friends already in the movement. We must trust our leaders and spokespersons to make good decisions, remain well informed, and represent our goals to outsiders and the media. We must trust fellow protestors to show up and do their part. Mistrust, conversely, informs many of the grievances that movements have: they do not trust the information offered by experts; they do not trust their government to protect them from nuclear and other accidents; they do not trust the news media to report objectively on important events. Every social interaction differs depending on the level of trust each player has for the others. We select different tactics depending on how much we trust the police, the media, the legal system.

SOLIDARITIES OF COMPOUND PLAYERS

Formal organizations and informal groups build on our affective commitments in several ways. Our existing commitments—whether to our neighborhood or to socialism—are often the basis on which new groups form, sparked by the grievances the groups address. This is the most common way of examining collective identities: as preexisting. But groups and organizations also try to create their own loyalties, so that members have positive associations not only with imagined communities but with real organizations. Leaders also try to reinforce commitments to the ideas of the group, partly independently of loyalty to the group or the category of people it claims to represent.

Solidarity is key to all compound strategic players. Economic historians Dora Costa and Matthew Kahn, using a massive sample of soldiers, have asked what increased the cohesion of Union fighting units during the American Civil War, with the effect of decreasing desertion and keeping men alive in Confederate prison camps. They "assess the relative importance of group loyalty, ideology, morale, and leadership in the Civil War. They all mattered, but a tightly knit company, one in which men had much in common and knew each other, was the most loyal company, even in one of our country's more ideological wars." This kind of cohesion, they admit, could just as easily lead men to their death in battle—but then, some sacrifice is required in most collective endeavors, including less deadly ones. Their other finding is that "loyalty to comrades extended only to men like themselves—in ethnicity, social status, and age."[62] Affective loyalty can be built up over time, but preexisting building blocks of trust such as shared religion or race or gender facilitate the process.

There is a tension in these close bonds that I call the band of brothers dilemma.[63] Those organizing a political party or social movement want to foster love and loyalty among members, and these commitments arise most effectively through face-to-face interactions among those close at hand. But loyalty, so desired by those at the top of the organization, may never extend any higher than these immediate companions: loyalty to the organization and loyalty to a small subunit of it often clash. Soldiers in combat sharing imminent danger are the paradigm. Comments one veteran: "Many veterans who are honest with themselves will admit, I believe, that the experience of communal effort in battle, even under the altered conditions of modern war, has been the high point of their lives. . . . Their 'I' passes insensibly into a 'we,' 'my' becomes 'our,' and individual fate loses its central importance."[64] People are willing to sacrifice for the cause because they are really sacrificing for their immediate group.

Combat is the origin of the term *band of brothers*, but it applies to many political groups as well. It may also apply generally to any large organization, as it touches on classic problems of command and control.[65] Local loyalties lead to favoritism and nepotism, to mutual back-scratching, the diversion of resources, and abuses of power—all of which in turn inspire additional apparatus for surveillance and control. In social movements, affinity groups or cells often attract affective loyalties stronger than those to the ideology or formal organization of which they are a part. The two commitments sometimes collide (just as all of an individual's commitments to groups can clash).

Bands of brothers can appear at the tops of political parties and movements as well as among the rank and file. In this case, the trade-off between local solidarity and more mediated connections helps explain the well-known iron law of oligarchy, as leaders are more loyal to each other than to lower-ranking members of their group or organization. That loyalty can also have benefits. We often see this among postrevolutionary rulers, a small group of whom can hold an ethnically diverse nation together due to their loyalty to each other built up through long struggles. Josip Broz Tito and the associates with whom he fought during World War II probably prevented Yugoslavia from fragmenting until after most of this group had died. South Africa today is perhaps held together by the same dynamic. The downside, which generates the dilemma, is that these groups do not easily incorporate their successors, exacerbating rather than fixing the challenge of fragmentation.

Bands of brothers, even when they included some sisters, governed SNCC and Students for a Democratic Society (SDS) in their initial phases in the early 1960s. The informal norms that could govern a small, affectionate group broke down as newcomers joined. Polletta shows how the vocabulary of participatory democracy became more explicit, and more contentious, as it expanded. Internal processes became an arena in which old and new cohorts (and in the case of SNCC, Blacks and whites) contended for control. In part, she implies, the founding bands of brothers had difficulty expressing disagreement directly: "The intensity of [SNCC] staffers' friendships made it easy for disagreement to be experienced as betrayal and easy to fight over things like decisionmaking rather than say or hear things that friends would find hurtful. It also made it difficult to integrate newcomers into the group."[66]

Polletta generalizes, too, about how bands of brothers develop and function: "The groups I studied did not begin as groups of friends. But the sense of finding allies in what seemed a wilderness of student apathy, combined with the long hours, the hard work, and, in some cases, the danger to which they were subjected as well as the excitement of launching a new movement, created strong bonds." These bonds of trust and affection made the groups more efficient, as "they relied on a participatory ethos combined with the natural goodwill, trust, and respect that friends have for each other." They not only knew each other's skills and preferences, she observes, but tolerated them when they disagreed.[67]

Groups seem to be strengthened when their members share reflex emotions in response to events *and* when they share affective commitments to one another (what I call *shared* and *reciprocal* emotions, respectively), with each one contributing to the other.[68] Shared emotions are about the rest of the world; reciprocal emotions are about one's own group (feelings about individual members and about the group as a whole). The two interact. You often develop affective attachments with others by sharing an emotional experience: moods, of course, but also urges, reflex emotions, and moral emotions. Even negative shared emotions can strengthen positive reciprocal emotions, as Ron Eyerman observes: "The experience of fear and anxiety, not uncommon in the midst of protest, can be a strong force in creating a sense of collectivity and be an attractive force in collective actions."[69] After all, it is negative shared feelings such as indignation against repression or stigma that often *inspire* protest groups in the first place.[70]

Group leaders usually try to minimize affective loyalties to anyone outside the group and maximize them to the group or its leaders, to generate a simplified sense of personal identity that lines up with the collective identity. Understanding these dynamics well, Janja Lalich compared the group Heaven's Gate, which expected to be transported up to the Hale-Bopp comet to start new incorporeal existences, to the Democratic Workers Party, a Marxist-Leninist cellule in the San Francisco Bay Area in the 1970s and 1980s.[71] Both required members to take new names, cut outside ties, and remain silent about prior affective commitments. (Both groups discouraged any talk of feelings, even as leaders manipulated affective loyalties.) She lists dozens of financial, organizational, ideological, and emotional mechanisms by which the groups' charismatic leaders built loyalty, as well as the costs of each, which I provide here in table 2. By negative, Lalich means damaging to the individual, not that these necessarily undermine the person's loyalty to the group: emotions that are useful means for group leaders may simultaneously be damaging to the rank and file as individuals. Although these two cults were especially destructive of their members, all groups deploy some of these means to create loyalty.

I do not mean to imply that the emotional dynamics of groups consist only of leaders' manipulation of the others. Subordinates frequently have nothing but emotional performances and appeals in their tool kits and use them often to influence their leaders. Plus there are plenty of horizontal interactions in which emotions are created and deployed. I mean to point to the many emotions that create groups, hold them together, and split them apart. Even without manipulation or selfish leaders, intensive group life can take a toll on individuals, the syndrome often referred to as *burnout*; in many cases our feeling-thinking processes warn our conscious selves about our fatigue.[72]

TABLE 2. Positive and Negative Characteristics of Transcendent Belief Systems, Systems of Control, Systems of Influence

| | Influence | |
	Positive	Negative
Transcendent Belief Systems	Higher calling	Overly righteous
	Sense of purpose	Becomes dogmatic
	Special	Exclusive
	Provides answers, meaning	All-or-nothing, totalistic
		Push to become a true believer
	Offers path to salvation	Self-renunciation outweighs
	Lure of freedom	freedom
	Hope for future	Closed worldview; dead end
Systems of Control	Sense of purpose	Reified and dogmatized
	Orderliness of life	Little or no independent action; no
	Sense of accomplishment	democracy
	Security of strength in numbers	Overworked, burned out
		Elitist attitudes; weak elements
	Most if not all personal needs met	purged
		Little or no personal time (or money)
	Group system of justice	Fear of rejection; ejection
	Hierarchical structure; clear lines of authority	Reinforces class relations; leadership secrets and privilege
	Increased sense of responsibility	Anxiety; guilt; fear of making mistakes
Systems of Influence	Sense of belonging	Loss of sense of self, individuality
	Enjoys sense of comradeship	Peer monitoring and reporting to leadership
	Strives to be better	Pressure to change; tension
	Role models for each other	Overly conformist; cut off from outside
	Sense of commitment	Becomes overly obedient;
	Born again; renewed self	deployable agent
	Part of something greater, so submit to authority	Self-exposure; constant confession
		Potential for exploitation, abuse

Source: Janja Lalich, *Bounded Choice* (University of California, 2004), appendix tables 2, 3, and 4. Reproduced with permission.

HATE

Negative commitments are influential as well—and are frequently even stronger than positive ones. In a letter to his lifelong friend Atticus, Cicero complained about the First Triumvirate, "My sole form of political activity is to hate the rascals, and even that I do without anger." For him, hatred had become a principled political stance, divorced from reflex emotions like anger that might have first stimulated it. Cicero expresses frustration, since hatred is an inner seething without the action orientation of anger (actions for which he would have been killed). But hate is still political, he recognizes, since it is a basic orientation to the world that he can share with others—Atticus at least—and which might inform future actions.

We also have a number of prejudices that fall short of full hatred: suspicion, mistrust, distaste, disliking. In 1954, Gordon Allport famously defined prejudice as "thinking ill of others without sufficient warrant."[73] Allport lived in a time before the cultural turn, when judgments like these were considered either right or wrong, not culturally constructed. Stereotypes, because they are judgments about a group as a whole, were in his view mistakes that well-functioning brains-as-calculators should not make. Cultural contact, replacing inaccurate with accurate information, was the cure. More recently, the trend in research has been to show the many uses we make of stereotypes in trying to grapple with the world despite our limited cognitive power—just as we use other carriers of cultural meanings.

Allport's "faulty and inflexible generalizations," often based on the authoritarian personality, have since been dislodged by theories that show stereotypes to be a natural part of human feeling-thinking, observable even in children as young as three months, rather than as a pathology. They are working hypotheses that we use when we encounter others, especially when our conscious brains are preoccupied with other issues and are not paying close attention to the individual in front of us.[74] By acknowledging stereotypes as universal rather than as frightening aberrations, researchers could ask *when* stereotypes lead to abiding hatred or aggression. The answer turns out to depend on group goals, competition over resources, a sense of threat from other groups, moral indignation over perceived unfairness from other groups, and the physical and cultural traits of the strategic arenas where organized groups engage one another. Moving beyond the calculating-brain model allows us to see many uses of stereotyped feeling-thinking, including affective commitments rhetorically accomplished.

The same feeling of "groupness" whose advantages we observed earlier can make the group a target of negative feelings. Susan Fiske and Mark Pavelchak suggest that we use different forms of processing when we see other people as part of a category to which we have a positive or negative affective commitment: they contrast "category-based" and "piecemeal" processing. In the former, we quickly evaluate someone on the basis of the feelings we have toward a group to which that person belongs; in the latter, we look for a number of individual traits to compile an evaluation.[75] As long as we see people as simply representatives of a group, we stereotype them, whether positively or pejoratively.

Kathleen Blee studies American hate groups that inflate everyday prejudices into what she calls "extraordinary racism": "an ideology that interprets and gives meaning to a wide variety of phenomena that seem unconnected to race, ranging from the global economy and the growth of media monopolies to more immediate personal issues such as the quality of family life, city services, and medical care." The white supremacists distinguish among their enemies. Some are dangerous, such as the worldwide Jewish conspiracy said to control finance and the media, while others are merely disgusting, such as gay people. One *causes* "social degeneracy," the other *results from it.* Even among the powerful villains, the supremacists had an immediate, visceral fear of African Americans but a distant, abstract fear of Jews. One was closer to reflex fear and anger, the other to moral indignation.[76]

It is almost certainly easier to stir up anger and aggression against those we already hate. Years of cultural construction can build contempt or disgust for groups whom we come to view as subhuman. The lynchings, pogroms, and other horrific massacres that humans have inflicted on each other are never random; the groups are sadly predictable.[77]

Paul Hoggett lists the dynamics that build on hate to prolong conflicts between groups: group boundaries become "electric" (that is, objects of affective commitment); identity markers become historicized in the sense that history is ransacked for events that reinforce those boundaries, especially in commemorations; both "us" and "them" become homogenized, as between-group differences loom larger than within-group ones; boundaries and group differences are policed, as physical mobility is restricted and the affective resonance of group symbols grows; each group projects hostility onto the other (each sees itself as the victim of the other's aggression).[78]

A team of psychologists, studying Israel, found that hatred for other groups is associated with political intolerance and that fear and anger operate through hatred and perceived threat.[79] These findings fit with other work showing that hate is aroused during wartime, when mobilization against an outsider is necessary.[80] Some regimes declare war against internal enemies. The Nazi Joseph Goebbels wrote, "Oh, I can hate, and I don't want to forget how. Oh, how wonderful it is to be able to hate."[81] Hatred is necessary for a moral crusade against an enemy who is constructed as totally evil.

Stuart Kaufman pulls together several levels of explanation to account for the gruesome ethnic violence in the former Soviet Union and former Yugoslavia in the 1990s. Preexisting hostilities must be there, he says, but they must be manipulated by political and media elites, around an economic conflict of interest: "Without perceived conflicts of interest, people have no reason to mobilize. Without emotional commitment based on hostile feelings, they lack sufficient impetus to do so. And without leadership, they typically lack the organization to act." Affective commitments feed the reflex emotions that (local or national) leaders transform into acts of violence. But the commitments remain central, elaborated through symbols, myths, and identities.[82]

In today's world, torture (the horrors of which we examined in chapter 3) is more commonly used against groups considered outsiders. Although overall rates have declined, thanks partly to human rights movements, civil wars in nations divided along race-ethnic and religious lines still often revert to torturing opponents. These outsiders join a long, sad list of groups considered something less than human and so available for mistreatment, such as slaves, foreigners, prisoners of war, and women. Hatred and pseudo-speciation are elaborated into a definition of a group as evil or nonhuman.[83]

Hatred for a group is inevitably entwined with a package of prejudicial stereotypes, anger over specific actions, and some sense of competition. It appears in politics as part of a "social dominance orientation," defined as "a generalized orientation towards and desire for unequal and dominant/subordinate relations among salient social groups, regardless of whether this implies ingroup domination or subordination."[84] Hatred for other groups is connected to a vision of the world as a ruthless competition.[85] It is useless to try to decide whether personal hatred or group competition comes first: they feed each other over time. A sense of external threat seems to lead to hatred for outsiders but also to love of one's own group, as both sides of a sharp boundary.

Historian Jan Gross, describing a 1946 pogrom in Poland, tries hard to attribute it to a fairly immediate sense of fear and threat, but in the end he cannot avoid the underlying affective commitments to hatred: "I see no other plausible explanation of the virulent postwar anti-Semitism in Poland but that it was embedded in the society's opportunistic wartime behavior. Jews were perceived as a threat to the material status quo, security, and peaceful conscience of their Christian fellow citizens after the war because they had been plundered and because what remained of Jewish property, as well as Jews' social roles, had been assumed by Polish neighbors in tacit and often directly opportunistic complicity with Nazi-instigated institutional mass murder."[86] Although Gross downplays prewar attitudes, they pop up again and again in his account, in the Christians' expectations and anxieties over what Jews were capable of.

"The postwar hatred of the Jews in Poland was too lethal, too widespread, too untamed to be grounded in anything else but concrete, palpable fear. It would have mellowed, subsided, or ossified had Jews not represented an existential threat to the Poles. Such hatred could not have sustained itself on figments of people's imagination, unsupported by evidence or everyday experience. There had to be real reasons for it or else it would have paled, if only out of pity for the boundless suffering that the Jews had experienced." I think Gross underestimates the power of the imagination, especially when we think of the peculiar case of Japanese anti-Semitism.[87]

People can hate a group they have never met, and when they do interact with a hated group, as Gross suggests, human sympathies sometimes kick in. But sometimes they do not. Two types of factors seem to be part of an explanation. One is precommitments such as hate or guilt. The other is the microlevel interaction that Collins describes: the tense fear, the anger stoked up by certain "brave" acts of violence, and so on. Hostile engagements will create negative affective commitments in cases when these do not already exist.[88]

As Gross later admits, "People don't avail themselves of every opportunity that comes their way. That Polish society proved vulnerable to totalitarian temptation and that numerous Poles joined in Nazi-organized victimization of their Jewish fellow citizens was facilitated by indigenous anti-Semitism."[89] That so many Poles cooperated with Nazi extermination efforts reinforced anti-Semitism rather than moderating it. Long-standing hatreds, simmering hostilities, disgust and contempt, dehumanizing stereotypes: these are all essential background conditions that trigger anger in the right circumstances. Perhaps it simply appears faster or more directly than it otherwise would.

Scholars are quicker to analyze right-wing groups as hateful, but the Left is capable of its own hatreds. I could easily have used the example of the Khmer Rouge, who had a long list of groups they considered vermin, viruses, and other nonhuman species. I may be horrified by examples of hate on the right and on the left, but that does not make them irrational. Hate is extremely effective in mobilizing people.[90]

Fortunately for humanity, the strength of us/them boundaries, along with the hatred that can arise toward outsiders, varies considerably. Those who have studied the rescuers during the Holocaust find that they valued the sanctity of all human life, refusing pseudo-speciating distinctions. In response to one rescuer's comment about those she saved, that "they were just people," Kristen Renwick Monroe concludes, "For rescuers, all people within the boundaries of their community of concern were to be treated the same, and their circle of concern included all human beings. This perception of a shared humanity triggered a sense of relationship to the other that then made the suffering of another a concern for the rescuers." The relevant boundary encompasses all humankind.[91]

There is another twist on us/them boundaries. Most research expects positive commitments to our own group and negative ones to outsiders, fairly enough. Sadly, those in oppressed or stigmatized groups often develop an admiration for the very groups who oppress them. And those on top, realizing that persuasion is more effective than coercion, work hard to cultivate those loyalties.[92] Acknowledging that thinking is below full awareness, researchers have used implicit attitude techniques to discover, for instance, that more than a third of African Americans implicitly favor whites, virtually the same proportion as those who favor their own group. Roughly the same proportion of gay respondents implicitly favored straights, confirming Deborah Gould's view that shame is still alive in the LGBTQ community.[93]

Patterns of affective loyalties like these help explain why there is never as much protest as observers think there should be, why so many injustices and inequalities are never attacked. Scholars of protest devote far too much attention to the positive cases, not these absences. Our emotional commitments help explain our patterns of action and inaction, partly because they shape our reflex emotions that can be created as part of our political programs.

ANXIETIES AND OTHER COMMITMENTS

A number of other emotions operate as fairly stable affective commitments. We may have wistful nostalgic feelings about heroes or other players from the past, who are now only symbolic references. We may respect other players' power while not especially liking them. They may inspire gratitude or humility in us, we may feel respect for them or feel responsible for them. We may feel competitive with other players, for instance, with envy or jealousy. Or we may feel downright sadistic toward them.

Some of our ongoing feelings toward them may be moral in tone, the subject of the following chapter. For instance, we may feel disgust for another group of humans, going beyond immediate gut repulsion into a permanent repulsion for who they are. We may feel contempt for them, placing them outside the circle of human moral concern. We will return to feelings like these.

Anxieties are a recurrent affective commitment that drives many mobilizations. We have seen reflex forms of fear, and panics that approach something like an all-encompassing mood, but anxieties are more abiding forms of fear. Just as there are things and people that we dislike or hate, others make us anxious or nervous. Normally, these anxieties are in the background, but they can be aroused or even whipped into reflex fears. As we saw in chapter 2, social scientists have used the term *moral panics* to get at episodes in which background anxieties are heated up by the media, self-appointed guardians of morality, politicians, and others who can garner public attention.

Each mobilization builds upon and reinforces existing anxieties. The image of a predatory "sex beast" that emerged in the United Kingdom in the 1970s and 1980s was successively applied to gay men, foreigners, Satanists, and elite criminal networks. Even supposed Satanic rituals, for which there was never any plausible evidence, reverberated emotionally and left anxieties on which future panics could build. The repetitions increased the plausibility of future claims, largely because the symbolic traces changed patterns of anxieties.[94]

* * *

Background emotions of affective and moral commitments shape our other, shorter-term feelings. Our bonds to our group will influence whether we get angry when we feel it is insulted or harmed. Our confidence in its strength will encourage us to participate in its actions. Feelings of trust help us act in concert with some people, even strangers, and avoid engagement with others. We may be aggressive, even violent, when we are dealing with despised groups.[95] Leaders have numerous ways of "retrieving" these affective convictions when they want to.

Affective commitments have low regret and disruption potential. We regret our feelings about groups primarily after we switch allegiances, often as a result of a betrayal or revelation about our group that we cannot forgive. Defectors must usually feel some regret. Many whistle-blowers feel this way about the organizations for which they work, or worked; they are transformed from loyalists to shocked victims. But when we remain part of a group, our loyalty is such a basic commitment that we cannot imagine regret. It is who we are.

As for disruption, our loyalty to a group rarely disturbs things for that group. We work hard to fit in, to help the group. Yet there can be too much of a good thing. Someone whose loyalty to the group conflicts with other appropriate emotions, sometimes moral commitments, can become the true believer who is more loyal to a group than to its principles. Extreme loyalty to one group can prevent appropriate feelings about other groups to which we belong. The same is true of loyalty to an idea.

Humans are many things, embedded in a variety of contexts. We have observed a series of emotions that reflect these contexts, of our own bodies and their urges and pains, of our immediate physical and social environments, and next even the context of our moral imaginations. Idealists could, I suppose, dismiss immediate physical contexts as unimportant, and actions oriented to them as irrational. But no one can say the same about our affective and moral attachments. In any vision of human nature, these are the deepest components of our humanity.

6: MORAL COMMITMENTS

Here dead we lie because we did not choose
To live and shame the land from which we sprung.
Life, to be sure, is nothing much to lose;
But young men think it is, and we were young.

A. E. HOUSMAN

A Notre Dame football star and idealistic recruit to the Central Intelligence Agency (CIA) in 1952, Ralph McGehee took a long road to becoming a whistle-blower, protestor, and creator of a public database on CIA operations. First in Thailand and then in Vietnam, McGehee's research on communist insurgents led him to conclude that, far from being an outside military intervention, they were popular and indigenous. He had developed a method unusual for the CIA, of surveying local villages, and he had confidence in his empirical results. After years of resistance and harassment by his superiors, he concluded that the rhetorical purpose of analysis in the CIA was to justify its larger, lethal program of covert involvements, not to learn the truth.

Despite his mounting frustration, he remained at the CIA for twenty-five years. He confesses, "I hated my inaction and myself," and he often took refuge in alcohol and thoughts of suicide. But with four kids to put through college and a résumé that was almost entirely classified, reducing the chance of outside employment, he stayed. And fumed. When severe back pain made him even more irritable, he sent an angry memo to a superior, effectively ending his hopes of advancement. The only colleague who would speak to him had also given up on advancement within the CIA. When the agency was downsized after a series of scandals in the mid-1970s, he eagerly grabbed an offer of early retirement, putting behind him a decade "which had been filled with anger, bitterness, self-doubts, mistrust, disbelief, disgust, and struggle." He wrote a book and some popular articles about the CIA and launched a database containing all publicly available information about CIA activities. It had taken him a long time, but he finally felt proud of himself.[1]

Morality depends on emotions to have an impact on social and political life. Even more than affective solidarities, most moral commitments change rarely and gradually. Although most remain intuitive, they are amenable to elaborate cognitive processing. Social movements never arise without them. Yet they are bodily feelings as surely as urges, reflexes, moods, and affective commitments are. Scholars of protest have used the word *moral* extensively, as I did in *The Art of Moral Protest*, without adequately demonstrating the mechanisms through which it operates. Social movements devote enormous ideological work to articulating moral intuitions, stabilizing them, and elaborating them through arguments, symbols, frames, moral characters, and didactic stories. These resonate when they tap the right emotions.

Nothing is more central to social movements than moral emotions. They operate as individual motivations, the ultimate goal of movements, indeed the very raison d'être of movements, which reflect and articulate existing moral commitments and at the same time try to transform them.

Moral emotions include shame and pride but also compassion, outrage, contempt, and more complex, cognitively processed forms of disgust, fear, and anger. Our anger may begin as a quick reflex, but sustaining it requires a deepening tincture of hate or moral indignation. As background commitments, moral emotions will now shape what makes us angry in the first place, and so they will influence future interactions. Reflex emotions, especially anger, can thus have a moral impact.[2]

Just as our affective commitments map our fundamental attractions and repulsions, moral commitments relate us to ideals of good and bad. Another way to put this: *we have affective commitments toward particular others, moral commitments toward general others.* I see special things in those people or places I love. In contrast, as T. M. Scanlon points out, "in the case of morality the relevant conditions do not concern the parties' existing attitudes toward one another but only certain general facts about them, namely that they are beings of a kind that are capable of understanding and responding to reasons."[3] Moral commitments are relationships to others, as well as to certain intuitions and principles about how we should treat those others.

Affective and moral commitments are woven together. On the one hand, we can view the emotions of morality as a subset of affective commitments, as applied to moral ideas. On the other hand, many of those moral principles are *about* loyalty to our groups. In most societies in history, loyalty to one's group has been considered the essence of morality. The ancient Greeks defined morality as helping friends and hurting foes; the ancient Jews focused more on following the rules of the group. In the modern world, some of our loyalties are to ideas about right and wrong. In all cases, some affective commitments are considered especially consequential, or sacred—Charles Taylor calls them "hypergoods"—and are thus "moral."[4]

Once we appreciate feelings as forms of thinking, we can see morality as consisting of emotional processes. Nussbaum draws this conclusion on the first page of her treatise, *Upheavals of Thought:* "Instead of viewing morality as a system of principles to be grasped by the detached intellect, and emotions as motivations that either support or subvert our choice to act according to principle, we will have to consider emotions as part and parcel of the system of ethical reasoning."[5]

The moral emotions are especially important when we try to connect micromotives to broader political systems. Our places in hierarchies and polities condition the emotions we feel, and many emotions arise out of structured strategic interactions in a number of institutional arenas. Many of our moral emotions develop out of our reactions to and beliefs about the social systems in which we live, especially outrage, indignation, and other feelings tied to our sense of justice.

Morals have stabilizing effects, making human action more predictable and aiding cooperation. The internalization of social norms and values was the glue keeping society together, according to Parsonian functionalism. The weakness in this theory was not only to exaggerate the homogeneity of moral commitments throughout a "society" but also to ignore a range of other emotional processes that frequently work against the moral emotions. As Dennis Wrong pointed out in 1961, humans are social but never fully socialized. In the sociology of his time (and perhaps ours), Wrong says, "Durkheim's whole stress on inner conflict, on the tension between powerful impulses and superego controls, the behavioral outcome of which cannot be prejudged, drops out of the picture." He draws on Sigmund Freud, of course, for an image of the inner life as "a battleground of conflicting motives." Sociologists have kept the superego but dropped the id from their models. Unfortunately, by relying on Freud, Wrong necessarily accepts the dualistic view of emotions as eruptions from within. We can instead view these conflicts as grounded in other emotions.[6]

I see three broad categories of moral emotions, each with its own potential impacts on political action. Each has a positive and a negative cluster. One concerns our own reputation, especially our sense of pride or shame about ourselves and our groups. This kind of pride is closely connected to dignity, involving our proper place in the world. The second involves our compassion or pity for others, sometimes feeding altruistic action just as anger frequently feeds aggression. Unlike pride and shame, the negative commitments here are not on the same continuum as compassion: contempt and disgust are distinct feelings, although their effects are largely the opposite of compassion's. A third set of moral feelings have to do with justice; in other words, how people are treated when they interact. Indignation is tied to a sense of injustice or unfairness. (Pride and, even more, compassion feed into our sense of justice by informing us about what treatments particular categories of beings deserve.) The remainder of this chapter follows these categories, with a final section on praise and blame, processes that run throughout the others. But let's start with Immanuel Kant, who applied the calculating brain model to morality more thoroughly than anyone else.[7]

KANT'S DUALISM

Before and after the Kantian era, philosophers typically acknowledged the role of emotions in morality. Pre-Kantian theorists, including the French "moralists" who pushed this idea to a cynical extreme, recognized that we only obey moral precepts because of the accompanying emotional pleasures. As Benedict de Spinoza put it, "Blessedness is not the reward of virtue, but virtue itself; neither do we rejoice therein, because we control our lusts, but contrariwise, because we rejoice therein, we are able to control our lusts."[8] Doing the right thing feels good *directly*; it is not the side effect of other actions. When we do the right thing, it is because we are driven by the accompanying emotions.

At the end of the eighteenth century, Kant applied the familiar dualism of emotion versus thought to matters of morality: our bodies live in a realm of natural causal necessity, but our reason resides in a realm of perfect freedom. As a moral philosopher, he was more interested in postulating how people *should* act than in explaining how they *do*, but his paradigm of moral action is interesting because even he falls prey to his emotions. We should act, he says, according to principles that we would wish to see made into universal laws to be followed by all rational people. We should derive our actions from those first principles in a logical fashion. There are many problems with "universal" (Are children supposed to follow the same moral maxims as parents? The poor as the rich, who have more means to act morally?) as well as with "rational." In defining what is rational, Kant surreptitiously followed his own moral intuitions, presenting them as what any rational being would do. This is clear in his arguments against suicide or rebellion *under any circumstances*.[9] Kant also *opposed* emotion and morality: an action is not distinctively moral if we enjoy it. Our only motive must be a sense of duty, from which we are not allowed to derive any smug pleasure. Far from refuting David Hume's claim that we follow our emotions and that we rationalize our actions to do so, Kant in his argumentation seems to confirm it. "Morals excite passions," Hume famously said, "and produce or prevent actions."[10]

In the twentieth century, Lawrence Kohlberg articulated a psychology that corresponded to Kant's view of morality, including its preachy normative intrusions. At the lowest levels, children define what they themselves like or want as what is right. They mature into conventional morality, following the rules laid down by society. When we attain the highest morality—and Kohlberg thought that most adults do not—we define what is right in terms of abstract, universal principles and derive our actions from them: to be moral, you have to work your way up from first principles, and to be supermoral, you have to develop your own first principles, too. Kohlberg measured morality by asking people to talk about moral situations and dilemmas, meaning that he had no room for inarticulate moral intuitions.[11] Yet this *is* morality for most people: we sense that something is right or wrong without being able to say why, exactly. We feel angry or disgusted by certain actions; we *feel* our disapproval. We think through our feelings. And a great deal of that thinking involves following the conventions of the groups with which we identify—a loyalty that Kohlberg found immature.

Post-Kantian philosophers have backed away from Kant's icy dichotomy between emotions and morality. Bernard Williams insists that moral education is emotional education, revolving around "such issues as what to fear, what to be angry about, what—if anything—to despise, where to draw the line between kindness and stupid sentimentality."[12] Carol Gilligan posited an ethic of care and connection to others that contrasted with the abstract rights ethic that Kohlberg thought superior. And a number of modern Aristotelians have described a morality based on moral training, on character and its attendant virtues. They insist that we learn *habits* of right action, so that we do not have to calculate the right moral move but instead know it intuitively. Good character is a training of the feeling-thinking processes that already guide us.[13]

Mark Johnson takes us partway down the path away from Kant and toward feeling-thinking by emphasizing metaphors, since these operate in more subtle ways than the moral judgments which, in Kant's view, merely apply moral laws to concrete cases. Johnson sees the aesthetic imagination as helping us feel our way through the world: "Morality is not the search for moral laws to guide our lives, but rather the ongoing imaginative exploration of possibilities for dealing with our problems, enhancing the quality of our communal relations, and forming significant personal attachments that grow." We could almost substitute feeling-thinking processes for imagination in what Johnson says here: "It is precisely that capacity which allows us both to experience present situations as significant and to transform them in light of our quest for well-being." Another word that had done the same work, for John Dewey, is *aesthetic*. By the 1990s, cognitive science was groping toward emotions.[14]

Jonathan Haidt observes that Kohlberg's approach has no room for emotions, especially loyalties to one's own group. It fits an American and Western image of social life as interactions among autonomous individuals, not people who define themselves primarily as part of a group, with its attendant authority, hierarchy, and tradition—all of which are denigrated in Kohlberg's moral scheme. Haidt notes that people often have a gut intuition about right and wrong but feel that the only way they can articulate those intuitions is by finding explicit principles or a victim who has been wronged. In one of his research vignettes, he describes a woman who rips up an American flag that she no longer needs. His American subjects had a sense that this was wrong but tried to justify their intuitions by searching instead for principles based on personal injury: she might later come to regret throwing out the flag; someone might see her do it and be offended. They were confident in their emotional judgments and then flailed about to find a calculating rationale for them. Their emotions came first. Haidt's interest, however, is in showing that humans are not selfish but "groupish." They care about their group and about symbols of that group. Their affective attachments are a key part of their moral intuitions.[15] This only begins to suggest the panoply of feelings that comprise the moral dimension of human action.

PRIDE

A desire for good reputations in our own and others' eyes is a deep and persistent motivation. We have lost track of this in a world of Freudian drives and Marxist materialism, but pride and honor continue to propel and enhance individual and collective projects throughout the world. They situate us in relation to other individuals, groups, and our ideals. Even money and power, usually viewed as ends in themselves, are sought mostly because they raise our status in the eyes of others. Pride and shame are our feelings about our own reputations. As table 3 suggests, we can apply our feelings of approval and disapproval to ourselves or to others. Many of the moral batteries that drive protest incorporate the upper-left and lower-right quadrants.

As we saw in chapter 2, pride (and shame) include at least three distinct kinds of feelings. They can be reflex emotions easily read from a person's face and body; they can derive from membership in a group, which can provide either shame or pride; or they can accompany particular actions, in which case they are most clearly moral emotions. In general we avoid actions we anticipate will lead to shame, and we seek those that will make us proud.

According to social psychologist Thomas Scheff, pride and shame are master emotions that drive social life because they help or hurt our connections to others. "Pride signals and generates solidarity. Shame signals

TABLE 3. Basic Moral Judgments

	Approval/Praise	Disapproval/Blame
Self	Pride	Shame, Guilt
Others	Admiration	Indignation, Disgust, Contempt

and generates alienation. Shame is a normal part of the process of social control; it becomes disruptive only when it is hidden or denied."[16] Drawing on Erving Goffman, who used embarrassment much as Scheff uses shame, Scheff builds up from personal encounters. He insists that there are good and bad forms of pride. One is a justified sense of having a secure place in the social order, the other is mere egotism or hubris.[17] Appreciation that one has a secure place in the world—the fullest form of pride—is what we often think of as *dignity:* having the full social and moral attributes of a human being. "Shame is the emotion that occurs when we feel too close or too far from others," Scheff explains. "When too close, we feel exposed or violated; when too far, we feel invisible or rejected. Pride is the signal of being at the right distance: close enough to feel noticed but not so close as to feel threatened."[18] Shame is an extremely demobilizing emotion, and it must be overcome for political mobilization to occur, as we'll see.

Pride and honor are usually judgments about a whole person, in contrast to esteem for particular actions or areas of life. We can have esteem for a person's ability in a particular situation—say, to arouse others with a speech—but that person does not thereby gain a general reputation or honor.[19] Shame, like pride, "pertains to the whole self, rather than to a specific act of the self." It "is a painful emotion responding to a sense of failure to attain some ideal state."[20]

Pride and shame arise from our ability to feel about ourselves as others feel about us, even if our judgments about how others feel are not always accurate. In the *Protagoras*, Plato saw this ability as arising especially from friendship, which to him entailed moral accountability in a way that few moderns would recognize. The same idea forms the core of symbolic interactionism, and one of its founders, Charles Cooley, pointed to shame and pride as fundamental emotions that we feel when we imagine how others are seeing us (his famous "looking glass self"): are they judging us favorably or unfavorably? Our concern for positive judgments, which give us pride, drives us to follow social rules.[21]

Moral pride (or *deontological pride*: pride in doing the right thing in and of itself) is a complex accomplishment, based on values that we share with others.[22] Living up to those values, or our own interpretation of them, yields moral pride. There are two ways to feel morally valuable. One is simply to belong to a valued status group, to have the right blood flowing through our veins. The other is to do things that others admire. Both sources can operate simultaneously: an aristocrat may or may not "live up to" aristocratic ideals. When he does, he is admired for being an aristocrat *and* for doing it well. Or he might have the status of an aristocrat, but combined with shame for playing the role badly. One must encounter or imagine an other, whose opinion one respects, in order to feel shame from that person's disapproval. Even when no one actually knows who we are or what we have done to be ashamed of, we can *imagine* that they might, and we still feel private shame.

What does moral pride feel like when it arises from our actions, rather than being due to our birth? We do not follow the moral rules of our group automatically. We either obey moral rules because we fear sanctions if we do not, or because it feels good to do the right thing—Spinoza's "rejoicing." In the latter case, doing the right thing may feel good intuitively rather than because of some explicit principle. The Kantian tradition, which posits that we do what we believe is right simply because of that belief, has discouraged attention to the many satisfactions that accompany this kind of action. We can be proud, sometimes smugly or invidiously so, in comparing ourselves to those less righteous. We may feel joyful, happy, or simply relieved to have overcome temptations to act another way. We may get a charge from being active agents rather than passive victims, related to a mood of confidence. We get these feelings especially when we obey explicit moral rules recognized by those around us, but also sometimes when we follow our own moral principles and intuitions. Some people are *especially* pleased to follow their own moral rules in the face of opposition (in a way that Kohlberg would have respected). Following moral norms when we have little choice in the matter doesn't have the same satisfactions (although it has others) as when we choose to obey them. All these deontological emotions can be observed in protestors, including occasionally the smug self-righteousness.

In chapter 4 I argued that happiness can be a mood, a reflex emotion of joy, or a broad judgment of satisfaction about how one's life has gone. It is this last feeling, in fact, that most happiness surveys capture. For most people, this kind of satisfaction must contain a heavy dose of moral pride. We are happy because we have lived up to our own hopes and to the expectations of those around us, as we have moved through a series of roles in life, including political roles. We have not messed up in any serious way. Martin Buber's formulation of conscience links it to this kind of reflection: "Conscience means to us the capacity and tendency of man radically to distinguish between those of his past and future actions which should be approved and those which should be disapproved," in other words a kind of contemplation and judgment of one's actions.[23] So pride can become encrusted with cognitive elaborations over time.

Pride helps us persist in a course of action despite enormous adversity or risk. Even torture is more tolerable if we think our suffering is for a good cause.[24] We resist the shame of breaking down as we imagine an audience of comrades watching us. Plus our solidarity with that group bolsters our strength. Pride and dignity may yield the confidence that is so important to strategic action.

Jon Elster has written interestingly about moral emotions, especially about humans' ability to have moral emotions—notably shame and pride—about their reflex emotions. We are ashamed of our anger or fear, say. We monitor our actions, thoughts, and even feelings, in the kind of reflexivity dear to social constructionists. Elster comments that conscious efforts to humiliate others can misfire, arousing anger instead of shame. If the person I try to shame realizes that I am trying to shame her, she may be able to deflect the feeling and instead blame me for bad intentions. For that reason, disgust is more effective at shaming someone because it seems more genuine. It also seems to encompass the target's entire being rather than a single action. "Involuntary recoil is more effective in inducing shame, because it does not give the target the option of rewriting the script in terms of a blamable intention to slight on the part of the sanctioner."[25] Those with stigmatized identities may nonetheless begin to feel their shame to be an unfair oppression, consciously used against them, rather than as inhering in their own character. This emotional transformation can open the door to political action.

Table 3 suggests that we apply the same moral commitments to ourselves and others (even if we are more lenient or less lenient on ourselves, depending on personality quirks). I also want to show the close connection between feelings of approval or disapproval and the actions that typically accompany them, praise or blame. There is some overlap: we can feel contempt or disgust for ourselves as part of our shame, and we admire ourselves as part of pride. Plus we can feel proud of loved ones and shame for a group with which we identify. We'll return to praise and blame later in the chapter.

SHAME

Failure to live what is recognized as a moral life yields shame. A single action can so violate a group's moral system that it permanently taints the person who committed it, making her a defective individual. Or she may simply belong to a group so stigmatized or deprived that its members are prohibited from living the kind of life that is recognized as morally decent or dignified. Either way, she is like an untouchable, who arouses moral disgust in others—even though the source of the contamination differs in the two cases.

Even the *victim* of a shameful act—those who have been in concentration camps, those who have been raped—can feel shame. "The shame of passivity, the passivity of shame, is intolerable," remarks philosopher Arne Johan Vetlesen. "It is felt as incompatible with dignity, with self-respect." There is shame in not being able to prevent something terrible from happening, either to oneself or to others. An Auschwitz survivor compares his torture to rape: "Logically, it is the rapist who ought to feel shame, but in reality it is the victim who does, for she cannot forget that she was reduced to powerlessness, to a total dissociation from her will."[26] To something less than fully human, robbed of dignity.

Vetlesen describes the bodily component to this shame. "No longer a natural and trustworthy source of pride, of self-esteem and self-identity, the body is all of a sudden turned into the opposite: a thing-like 'object' that one drags around, reminding oneself only of the body's fall from grace; a transition, that is, from a subject of willed action in the world whose every move exhibits her sovereignty, to an object of abuse at the hands of an alien will."[27] The forms of shame reinforce each other. The many bodily limits and failures observed in chapter 3 can become sources of moral shame, whether or not they begin as physical humiliation.

Because it pollutes our entire being, shame has an obsessive quality. Amélie Rorty points out that it "tends to involve obsessive imagistic replays of the moment of exposure, to be expressed in the focused remembering of the event, as if time were arrested."[28] The spoiled identity makes it hard to work back from shame. Although their sources differ, group- and action-based forms of shame both lead to the same sense of an inherently bad self: a self so damaged that we cannot undertake coordinated actions with others, cannot be part of a parade or rally; instead we try to avoid others. We fall into a deep mood much like depression.

Guilt is a version of act-oriented shame, but the damage does not pollute the entire person. In contrast to shame, guilt does not seem to have a primate counterpart; it necessarily entails complex moral and cognitive judgments. For this reason Derek Phillips sees it as the epitome of a moral emotion: "the rational and appropriate (in short, the 'correct') emotion for people to experience when they violate the generic rights of other persons or fail to give them the esteem to which they are entitled."[29] Through confession, apology, or reparation, the perpetrator can expiate guilt and be accepted again as a normal member of the group. One way to make amends is to work harder on behalf of the group, a mechanism with possible ramifications for protest groups and political parties.[30]

Guilt is about what I have *done*, shame about who I *am*. "We can feel both guilt and shame towards the same action," Bernard Williams explains. "In a moment of cowardice, we let someone down; we feel guilty because we have let them down, ashamed because we have contemptibly fallen short of what we might have hoped of ourselves."[31]

The contrast between reflex and moral shame can be seen in *humiliation*. Someone can humiliate me by saying things or threatening me physically in a situation when I cannot talk or fight back. I am cowed and feel degraded. It is a form of fear. My feeling is different when I have done something of which I myself am ashamed, something I know violates certain expectations that I share with others. I *may also* feel shame about my inability to fight back, as we saw earlier, but I may instead have a political analysis that allows me to avoid this feeling.

Shaming someone can be a devastating strategic move. These acts of shaming operate publicly, especially where honor is used to reinforce status hierarchies. When actions bring shame not just on the individual but on her family or caste, revenge is often used to clear their name. In parts of the Muslim world, so-called honor killings target young women who have attempted to control their own sexuality through acts such as premarital sex, modern styles of dress, adultery, or resistance to arranged marriage (although victims of rape are frequently seen as polluted, dishonored in much the same way). Some are murdered by their own brothers or fathers, with the explicit or implicit approval of the rest of the family. A student of Bedouin society, Gideon Kressel, suggests that honor killings are more likely if the infraction is widely known (more shameful) and among social groups trying to ascend the social hierarchy.[32] Honor is a precious resource for them.

If many movements try to eliminate shame, others deploy shame as part of their tactical repertory against those who violate widely shared norms. Whistle-blowers, watchdog groups, election monitors, and muckraking journalists all look for malfeasance, lies, and cover-ups. While some social movements face the job of changing public norms and tastes, others merely reinforce existing (consensual) ones—usually an easier task. Since the mid-twentieth century, a presumption of "the right to know" has spread internationally, stimulating protestors such as Ralph McGehee to devote themselves to information gathering, a burden made easier by the Internet (and by hackers). Targets are more easily shamed when they are accountable to the public, but even those who are shameless can often be brought in line by the threat of legal penalties.[33]

The anticipation of pride or shame, Cooley said, tends to drive our actions down socially approved paths.[34] When we feel either pride or shame, there are numerous effects. Pride strengthens and shame corrodes affective attachments. Pride puts us in a good mood and shame in a bad, contributing to either confidence or lassitude. Pride and shame even help us interpret our urges, and especially their expressions. And they define what situations will trigger which reflex emotions. So it is crucial for protest movements to

rework the moral intuitions of recruits so that they feel proud of membership in the movement or its associated group.

THE SHAME-PRIDE BATTERY

The energizing power of pride and the devastation of shame together form
a moral battery and lay out a basic strategy for many movements of the oppressed: transform shame into pride. This is one of the strongest of moral
batteries that juxtapose strong negative and positive feelings in a way that
encourages passage from one to the other.

The shame-pride battery has been dissected most thoroughly for
American gay and lesbian rights (and later, lesbian, gay, bisexual, transgender, and queer, or LGBTQ rights), in part because these movements
have been such a laboratory for theorizing, even though we can find the
same dynamic among workers, women, ethnic-racial minorities, lower
castes, and many other movements. In her study of the AIDS Coalition
to Unleash Power (ACT UP), Deborah Gould shows that, as late as the
1980s, many gays and lesbians still felt "an anxiety that something about
homosexuality—something that was revealed by AIDS—was indeed
shameful and must be obscured in order for gays to be deemed deserving
of rights and state assistance." They pursued a safe politics of respectability
that downplayed differences between gay and straight America: "Anger,
even in the face of death—indeed, the murder—of one's lover and perhaps
oneself, should be channeled toward phoning one's elected representative." Mostly, shame discouraged anger: "It is hard to be angry if one thinks
that what is happening to oneself flows naturally from what one is."[35]

At first, pride meant quiescence. "A politics of responsibility," Gould says,
"is almost always deeply ambivalent: concerned above all with social acceptance, it entails efforts by some members of a marginalized group both to dis-
prove dominant stereotypes about the group and to regulate and 'improve'
the behavior of its members in line with socially approved norms."[36] But
in one important arena, LGBT claims to acceptance were harshly rejected.
When the US Supreme Court, in its 1986 *Bowers v. Hardwick* decision, de-
clared, "there is no such thing as a fundamental right to commit homosexual
sodomy," many lesbian and gay activists shifted to less respectable, more
disruptive tactics, founding ACT UP. They became proud of their difference,
not their similarity, thanks to the moral shock of *Hardwick*.

The appeal of ACT UP, and the label "queer" that it embraced, was to
combine pride in queer difference with indignant anger over homophobic
oppression. It offered new answers to two strategic dilemmas: the naughty-
or-nice dilemma and the dilemma of stigmatized identities. Naughty or
Nice pits respectability against aggressive tactics, love against fear from

other players. ACT UP decided that queer Americans were not getting any love from American society, so why not go for media attention and disruption instead? Anger is the usual stepping-stone from shame to pride.[37]

As groups go about this kind of emotion work, they face the stigmatized identity dilemma, as I have described elsewhere: "You want to mobilize to change or eliminate the identity, but you need to use that same identity to mobilize people. So you run the risk of strengthening the label you are opposed to. This is a dilemma both at the level of means, of how to get what you want, and at the level of ends, since moral dignity arises both from abolishing the stigma and from organizing politically."[38] Successful movements would make themselves obsolete by eliminating stigma, even if their organizations continued by adopting new goals (or focusing on remaining pockets of stigma). For many groups, including gays, African Americans, and India's Dalits, new self-labels are often part of the effort to create pride without giving up the affective solidarity. This identity work may consist of recharging pejorative terms with positive means, inventing scientific or technical labels, introducing new variations on old names, or promoting designations that connote proud pasts.

Dignity is a form of pride, a feeling that others respect you, but it also includes the feelings that others have toward you. (Like its ancestor, the idea of natural rights, it is not entirely clear where it resides, but it entails some interaction with others.) It can arise from pride in one's group, but it can also be part of an individual identity, too, a sense of mastery. This search for personal meaning used to be considered a reason to condemn protest, as confused young people thrashed about.[39] But William Gamson finds a kernel of truth in collective behavior traditions: "Cleansed of its assumptions about a spoiled or ersatz identity, there is a central insight that remains. Participation in social movements frequently involves enlargement of personal identity for participation and offers fulfillment and realization of the self."[40] According to Elisabeth Wood, their yearning for dignity drove many Salvadorans to the extreme risks of participation in a revolutionary guerilla movement.[41]

To reduce and eliminate shame for stigmatized groups, movements often try to change sources of disgust. Like anger, disgust comes in several forms, ranging from gut-level bodily revulsion, a kind of gagging, up through abstract moral repugnance. The most successful status hierarchies fuse these forms, so that the low-status group is considered not only morally but also physically disgusting. Groups that challenge such systems attain dignity by erasing the disgust previously felt toward them.

"Coming out" is a movement tactic intended to take advantage of the shame-pride battery, especially when shame takes the form of invisibility. Originally a lesbian and gay term, the phrase has been adopted by other movements for its ability to link personal with collective identities, private choices with public statements. "When activists come out," remarks Nancy Whittier, "they publicly display a politicized, redefined version of what it means to be part of their group, and they declare that their individual fates—both their position in hierarchies and their happiness—are bound up with the fate of the collectivity." Coming out not only brings pride to individuals, it also increases the solidarities of the group. It is the essential shame-pride battery.[42]

Pride parades have proven a powerful tool for rejecting shame, adopting a celebratory mode of "parade" instead of the more usual, earnest "march." Starting in 1970—on the first anniversary of the Stonewall riots in Greenwich Village, —gay pride parades soon spread around the world, involving millions of participants annually in revelry, sheer fun, and public insistence on pride.[43] Like many emotions, pride is both an end in itself and a means to further action.

COMPASSION

Philosophers of the Scottish enlightenment, notably David Hume and Adam Smith, believed that morality arises from the basic human capacity to feel sympathy for others. Although the details differ, the central idea is that our own life experiences allow us to gauge what someone else is going through, as signaled by their expressions, body language, and utterances. Recently, this view was given support by the discovery of "mirror neurons" that fire *both* when we experience something *and* when we see another person experience it.[44] These neurons help explain the imitation and emotional contagion found during many human interactions.

Empathy is one pathway to fellow feelings. It includes our feeling-thinking capacities to understand or reconstruct what another person is feeling and, in some definitions, to actually feel it ourselves. Although it need not lead to action to help the other, Nussbaum insists that it is "a very important tool in the service of getting a sense of what is going on with the other person and also of establishing concern and connection."[45] But empathy is value neutral, and a sociopath can use it to manipulate others as easily as normal people rely on it as a path to sympathy. Empathy is necessary but not sufficient for moral sympathy.

Empathy forms the starting point for some types of love, in which we feel solidarity with others. Social structure directs our fellow feelings. We are more likely to develop empathy for family members for a variety of reasons, and even Hume suggested, quite sociologically, that we are more apt to empathize with those who are similar to us and whose place we can imagine occupying. Other emotions can block empathy—for instance, when we are angry with someone and desire revenge.

Psychologist Simon Baron-Cohen says that we feel empathy when we are able to imagine someone else's mind at the same time as we attend to our own; in other words, putting aside our usual single-minded focus of attention from our own perspective. He is suggesting what we already know about feeling-thinking: multiple pathways provide different kinds of information at the same time. He further insists that we not only *recognize* what another is feeling and thinking, but that we *respond* to it in some way—although others would see that response as sympathy rather than empathy.[46] We think we feel what they feel, and we expect them to reciprocate. Other kinds of love do not require empathy, like adoration of a loved one, whom we love precisely because that person is so different from us.

Fortunately, sociopaths are rare. For most of us, empathy leads to sympathy, toward tolerance and away from prejudice, opening us to the possibility of action on others' behalf. Sam McFarland, in research on sources of prejudice against other groups (homophobia, racism, sexism, xenophobia, and so on), found that empathic abilities moderate prejudice, as does principled moral reasoning. Greater capacity for empathy, instilled since infancy, is one reason that women tend to have less prejudice toward many out-groups than men do, and perhaps why they are uncomfortable seeing people punished—even when they otherwise approve of the punishment.[47] Sociologists tend to attribute prejudice to a dominant group's efforts to control resources, but there is a world of interesting emotional mechanisms involved in bolstering one's own group and denigrating others, some of which we examined in the last chapter.[48]

Sympathy involves having a feeling as a result of someone else's feeling, but it is not neutral: it involves a judgment that the other person is feeling bad. Unlike empathy, which is a path to emotions rather than an emotion itself, sympathy is an emotion of sadness and compassion. It is not necessarily the *same* emotion the other is feeling but rather a *response* to that emotion—although we may partly also feel what the other person is feeling. We may feel other people's shock or disappointment, but we might also feel sympathetic indignation in response to their anger or frustration. It turns out that sympathy increases the impact of trust on cooperation.[49]

Sympathy is close to compassion, with the main difference being the greater intensity of the latter and the greater empathy of the former.[50] According to Nussbaum, there are three components to compassion: we must think the other person's plight is serious rather than trivial; that it is undeserved; and that this person has some relevance to our own projects. One of the accomplishments of the modern world is the potential extension of this relevance to all humans, and even beyond, to all sentient beings. In my view, this relevance must entail some identification with those others, at least as fellow sufferers. Nussbaum observes that imagination may "help us bring a distant individual into the sphere of our goals and projects, humanizing the person and creating the possibility of attachment. This imaginative leap may aid, but it does not define, compassion."[51] Compassion affects what policies we favor by focusing our attention and defining worthy recipients of aid.

Compassion for others, and outrage on their behalf, can come to rest on strangers, but most often it applies to people we know. There is a social structure to compassion and related feelings. When an immigrant faces deportation, it is friends, family, fellow students, and sometimes neighbors who rally first to the person's aid: they experience more of a moral shock. On the other hand, people can be shocked into action on the basis of moral outrage but then continue their participation in a movement due to the social bonds they build there. Even their affective and moral commitments are not independent of their social networks, so that many US citizens were aware of events in Central America in the 1980s because of church ties such as missionary support, primed to feel moral shocks over Ronald Reagan's aggressive policies.[52]

In at least one case, documented by Chandra Russo, organizers ask protestors to wear others' shoes, almost literally, in a seventy-five-mile hike along the Migrant Trail on the US-Mexican border. Experiencing (part of) what migrants endure promotes solidarity by increasing compassion. In this case, affective bonds and moral emotions are tightly woven, as compassion reminds hikers of the basic human bonds that unite them with all the migrants who suffer (and often die) each year.[53]

Pity is similar to compassion and sympathy, but it has less empathic identification. In fact, it can involve considerable distance from the object of pity, sometimes even to the point of contempt. The very word *object* says it all: pity strips others of their full humanity and makes them into objects. We have full agency; they have none. They are victims. Our pity for animals can rise to the level of compassion as we appreciate their mental capacities, but given the limits to that understanding, we can never be fully sympathetic. They will never be entirely like us.

Philosopher Jesse Prinz points to a related term, *concern*, a kind of anxiety or worry that another being is in a bad situation. Although it may not correspond to any emotion on the part of the object of concern, who may be oblivious to their own plight, Prinz thinks it "may be especially conducive to pro-social behavior."[54] In contrast to many cases of sympathy, which are gut level, concern often requires cognitive processing before it can emerge. It may also be more common in personal relations than in politics, although politics is based on face-to-face interactions as well as more mediated ones.

A final form of sympathy, a sensitivity to others, is summed up in Norbert Elias's notion of the "civilizing process." This has more to do with making other people "comfortable," avoiding actions that would disgust or even mildly disturb them. Elias examined etiquette books from the fifteenth to the eighteenth centuries, the period when Europeans learned to stop blowing their noses on their sleeves, spitting on the floor, or eating out of the common pot—niceties that filtered down gradually from courtly life to other social strata. They grew more private about sex and less immediately aggressive. Elias attributes the civilizing process—note his use of the singular—to social sensitivities at royal courts, demographic crowding, and increasing centralization of violence in the hands of monarchs, but he observes that "the social standard to which the individual was first made to conform by external restraint is finally reproduced more or less smoothly within him, through a self-restraint which may operate even against his conscious wishes."[55] These are new sources of empathy and disgust, but also of shame. Our moral commitments come to do the work that external constraints once did.

Not all the impetus for civilizing came from demography or courtly manners: intellectual and moral movements of the bourgeoisie also promoted the civilizing process. Some of this refashioning of manners was a self-help movement of ambitious bourgeoisie mimicking their social superiors, and some was a revolt by humanists against the violence and crudeness of the aristocracy. The decline of the old feudal aristocracy, Elias observes, gave "the representatives of a small, secular-bourgeois intellectual class, the humanists, and thus Erasmus, not only an opportunity to rise in social station, to gain renown and authority, but also a possibility of candor and detachment."[56] Pacifist movements trace their ideas to the same sources, especially Erasmus, since part of the humanists' moral disgust with aristocrats was over their role in perpetrating wars.[57] Compassion for others was part of the humanist movement, which was not precisely what we would today label a social movement but was certainly an intellectual movement.

In the period Elias studied, the increasing sensitivity to the feelings of others took the form of growing formality in manners, but in the twentieth century the same sensitivity began to require more *informality* in human relations. Moderns are expected to be finely attuned to those around them, whether that requires bluntness or tact, flexibility or rigidity.[58] Twentieth-century social movements criticized some of the formalities that earlier movements had promoted.

All these forms of fellow feeling are subject to framing processes, to every sort of cultural work that directs our attention to one individual or group rather than another. This is a large part of what politicians, protestors, and moral entrepreneurs do: offer new categories of victims to pity or classes of humans to respect compassionately. Through moral emotions they try to remap our affective commitments, to widen (or curtail!) our circle of compassion. The animal-rights movement would not have been possible without new extensions of compassion; Donald Trump would be impossible without impatience, anxieties, and backlash against similar extensions to immigrants and Muslims.

Pity and compassion inspire different types of social movements and strategies. If we pity a group we try to do something *for* them, often through experts and bureaucracies. They have objective interests that can be satisfied, whatever their own desires and activities. Compassion leads us to have a sense of their lives, their subjective point of view, and their dignity. We want to eliminate obstacles blocking them from attaining *their own ends*, through means that they themselves devise. Many movements have struggled with this difference in feelings, including animal *protection* versus animal *rights*, movements *for* versus *by* the disabled, and abolitionism.

CONTEMPT

The opposite of compassion may be contempt. Pride turned toward others is admiration; shame turned outward becomes contempt or disgust. Our shame disconnects *us* from the social world, our contempt for others expels *them* from the human group. Guilt over an action demands or allows reincorporation, while shame places the entire person beyond redemption. It is part of the process of treating others as subhuman. This is the essence of contempt. Pity and contempt can be combined, much as we might feel for a writhing animal without having any sense of its life projects. Convinced of our superiority, we can still recognize the suffering of an inferior.

Contempt often involves disapproval for those who have violated moral norms. Susan Fiske reports, "Students in both Japan and the United States reliably pick contemptuous faces and the word 'contempt' to describe their reactions to such norm violations as a child using obscenities to parents, an executive refusing to sit next to a laborer on a commuter train, a citizen burning the country's flag, or people not attending their own mother's funeral."[59] Yet cultures also contain many idiosyncratic moral norms—for instance, over appropriate roles for young and old, women and men. And some cultures place a wider range of practices in the category of moral as opposed to that of arbitrary social convention.[60]

Whatever their triggers, contempt and scorn often combine with disgust—not the reflex disgust that makes you gag, but a moral form that is close to indignation. "When people break a taboo," Fiske observes, "other people judge them by saying, 'That's disgusting,' a real conversation stopper." Like its reflex form, moral disgust "rejects, excludes, and repels." It also fascinates: people are more likely to pass along disgusting stories.[61] Like contempt, disgust implies that someone is not fully human.

Many progressive social movements aim to reduce contempt (by expanding compassion), but other movements are built on contempt. Donald Trump's 2016 campaign was based largely on his bullying disdain for others: "losers," low-energy candidates, women, men with small hands. (Many of his followers combined this disdain with resentment of others' perceived contempt for *them*, such as bureaucrats' supposed scorn for uneducated rural folks or blue-collar workers.) Hate groups find categories of people whom they consider not like them, not worthy of respect, and perhaps not fully human. The boundary between compassion and contempt, always subject to conflict and change, implies policies about how different groups should be treated.

CALCULATING JUSTICE

Fairness and justice are linked to a third set of moral emotions that can help or hinder protest or shape social movements. A generation ago, under the structural paradigm of protest, *justice* was the only word for talking about morality, and it was devoid of emotions. It fit well with that paradigm's sense that protestors largely pursue their economic and political interests, in that justice is largely about the distribution of life's rewards. Unlike pride or shame in oneself or one's group, and unlike gut-level compassion, fairness in particular tends to reflect a more abstract ideology of how rewards should be distributed, notably in market societies. Justice was largely seen as a goal for social movements, but one so general that it could safely be ignored in models of mobilization.

But even a sense of justice can move us to act only because of its associated emotions, such as indignation. Bert Klandermans, William Gamson, Charles Tilly, and other major theorists of protest have all recognized that some sense of injustice is key to mobilization. Much of the mobilizing power of injustice lies in a second type, *procedural* justice, rather than in *substantive* justice. As I said earlier, I believe that people tend to be more shocked when they encounter unfair procedures, especially in governmental practices that are supposed to protect them.[62] (Not everyone *expects* this, sadly, but they may still *hope* for it.) Procedural injustices tend to be discrete actions, while substantive injustices (such as a high level of economic inequality) tend to be ongoing states instead of specific decisions and actions. It is easier to ignore chronic states than dramatic events, perhaps because the reflex emotions spurred by the latter help focus our attention.

In the Kantian tradition, the calculating brain reduced morality to questions of the fair distribution of burdens and benefits and the fairness of procedures for arriving at those distributions. John Rawls suggested a procedure for arriving at fair social contracts by placing everyone behind a "veil of ignorance" that would somehow prevent them from knowing their own social position. Brian Barry similarly argues for impartiality as the key to justice; no group or individual should be favored by accidents of birth or other arbitrary advantages.[63] Justice is based on calculation, not compassion or dignity. The structural paradigm in protest research embraced this calculating imagery.

Even sociological theories, intended to describe how people actually act rather than to arrive at normative principles, tend to view us as calculators. We compare outcomes to our expectations, based on what we think we deserve, what others are getting, what we have received in the past, and other sources. A number of versions of relative deprivation theory and of status-value theory have tried to explain how we derive the references by which we evaluate justice. James Davies famously based a theory of revolution on these dynamics. None of these theories has much to say about how we react—what we feel—in making those judgments, their primary flaw.[64]

Yet the emphasis on expectations is promising for understanding feelings, which always emerge against background hopes. Debates inspired by the old dualisms asked whether cognitions or emotions come first in justice evaluations, a question we can safely set aside today. Karen Hegtvedt discovers predictable anger among those who feel they have been unjustly treated, and Jerald Greenberg finds that people are especially indignant when they feel that both procedures and outcomes are unfair. William Gamson took this finding further, into collective action, stimulating rebellion against authorities' actions that were perceived as unjust. Individuals led the resistance by claiming to speak for "the group," by using irony to separate "us" from "them," and by calling attention to the consensus of the group; they helped the group adopt an "injustice frame," which provided "a rationale for acting on the hostility or anger that participants feel." Gamson explicitly states that feelings come first, and they "in turn animate [participants'] suspicion, lead them to seek certain information, and alert them to flaws in the legitimating frame."[65]

Given its affinity with market exchange, justice as "fairness" has been popular in behavioral economics; experiments show that people are willing to pay a great deal to remedy or avenge perceived unfairness. The "ultimatum game" is a simple way to measure the price of fairness. One player proposes how to divide up a sum of money provided by experimenters, and the second player can either accept or reject the proposal. If the deal is rejected, neither player gets anything. If responders were out to maximize their gains, they would accept any offer above zero. Most proposers offer half or nearly half (40 percent on average)—already showing some concern for fairness—and responders tend to refuse offers of less than 20 percent. The amount of free money that they reject shows how much they value fairness. (Recall from chapter 5 that in the trust game, players consider a fifty-fifty split to be fair and reject offers that diverge too far from this.)

Countless experimental variations have uncovered variables that affect preferences for fairness, including cultural background, how the interaction is labeled (greater inequalities are tolerated when the game is labeled a "market exchange"), and the number of proposers and responders. One important factor is how much agency is attributed to proposers: when they do not choose the amounts they offer, they are not punished for unfair offers. They are not blamed; responders are disappointed but not indignant. Players punish unfairness to themselves more than unfairness to others, suggesting that anger and vengeance are at work in addition to abstract norms of fairness. When subjects are interviewed after playing ultimatum games, most admit that they rejected offers because they wanted to punish unfair behavior.[66]

Subjects are willing to pay explicit fees to punish those who act unfairly, especially in what is called the "public goods game." Players are given a lump sum, part of which they can "invest" in a common account that pays a dividend on the money contributed but which is distributed to all those playing whether or not they have contributed (an invitation to free riding). They then play over some set of rounds, usually ten. Typically, players invest roughly half their money in the common account, but the proportion declines over the rounds. The reason: they become angry with those who have contributed less, and the only way they can punish these other players is by contributing less themselves. Everyone ends up with less money.[67] (As we saw earlier, I call this the players-or-prizes dilemma in strategic action: players sometimes alter their own goals to concentrate on punishing other players instead of maximizing what they can derive from the arena.)[68]

Ernst Fehr and Simon Gächter added two interesting twists.[69] First, they divided the groups into those who remained with the same (but unknown) partners through all the rounds, those who were randomly reassigned after each round, and those who were told that they would definitely *not* play with the same partners again. Those who kept their partners throughout the game contributed the most to the kitty, while those who were assigned strangers in each round contributed the least.

Just as interesting is what happened, when, halfway through the rounds, the game was suddenly changed. Players were no longer allowed to punish defectors (through a fine that the finer paid to have imposed, while the proceeds from the fine went into the collective account). For the rounds in which punishment was possible, contributions to the collective account actually increased for those with set partners and remained the same for the other two groups. But when the punishment option was removed, the collective contributions of all three groups collapsed. When players feel they are part of an ongoing group, with shared rules, they contribute more to that group. Just think how much more they would contribute to real groups, outside the laboratory, when the membership is anything but anonymous, when long-standing grievances can fester, when anger and disappointment can be elaborated into pseudo-speciation. But also when love for a group can be elaborated into bedrock allegiances, for which one is willing to die.

Because it addresses distributional issues like these, fairness is one of the few moral topics that can be inserted into games with monetary payoffs—but there are many other steps to outrage. Affective loyalties to a group make us sensitive to unfairness directed at it. Such loyalties can be created even in the temporary, artificial setting of the laboratory, but they are much stronger in the real world. In addition, we must perceive outcomes as intentionally and maliciously biased: we must generate blame. And finally, we must find outlets for avenging the perceived wrongs. This is the stuff of political rhetoric and protest mobilization. But perceptions of unfairness are a crucial ingredient.

Anger over injustice and other moral affronts usually begins as a reflex emotion; it may take time and attention for our moral feelings to be explicitly aroused (except for compassion). There are even experiments purporting to show that, given time to reflect on their own actions, people cheat less in a dice game, as their moral commitments are engaged.[70] Our response to physical intimidation may be a reflex shame, but our moral pride and shame may require more conscious attention.

Procedural injustice probably stimulates actions through a more directly emotional route than substantive justice does. People's attention is already focused on the contest, they expect a certain decision, and—having been a player in an engagement—they are probably already mobilized. They are primed to be outraged. For instance, what pushes whistle-blowers to go public with their grievances is not their original complaint so much as the punishing way they are treated when they protest internally (they are demoted, harassed, fired, and defamed); this is what drives them from mild criticism to stubborn indignation. Whistle-blowers are of interest for a couple of reasons: they often end up in protest movements, and their emotional pathways as they respond to procedural injustices can help us understand the routes followed by many other participants.

INDIGNATION

The moral emotions we have observed so far all have an impact on action to the extent that they generate righteous anger—namely, indignation. Moral emotions are the "hot cognitions," as Gamson called them, that motivate engagement in politics and other strategic projects—a decision that is otherwise rather daunting. (To be sure, there is also a path that leads to fear and paralysis, often via moods of resignation, terror, or cynicism.) When the world proves to be different and more threatening than thought, moral shocks frequently lead to action, especially if victims and heroes can be identified, blame ascribed to human villains, and the infrastructure for action created or commandeered. Moral emotions are the core of political rhetoric. Indignation is the hottest of the hot cognitions; as a moral form of anger, it encourages action.[71]

Individuals often feel indignant before they know why; they sense a moral violation. This may be the first step toward articulating moral principles and values. But the next steps are rarely taken alone. Political organizers help us focus our anger, tell stories to explain it, and channel it into collective protest rather than individual griping. It is usually hard for oppressed people to express their anger because they are punished for doing so. This is a central tool in their oppression, one reason that disadvantaged players resort to gossip, jokes, and other weapons of the weak. Only collectively can they break out of this repertory.

One protest movement that had to nurture indignation among its members was the women's movement of the late twentieth century. As feminists pointed out, women had long been oppressed in part because they were associated with emotion. (Early crowd theorists had described mobs as feminine in their emotional volatility.) Yet ironically, one of the most useful political emotions, anger, was denied them. Women were expected to be both emotional and passive: a comment frequently made about crowds, capable of action but only when moved by a demagogue (again, a passivity considered feminine). True action, of the autonomous individual, was supposed to be motivated by thought rather than feeling. Yet how could women formulate the deep injustice they felt without expressing anger?[72]

Verta Taylor has applied this feminist analysis of anger suppression to the study of social movements.[73] In her book on postpartum depression, she documents efforts by women's self-help groups to transform paralyzing emotions such as shame, depression, and fear into mobilizing anger. The movement encouraged mothers to turn their blame outward toward unfair and unrealistic cultural norms concerning motherhood, rather than focusing it inward on their own inadequacies as mothers trying to fulfill those expectations. Anger allowed them to challenge cultural norms, medical authorities, and even their own marital habits. Feminism's efforts to make it acceptable for women to express negative emotions, especially anger, is merely the best documented of many movements' struggles to transform feeling rules.

Women are more likely to suppress anger, while men are more likely to mask fear.[74] Structural models of emotion insist that all subordinates suppress anger, but in this (American) case it may be especially white, middle-class women who are pressured to be passive and calm. Working-class and nonwhite women may find it easier to use anger as a strategic tool.[75] It is possible that certain categories of subordinates are subject to greater anger-suppression pressures than others, even while all are subject to some such pressures.

If anger is usually aimed downward in social hierarchies, as Aristotle insisted, the reason is obvious: anger is a useful means for asserting one's rights and status.[76] Calling self-help "the taproot of feminism," Taylor argues, "women's self-help plays a major role in challenging the emotion norms surrounding love and anger and is contributing to an historical shift in American society toward free expression, individualism, and self-development."[77] The ability to feel and display the emotions associated with political agency—anger, indignation, pride, and so on—represents a kind of emotional liberation every bit as necessary as cognitive liberation. As Peter Lyman says, "The anger of the powerless is an essential voice in politics, not least because angry speech contains a claim that an injustice has been committed."[78]

Anger, outrage, and other aggressive emotions are not always a winning approach. They embroil protestors in the naughty-or-nice dilemma.[79] Cheryl Hercus documents a number of emotional displays by which Australian women asserted their anger and identity as feminists but also restrained themselves for the sake of their family and work relations. Anger displays generated emotional energy, whereas self-control depleted it.[80] Protest groups with links to mainstream politicians and parties may have less need of anger and other aggressive tactics.[81] Naughty and nice strategies both have advantages, but protestors are certainly better off facing this dilemma than having their choices limited because "naughty" emotional expressions are precluded from the start, making them more predictable to opponents.

Like other naughty tactics, anger often works better with internal audiences than external ones: it can mobilize followers, but it scares other players, especially authorities. Naughty tactics are most successful when there is a significant victory to be gained that is not easily reversed later on, such as a new law or legal status. Naughty tactics tarnish a player's reputation in the long run—otherwise they are not naughty—so the short-run gains must be significant.

Historian Steven Ross shows how indignation is powerful enough to overcome a number of organizational dilemmas in political mobilization. In Cincinnati in 1886, skilled and unskilled workers were united by their shared indignation when the mayor sent local militia to put down May Day strikes. "The summoning of the militia produced strong reactions of outrage. Strikers and nonstriking workers alike demanded to know why Smith had brought in the troops when unions, strike committees, and committees of safety had repeatedly guaranteed that no violence would occur." The workers knew this was another case of collusion between capitalists and politicians, but they were shocked nonetheless. "It was the force of external events which precipitated the transformation from a series of working classes to a single working class." It was a procedural moral shock. The skilled and the unskilled would work together politically for the next two years, a solidarity unusual in American labor history. Moral emotions were strong enough to reshape the affective loyalties of Cincinnati's working class.[82]

PRAISE AND BLAME

We formulate our moral approval or disapproval as praise or blame, as a form of epidictic rhetoric. Typically, moral judgments like these are accompanied by emotions. Philosopher Jesse Prinz, observing that some theories say that emotions cause moral judgments while others say that judgments cause emotions, concludes, "What matters is that, when we come to regard something as morally good or bad, we have characteristic emotional reactions."[83] Leaving aside the implied dualism (which feeling-thinking theory is designed to avoid), moral evaluations have the potential to move us toward action.

Movements against injustices try to create or redirect the blame that their societies attach to social problems. Blame and credit are often seen as a kind of explanatory tally, but they are deeply emotional products.[84] Blame is a feeling of disapproval, with varying admixtures of contempt, hate, disappointment, anger, and more. Credit is a feeling of admiration, which might include love or liking, pride in a shared identity, even joy about particular actions. Due to what I call *the power of the negative*, blame is probably a stronger motivator of action than admiration for someone else.[85]

The moral indignation that moves us toward protest depends on our being able to find humans to blame for some bad outcome. We are upset by corporate policies and by forest fires, but one leads to moral indignation, the other to fear or sadness. One encourages political action, the other discourages it (although the forest fire may encourage nonpolitical action, such as community-wide efforts to help survivors). The perceived boundaries of human versus natural causes shift over time, often as the result of political work or advertising campaigns. For many years corporations have tried to persuade us, for instance, that markets are natural forces subject to their own laws rather than to human interventions—thereby deflecting blame for management's destructive choices.[86]

It is possible to blame others for causing some ill, but also for not fixing it. *Responsibility* has these two meanings: (1) causal responsibility and (2) ownership of a problem once it exists. In the modern world, the vast extension of the state's reach has made it the owner of many problems that were once merely the act of God or nature. Even forest fires are now frequently blamed on government policies. The US government did not cause hurricanes Rita and Katrina, but it was widely blamed for inadequate flood protection and especially for its ineffectual response to the "natural" disaster. In 2010, the Obama administration tergiversated, at times accepting responsibility for the Gulf oil spill in order to look powerful (efficient) but at other times insisting that oil company BP was responsible for the cleanup as well as for the initial explosion. (BP was willing to accept responsibility for cleanup—something it could brag about—but not for causing the accident, which had implications for legal liability.)

Praise and blame have lasting impacts in part because they affect whom we see as victims, villains, and heroes—the basic political characterizations that derive from rhetorical battles. Each character implies the emotions that we are supposed to feel for them. We are expected to hate villains and to wish vengeance and punishment on them. Anger, as an action inflator, has been shown to increase the desire for punishment, even when the anger is not connected to the action being punished.[87] We are supposed to feel pity or compassion for victims, depending on how much respect or strength we grant them. We admire heroes and are grateful to them (even when we don't necessarily like them).[88]

In a rough way, pride has to do with the power and autonomy we associate with heroes. Compassion tends to focus on victims, although in a way that can encourage us to transform them into heroes, or at least survivors. Fairness is more likely to focus our attention on villains, since those who live in modern market societies tend to view fairness as natural unless disturbed. Some protest movements try to establish victims first, in order to demonstrate injustice, whereas others first make claims about villains in order to arouse fears and a sense of urgency. Heroes are often left implicit.

Praise or admiration has received less attention than blame. Not only do negative emotions get our attention more powerfully than positive ones, mostly because of the threat, anxiety, and indignation involved, but we expect people to conform to moral norms and so we barely notice when they do. "Social stability depends on people conforming to norms," says Prinz, "not on performing remarkable acts of charity. A stable moral society can exist without heroes or saints."[89] And yet groups do have their heroes (saints are a subcategory of heroes), who exemplify the highest moral ideals and act on them in extraordinary circumstances. Protest literature contains plenty of stories of normal people who acted in abnormally good ways. Living up to your own values is not always easy; it is an accomplishment.[90]

Praise and blame operate in several ways. Their epidictic impact is to spread a general sense of right and wrong by pointing to examples of each. They channel our moral intuitions. But they also motivate individuals. We enjoy praise and dislike blame. Praise creates pride, blame creates shame. But foremost, people pursue rewards and punishments: they "seek to fix blame on the authors of their hardships, and to punish them appropriately." But praise is itself a reward, so that "they also seek recognition of their own merit, whether that merit consists of suffering borne bravely or of willingness to strike out at the rich and powerful. They ask for vindication. They ask for justice with regard to both blame and credit." These words come from Charles Tilly, in an uncharacteristically psychological moment.[91]

Juries, asked to allocate blame in tort cases, do so through their emotions more than through Kantian applications of the law. Neal Feigenson says that juries do not simply follow the legal instructions from judges but try to accomplish a sense of total justice by balancing accounts among litigants, using all available information, reasoning holistically rather than following the explicit procedures of the law, and paying a great deal of attention to fair procedures in their own deliberations. They try hard to "feel right" about their decisions, based on their moral intuitions. As Tilly sums it up, "Far from turning themselves into legal computers, jurors bring their common sense of justice into the jury room."[92] In part, they follow their feelings about the major characters in the courtroom drama: affective commitments and moral commitments interact.

One of Nussbaum's elements of compassion is a sense that someone's plight is "undeserved," a status that is often contested. The same Americans who contribute money out of pity for starving children in Africa, or those left homeless by tsunamis and earthquakes, may feel that the homeless they see around them in the United States are responsible for their own plight. Blame claims are filled with contradictions. Conservatives and corporations work hard to describe markets as natural forces outside human control but the victims of those forces as somehow deserving of their fate. Substance addictions are increasingly seen as a form of illness, yet those who are on the street because of them are rarely viewed as victims.

Attributions of blame are important to emotions in part because the same bundles of feeling-thinking processes take different paths depending on what we think caused them. Psychologists John Sabini and Maury Silver agree that emotional labels and experiences do not perfectly line up; the same feelings can become different emotions depending on how we interpret our situation. Participants in their research were likely to feel shame when they believed that one of their personal flaws had been revealed, but when they believed the same audience had no good reason for looking down on them, they instead reported righteous anger. With the right cultural work, the same feelings can lead to either shameful deflation or energizing indignation. As we have seen, considerable political work is devoted to creating the latter from the former.[93]

REVENGE

The outrage that drives our pursuit of justice is a form of anger, and Plato showed us that anger can go "too far." Instead of merely setting the injustice right, we may wish to hurt the perpetrator. Blame turns into hatred. And, especially when we feel humiliated, revenge may become our primary motive. The deep shame of impotence and frustration can only be set right in a fury of activity that puts passivity behind us, and possibly places our opponents in the same intolerable situation of passivity.[94]

This seems the case with many Palestinian suicide bombers, whom Robert Brym has studied extensively. He sums up his research findings in six lessons, beginning with "Suicide bombers are not crazy," and describing the political strategies involved. Lesson four states, "Sometimes it's retaliatory." He cites the representative case of Hanadi Jaradat, a twenty-nine-year-old lawyer who walked into Maxim restaurant in Haifa and detonated a belt of plastic explosives, killing herself and twenty diners, as well as injuring many more. "She carried out the attack," according to her relatives, "in revenge for the killing of her brother and her [fiancé] by the Israeli security forces, and in revenge for all the crimes Israel is perpetrating in the West Bank by killing Palestinians and expropriating their land."[95] While we immediately see the second grievance ("all the crimes") as more abstract and ideological, this does not mean it is false. If someone identifies with a group, forming deep affective convictions, then personal and political revenge fuse to some degree, as we saw in the last chapter. Humiliation in particular leads to an angry hatred that can encourage extreme tactics.

The same tension between moral righteousness and revenge persists after political conflicts end. When there are clear winners and losers, the winners may have the power to decide how to treat the losers, choosing between vengeance and forgiveness. Both can offer deeply satisfying emotions. When winners have based their campaign on moral indignation, it is difficult not to demand some form of punishment. When hatred dominated, some form of revenge may be necessary. But if the losers are large in number, say, as a proportion of the population, and if it will be necessary to cooperate with them in the future, then forgiveness and reconciliation may have more appeal. Vengeance and forgiveness satisfy different psychological impulses. Vengeance appeals to our affective commitments toward our group and against our opponents; forgiveness satisfies our commitments to justice. Our notion of justice may involve punishment but rarely the suppression or annihilation of an entire group. Affective and moral commitments often conflict.[96]

This dilemma has arisen acutely in nations that have faced traumatic, sometimes genocidal, acts perpetrated by their own governments: apartheid in South Africa, Communist Eastern Europe, the atrocities of the Balkan wars, the military repression that wracked much of Latin America, and virtually every other dictatorship. In these cases, there are additional needs, for the victims and their survivors to learn the truth about what happened to thousands of people who disappeared or were murdered.

Criminal prosecution of the perpetrators is not likely to reveal the full truth, so some nations have opted for forgiveness in exchange for the truth. The most prominent case is the South African Truth Commission, which gave amnesty to most of those who came clean about their role in apartheid. In these cases, there is a trade-off between remembering and forgetting the traumas of the past. Trials emphasize justice, truth commissions the truth, and reparations the need to help victims. Justice is blind, whereas forgiveness acknowledges the humanity of the losing side, including its ability to start afresh. It avoids the claim that there is something inherently evil about the former perpetrators. It matters whether the new regime took over through combat or negotiation with the old leaders, and whether the wrongdoing involved a small or large portion of the population; it matters whether the individual has a profound religious confidence in a divine realm of consequences for behavior on earth, or a strong desire to invest energy in surviving family members.[97]

A victim of repressive horrors has been stripped of personhood, and vengeance may be one way to restore her sense of agency. When it comes through official legal channels, vengeance can be constrained so that it does not spiral into excess or establish cycles of vendettas. But outside those channels it may.

CHANGES IN MORAL EMOTIONS

Social movements aim to transform our moral commitments. They try to help members articulate new moral visions, based on new ways of feeling-thinking, in the hopes that these will also spread to nonmembers. They deploy specialists—orators, intellectuals, artists—who know how to pull reflex emotions, moods, and affective convictions together into moral programs, grounded in symbols, frames, and artifacts. Of all the types of feelings, it is our moral emotions where we see the largest impact of successful movements. Movements affect both moral principles and intuitions, on the one hand, and the emotions that result from them, on the other.

In the shame/pride moral battery, we saw how the women's movement has tried to reduce forms of shame often forced on women. Analyzing postpartum depression, Taylor showed how women who did not have the "right" feelings battled American society's cheery norms about motherhood.[98] Her student Nancy Whittier has traced several decades of contention over child sexual abuse.[99] Far from an exclusive focus on internal repair, she found efforts to balance the Janus trade-off (a strategic dilemma over how much attention to pay to your own group's members versus to outsiders).[100] "The shame that victims felt about having been abused was not simply a psychological artifact, but a product of social forces. Thus, challenging that shame by undertaking emotional work in self-help groups and speaking publicly about one's experiences was not simply psychological change, but social change."[101] If shame is the central emotion that needs to be reduced, some public effort seems necessary, since shame entails imagining oneself in others' eyes. Struggles over identities must unfold on two fronts, both internal and external to a group.

Compassion, which has expanded markedly in the modern world, is the most obvious transformation in our moral emotions, the clearest moral legacy that generations of activists have left us. Beneficiaries include Catholics since the eighteenth century in Britain and the nineteenth in the United States, lower castes in India, Muslims in Europe, women since the nineteenth century, and racial/ethnic minorities everywhere. There are efforts on both sides of compassion, however. Movements aimed at oppressing minority groups tend to target affective commitments—hate and disgust for particular groups—whereas movements aimed at liberating groups usually deploy moral convictions that erase distinctions and reduce disgust. Ethnoracial groups are not the only beneficiaries of contemporary compassion: prisoners, the poor, the young, the insane, and so-called primitive peoples have all become objects of pity or compassion in the modern world. Political psychologist Sam McFarland discerns, since the fifteenth century, the "slow creation" of an encompassing concept of "humanity" as including all human beings, a definition that he says still should be expanded.[102]

At the extreme, animal protectionists hope to strengthen human compassion for other species, and ecologists for nature as a whole.[103] Moral philosopher Peter Singer posits an "expanding circle" of ethical concern that began, with the ancient Hebrews and Greeks, as a need to justify one's actions as based on something more than self-interest: "The idea of a disinterested defense of one's conduct emerges because of the social nature of human beings and the requirements of group living, but in the thought of reasoning beings, it takes on a logic of its own which leads to its extensions beyond the bounds of the group."[104] We expand our circles of concern in response to challenges, and political movements are often the cutting edge of those challenges. They explicitly confront what have been implicit or private practices, and abstract moral commitments can emerge out of affective loyalties to specific groups.

Historian Thomas Haskell and others have argued that markets help spread compassion by increasing a sense of personal interconnection and responsibility for others. Arguing against crude theories that humanitarianism served the interests of the rising bourgeoisie in the nineteenth century, Haskell sees a new cognitive style that recognized that market transactions have long series of consequences, in much the way that Adam Smith described. He unnecessarily distinguishes these ideas from the accompanying "upwelling of powerful feelings of sympathy, guilt, and anger." The two arose together in early nineteenth century America, always closely entwined.[105]

The empathic ability to feel something of what another is feeling—the key to compassion—can include disgust over mistreatment. It is difficult for many of us today to watch footage of a human or animal in great pain—exactly what most of our ancestors organized and watched as entertainment. It may be something about the daily life of the urban middle class—without productive interactions with nonhuman species or agricultural nature—that encourages the imaginative identification that supports the extension of compassion to other species. But it is a major emotional accomplishment, elaborated and promoted by a succession of social movements.

* * *

The regret potential of moral emotions is low. In the long run, we are more satisfied if we have followed impulses like pride and compassion. We are more likely to have regret when we have ignored these moral commitments in favor of reflex emotions or urges. This is the paradigm of regret: short-run feelings crowd out long-run allegiances.

Moral convictions carry some disruptive potential. My comrades may not share my stubborn moral resolve, and my tenacity may put an end to cooperation. I may refuse to dirty my hands with questionable means, or insist on radical demands instead of accepting compromises. Some actions become ends in themselves, an example of Max Weber's ethic of ultimate ends. As Frederick Saunders put it long ago, "Pride, like laudanum and other poisonous medicines, is beneficial in small, though injurious in large, quantities."[106]

Morality consists not only of principles but of intuitions, which bubble up through feeling-thinking processes. We often feel moral shock, disgust, or indignation faster than we can articulate our reasons—if we can articulate them at all. Our minds process facts, feelings, and moral principles and intuitions at the same time, all based on a jumble of smaller mechanisms. Our feelings often signal that we approve or disapprove of something before our conscious processes grasp it: and the latter sometimes grasp it due to the initial feelings.

Our affective and moral commitments can change, just as the other categories of emotions do. But they are just about as stable as anything in our lives. We develop our moral principles in the first decades of our lives and rarely change them after that. Our regrets almost always come from violating them, not from following them. They affect what we do whether we follow them or not. They are ongoing commitments, not sudden eruptions. They are neither calculation nor panic but rather one of the ways we feel our way through the world.

Moral emotions are powerful motivators because *they so often pit positive and negative feelings in a moral battery* that suggests some kind of movement from the negative to the positive, whether from shame to pride, injustice to justice, or humiliation to revenge. The contrast between how things are and how they should be is the *indignation gap*, the size of which should affect the potential for mobilization. There are all sorts of factors that can block action, especially fears of repression, but without some indignation gap, collective action loses its point. Activists continually try to construct a large gap to rouse their troops.[107]

Indignation, shame, revenge: these are the sorts of feelings that explain why some frames resonate and others fall flat, why one story appeals to us and another is a yawn. Culture matters because it can tap into our deepest moral convictions via emotions. A collective identity or boundary does not motivate us to act simply because we understand it; we must care about it. It *means* something to us.

Dignity is at the center of our moral commitments. Our own dignity gives us pride. Our compassion for others is based on a sense of their dignity as humans (or other beings), even or especially when it is threatened. And our feelings about justice and fairness reflect our intuitions about others' dignity. Yet despite its centrality in human affairs, there is nothing that we could call a sociology of dignity.

Scholars often talk about the "standing" of a protest movement: whether the media acknowledge it as speaking for the cause, or for a population; whether it has access to various arenas, most literally in the case of courtrooms. But movements also need emotional standing. They ask for respect from others, rather than contempt. They want honor, not disgust. They seek pride instead of shame. Protestors want to be treated as human beings, with all the trust, compassion, and dignity that implies.

We have come far from a model of emotions as necessarily short-run eruptions and distractions. Most are fundamental commitments that make us human. The political battles that really count are those over these moral feelings.

CONCLUSION

By now you have read about dozens of emotions that motivate us, help us appraise our situation, communicate with others, and provide the building blocks for paths of action. If you believe that action matters, then these emotional dynamics must also matter; you cannot understand action without them. If you believe that only structures matter in the long run, or that we maximize our material interests and simply hide them under a cultural veneer, then I have probably not persuaded you. If you believe that culture matters, you must recognize that emotions matter, because they explain why some meanings resonate and others do not.

Emotions motivate actions, especially because we anticipate what we will feel down different paths of action (in addition to our current feelings, such as moral pride in making a good choice). In much research on politics, the range of potential motives was drastically reduced in both the structural paradigm and rational choice theory. Yet a theory of action demands that we know something about motivation, and our emotions are a good place to start. We know a lot about them and their impact on action. If we hope to get a grip on motivation, we need to understand regrets and disruption, moral batteries that combine negative and positive feelings, sequences of emotions, and other feelings that arise during our interactions. Social psychologists have made a lot of progress, but their work is still largely unknown to sociologists and political scientists who study social movements.[1]

I have organized this book around five basic types of feelings, and then by specific examples of each type. Even though I think the emotion terms we use can be further broken down into underlying feeling-thinking processes, emotion labels have a commonsense reality familiar to readers. Once they are cleaned up a bit, especially along the time dimension—such as distinguishing reflex fear from long-term anxieties—they are useful for understanding action, including political action. The words and concepts that people have for their emotions guide what they feel. In the conclusion I want to elaborate on this utility, by linking emotions to three important topics in the study of protest and politics: types of arenas and interactions; causal mechanisms as a way to keep our explanations honest; and how we build up from psychological and interactive building blocks at the micro level to big outcomes such as revolutions at the macro level. These themes are not restricted to politics but have implications for all social life and our accounts of it.

EMOTIONS IN ARENAS

We experience a constant flow of feeling-thinking processes, but not randomly. We are likely to feel different things at a rally, during a small kitchen meeting, and when watching television alone, although there is considerable emotional overlap even across these settings. Most often we feel and react differently when we encounter authorities such as the police and when we are alone with our fellow protestors or our family. Most of our daily interactions occur in our personal and work lives, and even in the role of protestors, we engage with our fellow protestors far more often than with other players. Our opponents in particular are usually insulated from us, protected by security, distance, and spokespersons.

When I discussed such emotions as outrage and fear in earlier chapters, readers probably assumed that I was talking exclusively about interactions between protestors and other players, or protestors learning about the conditions that would become their grievances. But they can be angry with other factions and individuals within their group, too. In fact, dynamics within any group or movement can be emotionally intense, with diverse consequences for the longevity and strategic choices they make. Internal interactions are more likely to be face-to-face than interactions with other players.

I have used the terms *shared emotions* and *reciprocal emotions* to help us begin to understand these group dynamics. Protest groups form around shared emotions: their members feel the same way about a planned nuclear reactor, or about abortions. If they do not join initially because of those feelings, they eventually come to share them or they leave the group. Alongside these feelings, which include both reflex and moral emotions, group members also have feelings about one another, the reciprocal emotions. These include feelings about particular others, such as a friend or an affinity group, but also about the group as a whole, at least as we perceive it (the collective identity we attribute to it). In chapter 5, we observed potential tensions between these different attachments, especially in the band of brothers trade-off.

Typically, groups combine negative shared emotions (anger over their official grievances, especially) and positive reciprocal emotions (toward their fellow group members). This is a cultural revision of Neil Smelser's Freudian idea that protestors resolve Oedipal issues by rejecting authorities because they symbolize their fathers and by loving their movements in place of their mothers (see appendix 1). His theory suffered not only from adopting a dubious psychology but from exaggerating the love and hate in most movements, making them the primary emotional motivations.

Groups are unified players when facing the outside world (more or less), but they are contentious arenas when they turn inward to discuss and make decisions. At a planning session my anger is more likely to be aimed at the stubborn extremist who is wasting our time than at anyone outside the group. Given enough frustrating experiences with the same man and his misguided clique, I may develop an ongoing loathing for them that is as powerful as my hatred for our group's external opponents. I may even start writing diatribes to elaborate this dislike and link it to my moral commitments.

Political players also interact with people who have nothing to do with the movement or its targets, especially family members. They may express anger or admiration for my political work, influencing my mood and energy for continuing. I may choose the joy of playing with my kids over the deontological pride of attending another Black Lives Matter march. (More likely I must choose between two sources of joy and two forms of moral pride.) My emotions interact with theirs.

All these settings have their own particular feeling rules, individuals present, and emotional interactions that result. Protestors are not the only players who have emotions. The police become fatigued, angry, or pumped up. Journalists feel moral pride in covering important political issues. Corporate executives are embarrassed by a pointed question from a shareholder—or from their children. These players interact with one another to produce various decisions, policies, and other outcomes.

My concern to lay out players and arenas in detail is part of a broader program to develop a strategic perspective on politics and protest that is cultural and interactive. To highlight action, I have focused especially on the many trade-offs and dilemmas that players face (or deny). These dilemmas, numbering in the dozens, are mostly based on emotions: long- and short-run trade-offs, clashing allegiances to multiple groups, moral versus instrumental tensions, the needs of the individual body versus those of the group, and many more. Each option reflects and generates dozens of emotions. This is the stuff of action and decision, and it never boils down to simple calculations and comparisons. There are always long lists of good feelings and bad, current and anticipated, mine and yours, to take into account.[2] What's at stake is nothing less than a theory of action.

LESS MECHANISTIC MECHANISMS

I came to the study of emotions because I wanted to understand what a number of vague but ubiquitous metaphors really meant: How could a political "structure" constrain what people do? What do we actually mean when we call some collection of people and events a social "movement"? What does it mean to feel part of a group, or part of history? This curiosity first pushed me into the realm of culture and agency: how do real people view the world, and try to change it? Big outcomes such as repression, revolution, and social change made no sense to me without people and their action as the starting point. Eventually I realized that meaning and action in turn make no sense—people make no sense—without their feelings.

My research shifted from comparing national political systems (albeit with a dash of culture thrown in) to looking at what people say and do in interaction with each other. I began to look at demonstrations as a scholar, and not just as a participant. What was going on here? Why were all these people here? Instead of looking for correlations between such broad variables as political culture and policy outcomes, as I had once done, I gradually adopted a "tool kit" approach in which any small bits of theory could be used to explain what I saw. I came to understand this as a *mechanisms approach*, in which we drop from one level of reality (typically organizations and political structures) to a more concrete level (typically individuals and their interactions) to explain the correlations we observe. For me, this meant paying attention to individuals and the interactions among them.[3]

Giving priority to individuals does not mean seeing them as somehow outside social influence, as physical gyroscopes who only seek out others to satisfy preexisting desires. From the beginning of my career, I have used the term *biography* to emphasize that we carry traces of our past experiences, past interactions, along with us, in the form of memories, understandings, dispositions, affective convictions, moral intuitions, and more.

The term *mechanism* is misleading. It sounds like a mousetrap, sitting there unmoving until, with the right pressure, it snaps. It moves from state *A* to state *B* every time, almost without fail (even though there can be interferences). The word is too, well, mechanistic. There is little room for choice, discretion, subtle nuances. For most scholars, it is a way to sneak universal laws in at a small level (derived from Robert Merton's idea of middle-range theory).[4] Ekman's affect programs are a perfect example; once one of them is triggered it follows an unvarying pathway until it is extinguished.

Jon Elster has countered with devices that are more open-ended, especially paired mechanisms that represent the horns of a dilemma and the potential options that result from it. What makes something a useful mechanism, in his view, is simply that "it is more general than the phenomenon that it subsumes."[5] We readily understand people's anger or disgust because we imagine that we might feel the same way in their circumstances. Even if we are not angered by what enrages them, we can at least grasp what anger is and understand how it might make them act.

Our feeling-thinking processes are not so mechanistic, in part because there are so many of them that, even taken in the bundles they usually form, we could never derive invariant laws from them. But as they congeal into familiar emotions (familiar to both observers and the person feeling them), we begin to form expectations about what people will do. It's usually not a single thing but one of a very small number: two or three possible actions, not two hundred. Mechanisms help us to explain after the fact, not to make rigid predictions. They are familiar causal links, not inevitable ones.

Emotions may be the most pervasive mechanisms that we need in order to come to grips with the microlevel of individuals and their interactions, but they are not the only ones. Strategic dilemmas and choices, although generally defined by emotions, are a distinct subset of mechanisms; so are all the physical artifacts and metaphorical carriers of meaning we use to convey and stabilize our feeling and thinking. But once we have cataloged all these microfoundations of political action, can we get back to the big things that scholars of the past addressed?

BUILDING BACK UP TO THE MACROLEVEL

Certain chains of microinteractions are familiar from existing scholarship, especially that on political recruitment. Jocelyn Viterna, for instance, identifies three paths by which women came to join the Farabundo Martí National Liberation Front during El Salvador's civil war: those who were ideologically sympathetic, those who were actively recruited, and those who were more or less forced to join. Distinct emotional backgrounds and sequences accompanied each. Even this typology blurs considerable idiosyncrasy among her subjects; we are just beginning to appreciate the complicated sequences that unique individuals follow.[6]

All politics consists of interaction chains, which involve not only moves and countermoves but inventions, dissolutions, and recombinations of both players and arenas. These chains almost never end but instead simply move elsewhere, into new arenas, where restructured players continue to interact, even if they take up new symbols, goals, and names. Individuals, in particular, move from one organization to another, one social movement to another.

The challenge for a cultural-strategic approach, grounded in microlevel interactions, is how to "scale up" to broad outcomes such as national movements, regime changes, and policy impacts. Ideally we would trace the long chains of interactions. For protestors, these chains might begin with conversations around kitchen tables, move to exchanges between neighbors, proceed out into the streets, and then converge on central sites such as Tahrir Square. We would love to trace similar sequences for the police and militaries: from a private conversation among commanders, to their instructions to the troops, and on out to the engagements on the streets. And with politicians: from private interactions, to public debates, and finally to parliamentary decisions. We would track individuals as they join others to form compound players, then follow the compound players as they turn into arenas making decisions, and then as they try to implement those choices in their engagements with other players. We could identify many of the urges, reflex emotions, moods, and long-run commitments in these interactions. (The chains of interactions also move from public engagements back to more personal settings.)

So much for the ideal. Methodologically, there are a lot of interactions to which we will never have access; all strategic players have some moments they wish to keep secret. State players and private corporations have great advantages for doing this. That is why it is so easy for analysts to reduce them to black-box structures, a bit mysterious from the outside. *But we should not make a methodological limitation into a theoretical assumption.* More fundamentally, and secrecy aside, there are just too many individual chains to trace.

Social science offers two broad methods for linking the micro to the macro, short of following all those long chains. The more common is to *aggregate* the microactions. Market prices result from many, many individual transactions, providing a paradigm for economists to model all sorts of social outcomes and to describe paradoxes in which those outcomes are not the intent of any of the players. Voting is another form of aggregation, with its own rules and resources that produce outcomes. Most often, social scientists must sample some population to get the raw materials to aggregate; this is the point of surveys. Such techniques usually assume that the individuals are interchangeable, or that their idiosyncrasies average out in the aggregate. (Network analysis treats them as interchangeable in some ways but not others.)

The second solution is to insert microdynamics into structural models through *scope* factors. When George W. Bush decided to go to war against Iraq's Saddam Hussein, a great deal happened in both their countries (and others) due to the organizational positions of the two men, which allowed them to direct resources, personnel, and attention to their projects, unleashing organizational routines. Although there must be a structural component in our strategic story, the story begins with a tiny group of individuals talking with one another in a small number of meetings: Bush, Vice President Dick Cheney, and a handful of advisors (a shockingly small number of people, for such a momentous decision).

The implementation of their decisions also occurred through chains of personal interactions in several government agencies, in several armed forces, and within those forces, at the level of each corps, division, brigade, company, and platoon. Sometimes it is useful for an analyst to assume that organizations will respond the way they are expected to, but in many cases it is not. This black-box assumption can blind us. A full explanation would cover how compliance is achieved or not achieved at every level, at every stage. Most historical accounts combine microinteractive stories of key players with aggregate stories of the bit players (or stylized assumptions about them).

Arenas help stabilize chains of interactions by providing physical constraints, formal rules, and informal traditions. They offer places to sit or stand, to observe or participate. They have transmission and recording devices to preserve the actions and decisions or to convey them to audiences not physically present. Their lighting and acoustics also shape the action. Again, we are tempted to assume that actions follow the rules, but that's often wrong.

Margaret Archer suggests how to bring structure and agency together through her concept of an internal conversation. "Courses of action are produced," she says, "through the reflexive deliberations of agents who *subjectively* determine their practical projects in relation to their *objective* circumstances."[7] Unlike tangible structures, which make it physically impossible for us to do certain things, the "structures" that matter in social life exert their influence because we take them into account in making our decisions and in acting. A soldier pointing a gun at us does not make it *impossible* to step forward, but it takes a brave internal conversation for that to happen. Occasionally it does, even if usually it does not. We need to be able to account for both outcomes.

Our internal conversations include feeling-thinking processes, most of which we are unaware of. We feel the pull of different selves, past and future, of different possibilities. As in regular conversations between individuals, our internal life is full of pulls and pushes, of motivations and trepidations, hesitations and confidence. No two people can have exactly the same conversation, but there are patterns to be identified.

WHAT MATTERS?

We are a full generation into the cultural turn in the social sciences, and the central role of meaning and interpretation has transformed theories, methods, and empirical research in all fields. We have learned an enormous amount about frames and schemas, about the structure of narratives, about the risks and benefits of collective identities, about collective memory, about cognitive boundaries and distinctions. And yet we still know almost nothing about what actually helps a symbol or other carrier of meaning resonate with its audiences; almost nothing about the concept at the center of culture: meaning. This is not unusual. Paradigms grow faster by leaving their core idea ill defined. "Resource mobilization" theories allowed anything to count as a resource; "political opportunity" theories did the same for opportunities. Even Kuhn's idea of a "paradigm"—the paradigm for paradigms—was open to multiple interpretations.

The time has come to tackle meaning, and I think that emotions offer the key. There are two ways that an object, action, person, or artifact can "mean" something to us. In one, we simply understand it cognitively, as if we were walking dictionaries: we look up the word *dog* or search for memories of a face that we encounter at a convention. Are they familiar? But in another sense, they *mean* something to us because we *care* about them in some familiar way. I remember my pet waiting at home, or I recognize a classmate from graduate school beneath the wrinkles and gray hair. A dog is not simply a quadruped that differs from a cat but also a part of human lives and histories that makes us feel various bodily charges such as warmth or fear, oxytocin or cortisol and norepinephrine. Cultural models are misspecified because unacknowledged emotions do much of the explanatory work; I hope to have shown that emotions are the causal mechanisms beneath many familiar cultural processes. Meanings matter to us because of how they make us feel.

Emotions are also crucial to the normative work that social scientists do. Democracy is not simply a set of formal procedures along with the cognitive rules and understandings that make them function. It includes feelings, centering on respect for others, compassion for beings that are suffering, and the dignity of all citizens. Its failings also consist largely of emotions: the arrogance of those with too much power and wealth, the shame of those with too little. Democratic morality consists of emotions, not calculations of the greater good or the categorical imperative.

Human life is interesting, gratifying, and disturbing because of the feelings it involves. We will never run out of surprises and shocks to keep our interest in the stories that people tell and the actions they undertake. This is as true of the stories we tell, as researchers, as it is of the stories and lives that everyone crafts for themselves. Emotion-laden stories can get complicated. But they are more true, not less true, for that complexity.

AFTERWORD: TRUMP

While this book was out with reviewers, Donald J. Trump became president of the United States. His election looked like the triumph of emotions over reason, with his supporters driven by the fears and hatreds that Trump continually stirred up in his speeches and tweets. They seemed to accept at face value his claims to be a smart businessman who knows how to run things and create jobs, ignoring his billion-dollar loss on one leaked tax return as well as his notorious tendency to cheat contractors, students at his so-called university, and almost anyone he dealt with. He claimed to have numerous secret plans for making America great again. To journalists and scholars, there seemed no rational, evidence-based reason to support Trump, so his victory must have been due to the emotions of the moment.

Part of the accusation against Trump is that he reaches his supporters directly through his tweets, appealing to their emotions without the intermediary of the news media, a practice he has continued as president. Analysts said something similar about Hitler and other demagogues: they did not use intermediary institutions such as newspapers or unions but instead reached the masses directly through the radio. This idea was called *mass society theory,* and it also played a role in crowd theories in the form of a demagogue who appealed to emotion rather than to reason. All in all, Trump seems to pose a challenge to my argument that emotions and thoughts emerge out of the same feeling-thinking processes.

One sign of an emotional dynamic would be that Trump voters (only 26 percent of the country's eligible voters, by the way) soon regretted their choices. But in fact, they have continued to support him during his presidency, despite the inept chaos and patent lies of his first year. They seem to be getting what they had hoped for. They were not fooled. No regrets.

In fact, they have a lot of ideas woven with the emotions that receive so much media attention. Foremost, they hate the US federal government and are happy to see it in shambles because they think it is corrupt and inept, wasting our tax dollars. Many Trump supporters own or work for small businesses, and they view bureaucrats and experts as arrogant, contemptuous of people like them. (I am not sure they are wrong about this.) They include academics in this group, as people who are overeducated, cosmopolitan, and alienated from "normal" Americans. Trump fans believe in the efficiency and morality of free markets. They believe that immigrants take jobs from the native born and take more money from the government than they pay in taxes. They have faith in Jesus. They care little about the environment because they expect to be transported to a better world when the Rapture arrives, in the very near future. I reject almost every one of these beliefs, but they are indeed beliefs as much as they are emotions.

By now I hope I have convinced you that the distinction between beliefs and emotions is wrongheaded. Every one of these statements of belief is permeated with emotions. How could you think the government is corrupt without disliking it? Expect to be swept into heaven without feeling joy? Think that scholars find you ridiculous without resenting them? Loyalty to the town or farm where you grew up is an affective orientation supported by beliefs about the costs of geographic mobility as well as by a variety of feelings.

For generations, scholars have looked for an ideology behind this kind of collection of beliefs and feelings, for a few basic principles such as equality or liberalism or nationalism that hold them all together. A master frame, or a class interest, or at least a worldview. Because intellectuals are trained to make coherence out of odd assortments of ideas, we look for coherence in others, for some "logic" to their visions. When scholars can't identify a logic, they turn to dismissive psychological dynamics, usually unconscious, such as status anxiety, to explain people like the Tea Partiers. But what if that logic is not derived from first principles but reflects a web of feelings about the world: what do we fear, whom do we admire, where do we feel comfortable, what outrages us? Less of a logic than a bundle or package.

If we look for an emotional coherence instead of a logical one, we see that we cosmopolitans have our own feeling-thinking package just as Trump's locals have theirs. Our affective orientations and our moral emotions allow us to entertain some beliefs and policy conclusions and not others, to trust some politicians and news sources and to ridicule others. We eat what Jane Brody tells us to, we mistrust high finance because of Gretchen Morgenson's muckraking (both write for the *New York Times*, so demonized by Trump). We alter our exercise regimen or our vitamin supplements depending on new epidemiological findings. We trust Bernie Sanders from Brooklyn, not Donald Trump from Queens.

Each side is morally contemptuous of the other, lapsing into stereotypes made easier by America's polarization into "blue" neighborhoods and "red" neighborhoods. In blue communities it is considered dangerous and distasteful to express hatred for groups such as feminists or immigrants, while in red communities it appears harmful and naïve to allow the "deep state" to interfere in our markets and classrooms. Compassion for the poor or disabled is natural on one side, but on the other side, it makes you a loser, a sucker. A large part of each side's coherence is based on what emotions are appropriate to express, and how.

By rethinking emotions, and looking for their coherence as concepts in a larger constellation of moral and affective commitments, we can better study the cultural meanings that guide or at least accompany political action. We can see how skepticism about the Warren Commission report may be linked to reflex emotions when we watch the news, how moral distaste for Trump may be tied to our predictions of an economic recession now that he is in office. As humans, we feel our way through the world by using hundreds of feeling-thinking processes; we don't turn to a severe logic of first principles—either moral or cognitive—that we then apply in an ideology. This is true of Trump and his supporters, just as it is true for those of us who fear him.

APPENDIX I:
THE POLITICS OF EMOTIONS

The blood-dimmed tide is loosed, and everywhere
The ceremony of innocence is drowned;
The best lack all conviction, while the worst
Are full of passionate intensity.

WILLIAM BUTLER YEATS, "The Second Coming"

Neither a man nor a crowd nor a nation can be trusted to act
humanely or to think sanely under the influence of a great fear.

BERTRAND RUSSELL

Western thinkers have castigated the emotions of politics for 2,400 years, but the very fervor of their attack acknowledges the vital role of feelings throughout political life. Whether or not they are dangerous, emotions are central. After examining the emotions of politics in this book, I devote this additional essay to the politics of emotions: to some of the ways that observers have portrayed political emotions over the millennia. Analysts have all had their own political purposes, using claims about emotions to score a variety of ideological points for or against the people they study. Emotions have inevitably been portrayed as good or (more often) bad, rather than as a simple fact of political life.

DEMOCRACY'S SHADOW

The ancient Athenians feared the effects of emotions on politics, having seen the Assembly make a number of poor decisions in the heat of the moment. The disaster of the Peloponnesian War and the lack of an effective leader after Pericles brought on a crisis of democracy reminiscent of Europe in the 1920s. Extensive theorizing about rhetoric—the central tool of the Assembly—was frequently about its emotional consequences.

Plato (427–347 BCE) was the most famous skeptic. His family was wealthy and politically powerful, and his uncle had been one of the "thirty tyrants" who briefly overthrew democracy in 404 BCE, when Plato was in his early twenties. Only five years later, Plato was shocked when a jury, selected by lot from the citizens of Athens, condemned Socrates to death for "corrupting the city's youth," the end result of an ancient moral panic. Plato attacked rhetoric rather than emotions as we now think of them, which in his view were spread across three parts of the soul: reason, spirit, and appetite.[1] Aligned with poetry and drama, rhetoric was the opposite of philosophy: one aimed at the truth, the other at deception. Flattery was the main culprit, because this appealed to the emotion of pride. The problem with rhetoric was the emotions it stirred in audiences. Emotions could trick everyone except philosophers trained at Plato's Academy.[2]

In his equally famous response, Aristotle (384–322 BCE) analyzed how emotions are actually used, especially in rhetoric. He offered a highly sociological discussion of anger, for instance, as a healthy reaction to a slight to one's social standing; a normal man with any status to defend will lash out at an insult, as part of defending his due. In his interesting discussion of pity, Aristotle says we pity someone when we think he does not deserve his misfortune *and* we can imagine ourselves or our loved ones in the same situation. Aristotle is right to emphasize blame here, even though his ancient Greek vision of justice linked it to social standing (in contrast to universalistic modern notions in which no sentient being deserves to suffer unnecessarily). Moral feelings like compassion are closely linked to cultural settings.

Political rhetoric, Aristotle saw, aims at a number of effects on others, including arousing certain feelings in audiences. And yet Aristotle shared Plato's anxiety over rhetoric (and hence over democracy), admitting that emotions affect one's judgment and so sustaining the contrast between emotion and reason.[3] Aristotle begins his treatise on rhetoric by insisting that it should persuade by marshaling the facts of a case, not through theatrical effects that please the audience, yet he later shows how to accomplish those very effects, on the disapproving excuse that "the baseness of the audience" makes the tricks so powerful that every student must learn them.[4] Upper-class Athenians had every incentive to see reason as the master and emotions as the slaves, and to emphasize that one must remain in control of the other. It is a view that has long outlasted slavery.

Athenian thinkers like these used emotions to make two fundamental political distinctions. One was between citizens and the (much larger) remainder of the populace: the slaves, women, and children who were excluded from participation because they were too given to their appetites. The noted orator Demosthenes (384–322 BCE), who led Athens into disastrous resistance to Alexander the Great, suggested a number of proper roles for women—"We have mistresses for our enjoyment, concubines to serve our person, and wives for the bearing of legitimate offspring"—but politics was not one of them.[5] For citizens, this boundary was simply common sense: noncitizens were too passionate for political reasoning.

The distinction that troubled Athenian citizens much more was between decisions that citizens make which later turn out to be mistaken due to the passions of the moment enflamed by flowery rhetoric, and the right decisions that are apparently not affected by those passions. Even reasonable citizens can make mistakes, and emotions are to blame. They turn good democracy into bad. The great debate between rhetoric aimed at persuasion and philosophy aimed at truth was an effort to figure out what had gone wrong in Athens.[6]

Some thinkers rejected democracy altogether as a result, but others tried a more complicated patch. Inventing arguments that would accompany democracy down to our day, they attempted to introduce nondemocratic elements into democracy. Many of these elements had to do with shielding politicians from mass emotionality and accountability. With bad leaders, according to Thucydides, the *demos* (common people) tend to make bad decisions—as a mob. Pericles, who had no serious rival for leadership, was able to restrain the demos and lead them to make wise choices. But when would-be leaders must compete with one another; they must flatter the demos rather than telling it unpleasant truths.[7] Thucydides blamed "the lust for power arising from greed and ambition." Unscrupulous politicians flatter the citizens through their emotions.[8] Two thousand years later, the US Constitution would create a cumbersome model of how to protect rulers from popular emotions.

The long tradition of contempt for emotions that began in Athens has sometimes blamed orators as demagogues, sometimes blamed audiences as ignorant, easily swayed, and overly emotional—and frequently blamed both at the same time. Emotions, it seems, cast a shadow especially on democratic processes.

FROM ROME TO PHILADELPHIA

Emotions were even more dangerous in undemocratic regimes, but their power was aimed in the opposite direction. If elites feared the masses under democracy, everyone feared the Prince under autocracy. His emotions were arbitrary and potentially ruinous. In a nondemocratic world, rhetoric was no longer directed to the masses but to the equally fickle rulers. Appeals to *their* emotions still resulted in problems of deceitful flattery, as Plutarch (46–120 CE) suggests in his famous essay, "How to Tell a Flatterer from a Friend."[9]

It was also dangerous for the ruled to have or express emotions. Living under capricious dictators, the Roman Stoics thought that any emotions were likely to get you into trouble. (Seneca served the notorious emperor Nero and committed suicide at his command in 65 CE.) Politics in any normal sense of the word was impossible, or at least unhealthy, so the emotions that drive a person into politics should be avoided. The Stoics emphasized the risks of each emotion rather than the rewards: the vulnerability involved in love, the narcissism of fear, the arrogance of moral judgment that is part of anger. They were more concerned with personal feelings than the emotions stirred through public rhetoric, but both kinds were to be suppressed.

In both democracies and autocracies there was anxiety over rhetoric, whether it was aimed upward or downward: the same techniques that could be used to express truths could also be used to formulate persuasive falsehoods. In the search for some way to distinguish good rhetoric from bad, beginning with Plato, emotions were blamed as the source of falsehood.

After Rome, the useful complexities of Athenian debates were further eroded with the rise of Christianity, which turned the world into a battleground of good and evil. From Plato it borrowed a sense of objective ethical truth out there (in God); from Stoicism, a sense of human depravity yet also a potential inward serenity in the face of a harsh external world. The body is inherently weak and sinful; the soul is capable of escaping its limitations. Emotions were divided into a saving love, faith, and hope, on the one hand, and the bodily temptations of the deadly sins, on the other. Emotions still needed to be controlled, but they were a personal matter—and danger—more than a political one.

If the Christian world was divided into a Manichean battle between an arch-hero and an archvillain, the positive and negative emotions were together supposed to be a powerful moral battery propelling action, as we see in the periodic spasms of reform in the Western church. The greatest of these movements, Protestantism, succeeded by concentrating on believers' sudden conversion from bad to good as they are born again. "For those who have undergone this experience, the world, once in fragments, becomes whole; and sin, though always lurking to reestablish itself in the transformed heart, recedes like a nightmare upon waking."[10] But no amount of rhetoric, only God's love, can bring about this emotional conversion.

The good emotions were no longer even classified as emotions, becoming part of reason. Inevitably, more was written about the titillating seven deadly sins of individual desire: gluttony, sloth, greed, envy, anger, pride, and lust. These descriptions were mostly games for theologians. With few arenas that required oratorical justification, European politics for hundreds of years had little recourse to rhetoric or popular emotions; what mattered was that subjects feared or loved their sovereigns enough to obey them. They were expected to be passive, and when they were not, their rebellion was attributed to evil emotions.

When power is concentrated in a single ruler, that person's emotions have an extraordinary effect on policies. And when rule is hereditary, the monarch may have extremely arbitrary whims, having been raised to command. Advice to princes, whether in manuals or informal letters, aimed partly at shaping their moral character, acknowledged as the background source of emotions. With the right feelings, they might govern well; with the wrong ones, viciously. Hence the endless advice books to princelings in many parts of the world, as counselors have tried to curtail the worst excesses of those who would rule them one day. The emotional arbitrariness of the top can be quite as extreme—and deadly—as that of the bottom.

Yet this could never be said too directly. As a result, the systematic study of the ill effects of emotions has almost always been directed downward, as intellectuals have most often been aligned with elites who distrust democracy. Those who serve dictators have rarely been free to elaborate their mistrust of those rulers' emotional lives. As the most famous advisor to princes, Machiavelli, admitted, "Of peoples everyone speaks evil without fear and freely, even while they reign: of princes one always speaks with a thousand fears and a thousand respects."[11] Scholars have felt free to despise those beneath them on the social ladder.

This dualistic contrast between higher and lower—rational elites or rulers and emotional masses—shaped modern philosophy and social science. Emotions were caused, said René Descartes, by "animal spirits" in the blood, and so they were capable of disrupting the more strictly human processes of cognition and judgment. Immanuel Kant, 150 years later, based his categorical imperative on imagining the consequences of each decision were it to be applied universally, dismissing "the inclinations" as irrelevant and potentially confusing to moral issues. Charles Darwin portrayed emotions as hardwired instincts, with characteristic facial expressions and gestures, that humans share with other mammals. If emotions were involuntary instincts, launching us into a program of action with little warning, they could hardly be a component of rationality. A behavioral package that conferred an evolutionary advantage on a savannah one million years ago is unlikely to be helpful in today's world.

Dualistic ideas contrasting emotion and reason percolated through various traditions of political thought. Thomas Hobbes thought the "movement" of our bodies—based on desire and emotion—necessarily propels us into conflict with other bodies in motion, a constant source of friction that can be controlled only by an all-powerful state. James Madison, like the United States's other founding fathers as well as the ancient Athenians, worried that the mass of ordinary citizens would be easily "stimulated by some irregular passion . . . or misled by the artful misrepresentations" of demagogues.[12] In many of these descriptions, people are as likely to be mistaken out of ignorance, self-interest, and cognitive errors as their emotions. But their emotions make them scary.

Elite anxiety about the anger of the oppressed has led thinkers to imagine politics on the model of sudden, unpredictable, and dramatic reflex emotions. Criticizing the role of emotions in politics is itself a rhetorical act meant to frighten audiences. Those addressed are called upon to restrain the overly emotional, irrational "others." Emotions are just one strand in the long tendency for intellectuals to believe that "we" know what is best for "them." The fantasy of a politics without emotion is not only grim and unrealistic but probably contradictory, yet it has had a long life.

THE MOB

The mob is the central trope in the ancient but ongoing debate between democracy and autocracy, the terms of which the ancient Athenians formulated so persuasively. The emotional extravagance and volatility of crowds has been implicit or explicit in almost every political philosophy since. All these crowd theories have had a political agenda, usually of exclusion.[13]

Euripides had already crafted the defining image of the crowd in *The Bacchae* in 405 BCE. In it, Dionysus returns to Thebes to take revenge on his mortal mother's family for refusing to recognize his divinity, and especially on his cousin Pentheus for banning Dionysus worship. His followers are women, the Bacchantes, who turn into wild creatures under the god's alcoholic spell. A male leader turns a mob of impressionable women into murderous brutes who eventually tear Pentheus apart. His own mother carries his head back to the palace. This image of the crowd, with its female emotionality but a male demagogue leading it, would persist until the twentieth century.

Elites worked to curb urban crowds in early modern Europe, transforming drunken carnival revelry—"dancing in the streets," as Barbara Ehrenreich calls it—into more planned and disciplined political rallies. Protestant self-control, the need for an orderly workforce, and a concern with urban politics led the wealthy to seal themselves off in their city houses and palaces, frightened of "the great ruling class nightmare of the Renaissance: the marauding horde, the many-headed multitude, the insatiate, giddy, and murderous crowd."[14] With the halting spread of democracy across modern Europe and some of its former colonies, the old Athenian anxiety over emotions flourished even more, as those crowds made increasingly political demands. They had to be excluded from the polity, and their supposed emotionality remained the best excuse.

In the nineteenth century the fear of crowds gained a pseudoscientific veneer, reflecting Victorian veneration of crackpot science as practiced by armchair speculators. "Would-be scientific arguments," remark two well-known historians, "were used in the rationalization and legitimization of almost every aspect of Victorian life, with particular vehemence in those areas in which social change implied stress in existing arrangements."[15]

Nineteenth-century European cities focused the ancient anxieties on the image of the crowd: normal, reasoning individuals were thought to be transformed in a crowd, becoming angry, violent, impressionable, and generally unthinking. Crowds were assumed to create, through hypnotic processes such as suggestion and contagion, a kind of "primitive" group mind and group feelings shared by all participants. The mob overwhelmed individual personalities and moved them beyond reason and normal sensibilities. Through most of the twentieth century, crowds and their dynamics continued to be seen as the heart of protest movements, the core around which other forms of collective action were built. In this vision, individuals were calmly reasonable, crowds were emotional and irrational. They were also frighteningly working class.

In 1895 in *La Psychologie des Foules*, Gustave Le Bon described crowds as impulsive, irritable, suggestible, and credulous, guided primarily by unconscious motives and exhibiting "very simple and very exaggerated" emotions. "A commencement of antipathy or disapprobation, which in the case of an isolated individual would not gain strength, becomes at once furious hatred in the case of an individual in a crowd." Crowds are susceptible to the emotional appeals of demagogues. "Given to exaggeration in its feelings," wrote Le Bon, "a crowd is only impressed by excessive sentiments. An orator wishing to move a crowd must make an abusive use of violent affirmations. To exaggerate, to affirm, to resort to repetitions, and never to attempt to prove anything by reasoning, are methods of argument well known to speakers at public meetings."[16]

Virtually all scholars in the early twentieth century accepted this image of the mob. "When individuals come together in a group," Freud wrote, "all their individual inhibitions fall away and all the cruel, brutal and destructive instincts, which lie dormant in individuals as relics of a primitive epoch, are stirred up to find free gratification."[17] Emotions are disturbing reflexes coming from within, not socially approved moods, moral emotions, or group solidarities. Sociologists such as E. D. Martin embraced these ideas: "In the crowd the primitive ego achieves its wish by actually gaining the assent and support of a section of society. The immediate social environment is all pulled in the same direction as the unconscious desire." We see the far-fetched jump between individual emotion and a "section of society." Action is driven by the unconscious for its own regressive purposes, Martin contends: "The crowd is always formed for the unconscious purpose of relaxing the social control by mechanisms which mutually justify such antisocial conduct on the part of members of the crowd."[18] Beneath the mob image is the Durkheimian idea that "social control" operates along a continuum in which there is more or less.

Fears of mobs were reinforced by the romantic tropes that have dominated the arts in the West and beyond since the nineteenth century. One central image is the lone individual standing up against the group, whether that is society, tradition, inequality—or the mob. In these fictional plots, the individual is inevitably right, through special access to his own conscience, while the group is too fickle or cowardly to arrive at the correct moral stand. The image of the lonely hero, inevitably male, began with artists such as Wordsworth hiking in the Lake District or Beethoven at his piano, and eventually devolved into stars of Westerns like Tom Mix, John Wayne, and Gary Cooper in *High Noon*.[19]

Mobs were seen as feminine because women fell on the wrong side of the traditional rationality–emotion chasm. The central arguments against women's suffrage focused on their emotions. Sometimes their feelings were linked to ignorance. "If the great mass of ignorant women's votes are added to the great mass of ignorant men's votes, there will be constant demands for work, money, bread, leisure, in short, 'all kinds of laws to favor all kinds of persons.'"[20] The ignorant men here were, naturally, immigrants and the working class, feminine in their suggestibility. In this case, women's suspect emotion seems to have been compassion, a failing that would reappear in the "gender gap" in the late twentieth century, when women expressed greater preferences for welfare state protections than "rational" men did. A moral commitment was treated as if it were identical to a sudden, startling fear.

Others blamed women's emotions for a kind of ethic of ultimate ends. "The masculine represents *judgment*, the practicable, the expedient, the possible, while the feminine represents *emotion*, what ought to be, the dream of excellence, the vision of complete beauty. . . . The predominance of sentiment in woman renders her essentially an idealist. She jumps at conclusions. . . . She can make no allowance for slowness, for tentative or compromising measures. Her reforms are sweeping."[21] Women's emotions were often described as intuitive rather than logical. Their emotionality makes them hysterical: "In moments of excitement . . . it is liable to explode in violent paroxysms."[22] They lead to panic and other disruptive feelings.

Following ancient traditions, the modern study of "public opinion" developed in the early twentieth century out of American Progressives' suspicion of mob emotions. Progressives mistrusted the crowds that political parties assembled during elections to generate good moods through torchlit parades, tipsy rallies, and long speeches. They preferred policies to be created by educated city managers, and they wished voting to be a private choice based on information rather than a statement of solidarity with a party. Walter Lippmann formulated these arch attitudes toward crowds in his eponymous book on public opinion. The traditional themes were all there: people rarely pay much attention to the public world as opposed to their everyday lives; when they do, they are driven more by emotions than by reason and knowledge; as a result, they are open to manipulation by others—including both advertising professionals and machine politicians. In Lippmann's version of the usual dualism, the disorderly "drift" of democracy needed the "mastery" of science to guide it. Without it, the "mass" would follow its emotions in dangerous directions.[23]

Like research on voting and public opinion, public relations emerged out of the same supposition as crowd theory: the public is irrational and can be manipulated through emotional appeals. Edward Bernays, its early spokesman and nephew of Sigmund Freud, wrote a series of handbooks that were simply lessons in rhetoric. He assumed that, like crowds, the public follows trusted leaders rather than assessing the facts for themselves. The leaders' manipulation of opinion creates order out of chaos: "The conscious and intelligent manipulation of the organized habits and opinions of the masses is an important element in democratic society."[24]

Police and military officers were among the elites indoctrinated in crowd theories. According to sociologist Marnia Lazreg, a course in "crowd psychology" offered at the École Supérieure de Guerre in the 1950s taught the French military what to expect from the Algerians under their control: "The average Algerian was defined as dominated by emotions and given to mood swings. . . . Although he could be intelligent, he was gullible and deficient in the capacity for discernment. . . . Algerians thus emerged as a people living at a lower stage of psychological and social development than the French." Through behaviorist techniques, including pain, they could be reconditioned to be more civilized.[25] According to Edward Said, the orientalist mind cast the entire East as feminine, in its passivity but also its penetrability. Afrikaners depicted (and continue to view) their Black co-citizens as emotional and susceptible to mass hysteria. Once again, viewing a group as crowdlike in its emotionality serves as grounds for excluding it from politics.[26]

In Herbert Blumer's kinder formulation, crowds "short-circuit" symbolic communication, with participants instead responding directly to each other's physical actions, especially when spurred by rumors.[27] Even Ralph Turner and Lewis Killian, who rejected the distinction between rational individuals and irrational crowds, expressed hostility toward "mobs" (namely, crowds they disliked). As individuals "mill" about in crowds, according to Turner and Killian, their emotions are intensified and focused by their "circular reaction" to one another. Suggestible and uninhibited, crowds come to be "dominated by a uniform mood and uniform imagery" and, when frustrated, turn angry and aggressive. "Crowd behavior consists, *in essence*," they wrote, "of deviations from the traditional norms of society."[28] (Note the implication that people "normally" follow all of society's norms.)

In a devastating critique, Clark McPhail picked apart this "transformation hypothesis" through his own unprecedented observations of what crowds actually do. Most participants are neither anomic nor anonymous, attending with small groups of friends or coworkers who enforce many normal standards of behavior. Protestors often accept and even seek to defend traditional norms. Members of crowds may be afraid—for instance, when they gather because of a natural disaster or fire—but, far from diminishing their critical thinking, their situation may instead heighten it. Most crowds assemble, listen, cheer, and disperse. They are not so crazy or sinister.[29] Emotions such as fear, anxiety, and excitement are modes of paying attention. (Political scientists similarly find that more engaged voters have *more* emotions about politics than more ignorant voters: emotions do not crowd out "thought" but are a form of it.)[30] They are moods that support further action, not newly created motivations for action. In this book we have examined several crowd dynamics that are perfectly normal and helpful.

DAMAGED INDIVIDUALS

To understand mobs, some early twentieth-century scholars looked for peculiar individuals who might be susceptible to mass movements, predisposed to listen to extremist leaders or to act "aggressively." Psychologist Floyd Allport in 1924 rejected "group mind" accounts on the sensible grounds that only individuals have thoughts and feelings; the actions of crowds must reflect the interests and drives of the individuals comprising them. But he unfortunately concluded that these individuals participate because they have primitive, nonrational responses to thwarted drives, since Allport shared the assumption that crowds are dangerous and irrational. He accepted that crowds entail suggestion and enforce unanimity, due to the excitement they generate. They are also prone to violence and drastic action. They attract, he concluded, those predisposed to violence.[31] As with Freud, but in contrast to Aristotle, Allport saw anger lurking within some of us, ready to burst out.

Neal Miller and John Dollard argued that frustration leads inevitably or (in a later formulation) frequently to aggression, especially when reinforced by crowd dynamics. The frustration itself arises from being deprived of some desired reward, and the more time people spend feeling frustrated, the stronger their aggression becomes. Although "frustration" suggests external engagement, Miller and Dollard also concluded that only damaged individuals would place themselves in these situations. Borrowing from Allport's behaviorism, Miller and Dollard thought that crowds merely reinforce these feelings and compulsions to act aggressively. In their major work, an account of lynchings in the American South, they argued that only unusually sadistic individuals would act on their aggressive impulses. Lynch mobs, a most extreme case, were their exemplar for all crowds![32]

Other efforts to blame damaged individuals depended on Freudian psychology to portray participants as immature: as narcissistic, latently homosexual, orally dependent, or anally retentive.[33] In some versions, a generation was working out its identity issues by protesting against its parents and other authority figures.[34] What some reduced to a stage of life, others reduced, just as dismissively, to personality traits. Harold Lasswell in 1948 elaborated a personality "type" for whom politics was an effort to fulfill needs not met in private life.[35] Emotions resulted from inner conflicts more than from engagement with the external world, as Freud had been interested in the failures of adaptation and engagement, not the supposedly infrequent successes.

This tradition reached its apogee in Eric Hoffer, a popular writer (and social misfit) who described a desperate fanatic. Driven by inner needs, especially by frustrations due to a lack of a stable identity or to "barren and insecure lives," Hoffer's "true believers" hope to lose themselves in a collective identity, a "mass movement" in which they can believe with utter certainty. "Passionate hatred" is useful, as the emotion that "can give meaning and purpose to an empty life."[36] When one movement ends, they move on to another. Participation and its strong feelings are the motivation; the goals of protest hardly matter.

From the "damaged individual" perspective, even the social movements of the 1960s did not necessarily arouse sympathy, since they could be dismissed as the work of confused youngsters suffering from Oedipal fantasies. As late as 1969, Orrin Klapp described the signs of "identity trouble" that lead people to seek fulfillment in collective action: self-hatred, oversensitivity, a feeling of being blemished, excessive self-concern (including narcissism), alienation, a feeling that "nobody appreciates me," a desire to be someone else, a feeling of fraudulent self-presentation, Riesman's "other-directedness," and an identity crisis.[37] In academic traditions like these, protest is either a mistake, a form of acting out, or a sign of immaturity. Scholars' own moral panics over emotional crowds and youth—especially the youth in one's own classroom—masqueraded as serious social science.

Such glib dismissals of protestors as disturbed individuals have ebbed in serious scholarly circles, but they persist in the news media, applied to new villains. Here is Republican "terrorism expert" Neil Livingstone on the *CBS Evening News* on November 29, 2010: "The kind of people who become lone-wolf terrorists are people who generally have some deficiency or gap in their lives that they are trying to fill."

DAMAGED SOCIETIES

A less pejorative view emerged in the 1950s that shifted the blame for unruly emotions from damaged individuals to the social structures that cripple them. In "mass society," individuals supposedly are "atomized," cut loose from formal ties to others through "intermediary" organizations and left vulnerable to charismatic leaders like Hitler, who can manipulate them directly through mass media. (Radio was the favorite villain for the era's technological determinists, soon replaced by television and later by the Internet and social media.) The root cause shifted back a step, but the result was the same: irrational emotions. In the Athenian Assembly or the modern urban crowd, passions lead people to do or demand things that they do not "really" want, or which are not good for them in the long run. The "masses" sweep aside traditional sources of authority to rule directly or through their leader in "extremist" style. The affective ties of community supposedly break down, leaving many with an ill-defined sense of self.

When William Kornhauser tried to explain the propensity of isolated communities of miners and maritime workers to strike or to vote Communist, he blamed mass society, describing "mass behavior" (the term itself is confused but evokes images of crowds) as unstable, whimsically shifting its focus of attention and its intensity. He failed to distinguish the solidarity of local community from the formal organizations of "normal" politics, dismissing the affective ties of informal networks on the grounds that they opened workers to the appeals of rabble-rousers.[38] Only formal organizations were good—unless they were communist-infiltrated unions. Like Hoffer, Kornhauser and others set out to explain a form of politics which they had already decided was dangerous, so that everything associated with it had to be dangerous too, including strong emotions.[39] Psychological dynamics such as "self-estrangement" or "alienation" were poorly specified to start with, and Kornhauser applied them not to socially isolated individuals but to those whose primary groups (such as family, friends, and coworkers) had no broader linkages. Those with the strongest local bonds—such as mining communities—would have less allegiance to broader social institutions or the existing state. They had a dangerous, pugnacious solidarity. The affective bonds of community—normally seen as stabilizing emotions—were suspect when they led to radical politics.

This vision of society as an organic whole need not be politically conservative. Parts of the organic whole could be out of whack with each other
through no fault of the individuals involved. This was Émile Durkheim's
view of labor unrest and the "moral anomie" of modern industrial societies. His famous solution was to bolster occupational groups, "a moral
power capable of containing individual egos, of maintaining a spirited
sentiment of common solidarity in the consciousness of all the workers,
of preventing the law of the strongest from being brutally applied to industrial and commercial relations." In corporations, such groups can apply the
state's universal laws to local circumstances. In a formulation that inspired
Kornhauser and, later, Robert Putnam, Durkheim argued, "A nation can
be maintained only if, between the state and the individual, there is inter-
calated a whole series of secondary groups near enough to the individuals
to attract them strongly in their sphere of action and drag them, in this
way, into the general torrent of social life."[40] Without such attachments,
workers become disgruntled and take to the streets in mobs. In a properly
functioning social system, there should be minimal frustration, indignation, or protest. Moral commitments begin and end in group attachments
for Durkheim: keep people attached to something larger than themselves,
and they will never be outraged.

Parsonian structural-functionalists adopted a similar account of protest. In the most thorough effort, Neil Smelser chided crowd theorists for
assuming irrationality and unpredictability (although the two are hardly
the same). He rejected any assumption "that the persons involved in an
episode are irrational, that they lose their critical faculties, that they experience psychological regression, that they revert to some animal state, or
whatever." But he did assume "that perceived structural strain at the social
level excites feelings of anxiety, fantasy, hostility, etc." The social structure
is damaged, not individuals, who may simply be torn between multiple or
confused social roles as a result of social change. Even so, Smelser stressed
negative emotions as a sign that something has gone wrong. In contrast, positive emotions such as confidence, trust, and loyalty result when norms and
values are functioning properly; they apparently play no role in protest.[41]

In Smelser's model, anxiety is the mechanism that links social strain to
individual action, leading in different directions depending on the cognitive work that groups and individuals do in response. Although anxiety is a
promising mechanism to get at how people focus emotional attention, it is
insufficient, especially since Smelser wrote little about it—not even a nod
to connoisseurs of anxiety such as Freud or Harry Stack Sullivan.

Smelser's quick switch to cognitive processes, primarily "generalized
beliefs," at first seems to suppress the role of emotions, but it turns out that
generalized beliefs frequently follow emotional and symbolic pathways

rather than logical and empirical links. Like Kornhauser, Smelser missed the microlevel solidarities, interactions, and expectations that really account for emotions, all the stuff that actually connects individuals to larger groups. "Society" and "social system" are broad metaphors that hide most of this.

Six years after his 1962 book, and after he had himself entered psychoanalysis, Smelser tried to incorporate emotions into his theory, but in this period he had few tools at his disposal other than classical Freudian psychoanalysis. Protest "has a psychological dimension," he observed, "since the deepest and most powerful human emotions—idealistic fervor, love, and violent rage, for example—are bared in episodes of collective behavior, and since persons differ psychologically in their propensity to become involved in such episodes." Note the typical emphasis on "powerful" emotions, never mild ones. His *Theory of Collective Behavior*, he acknowledged in 1968, had failed to explain why the same social strains might affect different individuals in different ways or why people might choose different forms of participation; as a corrective, Smelser laid out some of the "psychodynamic meanings of the common elements of social protest movements."[42]

These meanings—actually feelings—came from Freud. Oedipal ambivalence felt toward one's father reemerges, split between two objects, Smelser argues: "On the one hand there is the unqualified love, worship, and submission to the leader of the movement, who articulates and symbolizes 'the cause.' On the other hand there is the unqualified suspicion, denigration, and desire to destroy the agent felt responsible for the moral decay of social life and standing in the way of reform, whether he be a vested interest or a political authority." Anxiety—a prime motivator for Freud—is reduced when strong positive and negative feelings toward the father are split and aimed in different directions. The Oedipal fantasy of obtaining the mother, usually severely repressed, can appear in the movement's utopian vision of "bliss, peace, and harmony." (Why women participate is less clear.) In *Love's Body*, Norman O. Brown made the same argument about community as a substitute for mother's love. "The striking feature of the protest movement," wrote Smelser, "is what Freud observed: it permits the expression of impulses that are normally repressed." External circumstances such as strain now mostly seem to provide an opportunity for the expression of internal emotional dynamics.[43]

BLAMING THE DEMAGOGUE

Strained societies allow demagogues to appear. If mobs are like children or women, they must have a strong male to lead them. If they are suggestible, they must have demagogues manipulating them. These are the real villains of the story, with awareness and intention, unlike their supposedly entranced followers. Demagogues come in two forms, venal and mortal we might call them, since they vary in seriousness (although Donald Trump manages to combine them).

Some demagogues are seen as simply selfish, trying to manipulate public decisions in order to benefit themselves and their cronies, or motivated only by the desire to remain in power. They substitute private gain for the public good. Venal sins.

Other demagogues are criticized for stirring up hate, especially in what Andrew Delbanco calls "the century of demagogues," the twentieth. They speak in the voice of despair, attacking their "catalogue of demons— capitalists, industrialists, prohibitionists, usurers, tax-evading financiers, blacks, Jews, and other devils innumerable."[44] They make the crowd feel that they are victims of unspeakable suffering, whose only hope is to punish an enemy who is totally evil. Mortal sins.

In the 1950s, demagogue theory flourished: if crowds were largely acting out or responding to contagion or internal Oedipal drives, someone had to be making decisions, and theorists often focused on the leader—easily enough in the aftermath of Hitler and Mussolini. For Hoffer and Kornhauser, the existence of a demagogue was a defining element of extremist politics. Even Smelser saw idolatry of the leader as a crucial psychological mechanism. For those who believe human nature is essentially good, and for those trying to avoid blame themselves, former leaders are often a perfect scapegoat. It certainly must have seemed that way to the postwar generation of Germans.[45]

Over the centuries the feared targets have changed: from Greek slaves to Renaissance revelers, from the working class to lynch mobs, to communists and fascists, to alienated youths, to radical Islamic terrorists. But the analysis has remained the same. They are acting out their emotions rather than formulating rational demands and policies. They are politically dangerous and immature.

THE WRONG EMOTIONS

The pernicious effects of emotions have always been central to Western thought. As a dark shadow over democracy, emotions were thought to emerge from crowds and their demagogues, having little to do with individuals' own lives and goals. They appear and disappear in response to what is happening in participants' immediate surroundings, with little lasting resonance. Because social movements were thought to embody particular emotions such as anger or frustration or hate, it was assumed that the individuals in the movements—unified in a crowd—all shared these feelings.

Freud added the twist that emotions result from internal personality conflicts rather than as responses to the social environment. Thus only certain kinds of flawed people are susceptible to movement appeals. Their emotions are inevitably negative or troubled rather than positive and joyful; they reflect a psychological problem, albeit one that might go away with maturity. Participants do not *enjoy* protest, they are *compelled* to it by their inner drives.

Strain theorists moved in the opposite direction, finding pathological social structures that lurk behind the emotions of crowds. The result—the irrationality of passionate politics—was the same. Generations of writers who mistrusted protestors turned to their patent emotions as the best way to condemn and dismiss them.

In all these currents, the salient emotions were often vague and difficult to identify except through the actions they were meant to explain. Can we recognize a propensity to violence except when it results in violence? Contagion in crowds except when it leads to collective action? Can we identify states of anomie or alienation before they lead to movement participation? In the absence of empirical investigation, what Le Bon and Hoffer thought they saw in crowds was more a projection of their own fears and anxieties—their own moral panics—than an accurate psychological portrait of protestors. Democracy's shadow darkened their vision.

If efforts to apply psychological insight to politics usually reduced the latter to little more than internal personality dynamics, group psychology ignored preexisting traits of individuals altogether: their norms, goals, convictions, and knowledge. Plus little was recognized between the individual and the social: no social networks, organizations, shared cultural meanings (including most emotions), processes of negotiation and especially of interaction. Driven by forces outside their control, whether the individual's unconscious or the mysterious pull of the crowd, protestors were not rational agents with purposes of their own. The actual stuff of politics—moral commitments, stated goals, processes of mobilization, group solidarities, the pleasures of participation—was ignored.

Every emotion that protestors were acknowledged to feel—primarily the dramatic emotions of anger and fear—had enormous regret and disruption potential. Emotions were described by a panic model, contrasted with the calculating brains of cognition. Through Freudian models, participants were so divided in their own psyches that they were likely to regret their actions even while they were carrying them out. They would certainly regret them as they matured. The disruption was primarily of society's normal institutions, assumed to function in healthy ways most of the time.

The essence of crowd theory was a confusion between reflex anger and the moral emotion of indignation. In mass society theory, a similar conflation placed reflex emotions such as anger and fear in the same category as moods of resignation or cynicism and affective bonds (for one's own group, against outsiders). Among scholars, most such portrayals today are straw targets trotted out to make a point. Thus Jasbir Puar, attempting to demonstrate "homonationalism," relies heavily on a Library of Congress report on terrorism. Puar rightly castigates the "negative identity hypothesis" and the "narcissistic rage hypothesis" from the report. But it turns out that the report, intended as a literature review, even of outdated materials, itself was trying to cast doubt on these ideas.[46]

Let's be clear about the problem with crowd and strain theories. They implied that individuals have emotions, for internal or external reasons, and then go out and engage in politics to try to satisfy those emotions. The great structural turn has taught us that things are not so simple. Some emotions may propel people to seek out protest groups or political outlets. More commonly, participants are already part of social networks, they are already reading the posters or graffiti, they have already shown up at a rally, and they have the emotions appropriate to those settings. They already participate in some form of politics, and the emotions they feel or are encouraged to feel keep them engaged; the emotions motivate them to return or to move to the next level of commitment. They go to rallies and meetings to feel the joy, love, or outrage that will keep them going. Emotions do not stop when participation begins.

Yet when irrationalist theories went out of fashion in the 1970s, some of the topics they had addressed also disappeared, including the power of strong emotions to mobilize or inhibit collective action, and the ways in which followers admire and identify with their leaders. Even if they pathologized the emotions accompanying protest (indeed, emphasized emotions *in order to* pathologize protest), early theorists had at least paid attention to them. This would not be the case for the next generation of scholars of protest.

STRUCTURAL CONFLICT

By the early 1970s, many social scientists were writing about protest movements in which they had themselves been active. Civil rights, antiwar, New Left, and feminist activists did not see themselves as atomized individuals, defeated in their personal aspirations, or swept up by charismatic demagogues. In their view, activists campaign outside institutional politics when they are excluded from regular political channels, not because they are personally alienated or overly emotional. Rather than being studied alongside fads, crazes, and panics, social movements were now perceived as "politics by other means."

To replace pathological explanations, most sociologists turned to implicit rational actor and explicit organizational models, shifting from motivational "why" to strategic "how" questions. Participants were assumed to be rational *instead of* emotional. Grievances, and the emotions that give them power, were causally uninteresting since they were seen as "relatively constant and pervasive."[47] Protest breaks out as soon as the means for doing something become available, such as the money to form oppositional organizations.

Dismissing emotions as motivating action, John McCarthy and Mayer Zald reversed the causal sequence: "grievances and discontent may be defined, created, and manipulated by issue entrepreneurs and organizations."[48] At the heart of the new "resource mobilization" models, powerless groups depend on the time, money, and political clout provided by powerful sponsors such as foundations, organized labor, or the government, or given by large numbers of otherwise passive supporters. McCarthy and Zald did not address sponsors' emotions, such as sympathy, any more than they looked at activists' emotions. They ignored *how* issue entrepreneurs "create and manipulate grievances," despite bringing attention to the centrality of this process, perhaps because emotions would have to be highlighted.

Political process theorists, elaborating on McCarthy and Zald's insight that protestors often need the help of elites, soon described dozens of openings that might be useful, especially elite allies, cleavages among elites, a lessening in repression, and new channels for participation. Aggrieved groups were viewed as rational actors pursuing long-standing interests, not constructing new ones (although some scholars included new grievances as "opportunities" for mobilization, stretching the definition of opportunity).[49] Charles Tilly recognized the importance of insurgents' interests, organization, and resources, as well as the ways in which the state facilitated or repressed them—yet he saw these, even interests, as structural and independent of individuals' beliefs and feelings. Doug McAdam came closer to emotions with his idea of "cognitive liberation," but this remained a calculation about likely repression or success rather than a set of liberating emotions.

In 1999 Jeff Goodwin and I criticized political-opportunity models for not recognizing the emotions that actually do much of the work of opportunities, by providing the basis for collective identities and alliances with elites, the anger for mobilization, the indignation over repressive violence by the state, and the energy that often creates opportunities rather than simply responding to them.[50] The rationalistic and organizational formulas of the structural paradigm discouraged any analysis of emotions.[51]

In these structural traditions, protestors search for the tactics that will be most effective in attaining their (instrumental) goals. Despite using the term *frustration*, Herbert Kitschelt also depicted protestors as searching rationally for effective strategies, with no emotional loyalties to their tactics, in a European version of political opportunity theory.[52]

In resource mobilization and political process accounts, emotions simply disappeared. Instead, the structural paradigm depicted shrewd entrepreneurs, rational actors coolly calculating the costs and benefits of participation, and people mobilized by incentives rather than by indignation.[53] McCarthy and Zald's metaphors of formal organizations and conflict over material interests encouraged an assumption of strategic purpose that did not seem to require attention to emotions. A view of collective actors as rational, political, and organized made sense as a counter to crowd theories. Activists are not bitter, crazy, or anomic. But by relying on the old contrast between rationality and emotions, structuralists misrepresented human action and motivation and misspecified their own models of participation.

Much as they disliked everything else the crowd tradition had done, the new generation of theorists shared with the older ones one big assumption: that emotions are irrational. While the earlier crowd theorists had portrayed protestors as emotional to demonstrate their irrationality, the new structuralists demonstrated protestors' rationality by denying their emotions. For the scholars of the structural school, virtually all of them men, emotions were unworthy of serious scholarly concern. Contemptuous of the "bleeding heart" imagery attached to protest, inevitably to discredit it, they set about to show that protest was serious business, a matter of hard-nosed calculation about "real" interests, especially material interests. They were eager to establish protest and revolution as central to politics, topics that future scholars would never be able to dismiss as youthful folly. Protest was a hard topic, and they approached it with hard methods and hard theories. Nothing soft for them.

Quantitative methods, for that generation, had the aura of rigorous facts, so the structuralists' inattention to emotions was partly methodological. As Olivier Fillieule has complained, "macro-comparisons based on quantitative analyses, statistical data, newspaper counts, surveys of organizations, etc." are a better means for getting at structural shifts than for understanding meanings and feelings.[54] Even their methods were "hard."

Structuralists eventually incorporated cultural meanings into their theories by stripping them of the emotions that give them their power. For instance, Ed Walsh tried to salvage the concept of grievances through his notion of "suddenly imposed grievances," an unexpected threat or affront that helps mobilize protest. In a critique of the structural image of bloc recruitment, Walsh saw—in nuclear accidents, oil spills, and revelations of damage such as Love Canal—situations in which residents were suddenly easier to mobilize. Emotions were hidden inside the idea, unacknowledged, since it is not really the grievance that spurs action but its suddenness: it is a shock, inspiring fear or indignation.[55]

But it was the idea of frames that most spurred the new appreciation of culture. David Snow and his collaborators argued that mobilization depends on organizers' and recruits' managing to agree on their diagnosis and prognosis of a problem by aligning their interpretive frames, or schemas. Hundreds of studies used frames, which are easy (perhaps too easy) to identify. Not much was said about why some frames resonate and others do not, perhaps because resonance involves emotional processes that were oddly ignored. Even "motivational framing," which is what actually produces action, was not explicitly linked to emotions.

Collective identities were the next hot cultural concept, but they, too, were initially treated as a set of cognitive distinctions among groups. First in studies of feminism and then in the growth of the lesbian, gay, bisexual, transgender, and queer (LGBTQ) movements, analysts unraveled the advantages and disadvantages of strong group boundaries: the rhetorical use of collective identities encourages mobilization from within the group, but it often reifies the very group stereotypes that the mobilization was meant to challenge. Oppression from the outside actually strengthens communities, as was clear for the US civil rights movement. As with frames, it soon became clear that emotional dynamics are responsible for the impact—good or bad—of collective identities: the love and trust of one's group, the hatred and mistrust for other groups, the elated mood of group gatherings, sometimes even the misplaced loyalty to one small part of a movement rather than to the movement as a whole.[56]

Narratives were next.[57] Humans readily understand the world through stories, which help them attribute causality and define characters. Stories of victimization and of heroic resistance against the odds have inspired many kinds of political mobilization. Early theories of narrative and politics drew on literary criticism, which emphasized plot over character: a small number of basic plots determined what the characters do, playing with reader expectations along the way. As with frames and identities, narratives had more emotions inside them than was first realized. Characters, for instance, tell us what we are supposed to feel: we pity victims, admire heroes, and detest villains. We feel afraid when the villains threaten the victims, relief when the heroes arrive to save the victims.[58]

The new cultural tools were easy to incorporate into structural models because most were based on a structural vision of culture as codes, whether in systems of language as the French structuralists like anthropologist Claude Lévi-Strauss had it, or in the metaphor of computer codes that instructed machines how to operate as schemas and other terms taken from psychology had it. Much of the early cultural turn grew out of cognitive science, a discipline based on the calculating-brain image. The idealism of this view is easy to understand, as it is always easier to see neat products on the shelf, page, or screen than to grasp the messy processes that created them.

Under the "code" model of culture, there was little room for humans, much less for emotions. Codes could be teased out, often through mysterious processes, and laid on the page for readers and viewers. Content analysis of texts became the preferred method for getting at meaning, and hundreds of studies of frames listed them in static summary form, like a glossary. Little was known about the rhetorical contexts in which they are used, or about how people feel about the cultural tools they deploy. Most strikingly, it was unclear why people care about their meanings. Why does one frame or story resonate with audiences while another does not? To understand this, emotions would be necessary.[59]

In retrospect, it seems inevitable that the cultural turn would arrive at emotions sooner or later. How could meanings possibly affect human action if they did not appeal to our emotions? How could collective identities matter if we did not feel differently about different groups? How could frames move us to action if they did not make us feel threatened, afraid, or indignant? What is resonance if not some emotional tingle? Pride and shame are things we feel, not words we write down in brochures.

THE SOFT REVOLT

At the same time that cognitive approaches were finding a place in structural paradigms, post-1968 movements were already inspiring a new way of understanding culture. In the 1970s, a range of new movements appeared, often influenced by scholar-activists, who cared about feelings, symbols, and group identities. Feminists came first, insisting on the affective bonds that are a defining part of being human. They were also able to see subtle forms of oppression that operated, not by excluding a group from formal political arenas but by shaping the emotions individuals were allowed to feel.

A wave of feminist philosophers in the 1980s exposed the individualist, male bias of Western moral and political philosophy, such as social contract theory. If we replace the root metaphor of individuals haggling in markets with one of parents nurturing their children, we can see that people already have emotional bonds with each other. Other people are not instruments to our own personal ends but a component part of our ends. Community forms an essential part of our character, and our capacity for compassion is central to moral decision making.[60] Neo-Aristotelians, notably Martha Nussbaum, picked up the torch by demonstrating that our moral selves depend on the lifelong training of our characters. Our sympathies can extend to those beyond the traditional frontiers of liberal justice, to beings such as foreigners, other species, and those with mental handicaps. Morality depends on emotions as much as or more than on calculation; political and moral autonomy depend on our relationships with others.[61]

Around the same time, Alain Touraine, Alberto Melucci, and other European scholars noticed that social movements were no longer concerned with seizing state power. The so-called new social movements were more interested in shaping cultural meanings, such as what it means to be human, what our relationship to "nature" is, what kinds of military weapons are beyond moral bounds. Economic and political power, the core of the structural models, no longer seemed fundamental to protest. A more humanistic image of protestors began to emerge, driven by feelings and not by the calculation of interests.

The philosopher Michel Foucault helped articulate new concerns with how humans come to have the desires, the sense of themselves as subjects, that they do. Although couched in terms of a critique of the practices of power that create subjects, Foucault's project was motivated by humane emotions of solidarity with his fellow humans and their sufferings. His tone of indignation was perfect for post-1968 readers.

Among other things, Foucault inspired queer studies, which along with the expansion of LGBTQ movements helped to further soften social movement studies in the 1990s. It is even tempting to call these developments the "queer turn" in movement research. As usual, intellectual trends depended on the politics of the moment. In the United States, the AIDS Coalition to Unleash Power (ACT UP), Queer Nation, and related groups were the most exciting protests of the late 1980s and early 1990s, planting the seeds for a harvest of books and articles in the mid- and late 1990s that highlighted the joy of participation, its erotic attractions, the mechanisms and dilemmas of collective identities, even the microlevel conflicts that all movements must work out. A wave of LGBTQ activists went off to graduate school.

In the mid-1990s, Verta Taylor began to apply feminist insights into emotions to social movements, especially through the lens of LGBTQ movements.[62] For example, she and her student Nancy Whittier wrote about the centrality of collective identities by studying the lesbian rights movement as it distinguished itself more and more from the rest of the women's movement. Taylor chaired the sociological group that in 1997 awarded Mary Bernstein a best-article prize for her analysis of the strategic uses of identities in gay and lesbian rights groups. Josh Gamson was in ACT UP as the term *queer* emerged, quickly assessing the challenge that it posed to any and all claims to collective identities: any label that fits some individuals will discomfit or exclude other potential participants. Many other young scholars found inspiration and evidence in the LGBTQ movements of the 1990s.[63]

This surge of research culminated in Deborah Gould's investigation of the rise and fall of ACT UP through its emotional dynamics. These include the interplay of shame and pride, the moods of meetings—"the energy in the room" that so attracted participants—a variety of reciprocal feelings that members had for each other, and a deep mood of desperation that loved ones were dying while the Reagan administration was in denial about the whole epidemic. Central was the production of anger, which not only had to displace fear, anxiety, and embarrassment but also transformed gay pride, identity, and respectability. With unique candor, Gould even documents the feelings of betrayal, mistrust, and grief that surfaced as ACT UP began to splinter and decline.[64]

Gould's use of multiple research techniques—including interviews and participation as well as texts—contrasts with "affect theory" as practiced in cultural studies and queer studies. Sara Ahmed, its best-known practitioner, takes considerable poetic license by relying exclusively on public texts to deconstruct the emotional underpinnings of common political boundaries such as nation, race, gender, and sexuality. She wishes to reassert bodily feelings against on overly cognitive vision of emotions, perhaps oddly since her evidence comes from texts rather than humans. Her intent is partly to show the inchoate, preverbal influence of affect, although she uses familiar pairings such as love and hate, pain and shame, fear and disgust.[65]

Queer theorists use the term *affect* to get at a variety of feelings that have not yet been labeled or which pass too quickly to ever be acknowledged and labeled. "The body," remarks Brian Massumi, "is as immediately virtual as it is actual. The virtual, the pressing crowd of incipiencies and tendencies, is a realm of potential . . . a lived paradox where what are normally opposites coexist, coalesce, and connect."[66] He seems to be describing feeling-thinking processes, but he places them all in the "body" in contrast to the labels in our brain—ironically retaining a mind-body dualism. He even stoops to the ancient Sophists' trick of pointing out how our object of study is a flow more than a thing, so that any description of a person's emotions is necessarily out of date. Feeling-thinking processes promise that we may be able to describe the mysteries of affect rather than simply marveling at them.

If the hard, structural theorists ignored questions about motivation—by default restricting them to material interests and political power—the soft revolution introduced a range of additional reasons that people have for protesting and engaging in politics. All sorts of personal and cultural motives engage us, many of which revolve around personal and collective identities but also extend to all sorts of additional emotions.[67]

If the soft theorists were revolutionary in their willingness to recognize emotions as a positive force in political action, in another way they were in line with the other traditions we have examined in this appendix: acknowledgement of emotions had powerful political implications. The incorporation of feminist and queer issues into politics accompanied a defense of feelings; the expression of emotion no longer disqualified one from participation. A politics of compassion, derided in the nineteenth century as a matter for women and other bleeding hearts, followed from a candid recognition of moral emotions. The feeling brain encouraged a softer politics in defense of the welfare states that had been savaged by the "hard" Thatcher-Reagan onslaught in the 1980s.

After millennia in which the majority of every population was excluded from politics because they allegedly followed their emotions, there was now a rallying claim that politicians (mostly men) who were deficient in normal human empathies were the ones incapable of ruling well. In management studies, a parallel finding emerged: the feeling brain had better people skills than the calculating brain. "Emotional intelligence" suddenly mattered.[68] Rosabeth Moss Kanter had described a "masculine ethic" that "elevates the traits assumed to belong to some men to necessities for effective management: a tough-minded approach to problems; analytic abilities to abstract and plan; a capacity to set aside personal, emotional considerations in the interests of task accomplishment; and a cognitive superiority in problem-solving and decision-making."[69] Women, in contrast, are often assumed to be more empathic listeners, better able to communicate with coworkers in ways appropriate to flexible, participatory, nonhierarchical workplaces. Whether or not men actually had less emotional intelligence to start with, many male managers now tried to master it.[70]

In the late 1990s, emotions reappeared, partly through the evolution of cultural theory and partly through the feminist and queer turn. It was a new vision of emotions, more likely to view them positively as tools that activists could use to craft arguments and actions, as positive bonds that kept groups together, as moral indignation that was a justified response to unjust situations and actions.[71]

Emotional dynamics that had been disparaged for generations could now be reevaluated. Many emotions, such as those marked by clear facial displays, are indeed contagious, but what is wrong with that? A smile of joy is as contagious as a frown of anger. Social life depends on our ability to read the emotions of others and to feel empathy for what they are experiencing. This is a central mechanism for coordinating action. Leaders can inspire wonderful, altruistic acts as well as destructive ones (as Le Bon himself acknowledged). For every Adolf Hitler there is a Winston Churchill, who stirred Great Britain to feats we now admire. Paul Hoggett complains that Freud "never quite provides us with a convincing account of forms of identification with leaders that are nonpathological, that is, founded upon ordinary admiration and respect rather than abject devotion."[72] We briefly looked at leaders in chapter 5, trying to explain these dynamics rather than judge them.

Groups, too, can inspire great action as well as providing the satisfactions of collective identity. There is no need to assume, with Hoffer, that anyone who enjoys belonging to a group must be deranged. More likely, social isolates like Hoffer are the ones who are screwed up. Any form of self-sacrifice seemed irrational to Hoffer, but social life and civilization are based on continuing sacrifices for group goals. Humans frequently adopt group identities and priorities, which often conflict with their more personal projects. Kornhauser, too, seemed to believe that collective identities based on small groups are unhealthy, compared to identities based on society's official, legal institutions, but this is a cheery view of mainstream institutions that few would accept today. To the contrary, it is the ability of smaller groups to challenge these institutions to live up to their own proclaimed standards that appears healthy for a society.

*   *   *

For centuries, *the crowd trope has expressed the fears of those in control about those they control*, especially their fears of property damage. Now that most of those frightening groups hold full citizenship rights, they seem less scary—and less emotional. The most disruptive emotions have migrated to Islamic terrorists and illegal immigrants, who can still be vilified as unworthy outsiders. Elites still use the alleged emotionality of the masses to exclude them from other forms of power. With so much to lose, elites fear everyone else. For this reason, they are subject to moral panics over threats to their economic and political positions. Ironically, their response is to attribute panic to the general public. As a result, "disaster preparation," observe Lee Clarke and Caron Chess, "means concentrating resources, keeping information close to the vest, and communication with people in soothing ways, even if the truth is disquieting."[73] In fact, generations of research into responses to disasters demonstrate that regular people help each other out, invent new ways of coping with their challenges, and commit fewer crimes, without waiting for authorities to come to their rescue.[74] Typically they cannot wait that long. It is the fears of elites that look more like panic, or at least anxiety.

During this same long span of time, protest frightened those who wrote about it. It had to be bad, so the forces driving it, such as emotions, also had to be bad. After the 1960s, as more and more observers began to see the positive side of protest, they still saw emotions as bad. The structuralists had to deny emotions to establish protest as a valid thing to study in the academy. The culturalists had to deny them to establish meaning as a valid field of study. Today, protest and meaning are respectable topics for investigation. So are emotions, thanks to the efforts of psychologists and others. So we can now incorporate emotions into the mainstream of political research as well. Emotions have both good and bad effects, they are involved in our triumphs and our regrettable mistakes—just as we would expect from such a diverse and pervasive set of feelings. They are not necessarily bad or good, just normal.

APPENDIX 2: RESEARCH TECHNIQUES

The rhythmanalyst calls on all their senses. They draw on their breathing, the circulation of their blood, the beating of their heart and the delivery of their speech as landmarks. . . . They think with their body, not in the abstract, but in lived temporality. . . . They garb themselves in the tissue of the lived, of the everyday.

HENRI LEFEBVRE

Whenever I give a talk about emotions and politics, a couple key questions always come up afterward: What methods can we use to study emotions in political settings? Aren't they hard to observe, compared to the other kinds of things we study in politics? Fortunately, the answer is easy: we can use any of the same techniques we use to study anything else. Students of emotion have used every known method of research—and invented some new ones.

Psychologists and social psychologists have largely deployed quantitative techniques, especially questionnaires and experiments, following the customs of their field. At the neurological end of psychology, subjects are hooked up to functional MRIs, along with other apparatuses and tests to gauge skin responses, brain activity, adrenaline levels, and so on. Sociologists who study emotions in politics have preferred interpretive techniques, essentially the same range as other cultural approaches to politics have used. If feeling and thinking are not so different—and I hope I have persuaded you by now—then all the techniques used to study cultural meanings can be applied to feelings.

These cultural methods bring frictions and debates. For example, one of the tensions in research on emotions involves whether to view them as inner feelings, not easily identified by observers, or as public displays not easily linked to inner states. We know what emotions an orator is displaying, but are they what she actually feels? Or is she simply a good actor? Many analysts of emotion and politics have given up on the inner states, preferring to examine emotional displays purely as rhetoric.

Debates like these echo disagreements in cultural sociology. Are cultural meanings interior states of mind, or are they external, public embodiments and claims? Until the 1970s, scholars interested in meaning turned to psychology and psychoanalysis because there were so few tools of cultural analysis, but in the 1980s, cultural pioneers legitimated their topic in Durkheimian fashion as something external and objective.[1] As Francesca Polletta put it, "Culture is not just in your head," pointing to "traditions, principles, codes, and arrangements [that] cannot easily be 'thought away' by insurgents. They are supra-individual and constrain individual action."[2] The in-your-head crowd would counter by asking how codes and so on constrain us unless they *also* find their way into our heads.

My own approach to the cultural debate was to say that meanings are both interior and exterior. We need different methods to get at the two—such as interviews and participant observation to get at the inner states, and textual analyses and other observations to get at the public ones. Then we can triangulate from these kinds of evidence. Sometimes they will line up and sometimes they will not, but we learn something important either way. We can figure out why they do not agree, in those cases when they do not. The same seems true for emotions: we need to gather evidence about interior feelings as well as exterior manifestations, and we can make a research question out of the relationships between them.

I am a methodological pluralist: we should exclude no method a priori but instead see what it can show us. For every technique, we always need to qualify and interpret the findings, in awareness of its strengths and limitations. We also need to try to improve our techniques, as we become aware of their limitations. None should be taken as the empiricist truth, but all should be mined for their empirical products.

URGES AND REFLEX EMOTIONS

Certain techniques are necessarily better for studying particular types of emotions. The methodological challenge for the short-run feelings is this: feeling-thinking processes unfold rapidly during the course of our interactions. Even the conscious labels that we call emotions combine and change in complex ways. Yet most of our research techniques interrupt that flow, or reconstruct it after it is over. Many of the most innovative techniques try to shrink that gap.

The reflex emotions are the most studied category, amenable to both physiological and observational techniques. Thanks to Paul Ekman and others, we have good lists of cues for most reflex emotions, even if they are not as definitive or exhaustive as he thought. In order to observe brief facial expressions, Ekman pioneered the use of videos of people's reactions.

More than faces, videos can also capture bodily rhythms and postures that express emotions. According to Randall Collins, cheap video cameras sparked the sociology of emotions much as portable audio recorders did ethnomethodology and conversation analysis in the 1960s.[3] Videos can be slowed down so that even fleeting expressions can be detected.

Jack Katz used videos to show how small groups employed laughter to reinforce their solidarity, and how a criminal under interrogation engaged in weeping to express meanings that he could not put into words.[4] Couples have been videotaped as they discussed problems in their relationships, obviously a topic of intense emotions.[5] Thomas Scheff and Suzanne Retzinger even analyzed tapes of *Candid Camera* in their work on expressions of shame.[6] A wealth of recordings of both public meetings and private conversations (such as presidential tapes) are rich data for recognizing the emotions that accompany face-to-face interactions.

Anne Nassauer carefully reconstructed protest marches by piecing together short segments of videos posted on YouTube. Following Collins' suggestions about the origins of violence, she calculated the microsequences that lead to violent encounters between police and protestors, as we saw in chapter 2. You can see the suspicion, anger, and frustration on the faces of both police and protestors, and count the time it takes for these encounters to ignite into violence (typically two to three hours).

Images of faces are not the only way to observe reflex emotions. We gesture, hold our bodies in certain ways, and use our tone of voice to express emotions. Video recordings typically have sound as well as visual images, and so voice analysis can be included.[7]

Participant observation is also useful for studying reflex emotions, which appear and disappear so quickly. Being there allows us to expect certain emotions, so that we can prepare to observe them. Of course, we can also be surprised. Embedded in the field, we undergo our own emotions, either by experiencing what those we study experience or by interviewing them.

Thomas Scheff provides a useful list of verbal, visual, and paralinguistic markers for anger and humiliation (or what he calls the "subordination-form" of shame), which I reproduce here (see table A.1).[8] Scheff insists that, like all human expressions (including words), the meaning of these markers is context related; some interpretation is always required. His categories point to particular feeling-thinking processes, including verbal markers. A complex emotion such as shame or anger is not going to be judged present or absent by a single feeling-thinking process; the more markers there are from each category, the stronger the evidence is for the emotion.

Before Scheff, none other than Erving Goffman listed indicators of embarrassment (for him, perhaps the central emotion) in 1956: "An individual

TABLE A.1. Thomas Scheff's Markers for Shame and Anger

	Shame	Anger and Shame-Rage
Verbal markers	*Alienated:* rejected, dumped, deserted, rebuffed, abandoned, estranged, isolated, separate, alone, disconnected, disassociated, detached, withdrawn, inhibited, distant, remote, split, divorced, polarized *Confused:* stunned, dazed, blank, empty, hollow, spaced, giddy, lost, vapid, hesitant, aloof. *Ridiculous:* foolish, silly, funny, absurd, idiotic, asinine, simple-minded, stupid, curious, weird, bizarre, odd, peculiar, strange, different. *Inadequate:* helpless, powerless, defenseless, weak, insecure, uncertain, shy, deficient, worse off, small, failed, ineffectual, inferior, unworthy, worthless, flawed, trivial, meaningless, insufficient, unsure, dependent, exposed, inadequate, incapable, vulnerable, unable, inept, unfit, impotent, oppressed. *Uncomfortable:* restless, fidgety, jittery, tense, anxious, nervous, uneasy, antsy, jumpy, hyperactive. *Hurt:* offended, upset, wounded, injured, tortured, ruined, sensitive, sore spot, buttons pushed, dejected, intimidated, defeated.	ANGER: cranky, cross, hot-tempered, ireful, quick-tempered, short-fused, enraged, fuming, agitated, furious, irritable, incensed, indignant, irate, annoyed, mad, pissed, pissed off, teed-off, upset, furious, aggravated, bothered, resentful, bitter, spiteful, grudging (the last four words imply shame-rage compounds).
Other verbal markers	Mitigation (to make appear less severe or painful); oblique, suppressed reference, e.g. "they," "it," "you"; vagueness; denial; defensiveness; verbal withdrawal (lack of response); indifference (acting "cool" in an emotionally arousing context).	ANGER: interruption; challenge; sarcasm; blame. SHAME-RAGE: temporal expansion/condensation or generalization ("You always . . ."; "You never . . ."); triangulation (bringing up an irrelevant third party or object).

(continued)

TABLE A.1. (*continued*)

	Shame	Anger and Shame-Rage
Paralinguistic markers	Vocal withdrawal/hiding behaviors, disorganization of thought: oversoft irregular rhythm; hesitation; self-interruption (censorship); filled pauses (-uh-); long pauses; silences; stammering; fragmented speech; rapid speech; condensed words; mumbling; breathiness: incoherence (lax articulation); laughed words; monotone.	ANGER: staccato (distinct breaks between successive tones); loudness; heavy stress on certain words; singsong pattern (ridicule); straining; harsh voice qualifiers. SHAME-RAGE: whine; glottalization (rasp or buzz); choking; tempo up/down; pitch up/down.
Visual markers	(1) hiding behavior: (a) the hand covering all or parts of the face; (b) gaze aversion, eyes lowered or averted. (2) blushing. (3) control: (a) turning in, biting, or licking the lips, biting the tongue; (b) forehead wrinkled vertically or transversely; (c) false smiling; or other masking behaviors.	ANGER: (1) brows lowered and drawn together, vertical lines appearing between them; (2) eyelids narrowed and tense in a hard fixed stare and maybe with bulging appearance; (3) lips pressed together, the corners straight or down or open but tense and square; (4) hard direct glaring; (5) leaning forward toward other in challenging stance; (6) clenched fists, waving fists, hitting motions.

Source: Thomas J. Scheff, *Bloody Revenge* (Westview, 1994), 151–152.

may recognize extreme embarrassment in others and even in himself by the objective signs of emotional disturbance: blushing, fumbling, stuttering, an unusually low- or high-pitched voice, quavering speech or breaking of the voice, sweating, blanching, blinking, tremor of the hand, hesitating or vacillating movement, absent-mindedness, and malapropisms."[9]

Sociologists Jody Clay-Warner and Dawn Robinson have used infrared cameras to measure facial skin temperature, based on changes in blood flow, without the need to hook people up to electrodes and wires. Researchers posit that deception increases the blood flow around the eyes, that frustration warms the forehead, and that arousal including fear cools the nose (by directing blood to surrounding areas). In general, techniques like these seem better at detecting general levels of emotional arousal than identifying specific emotional packages.[10]

Urges are rarely considered dignified enough to be studied in political contexts. There has been enormous research on addiction, since it is considered a medical issue, and some research into the effectiveness of techniques of torture, but these techniques are difficult to apply to politics.

MOODS

Because moods typically last for hours, additional techniques are open to us. At the end of a day, we can recollect many of the moods we experienced as the day unfolded, along with the events that shifted them. Interviews and daily diaries get at this time frame efficiently.

As we saw in chapter 4, happiness studies use two primary methods that seem to get at different feelings, one a moral emotion and the other a mood. Surveys ask how satisfied people are with how their life is going, which seems to me to get at a kind of moral emotion of appraisal. My life is going well, given standards that I held when young, or hold now, or which I imagine others hold. More interesting, as a technique, is to prompt people for their current mood through "experience sampling." Happiness researchers contact respondents at various points in a day, to ask how they feel and what they are doing. This seems a robust way to identify the moods that various activities arouse. Daniel Kahneman and his coauthors have ranked a number of activities in this way, ranging from "intimate relations," which unsurprisingly yield the best mood, through (in order) socializing after work, dinner, relaxing, lunch, exercising, praying, socializing at work, all the way down to working and commuting.[11]

There is no reason this kind of research could not be conducted on political activities, so that we could ascertain how marching, chanting, singing, writing letters, listening to speeches, sitting through meetings, and so on all affect moods. We can speculate that some political activities are like socializing after work, others are like exercising, and some—alas—are like working. "Happiness" may be too complex a construct to measure in a satisfactory way, but good and bad moods can be identified.[12]

Collins discusses how to measure emotional energy, which I classify as a mood. Facial expressions are not useful, as they are associated with more dramatic reflex emotions. Changes in hormones would be a useful measure, especially testosterone; the relevant comparison would be in an individual over time rather than across individuals, when baseline differences would interfere. Collins embraces Scheff's measures of pride and shame as indicators of emotional energy and attunement, adding rhythmic coordination at several different time scales, as well as "a close pattern of turn-taking with minimal gap and overlap; rhythmic entrainment in shared laughter, applause, and other simultaneous vocalizations." Finally, self-reporting can get at subtle shifts in emotional energy.[13]

AFFECTIVE LOYALTIES AND MORAL EMOTIONS

In my final two categories of emotions, with their longer time frames and more elaborated cognitive content, we can deploy a broader range of techniques. Surveys, interviews, textual analyses, and more can get at affective and moral commitments. Every conceivable technique has been used to study collective identities, as one type of affective loyalty. In cases in which we are not consciously aware of our orientations, other techniques can be deployed. Implicit attitude tests get at feelings we cannot admit to ourselves or to interviewers, notably prejudice against other groups.

Trust and indignation have been measured, to some extent, in experimental games, several of which we discussed in chapters 5 and 6. Game experiments can often get subjects to reveal their feelings, such as how much they value fairness, rather than having to ask it explicitly as in traditional surveys. It may be more accurate to speak of game *methods* than game *theories*, as experiments use games to get at feeling and thinking, in contrast to older versions that made predictions about human actions—usually normative and often unhelpful predictions.

Place loyalties have also been measured through surveys. Edward Lawler and his coauthors, for instance, examine expressed loyalty to one's neighborhood, town/city, county/province, and country (finding, by the way, a strong and continuing loyalty to one's nation above and beyond those other geographical units).[14]

Although Scheff's markers for shame apply primarily to the gut-level variety, some might also indicate the more elaborated, moral form as well. He discovers numerous instances of shame, anger, and shame-anger sequences in Adolf Hitler's *Mein Kampf* that help explain the Nazi leader's appeal to many Germans still ashamed of their defeat in World War I. He links these feelings to Hitler's biography, and he finds them as well in Hitler's speeches, in not only his words but also his gestures and stances.[15]

OBJECTIVE TECHNIQUES

Surveys have the advantage of being techniques developed across generations of social scientists, and they remain the premier tool for examining the distribution of beliefs in a population. There is little reason to think that self-reports of feelings face greater limitations than those of beliefs—although they are substantial.[16] Surveys of random samples of any population are good for tracing changes across time, but less adept at probing feelings that are difficult (or sensitive) to articulate.[17] They have been especially useful for establishing the background expectations that set the stage for our emotional reactions. Affect control and identity control theorists deploy surveys to probe the expectations about identities and actions that form a central part of our culture—the affective and moral expectations that in turn shape our reflex emotions, developing useful catalogs of assessments in many countries.[18]

The advantages of *experiments* are well known, focused on the control of key variables. They have been used to generate a variety of emotions in experimental subjects, not only through interaction with confederates and other subjects but in interaction with computers. Most evidence about emotions in behavioral economics comes from this source.[19] Two disadvantages of experimental settings are that the emotions elicited are typically mild (due in part to limitations imposed by institutional review boards) and that the interactions are with strangers (or computer-simulated strangers). Interactions with intimates, or anyone we have known a long time, can be both more intense and constrained by different norms of politeness. In other disciplines, laboratories have allowed various physiological measurements, but sociologists rarely gather these kinds of data.

Network analysis has demonstrated the importance of networks for recruitment and collective action.[20] What travels across those networks is not only information but also affective bonds such as trust and collective identities.[21] Ann Mische even suggests that we view networks as "composed of culturally constituted processes of communicative interaction," in which understandings and decisions are negotiated—which should include emotions.[22] Unfortunately, the elaborate techniques developed for mapping networks are not the most subtle for getting at those meanings and feelings.

Historical research necessarily narrows our techniques, excluding introspection, participant observation, and—for distant periods—interviews and focus groups. Yet documents and video recordings can be scanned for the expression of emotional meanings just as they regularly are for the expression of any other cultural meaning (Norbert Elias famously used etiquette books).[23] Affective and moral commitments can be expressed in this way. Reflex emotions are visible in visual records but not necessarily in textual records that have undergone editing and reductions. Most urges are less visible; moods are visible only when they are extreme. Benjamin Lamb-Books analyzed abolitionist speeches from the nineteenth century for their emotional content as well as their more cognitive arguments. He was able to find reflex emotions as well as moral and affective commitments.[24] But the reflex emotions that arise between orators and audiences do not get recorded in transcripts, except in stylized versions of angry-crowd theories.

Although I have referred to these techniques as *objective* because they were developed in a more positivist era, when their practitioners thought of them as getting at a social reality independent of our interpretations, most social scientists have changed their view of these practices, recognizing the interpretive work that goes into the construction of every sort of data, even those of natural science. But we turn now to methods that have always been explicit about the need for interpretation, and which have always had meaning as their central goal.

INTERPRETIVE TECHNIQUES

Cultural approaches to social explanation have refined many interpretive techniques meant to get at subjective meanings. Because of the overlap between thinking and feeling, the techniques of getting at the former have been readily applied to the latter.

Focus groups redress some of the drawbacks of quantitative techniques by allowing deeper probing in a group setting in which new feelings might emerge that researchers had not initially expected. Focus groups can also allow researchers to confront participants in order to observe their emotional as well as cognitive reactions, as in Alain Touraine's sociological interventions.[25] As Jenny Kitzinger and Rosaline Barbour observe, although with an overly cognitive emphasis, "Focus groups are ideal for exploring people's experiences, opinions, wishes and concerns. The method is particularly useful for allowing participants to generate their own questions, frames and concepts, and to pursue their own priorities on their own terms, in their own vocabulary."[26] They can also generate their own feelings.

Various forms of *content analysis* have looked at publicly expressed meanings and feelings, often formulating them as frames.[27] The advantage here is that the researcher need not probe subtle mental representations, only their public embodiments—although there remains some assumption of a connection between the two. For that reason, it is more useful for examining affective and moral commitments that have been well articulated and stabilized than for catching emotions on the fly. Yet content analysis is not a search for static meanings but an effort to show how people *do things* with words, including creating and displaying feelings, in interactions with each other.

The best way to get at the meanings and especially the feelings of participants remains some form of involvement, through *ethnographic* observation, direct *participation, depth interviews*—or some combination of these. The lengthy time commitment allows adjustment between hypotheses and evidence, especially in the form of interrogating activists about their feelings. Janja Lalich's detailed study of Heaven's Gate and the Democratic Workers Party, for instance, was only possible through her unique (and extensive) contact with each group.[28] Few social scientists have therapeutic training, so therapists like Lalich are uniquely positioned to probe guilt, pride, shame, sexual attractions, and some other feelings that permeate groups.

Semistructured interviews represent an effort to combine some of the representativeness of surveys with the depth of open-ended interviews.[29] Researchers can get at the feelings and understandings of participants, especially by adding some degree of context unavailable to most surveys. By carefully choosing whom to interview, researchers can probe beneath the official statements of a group—for instance, by delving into factional hostilities and solidarities. But as with surveys, the more structured the interview, the less likely it is to reveal something new to the researcher.

Mary Holmes recommends joint interviews, not merely as a way to generate surprises for the researcher but also to allow observation of how two people interact with each other and reflexively discipline their emotions as they constantly emerge. In this case, subjects have feeling-thinking sequences and apply labels to many of them, but in interaction with each other rather than in interaction with a researcher. Researchers, she says, "can observe participants taking account of each other's feelings in embodied, not just verbal ways."[30] We can jointly interview more than two people, of course, a technique that shades into focus groups and sociological interventions.

Shadowing is another method that might be useful in the study of emotions: the researcher follows subjects for some period of time to be able to observe their choices and actions up close. The researcher can also ask occasional questions, especially for emotions that are not visible in the face. Shadowing can replace participant observation when the subject performs a special role, such as a protest leader or public official, that the researcher cannot adopt. Shadowing seems especially appropriate for studying individuals in political arenas.[31]

Produced as part of participation, *field notes* are a cult object for most qualitative researchers, treated as a source of truth and authenticity. They are not usually (or ever) a straightforward recording of what happened but part of an interaction with those we study and those we write for. Researchers have developed techniques for thinking and feeling about their own notes, such as reading them in small groups of trusted colleagues or writing the notes in one column next to a column that records the researcher's interpretations and feelings.[32]

Some researchers have asked subjects to keep *diaries* of their emotions, often written at the end of each day. In diary methods, subjects must be trained to recall emotions, although this is something they learn to do just because they know they will have to write something down later. But some emotions are fairly fleeting or faint, and so they are forgotten, especially during a day of intense interactions, such as protest events or contentious meetings. It might be possible to ask for writing at more than one point in a day, keeping the emotion memories fresher. As I said earlier, this method might be especially suited to the study of moods.

One advantage is that diarists, writing privately, may vent feelings that they suppress during interpersonal engagements—including interviews and surveys. In writing, they may relive the emotions in part. Catherine Theodosius asked the nurses she studied to audiotape their diaries, finding that the spoken word allowed more immediacy. "The 'here and now' was captured through their verbal communication, their intonations, emphasis, tone of voice and speed of their words, conveying their emotion much more readily than if they had written them." Audio diaries may also require less time, allowing more frequent or more extensive entries.[33] Because she was studying nurses on shifts, she could provide format sheets to jog their memory by leading them through their rounds.

In all these interpretive methods, researchers try to get at the meanings and feelings of protestors by taking "the actors' point of view."[34] Ethnographic and similar approaches share the assumption that only through our own participation can we fully understand what protestors are going through, what they are thinking and feeling. There are two possible ways to adopt the actors' points of view. One is to sympathize with them, a natural stance for scholars who are also activists, as many are. The risk is that analyses of movements become moral cheerleading aimed at showing that their arguments are right rather than at explaining them objectively (or worse, they are opportunities to settle old scores). The other way to get inside actors' heads is simply to empathize, to understand their goals and sensibilities as well as possible, but to fit this empathy into causal models that would work whether the protestors' own arguments are right or wrong. Besides, if sympathy is necessary, it becomes harder to understand opponents, state officials, and others who help determine the outcomes of struggle, much less groups we dislike.

Perhaps the best way to get at someone's point of view is to let people tell their own story, which is what interviews and diaries are intended to do. Sometimes people publish their own stories independently of our research. I mentioned in chapter 4 a wave of memoirs that have delved into the most extreme mood, depression, but other moods are not dramatic enough for that.

MULTIPLE METHODS

Because one of our goals is to observe how particular types of emotions interact, it is useful to deploy diverse techniques that are adept with those types. Some of the most influential research on emotions has relied, not surprisingly, on multiple methods. In her work on sympathy, for instance, Candace Clark used survey data, interviews, observations, ethnographic data, and texts such as greeting cards.[35]

Arguing for multiple methods, Theodosius comments, "While it was possible to observe emotions as they were expressed spontaneously, it was not always possible to identify those that were being managed. . . . Suppressed emotions are not visible emotions."[36] Thomas Scheff would disagree with the latter statement, at least for shame and anger. But the first point, that good acting hides the fact that it is acting, suggests that inner and outer forms of evidence need not line up perfectly.

Theodosius insists that her participant observation enhanced her nurses' diaries because they often addressed her, anticipated her reactions and questions, and wanted to tell her pointed stories. Diaries, interviews, and participation are distinct forms of research interactions that can inform one another.

Although most of Jack Katz's evidence comes from videos of people interacting, he also asked his undergraduates to gather accounts of angry driving. He uses various episodes to add layers of complexity and understanding. As he says, "In qualitative research what one worries about is not how high the pile of confirming evidence can be mounted but that one will have missed a way of life, an interaction strategy, or a kind of event that the reader knows intimately."[37] I would also hope not to miss important strategies or events that the reader does *not* know intimately.

Daniel Gilbert wrote a popular book about happiness, but his methodological premises apply to emotions research more generally, suggesting that we combine more subjective and objective techniques. "The nature of subjective experience," he begins, "suggests there will never be a *happyometer*—a perfectly reliable instrument that allows an observer to measure with complete accuracy the characteristics of another person's subjective experience." But this is no reason to give up on methods altogether, he says: even a flawed tool is better than none. "Of all the flawed measures of subjective experience that we can take, the honest, real-time report of the attentive individual is the least flawed."[38] Elaborate machines for observing slight changes in brain activity, facial muscles, the autonomic nervous system, and so forth only *appear* more rigorous and scientific. We usually throw the results out if they do not correspond to what people tell us they are feeling.

Speaking of research subjects, Gilbert insists, "She may not always remember what she felt before, and she may not always be aware of what she is feeling right now. We may be puzzled by her reports, skeptical of her memory, and worried about her ability to use language as we do. But when all our hand wringing is over, we must admit that she is the *only* person who has even the *slightest* chance of describing 'the view from in here,' which is why her claims serve as the gold standard against which all other measures are measured."[39]

Gilbert's solution is the time-honored one of large samples. "No individual's report may be taken as an unimpeachable and perfectly calibrated index of his experience—not yours, not mine—but we can be confident that if we ask enough people the same question, the average answer will be a roughly accurate index of the average experience."[40] For theory testing, his solution may be unimpeachable (although we may wonder what an "average experience" of an emotion is: can you average anger, fear, and shame together?). For theory generation, however, it is hard to avoid more intensive qualitative techniques.

Multiple methods are a wise approach in general in social science, and they are probably unavoidable for examining the interplay of different types of emotions, especially that between short-run and long-run feelings.

INTROSPECTION

One technique especially suited to the study of several types of emotion at once is *introspection*, which eliminates the need for empathic imagination. Jon Elster calls it "both indispensable and insufficient."[41] Still a staple among philosophers, introspection has a terrible reputation among social scientists. In psychology, experimentalism and behaviorism thoroughly vanquished it.[42] Among scholars of social movements, it reeks of the "armchair theorizing" about crowds that prevented progress in understanding social movements for so long.

But armchair theorizing becomes introspection when those in the armchairs have participated in the processes about which they are theorizing: William Wordsworth's famous "emotions recollected in tranquility." Today, many of those who write about social movements have participated extensively in them. They use introspection to derive theories on the basis of what they believe is plausible, although they usually seek independent evidence to test them (if they want to get tenure). But since many scholars test their theories on the same movement from which they derived them, they do not always move very far from introspection.

In his discussions of practices and habitus, Bourdieu suggested that scholars who observe activities without participating in them tend to draw logical models of them that miss much of their driving force. Speaking of science, for instance, he warned, "One has to avoid reducing practices to the idea one has of them when one's only experience of them is logical."[43] Meanings must be interpreted, and outsiders must exercise empathy at the very least. Even then, they get things wrong a lot. Participation is useful because it allows introspection.

Introspection may be especially helpful for identifying new or unexpected feelings. Christian Borch sees Elias Canetti's use of it to understand crowds as a form of Andrew Abbott's lyrical sociology: Abbott's sociologist "looks at a social situation, feels its overpowering excitement and its deeply affecting human complexity, and then writes a book trying to awaken those feelings in the minds—and even more the hearts—of his readers." I'm not sure why Abbott thinks only men can do lyrical sociology, apparently, but he is right to emphasize the emotional aspect of our experience.[44] Introspective reports arouse informative empathy in others.

Aside from the handful of reflex emotions, feelings are usually difficult to discern from the outside through visual observation. Combinations and sequences of emotions are even harder for an observer to interpret correctly, but cautious inspection of our own feelings may allow us to tease them out with a fair degree of complexity. We can actively examine and interrogate ourselves to try to understand our feelings, motives, dilemmas, and so on. Margaret Archer suggests that we replace introspection (a visual metaphor that suggests a passive observer) with that of an internal conversation, which allows us to be both subject and object at the same time.[45]

When player and analyst are the same person, we can discipline our scrutiny of our mental processes, label our impulses, and trace our rationales. We can look for the dilemmas behind our choices. No method is perfect, but introspection sometimes offers access to mental processes that no other method does. We need to be explicit and systematic about it—for instance, by specifying which of our experiences and emotions we are drawing on.

Introspection can be trained and articulated, becoming "autoethnography," as we systematically observe our own feelings as we engage in various interactions. Carolyn Ellis points out the advantages for understanding the complexity and ambiguity of emotions, because they are embedded in elaborate social processes. In addition to individual introspection, she recommends interactive introspection, which "offers a cross-check on self-introspective feelings." This looks like a depth interview, but "the goal is for subjects to relive their emotion and talk about it as they experience it."[46]

One drawback of introspection is that it is limited to our own experiences. We might have difficulty comprehending what it is like to be a suicide bomber, for instance. Another drawback is that we are not always honest with ourselves—but this is even more of a problem when we interview others, who bring their own strategic goals to the interview.

Almost all our techniques are aimed at eliciting emotion labels, not uncovering the full range of feeling-thinking processes. This is the complaint of affect theorists; we do not know much about how certain bundles of these processes do or do not end up triggering conscious awareness or verbal labels for our feelings. Introspection may get us further than most social techniques, but only neurological research gets at most of the underlying feeling-thinking processes. We remain a long way from combining the two.

RESEARCHERS' EMOTIONS

Several sociologists have written about their own emotions during research, especially participatory and ethnographic research. Their emotions can be vital evidence, since the point of participation is to place yourself in the position of those you are studying so that you can feel (and think) what they do. Experiencing something is different from observing it from the outside. Participation consists not only in doing what our subjects are doing but also in doing it *with* them, typically including some contagion and more verbal forms of communication. We follow them, mimic them, but also talk to them about what they are doing and why.

There are still limits, in large part because we are unlikely to share their full set of background emotions: the affective convictions and moral commitments that shape reflex emotions and moods and sometimes even urges. Over time we may be able to develop or at least understand these background emotions, but if we shared them from the start, we would barely need to do research. We could simply write our own memoirs based on introspection.

On many occasions we have emotions that our subjects do not. At the extreme, we may be studying people who disturb or even disgust us, such as Kathleen Blee's hate groups or those who employ violence. In this case, we need to refrain from expressing our feelings for long periods. Blee also recounts that her subjects played on her fears to limit the kinds of information she could obtain, although this tactic also allowed her insight into how fear was deployed more generally in these groups.[47] Emotions are another way that we learn what is happening in our interactions with those we study.

Sherryl Kleinman and Martha Copp also suggest that we use our own emotions as fieldworkers to better understand our social settings.[48] Although much of their concern is with the distortions that arise when fieldworkers ignore their own emotions or report only positive experiences, they also recount how awareness of their own feelings helps them understand the feelings of those they study. Emotions are a core part of participant observation. Interactionist traditions are especially attuned to these kinds of embeddedness in field research.[49]

Affective commitments can arise during research, bringing subjects to trust the researcher through a common bond. Fellow protestors might assume we share their commitments just because we are at the same rally. When I surveyed participants at an antinuclear demonstration in 1984, they were enthusiastic to help. Most simply assumed that I shared their views (true enough), but the survey also said (at the end) that I would share the results with the Abalone Alliance, the day's sponsor. While many researchers have worked hard to establish bonds of trust like these, others have criticized the same practice as exploitative, although this seems truer of research into personal lives than research into political ideologies and participation.[50]

LIMITATIONS

We would love to have prospective research that takes the measure of individuals at some point in time and then watches them interact with others to see how they react and change. Outside the lab, which has its own artificialities, it is difficult to conduct prospective longitudinal research on political action, although a researcher could conceivably interview new recruits to an organization and then follow them through a number of months or years of engagement.[51] Introspection is a kind of substitute for all this.

Another challenge is the depth of information we would like to have about individuals as they engage others. The ideal would be almost constant surveillance to get at their reflexes, urges, and moods in both private and public settings, combined with a catalog of their background commitments. But since much politics occurs in public settings, we can indeed videotape considerable action, from group meetings to large demonstrations—even piecing together long segments from snippets on the Internet, as Anne Nassauer did. Clark McPhail has coded vocalizations such as oohs, ahhs, and laughs, singing, chanting, gesturing, and so forth: many of these actions could be coded as emotional expressions.[52] Close-ups of faces are not the only available evidence of emotional displays.

But it is difficult to link these external observations with internal thoughts and feelings. Richard Lazarus perceives progress toward this kind of longitudinal, prospective, day-to-day, and in-depth research in the field of stress and coping, but we are far from it in the field of politics and protest.[53] Multiple methods and introspection will help.

Finally, we must be careful not to reify all feeling-thinking processes into a short list of emotions with well-known labels. We must remember that this labeling is one process among others, but once we identify "an emotion" and give it a name—for instance, in our field notes—we tend to use it as a solid thing. This is why good field researchers continuously revisit and reinterpret their own notes, why we use introspection to try to get beneath these labels. The most important method is to constantly reflect on our own methods, to be aware of what they can and cannot tell us, to combine techniques to fill gaps, and to strive constantly to improve all our methods of research. Emotions are as real as anything social scientists study, and once we start looking for them, they show up in all our research techniques.

NOTES

INTRODUCTION

1. I have developed this strategic approach in articles and the book *Getting Your Way* (University of Chicago Press, 2006), in the edited volumes James M. Jasper and Jan William Duyvendak, *Players and Arenas* (Amsterdam University Press, 2015) and Jan William Duyvendak and James M. Jasper, *Breaking Down the State* (Amsterdam University Press, 2015), and in a forthcoming coauthored book on the impacts of social movements, James M. Jasper, Luke Elliott-Negri, Isaac Jabola-Carolus, Marc Kagan, Jessica Mahlbacher, Manès Weisskircher, and Anna Zhelnina, *Gains and Losses*.

2. My debt to symbolic interactionist theories of emotions should be clear, and this is the dominant approach in sociology. Tim Hallett ably summarizes this view in "Emotional Feedback and Amplification in Social Interaction," *Sociological Quarterly* 44 (2003):705–726.

3. Kristen A. Lindquist, "Emotions Emerge from More Basic Psychological Ingredients: A Modern Psychological Constructionist Model," *Emotion Review* 5 (2013): 359.

4. Lisa Feldman Barrett, *How Emotions Are Made* (Houghton Mifflin Harcourt, 2017), 141.

5. Martha C. Nussbaum, *Upheavals of Thought: The Intelligence of Emotions* (Cambridge University Press, 2001), 23, 30.

6. Antonio Damasio, *Looking for Spinoza: Joy, Sorrow, and the Feeling Brain* (Houghton Mifflin Harcourt, 2003), 54.

7. Jonathan Haidt, *The Righteous Mind* (Random House, 2012).

8. It is beyond my expertise to trace the debates over the rationality of voters, but it seems to triangulate between affective commitments to parties, economic interests, and—more recently—a variety of emotional processes that focus attention, filter information, lead us to stereotypes, draw us to some candidates and not others, and the like.

9. Throughout our journey we will see women who have led the study of emotion, such as Magda B. Arnold, who created appraisal theories of emotions with *Emotion and Personality* (Columbia University Press, 1960), Arlie Hochschild in sociology, and psychologist Lisa Feldman Barrett (e.g., see n. 4); see appendix 1 for other gender links. Gerd Gigerenzer traces the history of the calculating-brain image in the second half of the twentieth century in *Adaptive Thinking: Rationality in the Real World* (Oxford University Press, 2000), chap. 2. For an early challenge from within cognitive psychology, see Ulric Neisser, "Memory: What Are the Important Questions?" in *Memory Observed*, ed. Ulric Neisser (W. H. Freeman, 1982).

10. As an undergraduate in one of Ellen Langer's courses, I participated in several of those experiments. "Mindless" autopilot is useful when doing math problems, but at other times it can be a hindrance, as when we stereotype strangers (although this too may be useful in some circumstances. See Langer's *Mindfulness* (Perseus Press, 1989).

11. Roger Giner-Sorolla writes about the conflicts between these emotional functions (which he derives from evolution) in *Judging Passions: Moral Emotions in Persons and Groups* (Psychology Press, 2012). His four functions (p. 4): "Emotions can help us appraise new developments in the world; learn about the world in a rapid, associative way; regulate our own behaviors; and communicate our sincere intentions to others."

12. In *Getting Your Way* I use the terms *compound players* and *simple players*. They operate differently, not least because compound players are always composed of simple players, who have different degrees of identification with and loyalty to the compound player.

13. Among his many contributions, Pierre Bourdieu tried to show how humans innovate within social rules. But in the habitus, our dispositions are closely tied to the structured social settings of our past. The potential for innovation comes primarily from the clash between past and present situations. Despite its gaps as a theory of action, his theory of dispositions can help us understand why certain groups seem primed for certain emotions compared to other groups that were socialized differently. It would not be far off to understand the habitus as a configuration of feeling-thinking processes—which highlights the way that Aristotle and Norbert Elias used the term.

14. Martin cites the urge of hunger, as something inside us, sensitizing us to properties in objects that we might eat. "Thus, both the self and the object must be placed in some sort of social, as opposed to psychological, field." Had he taken emotions seriously, he would have found any number of mechanisms for these interactions, compatible with the first-person point of view that he values. John Levi Martin, *The Explanation of Social Action* (Oxford University Press, 2011), 247.

15. Barrett also chides social constructionists for ignoring biology, preventing us from seeing how our "perceptions, thoughts, and feelings are themselves constructed from more basic parts." (*How Emotions Are Made*, 33).

16. Jon Elster has consistently insisted, "The theory of rational choice is first of all normative, and only secondarily explanatory." *Reason and Rationality* (Princeton University Press, 2009), 14.

17. Elster wrote two important books on emotions. I especially draw on *Strong Feelings* (MIT Press, 1999) in my chapter 3 and on *Alchemies of the Mind: Rationality and the Emotions* (Cambridge University Press, 1999) in my chapter 6.

18. I hope I can justify skirting some of the issues of cultural meaning and interpretation by referring the reader to James M. Jasper, *The Art of Moral Protest: Culture, Biography, and Creativity in Social Movements* (University of Chicago Press, 1997).

CHAPTER ONE

1. Kristen Renwick Monroe, *The Hand of Compassion: Portraits of Moral Choice during the Holocaust* (Princeton, 2004), 112, 259. Although she contrasts character and calculation here, her work suggests the kind of feeling-thinking processes that underlie both.

2. Acknowledgement of the full range of feeling-thinking processes promises to resolve a number of debates over emotions. Robert Zajonc famously argued that emotions operate faster than thoughts, leading him to criticize cognitive appraisal theories

of emotions: "Feeling and Thinking: Preferences Need No Inferences," *American Psychologist* 35 (1980):151-175. But most cognitive appraisal theorists recognize that appraisal can be intuitive and preconscious. Once we see the many components of both feeling and thinking, we no longer need to contrast them as Zajonc does in seeing them as independent systems. Colin Barker speaks of emotions as adverbs rather than nouns, in an effort, similar to affect theory's, to avoid reifying emotion labels: "Fear, Laughter, and Collective Power," in *Passionate Politics: Emotions and Social Movements*, ed. Jeff Goodwin, James M. Jasper, and Francesca Polletta (University of Chicago Press, 2001). Once we recognize the emotion labels as one kind of feeling-thinking process among others, all of which are registering and appraising our situation, and which permeate our brains and bodies, these objections no longer hold.

3. Lisa Feldman Barrett and Peter Salovey, eds., *The Wisdom of Feeling* (Guilford, 2001). Barrett further integrates thinking and feeling in "The Future of Psychology: Connecting Mind to Brain," *Perspectives on Psychological Science* 4 (2009): 326-339; Seth Duncan and Lisa F. Barrett, "Affect Is a Form of Cognition: A Neurobiological Analysis," *Cognition & Emotion* 21 (2007): 1184-1211; and Kristen A. Lindquist, Tor D. Wager, Hedy Kober, Eliza Bliss-Moreau, and Lisa F. Barrett, "The Brain Basis of Emotion: A Meta-Analytic Review," *Behavioral and Brain Sciences* 35 (2012): 121-143. Barrett summarizes her theory and research in a recent trade book, *How Emotions Are Made* (see intro., n. 4).

4. Gerd Gigerenzer, *Gut Feelings: The Intelligence of the Unconscious* (Penguin, 2007), 19. See also Malcolm Gladwell, *Blink: The Power of Thinking without Thinking* (Little, Brown, 2005).

5. Daniel Kahneman and Amos Tversky, "On the Reality of Cognitive Illusions," *Psychological Review* 103 (1996): 582-91.

6. Daniel Kahneman, *Thinking, Fast and Slow* (Farrar, Straus and Giroux, 2011), 79. David G. Myers takes a balanced view in *Intuition: Its Powers and Perils* (Yale University Press, 2002). The powers and perils of feeling-thinking processes don't matter to us nearly as much as their ability to explain human action. Gigerenzer criticizes Kahneman in *Adaptive Thinking*, chap. 12 (see intro., n. 9).

7. Gigerenzer amusingly complains, "Given the message that ordinary citizens are unable to estimate uncertainties and risks, one might conclude that a government would be well advised to keep these nitwits out of important decisions regarding new technologies and environmental risks": *Adaptive Thinking*, 237. One might, except for all the research showing that experts are subject to many of the same biases.

8. Antonio Damasio, *Descartes' Error: Emotion, Reason, and the Human Brain* (Putnam, 1994), xix. To be precise, as Damasio points out, our minds are not responding directly to the physical and social world, but to feeling-thinking signals that are filtered through our bodies. Theories of "implicit cognition" have demonstrated all sorts of fast thinking, which have been used for example to develop "implicit attitude" research to take advantage of differences between our explicit and implicit attitudes: Bertram Gawronski, Wilhelm Hofmann, and Christopher J. Wilbur, "Are 'Implicit' Attitudes Unconscious?" *Consciousness & Cognition* 15 (2006):485-499.

9. Robert C. Solomon, *The Passions*, 2nd ed., with new preface (Hackett, 1993), ix, 126.

10. Much of the criticism of the cognitive approach perpetuates a mind-body dualism, finding that emotions emerge without or before we become aware of them. Philosopher Jesse Prinz portrays the cognitive theorist as saying, "Fear arises when, and only when, this cognitive appraisal is added to our experience of the somatic

response": *The Emotional Construction of Morals* (Oxford University Press, 2007), 58. In his alternative, an "embodied appraisal approach," "emotions represent concerns, such as losses, dangers, and offenses" (65). This approach seems to retain an overly strong distinction between conscious and unconscious processes, especially if we think of appraisals as one type of feeling-thinking process interacting continually with others: it makes no sense to speak of one as coming first. In *Upheavals of Thought* (see intro., n. 5), Nussbaum cautions that she means by "cognitive" nothing more than "concerned with receiving and processing information." She does not "mean to imply the presence of elaborate calculation, of computation, or even of reflexive self-awareness" (23). She is reluctant to include nonconscious emotions, largely because they invalidate experience as the primary source of information about emotions. "This would be a problem," she reflects, "if the nonconscious cases were central or ubiquitous; and it would also be a problem if, even though not central, they were such that people could rarely be brought to acknowledge their presence and the role they play in their own experience" (71). This is the reason that Freudian approaches see irrationality in emotions: there is no way to get at them, or rather, normal people need experts to tell them what they are "really" feeling. Prinz seems to ignore our many feeling-thinking processes in favor of only one of them, our verbal, conscious labeling. For him, it counts against cognitive appraisal theory that many of our feelings take place outside the prefrontal cortex. But in the end, his view is similar to mine: "Each emotion is both an internal body monitor and a detector of dangers, threats, losses, or other matters of concern. Emotions are gut reactions; they use our bodies to tell us how we are faring in the world": Jesse Prinz, *Gut Reactions: A Perceptual Theory of Emotions* (Oxford University Press, 2004), 69.

11. Nussbaum, *Upheavals of Thought*, 2, 3.

12. *Upheavals of Thought*, 4. For her refutation of the view of emotions as non-reasoning eruptions of the body, the reader should consult pages 24-33, especially as I do not recapitulate the full argument here. The key is to see living bodies as "capable of intelligence and intentionality" (25).

13. Nussbaum, *Upheavals of Thought*, 65.

14. Nussbaum, *Upheavals of Thought*, 70.

15. According to Leonard Mlodinow, another aficionado of the unconscious: *Subliminal: How Your Unconscious Mind Rules Your Behavior* (Pantheon, 2012), 33.

16. Frans de Waal, *Are We Smart Enough to Know How Smart Animals Are?* (W. W. Norton, 2016).

17. Nussbaum dislikes talk of the appropriateness of emotions (*Upheavals of Thought*, 47), but she is discussing right or wrong emotions about values, which she thinks "appropriateness talk" confuses. But it seems useful for understanding social interactions, where clearly we can have appropriate or inappropriate emotions, governed by "feeling rules" and display rules: Arlie R. Hochschild, "Emotion Work, Feeling Rules, and Social Structure," *American Journal of Sociology* 85 (1979): 551-75.

18. Nussbaum, *Upheavals of Thought*, 58, 61.

19. In an important summary, Agnes Moors, Phoebe C. Ellsworth, Klaus R. Scherer, and Nico H. Frijda speak of the various components of emotions: appraisal, motivation, somatic and motor components, and subjective feeling, commenting that "the emotion process is continuous and recursive. Changes in one component feed back to other components": "Appraisal Theories of Emotion: State of the Art and Future Development," *Emotion Review* 5 (2013): 120.

20. Barrett, *How Emotions Are Made*, 86, 104.

21. Matthew Ratcliffe similarly calls for abandoning the distinction between cognition and affect in *Feelings of Being: Phenomenology, Psychiatry, and the Sense of Reality* (Oxford University Press, 2008).

22. The relationship between our social categories of "race" and the underlying clusters of genetic material may be parallel to the relationship between our emotion labels and the underlying feeling-thinking clusters. In both cases, there is no one-to-one correspondence, and we can see all the cultural work that goes into the labels without denying that there are small biological bits that lend them plausibility. As four students of race put it, we can "accept the existence of genetic clusters consistent with certain racial classifications as well as the validity of the genomic research that has identified the clusters, without diminishing the social character of their context, meaning, production, or consequences": Jiannbin Lee Shiao, Thomas Bode, Amber Beyer, and Daniel Selvig, "The Genomic Challenge to the Social Construction of Race," *Sociological Theory* 30 (2012): 67.

23. Maurice Merleau-Ponty, *The Structure of Behavior* (Beacon Press, 1963).

24. Merleau-Ponty, *Phenomenology of Perception* (Routledge, 1962), 108. In contrast to Martin Heidegger, Merleau-Ponty does not see bodies as an object like other, external objects in the physical world, for they are our vehicle for perceiving and dealing with those other objects. The world "is not what I think, but what I live through. I am open to the world, I have no doubt that I am in communication with it, but I do not possess it; it is inexhaustible" (xvi–xvii). This seems a plausible step toward feeling-thinking as the result of constant interactions between our nervous systems and our worlds (including our bodies), a process that only occasionally results in conscious awareness. What seems wrong is Merleau-Ponty's insistence that our bodies cannot be objects of these processes *as well as* their vehicles: Maximilian de Gaynesford, "Being at Home: Human Beings and Human Bodies," in *Oxford Handbook of Continental Philosophy*, ed. Brian Leiter and Michael Rosen (Oxford University Press, 2010), 545ff.

25. Merleau-Ponty, *Phenomenology of Perception*, 167.

26. Bourdieu adopted "habitus" to cover a range of dispositions, many of them embodied beneath consciousness. Many phenomenological sociologists approach the same processes but do a better job of recognizing how we learn through our bodies, as we'll see. This is not the occasion for a critique of the concept of habitus, but etymologically it has medieval and Aristotelian resonances of expressing the "essence" of an organism, rather than a learning, changing creature that nonetheless carries traces of its past with it. Bourdieu's use of the term reflects his lingering structuralism.

27. In his concern to reject phenomenology, Michel Foucault notoriously ignored most of the intention behind the great disciplinary practices he described, which came to include not only the physical ordering of individuals but their psychic ordering as well. Foucault devoted much of his life to showing how new "subject positions" emerged in the modern world. But as historically positioned and strategically constructed as those subjects might be, they are real. Once constituted, they act like subjects.

28. For an elaboration of Merleau-Ponty, especially showing how our embodied selves contain past action sedimented within us, see Mustafa Emirbayer and Ann Mische, "What Is Agency?" *American Journal of Sociology* 103 (1998): 962–1023.

29. Taylor Carman, *Merleau-Ponty* (Routledge, 2008), 80.

30. Jack Katz, *How Emotions Work* (University of Chicago Press, 1999).

31. Jack Katz, *How Emotions Work*, 237.

32. Jack Katz, *How Emotions Work*, 273, 315, 90.

33. Quoted in Eduardo Romanos, "The Strategic Use of Humor in the Spanish Indig-
nados/15M Movement" (paper presented at the Politics and Protest Workshop, CUNY
Graduate Center, New York, October 4, 2012).

34. David Sudnow, *Ways of the Hand: The Organization of Improvised Conduct* (Harvard University Press, 1978), 152.

35. Paul D. MacLean, *The Triune Brain in Evolution* (Springer, 1990).

36. Damasio, *Looking for Spinoza*, 76 (see intro., n. 6).

37. Just as they had once hoped to link emotions to parts of the brain, neurologists
still tend to downplay the fiendish complexity of the biochemistry of the brain and
body. So they started to speak of "dopamine circuits" and other chemical circuits. It
turned out that each of these so-called circuits involved many pathways in multiple
parts of the brain. Their reaction was to admit this, but to speak of certain pathways as
"primary" because they occur in the amygdala. Old images die hard.

38. Damasio, *Looking for Spinoza*, 63. Among the feeling-thinking processes are
changes in the temperature of various parts of the face, a fact exploited recently by
sociologists: Dawn T. Robinson, Jody Clay-Warner, Christopher D. Moore, Tiffani Everett, Alexander Watts, Traci Tucker, and Chi Thai, "Toward an Unobtrusive Measure
of Emotion during Interaction: Thermal Imaging Techniques," *Biosociology and Neuro-
sociology* 29 (2012): 225-266.

39. Damasio, *Looking for Spinoza*, 199.

40. As part of the move away from structural neurology, there is an emphasis today
on the brain's plasticity. If one part is damaged, other parts can take over many of the
same functions: Oliver Sacks, *The Mind's Eye* (Knopf, 2010).

41. Gerald L. Clore and Andrew Ortony, "Appraisal Theories: How Cognition Shapes
Affect into Emotion," in *Handbook of Emotions*, 3rd ed., ed. Michael Lewis, Jeannette M.
Haviland-Jones, and Lisa Feldman Barrett (Guilford Press, 2008), 634-35.

42. Elisabeth Norman and Bjarte Furnes, "The Concept of 'Metaemotion': What Is
There to Learn from Research on Metacognition?" *Emotion Review* 8 (2016): 187-193.

43. Matthew Ratcliffe, "The Phenomenology of Mood and the Meaning of Life,"
in *The Oxford Handbook of Philosophy of Emotion*, ed. Peter Goldie (Oxford University
Press, 2009), 363.

44. Lisa Feldman Barrett, "Solving the Emotion Paradox: Categorization and the
Experience of Emotion," *Personality and Social Psychology Review* 10 (2006): 20. She
observes that some "cognitive appraisal" theories also assume that, after we have recognized the triggers, our emotional appraisals launch us into an unvarying package of
behaviors. See also Lisa Feldman Barrett, "Are Emotions Natural Kinds?" *Perspectives
on Psychological Science* 1 (2006): 28-58. John Sabini and Maury Silver also argue that
there is no one-to-one correspondence between emotions and our labels for them, with
the latter especially affected by our understanding of the situation we are in: "Why
Emotion Names and Experiences Don't Neatly Pair," *Psychological Inquiry* 16 (2005):
1-10. The same intuition, that our verbal labels barely skim the surface of all that we
feel, animates many discussions of "affect" in queer theory and related endeavors, such
as Brian Massumi, *Parables for the Virtual: Movement, Affect, Sensation* (Duke University
Press, 2002), Patricia Clough, ed., *The Affective Turn* (Duke University Press, 2007);
and Nigel Thrift, *Non-Representational Theory: Space Politics, Affect* (Routledge, 2007).

45. Barrett, "Solving the Emotion Paradox," 23.

46. Barrett, "Are Emotions Natural Kinds?" 48, 49. Andrea Scarantino agrees that
our standard emotion terms are not natural kinds but suggests that we continue search-

ing for natural kinds "at both lower and higher levels of analysis": "How to Define Emotions Scientifically," *Emotion Review* 4 (2012): 364. Feeling-thinking processes seem a good candidate, as the building blocks of emotions.

47. For a longer version of this section, see "The Old Dualisms: Are Emotions Irrational?" posted on my academia.edu website under "Draft Papers."

48. Although he does not use the term, Bruno Latour observes that the common-humanity test was forced on sociologists when they began to study natural scientists, whose rationality could not be easily dismissed. Previously, "even when they were tycoons, artistic geniuses, movie stars, boxing champions, or statesmen, sociologists' informants were always branded by the stigma of being less rational, less objective, less reflexive, less scientific, or less academic than those doing the studying." Bruno Latour, *Reassembling the Social: An Introduction to Actor-Network-Theory* (Oxford University Press, 2005), 97.

49. In research on a parallel occupation, Julia Wrigley and Joanna Dreby found that, compared to casual, family-run operations or caregivers who come to the child's home, professionalized, bureaucratic day care centers reduce the rates of violent injury by weeding out those likely to lose their temper with children: "Violent Fatalities in Child Care," *Contexts* 5 (2006): 35–40.

50. Narrative theorists have shown all the arbitrary choices that go into constructing the beginnings and ends of stories. Game theory depends on games' having ends, when all the benefits can be tallied up. Both stories and games are inadequate metaphors for the long, never-ending series of actions and reactions that make up politics—and life. On the profound implications of this for theories of movement "outcomes" see Jasper et al., *Gains and Losses* (forthcoming).

51. For a discussion and comparison with other typologies, please see my brief working paper: James M. Jasper, "Five Types of Feelings: Notes on a Typology": https://www.academia.edu/26059900/Five_Types_of_Feelings_Notes_on_a_Typology. It is closest to Paul Griffiths's typology in *What Emotions Really Are* (University of Chicago Press, 1997), but I tweaked it for political explanations by distinguishing moral and affective convictions.

52. David Hume, *A Treatise of Human Nature* (1739–1740; repr., Penguin, 1969), bk. 2, pt. 3, sec. 3, p. 462. John Rawls has an excellent discussion of these and others of Hume's emotion distinctions in *Lectures on the History of Moral Philosophy*, ed. Barbara Herman (Harvard University Press, 2000), chap. 1.

CHAPTER TWO

1. Griffiths, *What Emotions Really Are* (see chap. 1, n. 51).

2. Lynn Owens, *Cracking under Pressure: Narrating the Decline of the Amsterdam Squatters' Movement* (Amsterdam, 2009), 77. Sue Wilkinson and Celia Kitzinger take an interactive approach to surprise, showing how it can be constructed during conversation: prepared for, referred back to, as well as expressed suddenly and directly. Narratives, too, set us up to be surprised, a major pleasure in reading or listening to them. See Sue Wilkinson and Celia Kitzinger, "Surprise as an Interactional Achievement: Reaction Tokens in Conversation," *Social Psychology Quarterly* 69 (2006):150–182.

3. Among many other works, see Paul Ekman, "Universals and Cultural Differences in Facial Expression of Emotion," in *Nebraska Symposium on Motivation* 19, ed. James K. Cole (University of Nebraska Press, 1972), and *Emotions Revealed: Recognizing Faces and Feelings to Improve Communication and Emotional Life* (Times Books, 2003); also Paul

Ekman, Wallace V. Freisen, and Phoebe Ellsworth, eds., *Emotion in the Human Face*, 2nd ed. (Cambridge University Press, 1982).

4. Paul Ekman and Wallace V. Friesen, "A New Pan-Cultural Facial Expression of Emotion," *Motivation and Emotions* 10 (1986): 159–168. Ekman was inspired by Charles Darwin, whose book *The Expression of the Emotions in Man and Animals* (published in 1872 and reissued two hundred years after Darwin's birth in a commemorative edition edited by Ekman) demonstrates parallels between the emotions of humans and of other species. Darwin's list is similar to Ekman's, except Darwin also thought he could distinguish happiness from joy. Darwin saw facial expressions as part of a broad, coordinated action response: the open mouth and wrinkled nose of disgust, for instance, are part of a vomiting response. The evolutionary contribution of facial expressions is to help us coordinate social interaction by providing information and eliciting action from others, ranging from mutual protection to mating. For such interaction to happen, expressions should be easily interpreted by others. Many mammals, according to Darwin, have similar reflex emotions. It was characteristic of this tradition to try to link the programs with evolutionarily distinct parts of the brain, an effort that has begun to unravel. See Charles Darwin, *The Expression of the Emotions in Man and Animals*, ed. Paul Ekman (Oxford University Press, 2009).

5. Ekman, "Universals and Cultural Differences."

6. For a nice summary, see David Matsumoto, Dacher Keltner, Michelle N. Shiota, Maureen O'Sullivan, and Mark Frank, "Facial Expressions of Emotion," in Lewis, Haviland-Jones, and Barrett, *Handbook of Emotions* (see chap. 1, n. 41).

7. Paul Ekman and his coauthors debunk experiments aimed to show that contextual information is more important or at least always adds something to facial information. Yet as they admit, "People rarely see a face alone without any context; when they do they usually make no inference about emotion." Paul Ekman, Wallace V. Friesen, and Phoebe Ellsworth, "What Are the Relative Contributions of Facial Behavior and Contextual Information to the Judgment of Emotion?" in Ekman, Friesen, and Ellsworth, *Emotion in the Human Face*, 135.

8. For the evidence against affect program theory, see Barrett, *How Emotions Are Made*, chap. 3 (see intro., n. 4); and the special issue of *Emotion Review* 5, no. 1 (2013).

9. Norman and Furnes, "Concept of 'Metaemotion'" (see chap. 1, n. 42).

10. The most prominent researcher in this field is Klaus Scherer: "Vocal Affect Expression: A Review and Model for Future Research," *Psychological Bulletin* 99 (1986): 143–165; and "Vocal Communication of Emotion: A Review of Research Paradigms," *Speech Communication* 40 (2003): 227–256. See also Casey A. Klofstad, "Candidate Voice Pitch Influences Election Outcomes," *Political Psychology* 37 (2016): 725–738.

11. Damasio, *Descartes' Error* (see chap. 1, n. 8).

12. Thucydides, *History of the Peloponnesian War*, trans. Rex Warner (Penguin Classics, 1972); William Desmond, "Lessons of Fear: A Reading of Thucydides," *Classical Philology* 101 (2006): 359–379.

13. Matthew Ratcliffe, "Phenomenology of Mood," 367 (see chap. 1, n. 42).

14. Desmond, "Lessons of Fear," 361.

15. Some researchers reject the term *panic* as a holdover from the days of pejorative crowd theory. It is typically used by elites in describing the masses, even though in most cases it is elites themselves who are panicking (if we can even use that word). See Lee Clarke and Caron Chess, "Elites and Panic: More to Fear than Fear Itself," *Social Forces* 87 (2008): 993–1014.

16. Jeff Goodwin and Steven Pfaff, "Emotion Work in High Risk Social Movements: Managing Fear in the U.S. and East German Civil Rights Movements," in Goodwin, Jasper, and Polletta, *Passionate Politics*. William Ian Miller reports on fear management in combat, including magical thinking, self-deception, bunching together with other soldiers, and the solidarity of small fighting units which are parallel to affinity groups: *The Mystery of Courage* (Harvard University Press, 2000), 214ff.

17. David L. Altheide, *Creating Fear: News and the Construction of Crisis* (Aldine de Gruyter, 2002), 14–15.

18. George E. Marcus, *The Sentimental Citizen: Emotion in Democratic Politics* (Penn State Press, 2002); George E. Marcus, W. Russell Neuman, and Michael MacKuen, *Affective Intelligence and Political Judgment* (University of Chicago Press, 2000); W. Russell Neuman, George E. Marcus, Ann N. Crigler, and Michael MacKuen, eds., *The Affect Effect: Dynamics of Emotion in Political Thinking and Behavior* (University of Chicago Press, 2007). There is some evidence that anxiety increases our attention in the short run but decreases it in the longer run, after we identify its source and try to avoid it: Violet Cheung-Blunden and Jiarun Ju, "Anxiety as a Barrier to Information Processing in the Event of a Cyberattack," *Political Psychology* 37 (2016): 387–400.

19. Barry Glassner, *The Culture of Fear: Why Americans Are Afraid of the Wrong Things* (Basic Books, 2000).

20. Anthony Giddens, *Modernity and Self-Identity* (Stanford University Press, 1991); *The Consequences of Modernity* (Stanford University Press, 1991).

21. Frank Furedi, *Culture of Fear: Risk-Taking and the Morality of Low Expectation* (Cassell, 1997), 52.

22. Philip Jenkins, *Intimate Enemies: Moral Panics in Contemporary Great Britain* (Aldine de Gruyter, 1992).

23. Hulda Thórisdóttir and John T. Jost, "Motivated Closed-Mindedness Mediates the Effect of Threat on Political Conservatism," *Political Psychology* 32 (2011): 785–811. They suspect the role of anxiety, even though they did not measure it directly.

24. Charles E. Osgood, George J. Suci, and Percy H. Tannenbaum, *The Measurement of Meaning* (University of Illinois Press, 1957). See also Lynn Smith-Lovin, "Behavior Settings and Impressions Formed from Social Scenarios," *Social Psychology Quarterly* 42 (1979): 31–43; David R. Heise, *Understanding Events: Affect and the Construction of Social Action* (Cambridge University Press, 1979); David R. Heise, *Expressive Order: Confirming Sentiments in Social Actions* (Springer, 2007); and Neil J. MacKinnon and David R. Heise, *Self, Identity, and Social Institutions* (Palgrave Macmillan, 2010).

25. Klaus R. Scherer, "On the Nature and Function of Emotion: A Component Appraisal Process Approach," in *Approaches to Emotion*, ed. Klaus R. Scherer and Paul Ekman (Erlbaum, 1984); and Klaus R. Scherer, "Appraisal Considered as a Process of Multilevel Sequential Processing," in *Appraisal Processes in Emotion: Theory, Methods, Research*, ed. Klaus R. Scherer, Angela Schorr, and Tom Johnstone (Oxford University Press, 2001).

26. Zoltán Kövecses, *Metaphor and Emotion: Language, Culture, and Body in Human Feeling* (Cambridge University Press, 2000), 23. His interest is in showing that we apply the same kinds of metaphors to emotions that we use in understanding our thoughts and actions. In our language for emotion, we tend to be the passive object of other forces, whereas our language for thought tells us that we are the actor (the mind is a "workshop" where we "work on" problems). In other words, the calculating-brain and panic models are still widespread as folk theories.

27. A number of writers have recognized the salience of anger in politics: see the special issue of the *European Journal of Social Theory* 7 (2004); Simon Thompson, "Anger and the Struggle for Justice," in *Emotion, Politics and Society*, ed. Simon Clarke, Paul Hoggett, and Simon Thompson (Palgrave Macmillan, 2006); and James M. Jasper, "Constructing Indignation: Anger Dynamics in Protest Movements," *Emotion Review* 6 (2014): 208-13. On the energizing force of anger, Nicholas A. Valentino, Ted Brader, Eric W. Groenendyk, Krysha Gregorowicz, and Vincent L. Hutchings find anger to motivate participation (voting) more than anxiety or enthusiasm do: "Election Night's Alright for Fighting: The Role of Emotions in Political Participation," *Journal of Politics* 73 (2011): 156-170.

28. Martha C. Nussbaum, *The Therapy of Desire: Theory and Practice in Hellenistic Ethics* (Princeton University Press, 1994), 404.

29. Nussbaum too speaks of the "doubleness of anger." On the one hand, anger is connected to brutality, to a delight in vengeance for its own sake, and often to hatred, as we distance ourselves from the humanity of those we wish to see suffer. "And this ferocity is, in turn, a diminution of one's own humanity." The Stoics made this point with great eloquence. And yet, "*not* to get angry when horrible things take place seems itself to be a diminution of one's humanity." So the Stoics *did* recognize indignation. See Nussbaum, *Therapy of Desire*, 403. The most thorough discussion of Greek and Latin anger is Harris, who also suggests that there are as many terms for fear as for anger: William V. Harris, *Restraining Rage: The Ideology of Anger Control in Classical Antiquity* (Harvard University Press, 2001), 55n27.

30. Nussbaum, *Therapy of Desire*, 423.

31. Jasper, *Getting Your Way*, 149ff (see intro., n. 1).

32. Harris, *Restraining Rage*, 58-59.

33. Leonard Berkowitz, "The Frustration-Aggression Hypothesis," in *The War System: An Interdisciplinary Approach*, ed. Richard A. Falk and Samuel S. Kim (Westview, 1980), 122. The cultural shaping of the triggers and displays of anger distinguish Berkowitz from Freudian theories of an innate aggressive drive but also from Dollard's overly tight link between frustration and aggression.

34. Randall Collins, *Interaction Ritual Chains* (Princeton University Press, 2004), 126, 127.

35. Kövecses, *Metaphor and Emotion*, 21. The ancient Greeks also used metaphors of fire and boiling liquids most often to describe anger, according to Harris, *Restraining Rage*, 68.

36. Charles Forceville, "Visual Representations of the Idealized Cognitive Model of Anger in the Asterix album *La Zizanie*," *Journal of Pragmatics* 37 (2005): 69-88. Forceville adopts the term "pictorial rune" from John M. Kennedy, "Metaphor in Pictures," *Perception* 11 (1982): 589-605.

37. On perceptions of inequity in families, see Mary Clare Lennon and Sarah Rosenfield, "Relative Fairness and the Division of Housework," *American Journal of Sociology* 100 (1994): 506-531; and Kathryn J. Lively, Brian Powell, and Claudia Geist, "Inequity among Intimates," in *Advances in Group Processes*, ed. Karen Hegtvedt and Jody Clay Warner (Elsevier, 2008).

38. Harris takes this as a contrast between shame cultures and guilt cultures, saying that injustice replaced slight as the primary trigger for anger in the Roman (and early Christian) period: *Restraining Rage*, 61.

39. Leonie Huddy, Stanley Feldman, and Erin Cassese, "On the Distinct Political Effects of Anxiety and Anger," in Neuman et al., *Affect Effect*, 228, 229.

40. Jasper, *Getting Your Way*, 106.

41. Owens, *Cracking under Pressure*, 95.

42. Even in relatively progressive Amsterdam, "The public emotions of anger were labeled masculine, while the emotions considered more appropriate in the home, like love and compassion, were categorized as feminine." Reflex emotions, with their vivid displays, are often part of strategic engagement, while affective commitments need not be made public: Owens, *Cracking under Pressure*, 125.

43. Julia C. Becker, Nicole Tausch, and Ulrich Wagner report that "collective action participation heightens the perception that the ingroup is treated unfairly, which produces corresponding 'negative' outgroup-directed emotions [i.e., anger] and increases the intention to engage in actions against this type of injustice in the future": "Emotional Consequences of Collective Action Participation," *Personality and Social Psychology Bulletin* 37 (2011): 1596. Anger at the out-group was a stronger motivation than positive feelings about the in-group.

44. Paul Rozin and April E. Fallon, "A Perspective on Disgust," *Psychological Review* 94 (1987): 24n1. Rozin is the preeminent psychologist of disgust. A common interpretation is that disgust reminds us of our own animal natures and, ultimately, our own death, as in William I. Miller, *The Anatomy of Disgust* (Harvard University Press, 1997). Although this is a bit fanciful for my taste, it has little bearing one way or the other on how we understand disgust as a political weapon. It may have implications for Martha Nussbaum's argument for abolishing disgust from politics, however: *Hiding from Humanity: Disgust, Shame, and the Law* (Princeton University Press, 2004). For an amusing romp through changing attitudes toward feces, take some hallucinogenic drugs and read Dominique-Gilbert Laporte, *Histoire de la Merde (Prologue)* (Christian Bourgois, 1978).

45. David Livingstone Smith, *Less than Human: Why We Demean, Enslave, and Exterminate Others* (St. Martin's, 2011). He plausibly argues that we are hardwired to categorize the world but implausibly that we are hardwired to see others as less than human. We often inflate others into powerful, superhuman villains: Jews control the world's financial system; communists have secretly and thoroughly infiltrated the US government.

46. Nussbaum, *Hiding from Humanity*, 110, 111. The new Nazi man, in contrast, was supposed to be hard and steely, without any of the "female-Jewish-communistic fluid, stench, and muck" (108). In *The Art of Moral Protest,* I discussed pseudo-speciation without specifying its link to disgust.

47. Simone Schnall, Jennifer Benton, and Sophie Harvey found that disgusted people were more condemning of mildly unethical acts: "With a Clean Conscience: Cleanliness Reduces the Severity of Moral Judgments," *Psychological Science* 19 (2008): 1219–1222. Even seeing a hand sanitizer seems to make respondents more conservative, according to Erik Helzer and David Pizarro: "Dirty Liberals! Reminders of Physical Cleanliness Influence Political and Moral Attitudes," *Psychological Science* 22 (2011): 517–522. Some individuals are more prone to disgust about objects in their environment, and they seem to be more prone to conservative beliefs: Yoel Inbar, David A. Pizarro, and Paul Bloom, "Conservatives Are More Easily Disgusted than Liberals," *Cognition and Emotion* 23 (2009): 714–725.

48. Gyanendra Pandey, *The Construction of Communalism in Colonial North India* (Oxford University Press, 1990), 265.

49. N. R. E. Fischer links the ancient Greek notion of hybris (or hubris) to this intentional humiliation of others in *Hybris* (Aris and Phillips, 1992).

50. I thank Thomas Scheff, who in personal communications persuaded me that shame exists in a reflex form, based on this kind of evidence from other species. But he sees it as *only* a reflex emotion, whereas I see a distinct moral form as well.

51. Jessica Tracy and David Matsumoto, "The Spontaneous Expression of Pride and Shame," *Proceedings of the National Academy of Sciences* 105 (2008): 11655-11660.

52. Deborah Tannen makes this point, perhaps too sharply, in *You Just Don't Understand: Women and Men in Conversation* (William Morrow, 1990).

53. Nussbaum, *Hiding from Humanity*, 206.

54. Thomas J. Scheff, *Bloody Revenge* (Westview, 1994), 151-152.

55. Erving Goffman, *Stigma: Notes on the Management of a Spoiled Identity* (Simon and Schuster, 1963), 4.

56. John Lofland, "Crowd Joys," in *Protest: Studies of Collective Behavior and Social Movements* (Transaction, 1985).

57. Collins, *Interaction Ritual Chains*, 53.

58. Erika Summers Effler, *Laughing Saints and Righteous Heroes: Emotional Rhythms in Social Movement Groups* (University of Chicago Press, 2010), 23ff.

59. Effler, *Laughing Saints*, 62.

60. Elaine Hatfield, John T. Cacioppo, and Richard L. Rapson, *Emotional Contagion* (Cambridge University Press, 1994), 10.

61. James Laird and Charles Bresler, drawing on William James, argue that our facial expressions help us interpret and label our emotions: "Facial expressions, and other expressive actions, arousal, action, and contextual information all contribute to the experience of emotion." James Laird and Charles Bresler, "The Process of Emotional Experience: A Self-Perception Theory," in *Review of Personality and Social Psychology* 13, ed. Margaret S. Clarke (Sage, 1992): 224. Acknowledgement of many feeling-thinking processes should move us beyond long-standing debates over whether action comes first or emotion comes first. Each is composed of many feeling-thinking processes that influence each other.

62. Jeanette M. Haviland and Carol Malatesta, "The Development of Sex Differences in Nonverbal Signals," in *Gender and Nonverbal Behavior*, ed. Clara Mayo and Nancy M. Henley (Springer-Verlag, 1981), 193.

63. Hatfield, Cacioppo, and Rapson, *Emotional Contagion*, 130.

64. Thanks to Jane McAlevey for recounting this remarkable tactic.

65. Randall Collins, *Violence: A Micro-Sociological Theory* (Princeton University Press, 2008), 85, 91.

66. Collins, *Violence*, 82.

67. Collins, *Violence*, 93. Anger is rare in combat, however, Collins observes (69).

68. Anne Nassauer, *Violent Clashes* (under review).

69. Sofia Salimovich, Elizabeth Lira, and Eugenia Weinstein, "Victims of Fear: The Social Psychology of Repression," in *Fear at the Edge: State Terror and Resistance in Latin America*, ed. Juan E. Corradi, Patricia Weiss Fagen, and Manuel Antonio Garretón (University of California Press, 1992), 74-75.

70. Collins, *Violence*, 40. Stefan Klusemann finds similar emotional dynamics in the Srebrenica massacre of 1995: "Atrocities and Confrontational Tension," *Frontiers in Behavioral Neuroscience* 3 (2009): https://www.ncbi.nlm.nih.gov/pmc/articles/PMC2776490/. He shows how the local Serbian commander came to dominate the UN commander through posture, words, facial expressions, and interruptions, opening the way for the massacre.

71. Frances Fox Piven and Richard A. Cloward, *Poor People's Movements: Why They Succeed, How They Fail* (Pantheon, 1977).

CHAPTER THREE

1. Alinsky described the tactic in a 1972 *Playboy* interview (March issue).

2. Damasio, *Looking for Spinoza*, 49 (see intro., n. 6).

3. Damasio, *Looking for Spinoza*, 49.

4. Damasio, *Looking for Spinoza*, 49–50.

5. Erving Goffman, *Encounters: Two Studies in the Sociology of Interaction* (Bobbs-Merrill, 1961), 55–56. See Jack Katz, *How Emotions Work*, chap. 5 (see chap. 1, n. 30).

6. Jack Katz, *How Emotions Work*.

7. Homer, *The Odyssey*, trans. Robert Fagles (Penguin, 1996), 288.

8. See, for example, Virginia Held, *The Ethics of Care: Personal, Political, and Global* (Oxford University Press, 2006), and more citations in appendix 1.

9. Miller, *Mystery of Courage* 112, 200 (see chap. 2, n. 17). In less dramatic workplaces, we can also push ourselves to fatigue and longer-term health problems, to the point that our bodies resist: Alexandra Michel, "Transcending Socialization: A Nine-Year Ethnography of the Body's Role in Organizational Control and Knowledge Workers' Transformation," *Administrative Science Quarterly* 54 (2011): 1–44. Although she examines investment bankers, the stress and strain of working in activist organizations can be similar.

10. Elster, *Strong Feelings*, 2 (see intro., n. 17).

11. Plato, *Republic*, 439a9–b1. Quoted by A. W. Price, "Emotions in Plato and Aristotle," in Goldie, *Oxford Handbook of Philosophy of Emotion*, 125 (see chap. 1, n. 20), who points out Plato's distinction between drinking and drinking something that is good for us: the former is a function of the appetite, the latter of reason. For Plato the appetites were not emotions but were closely accompanied by emotions.

12. Elster, *Strong Feelings*, 195.

13. As an aside, substance addiction demonstrates the complexity of the neurology and chemistry of feeling-thinking processes. Addiction centers on the neurotransmitter dopamine. Neurologists still speak of "dopamine circuits," in an effort to limit feelings to particular places in the brain, even though at least eight distinct dopamine pathways have so far been discovered that operate through many parts of the brain. There are other complexities. Amphetamines encourage the release of dopamine, cocaine sustains it by blocking its reuptake, and narcotics suppress the nerve cells that inhibit its release. Furthermore, the dopamine pathways are altered by use—the reason that most addicts need ever-greater amounts of a substance to get high. Dopamine is only one of the dozens of neurotransmitters and neuromodulators discovered so far. And all of this is an oversimplification.

14. Harry Levine, "The Discovery of Addiction," *Journal of Studies on Alcohol* 39 (1978): 154.

15. The very word *addiction* is political, of course. It is suitable to a moralistic (typically Protestant) culture that puts a premium on (what it sees as) rational individual decision making, any threat to which is disturbing. Americans have been especially prone to moral panics over addiction. In Japan, in contrast, men are allowed (perhaps even expected, in some circumstances) to become extremely drunk without running the risk of being stigmatized as "a drunk." Without that risk of shame, they (and their

patient companions) behave differently. Just as we display emotions in different ways, we satisfy urges in different ways.

16. Todd Gitlin, *The Sixties: Years of Hope, Days of Rage* (Bantam, 1987), 215.

17. Norman Mailer, "The Prisoner of Sex," *Harper's*, March 1971, 31. I hesitated to use the essentializing term "male lust," as though there were only one kind, and some other kind called "female lust." Instead I see a continuum ranging from immediate urges up to highly elaborated romantic versions that partake of many aspects of love. I find it plausible that men and women have different distributions along this continuum, given their different patterns of socialization.

18. Gitlin, *Sixties*, 109, 108, 371.

19. Philippe Braud, *L'Emotion en Politique* (Presses de Sciences Po, 1996), 10. Elaine Sciolino documents the French obsession with seduction in *La Seduction: How the French Play the Game of Life* (Times Books, 2011). In French, the word *seduction* has a much broader meaning than its English equivalent, encompassing almost all forms of persuasion, although sexuality is never far from the surface.

20. Jonathan Ned Katz, *The Invention of Heterosexuality* (University of Chicago Press, 2007), 190. Other good introductions include Mark Blasius, ed., *Sexual Identities, Queer Politics* (Princeton University Press, 2001); and Steven Seidman, *The Social Construction of Sexuality*, 2nd ed. (W. W. Norton, 2010).

21. See Almerindo E. Ojeda, ed., *The Trauma of Psychological Torture* (Praeger, 2008), for an overview of psychological forms of torture, although distinguishing psychological from physical tortures misses the bodily nature of the urges being manipulated in the former.

22. Lawrence M. Friedman, *Crime and Punishment in American History* (Basic, 1993), 48.

23. Michel Foucault, *Surveiller et punir: Naissance de la prison* (Gallimard, 1975).

24. Elaine Scarry, *The Body in Pain: The Making and Unmaking of the World* (Oxford University Press, 1985), 4. As Emily Dickinson put it:

> Pain — has an Element of Blank —
> It cannot recollect
> When it begun — or if there were
> A time when it was not —
>
> It has no Future — but itself —
> Its Infinite contain
> Its Past — enlightened to perceive
> New Periods — of Pain.

Emily Dickinson, "Pain—Has an Element of Blank," in *The Oxford Book of American Poetry*, ed. David Lehman (Oxford University Press, 2006), 177.

25. Scarry, *Body in Pain*, 54. "The point is that pain is not merely a private experience," insists Talal Assad, "but a public relationship as Wittgenstein taught long ago. . . . The person who suffers because of another's pain doesn't first assess the evidence presented to her and then decide how to react. She lives a relationship." Talal Assad, *Formations of the Secular: Christianity, Islam, Modernity* (Stanford University Press, 2003), 81, 82.

26. Jacobo Timerman, *Prisoner without a Name, Cell without a Number* (Vintage, 1982), 148.

27. Edward Peters, *Torture* (Blackwell, 1985), 4. John H. Langbein shows that torture

and Roman law declined together, as circumstantial evidence replaced confession as the favored form of proof: *Torture and the Law of Proof: Europe and England in the Ancien Regime* (University of Chicago Press, 1977).

28. Bush flunky Jay Bybee (later rewarded with a federal judgeship) oddly distinguished physical pain, which he had defended at the Office of Legal Counsel in 2001–2003, from disapproved techniques such as keeping detainees awake or unable to go to the bathroom: "Bush Aide Calls Some Methods Used by C.I.A. Unauthorized," *New York Times*, July 16, 2010.

29. Marnia Lazreg, *Torture and the Twilight of Empire* (Princeton University Press, 2008), 6. I do not address the longer-term psychological effects of violence, but there is some evidence that these effects differ according to how the victim understands the violence. A political ideology that frames violence as an unfortunate means to a worthy end may protect from trauma: Brian K. Barber, "Contrasting Portraits of War: Youths' Varied Experiences with Political Violence in Bosnia and Palestine," *International Journal of Behavioral Development* 32 (2008): 298–309.

30. Jack Whalen and Don H. Zimmerman, "Observations on the Display and Management of Emotion in Naturally Occurring Activities: The Case of 'Hysteria' in Calls to 9-1-1," *Social Psychology Quarterly* 61 (1998): 144. See also Jack Whalen, Don H. Zimmerman, and Marilyn R. Whalen, "When Words Fail: A Single Case Analysis," *Social Problems* 35 (1988): 335–362.

31. Whalen and Zimmerman, "Observations on Display," 150; they quote Goffman at 149–150.

32. Robert Sneden, quoted by Dora L. Costa and Matthew E. Kahn in *Heroes and Cowards: The Social Face of War* (Princeton University Press, 2008), 20.

33. Primo Levi, *Survival in Auschwitz: The Nazi Assault on Humanity* (Collier, 1961), 159.

34. Primo Levi, *The Drowned and the Saved* (Simon and Schuster, 1988), 49–50.

35. Robert Dirks, "Social Responses during Severe Food Shortages and Famine," *Current Anthropology* 21 (1980): 28.

36. In a formulation typical of the age, in which personality directly affects social structure, Sergius Morgulis thought that starvation "gnaws away at social ties by generating an irritable, unamicable, cantankerous disposition": *Fasting and Undernutrition: A Biological and Sociological Study of Inanition* (Dutton, 1923), 11.

37. See the remarkable study at the University of Minnesota in which volunteers were starved for twenty-four weeks: Ancel Keys et al., *The Biology of Human Starvation*, 2 vols. (University of Minnesota Press, 1950). Critics of institutional review boards should take a look at this work.

38. Yu-Sheng Lin, "The Rise and Fall of the Reds," *Social Movement Studies* 14 (2015): 291–310.

39. George Rudé, *Wilkes and Liberty* (Oxford University Press, 1962), 44.

40. Francesca Polletta, *Freedom Is an Endless Meeting: Democracy in American Social Movements* (University of Chicago Press, 2002), 138.

41. Nassauer, *Violent Clashes* (see chap. 2, n. 68).

42. Ariel Glucklich, *Sacred Pain: Hurting the Body for the Sake of the Soul* (Oxford University Press, 2001), 43, 77. Even extreme pain involves considerable cultural and psychological interpretation, fitting the model of feeling-thinking interactions rather than one of simple "periphery-to-center input." Glucklich argues, "Even the type of acute pain that is associated with clear physical causes and tissue damage is, to a very

large extent, a mental event." Not only do we produce natural opiates that moderate pain, but pain can be "masked or blotted out in the preoccupation with, or awareness of, more urgent or interesting matters" (52). "The success of the gate-control theory has led to the recognition that the intensity, duration, and nature of pain depend on decisions of the central brain, not just on peripheral stimulation" (53), Glucklich observes.

43. Psychologist Brock Bastian has performed experiments to show that pain can also relieve feelings of guilt: Brock Bastian, Jolanda Jetten, and Fabio Fasoli, "Cleansing the Soul by Hurting the Flesh," *Psychological Science* 22 (2011): 334-35. This finding helps explain some religious movements, especially Christian ones, although its implications for other political actions is less clear. Jean-Marie Apostolides comments that the "denial of everyday needs aims at an emotional rapport with the divinity. The soul seems to separate itself from terrestrial attachments": *Héroïsme et Victimisation* (Editions du Cerf, 2011), 63.

44. Steven Levenkron, *Cutting: Understanding and Overcoming Self-Mutilation*, rev. ed. (W. W. Norton, 1998).

45. E. Valentine Daniel, *Fluid Signs: Being a Person the Tamil Way* (University of California Press, 1987); quoted in Glucklich, *Sacred Pain*, 38. Daniel uses pain to adopt a new collective identity.

46. Maud Ellmann, *The Hunger Artists: Starving, Writing, and Imprisonment* (Harvard University Press, 1993), 17. I borrow her title, which she in turn borrowed from Kafka's famous short story, "A Hunger Artist."

47. Johanna Siméant summarizes the literature on hunger strikes in *La Grève de la Faim* (Presses de Sciences Po, 2009), translated in Johanna Siméant and Christophe Traïni, *Bodies in Protest: Hunger Strikes and Angry Music* (Amsterdam University Press, 2016). Looking only at cases reported in *Le Monde* from 1971 to 1992, she found roughly thirty a year in France—not including the much larger number occurring in French prisons, close to a thousand a year. On hunger strikes among undocumented immigrants, see chapter 6 of her *La Cause des Sans-Papiers* (Presses de Sciences Po, 1998).

48. Stephen J. Scanlan, Laurie Cooper Stoll, and Kimberly Lumm, "Starving for Change: The Hunger Strike and Nonviolent Action, 1906-2004," *Research in Social Movements, Conflicts and Change* 28 (2008): 275-323.

49. Sands quoted in Begoña Aretxaga, *Shattering Silence: Women, Nationalism, and Political Subjectivity in Northern Ireland* (Princeton University Press, 1997), 86. I also recommend the gripping 2008 movie about Sands, *Hunger*, directed by Steve McQueen and starring Michael Fassbender.

50. Oriana Fallaci, *Interview with History*, trans. John Shepley (Liveright, 1976), 351.

51. Abigail Richardson and Elizabeth Cherry, "Anorexia as a Choice: Constructing a New Community of Health and Beauty Through Pro-Ana Websites," in *Embodied Resistance: Challenging the Norms, Breaking the Rules*, ed. Chris Bobel and Samantha Kwan (Vanderbilt University Press, 2011).

52. Kevin McDonald, *Struggles for Subjectivity: Identity, Action and Youth Experience* (Cambridge University Press, 1999), 160. On anorexia as a career, see Muriel Darmon, *Devenir Anorexique: Une Approche Sociologique* (La Découverte, 2008).

53. Ellmann, *Hunger Artist*, 54.

54. Siméant, *La Grève de la Faim*, 73-74.

55. "Kyrgyzstan: Prisoners Sew Mouths Shut in Protest," *New York Times*, January 28, 2012.

56. Olivier Grojean, "Self-Immolations by Kurdish Activists in Turkey and Europe," *Revue d'Etudes Tibétaines* 25 (2012): 159-68.

57. Albie Sachs, *The Soft Vengeance of a Freedom Fighter*, 2nd ed. (David Philip Publishers, 2000), 41. My colleague Cynthia Epstein brought this book to my attention and lent me her copy, poignantly inscribed in Sachs's large, loopy, left-handed script.

58. Sachs, *Soft Vengeance*, 21.

59. Sachs, *Soft Vengeance*, 20.

60. Peter Burke's identity control theory suggests that our identities guide our behavior, as we constantly compare our expectations about ourselves with how we act and are treated by others. We have negative emotions when the two do not line up: Peter J. Burke, "The Self: Measurement Implications from a Symbolic Interactionist Perspective," *Social Psychology Quarterly* 43 (1980): 18-29; Peter J. Burke, "Identity Processes and Social Stress," *American Sociological Review* 56 (1991): 836-49.

61. Sachs, *Soft Vengeance*, 22.

62. Sachs, *Soft Vengeance*, 58.

63. In an earlier draft, I had cited Abraham Maslow's hierarchy of needs, but Johanna Siméant, who studies Mali, objected that the world's very poor also seek dignity, even if only through satisfying hunger; "basic" needs mean little in the absence of the higher, moral feelings.

CHAPTER FOUR

1. I was not at Tahrir Square, so my account here is brief and speculative. In the hundreds of eyewitness accounts, emotions play a central role, but in academic explanations they tend to disappear in favor of demographics, food prices, Facebook posts, cross-class coalitions, and the like.

2. For example, Christophe Traïni, "Opposing Scientific Cruelty: The Emotions and Sensitivities of Protestors against Experiments on Animals," *Contemporary European History* 23 (2014): 523-543.

3. Verta Taylor, "Emotions and Identity in Women's Self-Help Movements," in *Self, Identity, and Social Movements*, ed. Sheldon Stryker, Timothy J. Owens, and Robert W. White (University of Minnesota Press, 2000). Moods seem to involve the behavioral activation or the behavioral inhibition systems, as psychologists call them. See, for instance, Charles S. Carver and Teri L. White, "Behavioral Inhibition, Behavioral Activation, and Affective Responses to Impending Reward and Punishment: The BIS/BAS Scales," *Journal of Personality and Social Psychology* 67 (1994): 319-333.

4. William N. Morris, *Mood: The Frame of Mind* (Springer-Verlag, 1989). Peter Goldie, like most scholars, distinguishes moods by the lack of specificity of their objects: *The Emotions: A Philosophical Exploration* (Clarendon Press, 2000), 141.

5. Allan V. Horwitz and Jerome C. Wakefield, *All We Have to Fear: Psychiatry's Transformation of Natural Anxieties into Mental Disorders* (Oxford University Press, 2012).

6. William N. Morris, "A Functional Analysis of the Role of Mood in Affective Systems," in M. Clarke, *Review of Personality and Social Psychology*, 270 (see chap. 2, n. 63).

7. Anouk van Leeuwen, Bert Klandermans, and Jacquelien van Stekelenburg, "A Study of Perceived Protest Atmospheres," *Mobilization* 20 (2014): 81-100; Anouk van Leeuwen, Jacquelien van Stekelenburg, and Bert Klandermans, "The Phenomenology of Protest Atmosphere," *European Journal of Social Psychology* 46 (2016): 44-62.

8. David Hirschleifer and Tyler Shumway, "Good Day Sunshine: Stock Returns and the Weather," *Journal of Finance* 58 (2003): 1009-1032; Norbert Schwarz and Gerald L. Clore, "Mood, Misattribution, and Judgments of Well-Being: Informative and Directive

Functions of Affective States," *Journal of Personality and Social Psychology* 45 (1983): 513-523, experiment 2; Robert C. Sinclair, Melvin M. Mark, and Gerald L. Clore, "Mood Related Persuasion Depends on (Mis)Attributions," *Social Cognition* 12 (1994): 309-326.

9. At least in mice, a closer cousin than we like to admit. Mice with healthier guts were bolder (venturing into open spaces in a maze more often) and more persistent (swimming longer before they gave up and had to be rescued), suggesting more positive moods: Javier A. Bravo, Paul Forsythe, Marianne V. Chew, Emily Escaravage, Hélène M. Savignac, Timothy G. Dinan, John Bienenstock, John F. Cryan, "Ingestion of Lactobacillus Strain Regulates Emotional Behavior and Central GABA Receptor Expression in a Mouse via the Vagus Nerve," *Proceedings of the National Academy of Sciences* 108 (2011): 16050-16055, doi: 10.1073/pnas.1102999108. The thousands of bacterial, viral, and fungal species that compose each person's microbiome are a new frontier in biology, where we will learn about many new feeling-thinking mechanisms in coming years.

10. Quoted by Deborah Gould, *Moving Politics: Emotion and ACT UP's Fight against AIDS* (University of Chicago Press, 2009), 158.

11. Long Doan, "A Social Model of Persistent Mood States," *Social Psychology Quarterly* 75 (2012): 198-218.

12. David T. Lykken, *Happiness: What Studies on Twins Show Us about Nature, Nurture, and the Happiness Set Point* (Golden Books, 1999).

13. Paul T. Costa and Robert R. McCrae, "Influence of Extroversion and Neuroticism on Subjective Well-Being: Happy and Unhappy People," *Journal of Personality and Social Psychology* 38 (1980): 668-678; Robert A. Emmons and Ed Diener, "Personality Correlates of Subjective Wellbeing," *Personality and Social Psychology Bulletin* 11 (1985): 89-97.

14. Salimovich, Lira, and Weinstein, "Victims of Fear," 74-75 (see chap. 2, n. 71).

15. Collins, *Interaction Ritual Chains*, xiii, xv (see chap. 2, n. 36). Plato may have been the first to explicitly recognize the importance of rituals as a basis for civil order in a healthy city-state, in book 5 (738d) of his *Laws:* "The convocations of the various sections at stated periods may provide opportunities for the satisfaction of their various needs, and the festivities may give occasion for mutual friendliness, familiarity, and acquaintance. There is indeed no such boon for a society as this familiar knowledge of citizen by citizen." Plato, *The Collected Dialogues*, ed. Edith Hamilton (Princeton University Press, 1961), 1323-1324. Religions have relied on that insight implicitly for much longer.

16. Roland Neumann and Fritz Strack, "'Mood Contagion': The Automatic Transfer of Mood between Persons," *Journal of Personality and Social Psychology* 79 (2000): 211-223.

17. Collins, *Interaction Ritual Chains*, 42, 47. On copresence more generally, see Celeste Campos-Castillo and Steven Hitlin, "Copresence: Revisiting a Building Block for Social Interaction Theories," *Sociological Theory* 31 (2013): 168-92.

18. Jasper, *Art of Moral Protest*, chap. 8 (see intro., n. 18). Despite enormous overlap with Collins, I focused there on more formalized (although newly invented) rituals, appropriately since political organizers are well aware of the dynamics that Collins describes and craft interactions to maximize emotional energy. I pointed out that good weather enhances rituals, but now I would say that it also has a direct effect on moods, alongside the effects of interaction rituals.

19. William H. McNeill, *Keeping Together in Time: Dance and Drill in Human History* (Harvard University Press, 1995), 2. See also Barbara Ehrenreich, *Dancing in the Streets: A History of Collective Joy* (Metropolitan, 2006).

20. Collins, *Interaction Ritual Chains*, 105, 106.

21. Collins, *Interaction Ritual Chains*, 121. Kemper argues that our positions in status and power hierarchies affect the emotions we have when we interact with others in those hierarchies. Changes in our relative status and power also yield characteristic emotions. A decline in power leads to fear, a decrease in status leads to anger or shame, and so on. Theodore Kemper, *A Social Interactional Theory of Emotions* (Wiley, 1978).

22. Collins, *Interaction Ritual Chains*, 120.

23. Rachel Meyer and Howard Kimeldorf suggest, "What matters is not the rarity or scale of an event but rather its *novelty* in the context of the life experiences of participants": "Eventful Subjectivity: The Experiential Sources of Solidarity," *Journal of Historical Sociology* 28 (2015): 434. Further, Nicholas A. Valentino, Krysha Gregorowicz, and Eric W. Groenendyk find that a sense of efficacy boosts participation by increasing anger—but only among young people as they develop habits of participation: "Efficacy, Emotions and the Habit of Participation," *Political Behavior* 31 (2009): 307–330.

24. Bravery is central to Charles Kurzman's account of why the Egyptian uprising of 2011 succeeded, when none of the usual, more structural explanations helped much: "The Arab Spring Uncoiled," *Mobilization* 17 (2012): 377–390. He also cites three other articles in the same special issue that discuss individual acts of bravery. It is an important mechanism generating dignity, and perhaps especially moving us from shame to pride.

25. Rajagopal Ragunathan and Yaacov Trope, "Walking the Tightrope between Feeling Good and Being Accurate: Mood as a Resource in Processing Persuasive Messages," *Journal of Personality and Social Psychology* 83 (2002): 510–525; Barbara L. Fredrickson, "What Good Are Positive Emotions?" *Review of General Psychology* 2 (1998): 300–319; Yaacov Trope, Eric R. Igou, and Christopher T. Burke, "Mood as a Resource in Structuring Goal Pursuit," in *Affect in Social Thinking and Behavior*, ed. Joseph P. Forgas (Psychology Press, 2006). The latter authors highlight the trade-off between a good mood as a goal in itself and as a resource for the pursuit of other goals. Other research on the effects of moods appears in Joseph P. Forgas, ed., *The Handbook of Affect and Social Cognition* (Lawrence Erlbaum, 2001); for a good overview, see Joseph P. Forgas, introduction to *Feeling and Thinking* (Cambridge University Press, 2001).

26. The classic piece was Schwarz and Clore, "Mood, Misattribution, and Judgments of Well-Being," but see also Norbert Schwarz and Gerald L. Clore, "How Do I Feel about It? Informative Functions of Affective States," in *Affect, Cognition, and Social Behavior*, ed. Klaus Fiedler and Joseph Forgas (Hogrefe International, 1988); and "Mood as Information: Twenty Years Later," *Psychological Inquiry* 14 (2003): 296–303.

27. Alice M. Isen, "Some Ways in Which Positive Affect Influences Decision Making and Problem Solving," in Lewis, Haviland-Jones, and Feldman Barrett, *Handbook of Emotions*, 569 (see chap. 1, n. 41). See also Alice M. Isen, "Positive Affect and Decision Processes: Some Recent Theoretical Developments with Practical Implications," in *Handbook of Consumer Psychology*, ed. Curtis Haugtvedt, Paul M. Herr, and Frank R. Kardes (Psychology Press, 2008): 273–296.

28. Alice M. Isen, "Positive Affect, Cognitive Processes, and Social Behavior," in, *Advances in Experimental Social Psychology*, vol. 20, ed. Leonard Berkowitz (Academic Press, 1987), 203–253.

29. Eric J. Johnson and Amos Tversky, "Affect, Generalization, and the Perception of Risk," *Journal of Personality and Social Psychology* 15 (1983): 294–301; John D. Mayer, Yvonne N. Gaschke, Debra L. Braverman, and Temperance W. Evans, "Mood-

Congruent Judgment Is a General Effect," *Journal of Personality and Social Psychology* 63 (1992): 119–132; John D. Mayer and Ellen Hanson, "Mood-Congruent Judgment over Time," *Personality and Social Psychology Bulletin* 21 (1995): 237–244.

30. Summers Effler, *Laughing Saints and Righteous Heroes*, 43–44 (see chap. 2, n. 60). Extreme bad moods such as depression can freeze us in place, but milder bad moods such as sadness can motivate us to do something to snap out of it. Getting out of the house to attend a rally might appeal to those who appreciate the pleasures of collective events. On the other hand, psychologists point out that we are willing to do things that have short-term impacts on our moods, even at the expense of long-term projects. Spending money or seeking thrills are examples—not especially relevant to most political projects. See Roy F. Baumeister, C. Nathan DeWall, and Liqing Zhang, "Do Emotions Improve of Hinder the Decision Making Process?" in *Do Emotions Help or Hurt Decision Making?* ed. Kathleen D. Vohs, Roy F. Baumeister, and George Loewenstein (Russell Sage, 2007), 21ff.

31. On moral shock, see Jasper, *Art of Moral Protest*; Christophe Traïni, "Choc Moral," in *Dictionnaire des Mouvements Sociaux*, ed. Olivier Fillieule, Lilian Mathieu, and Cécile Péchu (Presses de Sciences Po, 2009); Gould, *Moving Politics*; Malene Vinther Christensen, "Mobilizing People for Social Movement Organizations" (master's thesis, Aarhus University, 2016).

32. Ratcliffe, "Phenomenology of Mood," 353 (see chap. 1, n. 42).

33. Ratcliffe, "Phenomenology of Mood," 355.

34. For example, William Styron, *Darkness Visible* (Vintage, 1992); Susanna Kaysen, *Girl, Interrupted* (Vintage, 1994); Elizabeth Wurtzel, *Prozac Nation* (Houghton Mifflin, 1994); Jeffrey Smith, *Where the Roots Reach for Water* (North Point Press, 1999); Andrew Solomon, *The Noonday Demon: An Atlas of Depression* (Simon and Schuster, 2002); Sally Brampton, *Shoot the Damn Dog* (W. W. Norton, 2008); Daphne Merkin, *This Close to Hell* (Farrar, Straus and Giroux, 2017).

35. David Foster Wallace, *Infinite Jest* (Back Bay, 2006), 695–696.

36. John Stuart Mill, *Utilitarianism* (Parker and Son, 1863).

37. Martin E. P. Seligman, *Flourish* (Free Press, 2011). After establishing the concept of learned helplessness, Seligman turned to the more upbeat topic of how to learn happiness.

38. Daniel Kahneman and Jason Riis, "Living, and Thinking about It: Two Perspectives on Life," in *The Science of Well-Being*, ed. Felicia Huppert, Nick Baylis, and Barry Keverne (Oxford University Press, 2005). Methodologically it is difficult to separate the mood from life satisfaction, as being in a good mood may also lead people to respond more positively to survey questions about their life satisfaction. Kahneman formulates the focusing illusion: "Nothing in life is as important as you think it is when you are thinking about it": Kahneman, *Thinking, Fast and Slow*, 402 (see chap. 1, n. 6).

39. Daniel Gilbert, *Stumbling on Happiness* (Knopf, 2006).

40. Distinguishing the two kinds of happiness also solves the so-called Easterlin paradox that higher income does not lead to greater happiness: Richard A. Easterlin, "Does Economic Growth Improve the Human Lot?" in *Nations and Households in Economic Growth*, ed. Paul A. David and Melvin W. Reder (Academic Press, 1974). Using a survey of nearly half a million Americans, Daniel Kahneman and Angus Deaton conclude that higher incomes do lead to better evaluations of life as a whole but contribute to happy moods only up to a certain threshold, around $75,000. Daniel Kahneman and Angus Deaton, "High Income Improves Evaluation of Life but Not Emotional Well-

Being," *Proceedings of the National Academy of Sciences of the United States of America*
107 (2010): 16489-16493.

41. Peggy A. Thoits and Lyndi N. Hewitt, "Volunteer Work and Well-Being," *Journal of Health and Social Behavior* 42 (2001): 115-131. It is also possible, these authors report, that those who are happy devote more time to volunteer work—possibly the energizing effect of a good mood.

42. Abbot L. Ferris, "Religion and the Quality of Life," *Journal of Happiness Studies* 3 (2002): 199-215. Research has found an independent effect of belief, which I would translate into a kind of confidence in one's own actions, including strategic actions. I discuss the rhetorical impact of "god terms" in "The Politics of Abstractions: Instrumental and Moralist Rhetorics in Public Debate," *Social Research* 59 (1992): 315-344, and what better god term than *god* itself?

43. John F. Helliwell and Robert D. Putnam, "The Social Context of Well-Being," in Huppert, Baylis, and Keverne, *Science of Well-Being*.

44. Derek Bok, *The Politics of Happiness* (Princeton University Press, 2010), 22, 23.

45. Charles D. Brockett, *Political Movements and Violence in Central America* (Cambridge University Press, 2005), lists a lack of state responsiveness, then state harassment or intimidation, and then state violence. Often, protestors' reaction to one leads to the next: "A group organizes around an economic concern, finds lack of government responsiveness, and then with more pressure on its part is met by state harassment and intimidation" (57). In discussing the impact of repression, Wendy Pearlman contrasts fear, shame, and sadness, on the one hand, with anger, pride, and joy, on the other: one typically amounts to a resigned mood and the other to a mood of energetic engagement: "Emotions and the Microfoundations of the Arab Uprisings," *Perspectives on Politics* 11 (2013): 387-409. On the shift to grievances about procedures and "procedural rhetoric" more generally, see Cynthia Gordon and James M. Jasper, "Overcoming the 'NIMBY' Label: Rhetorical and Organizational Links for Local Protestors," *Research in Social Movements, Conflict and Change* 19 (1996): 153-175; and Tom R. Tyler and Heather J. Smith, "Social Justice and Social Movements," in *Handbook of Social Psychology*, ed. Daniel Gilbert, Susan T. Fiske, and Gardner Lindzey (McGraw-Hill, 1998).

46. Daniel Kahneman calls the reflex form "hot regret" and the moral form "wistful regret": "Varieties of Counterfactual Thinking," in *What Might Have Been*, ed. Neal J. Roese and James M. Olson (Lawrence Erlbaum, 1995). Thomas Gilovich, Victoria Husted Medvec, and Daniel Kahneman recognize a large cognitive component in life regret. In contrast to the anger often involved in reflex regret, with life regret, "what grows over time . . . is not the regret associated with a particular consequence but the recognition that there is a large consequence to be regretted." Interestingly, they find that reflex regret is more likely to be about an action we have taken, whereas life regret is more likely to be about actions we did *not* take: Gilovich, Medvec, and Kahneman, "Varieties of Regret: A Debate and Partial Resolution," *Psychological Review* 105 (1998): 603.

47. Jasper, *Getting Your Way*, 108ff.

48. Albert Bandura, "Self-Efficacy: Toward a Unifying Theory of Behavioral Change," *Psychological Review* 84 (1977): 191-215. Although Bandura was most interested in therapy's impact on self-efficacy, the model seems to work well for political coping as well. I would add superstitious rituals and lucky charms to his list of confidence builders.

49. Ellen Langer, "The Illusion of Control," *Journal of Personality and Social Psychology* 32 (1975): 311-328. See also Daniel M. Wegner, *The Illusion of Conscious Will* (MIT,

2002), who examines multiple relationships between whether we are acting (exerting will) and whether we feel we are acting, and Shelley E. Taylor, *Positive Illusions: Creative Self-Deception and the Healthy Mind* (Basic Books, 1989). The term *illusion* suggests that there is always a sharp divide between accurate and inaccurate assessments of reality, but the self-fulfilling nature of confidence suggests otherwise.

50. Elizabeth Williamson, "The Magic of Multiple Emotions," *Sociological Forum* 26 (2011): 45-70. She studied forty-nine participants in Reclaiming meetings, weekend retreats spaced out over two years, so that she could measure the effect of these emotional sequences long after the moods themselves had subsided. Reclaiming combines pagan religion with feminism and ecology.

51. Quotations of Jouvenal, Lefèbvre, and Zolberg in Aristide Zolberg, "Moments of Madness," in *How Many Exceptionalisms? Explorations in Comparative Macroanalysis* (Temple University Press, 2008), 22, 24, 29.

52. Nancy Whittier, "Emotional Strategies: The Collective Reconstruction and Display of Oppositional Emotions in the Movement against Child Sexual Abuse," in Goodwin, Jasper, and Polletta, *Passionate Politics*; Helena Flam, "Emotions' Map," in *Emotions and Social Movements*, ed. Helena Flam and Debra King (Routledge, 2005). Flam (who cites a 1992 conference paper as her first use of the phrase) largely restricts the term to a shift in affective commitments: from loyalty to old institutions to attachment to the movement seeking change.

53. Russell R. Dynes, Bruna DeMarchi, and Carlo Pelanda, eds., *The Sociology of Disasters* (Franco Angelli, 1987); Russell R. Dynes, *Organized Behavior in Disasters* (Heath, 1970); Russell R. Dynes and Kathleen J. Tierney, *Disasters, Collective Behavior, and Social Organization* (University of Delaware Press, 1994); E. L. Quarantelli, "Some Images of Withdrawal Behavior in Disasters: Some Basic Misconceptions," *Social Problems* 8 (1960): 68-79. Daniel Cefaï is one of the few recent scholars to incorporate this research into theories of mobilization and protest: *Pourquoi se Mobilise-t-on?* (La Découverte, 2007), 130-136. When we understand what goes on in these situations, Cefaï observes, "The opposition between the institutional and the non-institutional decreases: most of the phenomena of collective behavior are based on a normative order (values, objectives and norms) and on social structure (interdependent roles)" (189). There is no reason to dismiss collective behavior as any more emotional or less rational than other forms of action. It was one of the most regrettable of the old dualisms to link institutionalized political action to rationality and noninstitutionalized action to emotions.

54. For example, Terri Mannarini, Michele Roccato, Angela Fedi, and Alberto Rovere, "Six Factors Fostering Protest: Predicting Participation in Locally Unwanted Land Uses Movements," *Political Psychology* 30 (2009): 895-920.

55. Bert Klandermans, *The Social Psychology of Protest* (Blackwell, 1997).

56. Studies into efficacy's impact on participation include Kristine Veenstra and S. Alexander Haslam, "Willingness to Participate in Industrial Protest," *British Journal of Social Psychology* 39 (2000): 153-172; Marilynn B. Brewer and Michael Silver, "Group Distinctiveness, Social Identification, and Collective Mobilization," in Stryker, Owens, and White, *Self, Identity, and Social Movements*; Miriam Liss, Mary Crawford, and Danielle Popp, "Predictors and Correlates of Collective Action," *Sex Roles* 50 (2004): 771-779; Matthew J. Hornsey et al., "Why Do People Engage in Collective Action?" *Journal of Applied Social Psychology* 36 (2006): 1701-1722. I see collective efficacy as a shared mood, involving self-efficacy in a particular (political) role.

57. Doug McAdam, *Political Process and the Development of Black Insurgency, 1930-1970* (University of Chicago Press, 1982).

58. David Darmofal, "Reexamining the Calculus of Voting," *Political Psychology* 31 (2010): 149-174.

59. Erik Neveu, "Life Stories of Former French Activists of '68: Using Biographies to Investigate the Outcomes of Social Movements," in *Conceptualizing Culture in Social Movement Research*, ed. Britta Baumgarten, Priska Daphi and Peter Ullrich (Palgrave Macmillan, 2014). Whatever we call the mechanism—militant capital or something else—there is a vast literature on the biographical consequences of activism. For some recent contributions, see Nella Van Dyke, Doug McAdam, and Brenda Wilhelm, "Gendered Outcomes: Gender Differences in the Biographical Consequences of Activism," *Mobilization* 5 (2000): 161-177; Marco Giugni, "Personal and Biographical Consequences," in *The Blackwell Companion to Social Movements*, ed. David A. Snow, Sarah Anne Soule, and Hanspeter Kriesi (Blackwell, 2004); Marco Giugni, "Political, Biographical, and Cultural Consequences of Social Movements," *Sociology Compass* 2 (2008): 582-600; Julie Pagis, *Mai 68, Un Pavé dans leur Histoire* (Presses de Sciences Po, 2014); Marco Giugni and Maria T. Grasso, "The Biographical Impact of Participation in Social Movement Activities," in *The Consequences of Social Movements*, ed. Lorenzo Bosi, Marco Giugni, and Katrin Uba (Cambridge University Press, 2016).

60. Hope is rarely measured directly, but for an exception see Katherine H. Greenaway, Aleksandra Cichocka, Ruth van Veelen, Tiina Likki, and Nyla R. Branscombe, "Feeling Hopeful Inspires Support for Social Change," *Political Psychology* 37 (2016): 89-107. Hope is also pivotal to conflict resolution, allowing more useful appraisals of the conflict, the ingroup, and the outgroup: Smadar Cohen-Chen, Richard J. Crisp, and Eran Halperin, "A New Appraisal-Based Framework Underlying Hope in Conflict Resolution," *Emotion Review* 9 (2017): 208-214.

61. Kari Marie Norgaard, *Living in Denial: Climate Change, Emotions, and Everyday Life* (MIT, 2011). She draws on Nina Eliasoph's research on the conversational work that Americans do to avoid politics in *Avoiding Politics: How Americans Produce Apathy in Everyday Life* (Cambridge University Press, 1998). Norgaard is more explicit about the emotional mechanisms involved.

62. Lynn Owens, *Cracking under Pressure*, 11, 92 (see chap. 2, n. 2). Gould also describes ACT UP's decline in *Moving Politics*.

63. Mao quoted in Richard H. Solomon, *Mao's Revolution and the Chinese Political Culture* (University of California Press, 1971), 191, 195, 196.

64. Elanor Kamans, Sabine Otten, and Ernestine H. Gordijn, "Threat and Power in Intergroup Conflict," *Group Processes and Intergroup Relations* 14 (2011): 293-310. See also Helena Flam, "The Politics of Grief and the 'Grieving' Mothers," in *The Blackwell Encyclopedia of Social and Political Movements*, ed. David A. Snow, Donatella della Porta, Bert Klandermans, and Doug McAdam (Wiley-Blackwell, 2013); and Rachel L. Einwohner, "Opportunity, Honor, and Action in the Warsaw Ghetto Uprising of 1943," *American Journal of Sociology* 109 (2003): 650-675.

65. Gould, *Moving Politics*, 49.

66. Gould, *Moving Politics*, 170. She points out that the new frame of "AIDS as genocide" worked because of its emotional resonance.

67. See Jo Fisher, *Mothers of the Disappeared* (South End Press, 1989); Marguerite Guzman Bouvard, *Revolutionizing Motherhood: The Mothers of the Plaza de Mayo*, (SR Books, 1994); Matilde Mellibovsky, *Circle of Love Over Death: Testimonies of the Mothers*

of the Plaza de Mayo (Curbstone, 1997). On the groups that emerged from it to track down the babies stolen from the disappeared, see Rita Arditti, *Searching for Life: The Grandmothers of the Plaza De Mayo and the Disappeared Children of Argentina* (University of California Press, 1999).

68. Dora de Bazze, quoted in Fisher, *Mothers of the Disappeared*, 28.

69. Guzman Bouvard, *Revolutionizing Motherhood*, 6.

70. Paul Hoggett, *Politics, Identity, and Emotion* (Paradigm, 2009), 20, 21, where he also quotes the Mothers.

71. Doron Shultziner, "The Social-Psychological Origins of the Montgomery Bus Boycott: Social Interaction and Humiliation in the Emergence of Social Movements," *Mobilization* 18 (2013): 117-142. I made the broader point about threats instead of opportunities in *The Art of Moral Protest*, 118: *Brown v. Board of Education* in 1954 did more to create White Citizens' Councils than to give hope and opportunities to Black Americans, although the two together formed a strong moral battery for Blacks.

72. Brym and Araj's research is summarized in Robert J. Brym, "Suicide Bombing," in *The Social Movements Reader*, 2nd ed., ed. Jeff Goodwin and James M. Jasper (Wiley-Blackwell, 2009). In the case of suicide bombers, the mood of desperation combines with a deep hatred for the occupying force.

73. Gloria Jimenez-Moya, Russell Spears, Rosa Rodríguez-Baílon, and Soledad de Lemus, "By Any Means Necessary? When and Why Low Group Identification Paradoxically Predicts Radical Collective Action," *Journal of Social Issues* 71 (2015): 517-535.

74. Hortencia Jimenez, Laura Barberena, and Michael P. Young, "'It Just Happened': Telescoping Anxiety, Defiance and Emergent Collective Action in the Student Walkouts of 2006,"*Social Problems* 61 (2014): 42-60. They use the example of anxiety, watching how anxiety as an affective commitment was focused into an anxious mood and then made into a frame for the events. It did not, however, become intensified into the reflex emotion of fear.

75. Doan, "Social Model of Persistent Mood States."

76. Hal Ersner-Hershfield, Joseph A. Mikels, Sarah L. Sullivan, and Laura L. Carstensen, "Poignancy: Mixed Emotional Experiences in the Face of Meaningful Endings," *Journal of Personality and Social Psychology* 94 (2008): 158-167.

CHAPTER FIVE

1. This chapter borrows several paragraphs from James M. Jasper, "Emotionen, Identitäten und Gruppen," in *Emotionen: Ein Interdisziplinäres Handbuch*, ed. Hermann Kappelhoff, Jan-Hendrik Bakels, Christina Schmitt, and Hauke Lehmann (Metzler, 2017).

2. Gyanendra Pandey, *The Construction of Communalism in North India* (Oxford University Press, 1990), 27.

3. Pandey, *Communalism in North India*, 65.

4. Paul R. Brass, *The Production of Hindu-Muslim Violence in Contemporary India* (Washington, 2003), shows how riots are produced by "conversion specialists" who can turn an insignificant incident into large-scale communal violence. It is not just historians who construct essentialist narratives but political players themselves, in this case especially Hindu nationalists. For a Putnamian view that active civic associations can prevent this kind of communal violence by creating Muslim-Hindu ties, see Ashutosh Varshney, *Ethnic Conflict and Civic Life: Hindus and Muslims in India* (Yale University Press, 2002).

5. Tomas Sedlacek, *Economics of Good and Evil* (Oxford University Press, 2011), 311.

6. Carl Schmitt, *The Concept of the Political* (1932; repr., Rutgers University Press, 1976), 29. For a psychoanalytic twist, a bit outdated, see Vamik D. Volkan, *The Need to Have Enemies and Allies* (Jason Aronson, 1988).

7. Jeff Goodwin, "The Libidinal Constitution of a High-Risk Social Movement: Affectual Ties and Solidarity in the Huk Rebellion, 1946 to 1954," *American Sociological Review* 62 (1997): 53-69.

8. For example, Vera B. Morhenn, Jan Woo Park, Elisabeth Piper, and Paul J. Zak, "Monetary Sacrifice among Strangers is Mediated by Endogenous Oxytocin Release after Physical Contact," *Evolution and Human Behavior* 29 (2008): 375-383.

9. Christopher Honts, Matthew Christiansen, Elizabeth Crider, Carey Fitzgerald, Christina Pfaff, Matthew Thompson, and Stephen Colarelli, "Effects of a Companion Animal on Individual and Work Group Outcomes" (paper presented at the International Society for Human Ethology meetings, August 2010).

10. In one of the classic experiments of social psychology, which review boards would not allow today, Muzafer Sherif and his colleagues created arbitrary group identities among two teams of boys and then observed the hostility each group developed for the other: Muzafer Sherif, O. J. Harvey, B. Jack White, William R. Hood, and Carolyn W. Sherif, *The Robbers Cave Experiment* (1961; repr., Wesleyan University Press, 1988). Group identities can congeal even when individuals know that they have been randomly assigned to the groups: Jacob M. Rabbie and Murray Horwitz, "Arousal of Ingroup-Outgroup Bias by a Chance Win or Loss," *Journal of Personality and Social Psychology* 13 (1969): 269-277.

11. A footnote to this literature could be book length. For recent work, see Aidan McGarry and James M. Jasper, eds., *The Identity Dilemma* (Temple University Press, 2015), especially the review in chapter 1. To take an example, Dan Lainer-Vos looks at one way that Ireland and Israel tried to make Irish and Jewish Americans feel as if they were part of those two new countries: financial support, especially the purchase of national bonds. *Sinews of the Nation* (Polity, 2013).

12. On love, see Benedict Anderson, *Imagined Communities: Reflections on the Origins and Spread of Nationalism* (Verso, 1983); Verta Taylor and Nancy E. Whittier, "Collective Identity in Social Movement Communities: Lesbian Feminist Mobilization," in *Frontiers in Social Movement Theory*, ed. Aldon D. Morris and Carol M. Mueller (Yale University Press, 1992); Mabel Berezin, "Emotions and Political Identity," in Goodwin, Jasper, and Polletta, *Passionate Politics* (see chap. 1, n. 2). On hate, see Scheff, *Bloody Revenge* (see chap. 2, n. 56); Oliver Le Cour Grandmaison, *Haine(s): Philosophie et politique* (PUF, 2002); and Michael Mann, *The Dark Side of Democracy: Explaining Ethnic Cleansing* (Cambridge University Press, 2005), the latter of whom argues, "When hatred and violence erupted, [individuals] were not so much freed from traditional socialization pressures as encouraged by new ones" (18).

13. Melvin L. Rogers discusses the "aspirational dimension" of references to "the people" in "The People, Rhetoric, and Affect: On the Political Force of Du Bois's *The Souls of Black Folk*," *American Political Science Review* 106 (2012): 188-203.

14. Henri Tajfel, *Human Groups and Social Categories* (Cambridge University Press, 1981). A small industry has developed around Tajfel's social identity theory, emphasizing among other things the social conditions under which social competition arises: when group boundaries are rigid, when the intergroup status system is unstable, and when it is seen as illegitimate: Henri Tajfel and John C. Turner, "An Integrative Theory of Inter-

group Conflict," in *The Social Psychology of Intergroup Relations*, ed. William G. Austin and Stephen Worchel (Brooks/Cole, 1979). In an interesting study of a student strike in Quebec, Benjamin Giguère and R. N. Lalonde find that the affective components of identification had a direct effect on participation, while strategic considerations had only an indirect effect through group identification: "Why Do Students Strike: Direct and Indirect Determinants of Collective Action Participation," *Political Psychology* 31 (2010): 227–247. Cultural approaches to social movements and political psychology have followed parallel paths in recent years without sufficient cross-fertilization: James M. Jasper, "The Doors that Culture Opened: Parallels between Social Movement Studies and Social Psychology," *Group Processes and Intergroup Relations* 20 (2017): 285–302.

15. Sophia Moskalenko, Clark McCauley, and Paul Rozin, "Group Identification under Conditions of Threat: College Students' Attachment to Country, Family, Ethnicity, Religion, and University Before and After September 11, 2001," *Political Psychology* 27 (2006): 77–97.

16. Christopher R. Browning, Seth L. Feinberg, and Robert D. Dietz, "The Paradox of Social Organization: Networks, Collective Efficacy, and Violent Crime in Urban Neighborhoods," *Social Forces* 83 (2004): 506–507. The collective efficacy tradition emphasizes social context and interactions, and so it is closer to a structural approach to trust than to a dispositional account. But we can observe dispositional effects on individuals, as in Mary R. Anderson, "Community Psychology, Political Efficacy, and Trust," *Political Psychology* 31 (2010): 59–84.

17. The many citations include Davide Mazzoni, Martijn van Zomeren, and Elvira Cicognani, "The Motivating Role of Perceived Right Violation and Efficacy Beliefs in Identification with the Italian Water Movement," *Political Psychology* 36 (2015): 315–330; Martijn van Zomeren, Tom Postmes, and Russell Spears, "Toward an Integrative Social Identity Model of Collective Action," *Psychological Bulletin* 134 (2008): 504–535; and Jacquelien van Stekelenburg, *Promoting or Preventing Social Change* (Vrije Universiteit, 2006).

18. Orla T. Muldoon and Robert D. Lowe, "Social Identity, Groups, and Post-Traumatic Stress Disorder," *Political Psychology* 33 (2012): 260.

19. Helena Flam, "Emotional 'Man,'" *International Sociology* 5 (1990): 39–56.

20. Farhad Khosrokhavar, *Quand Al-Qaïda Parle* (Grasset, 2006), 311ff. Translation mine.

21. Benedict Anderson, *Imagined Communities*, enlarged ed. (Verso, 1991), 51.

22. James M. Jasper, "Culture, Knowledge, Politics," in *The Handbook of Political Sociology*, ed. Thomas Janoski, Robert Alford, Alexander Hicks, and Mildred A. Schwartz (Cambridge University Press, 2005).

23. Andreas Wimmer, *Ethnic Boundary Making: Institutions, Power, Networks* (Oxford University Press, 2013).

24. Axel Honneth, *The Struggle for Recognition: The Moral Grammar of Social Struggles* (Polity, 1995).

25. Elisabeth Jean Wood, *Insurgent Collective Action and Civil War in El Salvador* (Cambridge University Press, 2003); James M. Jasper, "Strategic Marginalizations, Emotional Marginalities: The Dilemma of Stigmatized Identities," in *Surviving against Odds*, ed. Debal K. SinghaRoy (Manohar, 2010).

26. In *The Art of Moral Protest*, especially pages 92ff and chapters 5, 8, although in *Restless Nation: Starting Over in America* (University of Chicago Press, 2000), I argue that Americans tend to have less place loyalty than they should.

27. Terri Mannarini, Michele Roccato, Angela Fedi, and Alberto Rovere, "Six Fac-

tors Fostering Protest: Predicting Participation in Locally Unwanted Land Uses Movements," *Political Psychology* 30 (2009): 912. See also Richard C. Stedman, "Toward a Social Psychology of Place," *Environment and Behavior* 5 (2002): 561-581.

28. Jan Willem Duyvendak, *The Politics of Home* (Palgrave Macmillan, 2011). Also see Witold Rybczynski, *Home: A Short History of an Idea* (Penguin, 1986); Lynne C. Manzo, "Beyond House and Haven: Toward a Revisioning of Emotional Relationships with Places," *Journal of Environmental Psychology* 23 (2003): 47-61; Shelley Mallet, "Understanding Home: A Critical Review of the Literature," *Sociological Review* 52 (2004): 62-89.

29. J. Douglas Porteous and Sandra Smith, *Domicide: The Global Destruction of Home* (McGill and Queen's University Press, 2001), esp. chap. 2.

30. For a focus on the emotions of place resistance, see Alice Poma and Tommaso Gravante, "Analyzing Resistance from Below: A Proposal of Analysis Based on Three Struggles against Dams in Spain and Mexico," *Capitalism Nature Socialism* 26 (2015): 59-76.

31. Fernando J. Bosco, "The Madres de Plaza de Mayo and Three Decades of Human Rights' Activism: Embeddedness, Emotions, and Social Movements," *Annals of the Association of American Geographers* 96 (2006): 342-365.

32. Victor C. Ottati and Robert S. Wyer, "Affect and Political Judgment," in *Explorations in Political Psychology*, ed. Shanto Iyengar and William J. McGuire (Duke University Press, 1993); Donald R. Kinder, "Political Person Perception: The Asymmetrical Influence of Sentiment and Choice on Perceptions of Presidential Candidates," *Journal of Personality and Social Psychology* 36 (1978): 859-871; Donald R. Kinder, "The Continuing American Dilemma: White Resistance to Racial Change Forty Years after Myrdal," *Journal of Social Issues* 42 (1986): 151-172.

33. David O. Sears, "Political Behavior," in *Handbook of Social Psychology*, ed. Gardener Lindzey and Elliot Aronson (Addison-Wesley, 1969); David O. Sears, Richard R. Lau, Tom R. Tyler, and Harris M. Allen Jr., "Self-Interest versus Symbolic Politics in Policy Attitudes and Presidential Voting," *American Political Science Review* 74 (1980): 670-684.

34. David O. Sears and Jack Citrin, *Tax Revolt*, enlarged ed. (Harvard University Press, 1985), 169.

35. David O. Sears, "The Role of Affect in Symbolic Politics," in *Citizens and Politics: Perspectives in Political Psychology*, ed. James H. Kuklinski (Cambridge University Press, 2001).

36. Psychologists Charles W. Perdue, John F. Dovidio, Michael B. Gurtman, and Richard B. Tyler paired these words with nonsense syllables, which then took on positive or negative affective tones: "Us and Them: Social Categorization and the Process of Intergroup Bias," *Journal of Personality and Social Psychology* 59 (1990): 475-486.

37. Sears, "Role of Affect in Symbolic Politics," 25.

38. Richard S. Lazarus, "On the Primacy of Cognition," *American Psychologist* 39 (1984): 124-129.

39. Donald R. Kinder and Cindy D. Kam, *Us Against Them: Ethnocentric Foundations of American Opinion* (University of Chicago Press, 2009), 8. They believe that ethnocentrism affects public policy, increasing the odds of foreign interventions, decreasing support for foreign aid but also for domestic welfare provisions (seen as being "for them") but allowing aid to the elderly (seen as "us"). Debates continue whether ethnocentrism necessarily involves denigration of outsiders or merely positive feelings about one's

own group: Boris Bizumic and John Duckett, "What Is and Is Not Ethnocentrism?" *Political Psychology* 33 (2012): 887–909.

40. Donald Green, Bradley Palmquist, and Eric Schickler, *Partisan Hearts and Minds: Political Parties and the Social Identities of Voters* (Yale University Press, 2002), 48.

41. Green, Palmquist, and Schickler, *Partisan Hearts*, 6.

42. Green, Palmquist, and Schickler, *Partisan Hearts*, 48.

43. Arie W. Kruglanski and Donna M. Webster, "Motivated Closing of the Mind: 'Seizing' and 'Freezing,'" *Psychological Review* 103 (1996): 263–283.

44. Group norms and situational cues favoring cooperation can prevent this aggression: Agnieska Golec De Zavala, Aleksandra Cislak, and Elzbieta Wesolowska, "Political Conservatism, Need for Cognitive Closure, and Intergroup Hostility," *Political Psychology* 31 (2010): 521–541.

45. Polletta, *Freedom Is an Endless Meeting*, 207 (see chap. 3, n. 40).

46. Jack Barbalet, "A Characterization of Trust, and Its Consequences," *Theory and Society* 38 (2009): 367–382. Barbalet does not see trust itself as an emotion but as closely tied to the emotion of confidence—so closely that Susan Shapiro describes him as defining trust as an emotion: "The Grammar of Trust," in *New Perspective on Emotions in Finance*, ed. Jocelyn Pixley (Routledge, 2012); she found more than fifty thousand articles on trust in the *Social Sciences Citation Index*. Barbalet disagrees with cognitivist Russell Hardin, for whom trust is "essentially a matter of relevant knowledge about" those we trust and about whether they are trustworthy. We trust someone we feel is trustworthy, just as we love someone we find loveworthy. In both cases we may be wrong, and our feelings may never be put to the test. But they are feelings, not calculations.

47. Joyce E. Berg, John Dikhaut, and Kevin McCabe, "Trust, Reciprocity, and Social History," *Games and Economic Behavior* 10 (1995): 122–142.

48. Behavioral economists do not seem to have worked out a convincing explanation of these cultural differences. Koford found a group of Bulgarian students especially trusting, while Ensminger found Kenyan herders especially untrusting. Yet they attributed these opposite findings to the same factor, official corruption. Koford thinks their distrust of the *state* made the Bulgarians more trusting of *each other*. The experiments are reported in Colin Camerer, *Behavioral Game Theory* (Princeton University Press and Russell Sage, 2003), 87.

49. James C. Cox, "Trust, Reciprocity, and Other-Regarding Preferences of Individuals and Groups" (working paper, University of Arizona Economics Department, 1999).

50. Ingrid Seinen and Arthur Schram, "Social Status and Group Norms: Indirect Reciprocity in a Repeated Helping Experiment," *European Economic Review* 50 (2006): 581–602.

51. Camerer, *Behavioral Game Theory*, 100.

52. Most famously, Robert Axelrod, *The Evolution of Cooperation* (Basic Books, 1984); also Michael W. Macy and John Skvoretz, "The Evolution of Trust and Cooperation between Strangers," *American Sociological Review* 58 (1998): 197–209. Oddly, the recent *Handbook of the Sociology of Emotions* (Springer, 2014), edited by Jan Stets and Jonathan Turner, has almost no discussions of trust.

53. Edward J. Lawler, Shane Thye, and Jeongkoo Yoon, *Social Commitments in a Depersonalized World* (Russell Sage, 2009), 165.

54. Charles Tilly, *Trust and Rule* (Cambridge University Press, 2005), 12, 24.

55. Tilly, *Trust and Rule*, 4.

56. Lawler, Thye, and Yoon, *Social Commitments in a Depersonalized World*.

57. Harold H. Kelly and John W. Thibaut, *Interpersonal Relations: A Theory of Interdependence* (Wiley, 1978).

58. Robert Wuthnow, "Trust as an Aspect of Social Structure," in *Self, Social Structure, and Beliefs*, ed. Jeffrey C. Alexander, Gary T. Marx, and Christine L. Williams (University of California Press, 2004), 164.

59. Janine Willis and Alexander Todorov, "First Impressions: Making Up Your Mind after a 100-MS Exposure to a Face," *Psychological Science* 17 (2006): 592-598.

60. Paul Zak, who seems to be both an economist and a neurologist, has conducted a variety of experiments on the relationship between oxytocin and trust: *The Moral Molecule: Vampire Economics and the New Science of Good and Evil* (Dutton, 2012).

61. This is an understatement. A glance at the indexes of the *Oxford Handbook of Social Movements* and the *Blackwell Companion to Social Movements* yields one reference to trust: in a chapter I coauthored on emotions.

62. Costa and Kahn, *Heroes and Cowards*, 118, 6 (see chap. 3, n. 32).

63. On the same tension, see Clare Saunders, "Double-Edged Swords? Collective Identity and Solidarity in the Environment Movement," *British Journal of Sociology* 59 (2008): 227-253.

64. Jesse Glen Gray, *The Warriors* (Harper and Row, 1973), 52; quoted in William H. McNeill, *Keeping Together in Time* (Harvard University Press, 1995), 10. For a similar idea, McNeill also cites Edward A. Shils and Morris Janowitz, "Cohesion and Disintegration in the Wehrmacht in World War II," *Public Opinion Quarterly* 12 (1948): 280-315.

65. John N. Parker and Edward J. Hackett find the band of brothers trade-off in collaborative scientific and intellectual groups as well: "Emotions and social bonding were essential for the group's growth and development, but increased size and diversity have the potential to erode the affective culture that generated initial success": "Hot Spots and Hot Moments in Scientific Collaborations and Social Movements," *American Sociological Review* 77 (2012): 21. Band of brothers is a version of the extension dilemma: the larger a group, the less coherent it usually is.

66. Polletta, *Freedom Is an Endless Meeting*, 85. I suspect that all-male, all-female, and mixed groups have different versions of the band of brothers dilemma, based on somewhat different patterns of affective loyalties.

67. Polletta, *Freedom Is an Endless Meeting*, 207.

68. James M. Jasper, "The Emotions of Protest: Affective and Reactive Emotions in and around Social Movements." *Sociological Forum* 13 (1998): 397-424; "Emotions, Sociology, and Protest," in *Collective Emotions*, ed. Christian von Scheve and Mikko Salmela (Oxford University Press, 2014). In some cases, the shared emotions are better motivators than the reciprocal emotions: anger toward out-groups in the case studied by Becker, Tausch, and Wagner, "Emotional Consequences of Collective Action Participation" (see chap. 2, n. 45). But the key motivator here was anger.

69. Ron Eyerman, "How Social Movements Move: Emotions and Social Movements," in Flam and King, *Emotions and Social Movements*, 43 (see chap. 4, n. 53).

70. By isolating a group, repression can intensify its affective commitments: Hélène Combes and Olivier Fillieule, "Repression and Protest: Structural Models and Strategic Interactions," *Revue Française de Science Politique* 61 (2011): 1-24.

71. Janja Lalich, *Bounded Choice: True Believers and Charismatic Cults* (University of California Press, 2004). I reproduce here tables 2, 3, and 4 from the appendix, with permission from the Regents of the University of California Press. Sonia Roccas and Marilynn B. Brewer discuss the personal-identity consequences when a person does

not have multiple, divergent group memberships in "Social Identity Complexity," *Personality and Social Psychology* 6 (2002): 88–106.

72. Kathleen Rodgers, "'Anger Is Why We're All Here': Mobilizing and Managing Emotions in a Professional Activist Organization," *Social Movement Studies* 9 (2010): 273–291. She observes that the production, suppression, and modification of appropriate emotions often harms participants. For bodily harm in demanding organizations more generally, see Alexandra Michel, "Transcending Socialization: A Nine-Year Ethnography of the Body's Role in Organizational Control and Knowledge Workers' Transformation," *Administrative Science Quarterly* 54 (2011): 1–44.

73. Gordon W. Allport, *The Nature of Prejudice*, 25th anniversary ed. (Addison-Wesley, 1979), 6. For an update of Allport, see Rupert Brown, *Prejudice: Its Social Psychology*, 2nd ed. (Wiley-Blackwell, 2010).

74. Allport, *Nature of Prejudice*. "Cognitive busyness," according to Daniel Gilbert and J. Gregory Hixon, can lead us to fall back on stereotypes to process information, but so can emotional busyness. See Daniel Gilbert and J. Gregory Hixon, "The Trouble of Thinking: Activation and Application of Stereotypic Beliefs," *Journal of Personality and Social Psychology* 60 (1991): 509–517; and (on the impact of emotions) David A. Wilder and Peter N. Shapiro, "Effects of Anxiety on Impression Formation in a Group Context," *Journal of Experimental Social Psychology* 25 (1989): 481–499; and David A. Wilder and Peter N. Shapiro, "The Role of Competition-Induced Anxiety in Limiting the Beneficial Impact of Positive Behavior by an Outgroup Member," *Journal of Personality and Social Psychology* 56 (1989): 60–69.

75. Susan T. Fiske and Mark A. Pavelchak, "Category-Based versus Piecemeal-Based Affective Responses," in *The Handbook of Motivation and Cognition*, ed. Richard M. Sorrentino and E. Tory Higgins (Guilford, 1986). See also Susan T. Fiske and Steven L. Neuberg, "A Continuum of Impression Formation, from Category-Based to Individuating Processes," *Advances in Experimental Social Psychology* 23 (1990): 1–74.

76. Kathleen M. Blee, *Inside Organized Racism: Women in the Hate Movement* (University of California Press, 2002), 75–79.

77. Rebecca Littman and Elizabeth Levy Paluck observe that group identities can motivate violence, while violence in turn increases that group identification: "The Cycle of Violence: Understanding Individual Participation in Collective Violence," *Advances in Political Psychology* 36 (2015): 79–99. On Hindu constructions of disgust for Muslims, centering on their consumption of meat, see Parvis Ghassem-Fachandi, "On the Political Use of Disgust in Gujarat," *South Asian History and Culture* 1 (2010): 557–576.

78. Hoggett, *Politics, Identity, and Emotion*, chap. 4 (see chap. 4, n. 71).

79. Eran Halperin, Daphna Canetti-Nisim, and Sivan Hirsch-Hoefler, "The Central Role of Group-Based Hatred as an Emotional Antecedent of Political Intolerance: Evidence from Israel," *Political Psychology* 30 (2009): 93–123.

80. Asher Arian and Sigalit Olzaeker, "Political and Economic Interactions with National Security Opinion," *Journal of Conflict Resolution* 43 (1999): 58–77.

81. Quoted by Andrew Delbanco, *The Death of Satan: How Americans Have Lost the Sense of Evil* (Farrar, Straus and Giroux, 1995), 183. Delbanco comments that "the crusader who construes evil as a malignant, external thing—a thing alien to himself—is by far the worst kind of barbarian."

82. Stuart J. Kaufman, *Modern Hatreds: The Symbolic Politics of Ethnic War* (Cornell University Press, 2001), 12.

83. Christopher J. Einolf, "The Fall and Rise of Torture," *Sociological Theory* 25 (2007): 101–121.

84. Felicia Pratto, Jim Sidanius, and Shana Levin, "Social Dominance Theory and the Dynamics of Intergroup Relations: Taking Stock and Looking Forward," *European Review of Social Psychology* 17 (2006): 271-320. See also Jim Sidanius, Felicia Pratto, Colette van Laar, and Shana Levin, "Social Dominance Theory: Its Agenda and Method," *Political Psychology* 25 (2004): 845-880; and Chris G. Sibley and James H. Liu, "Social Dominance Orientation: Testing a Global Individual Difference Perspective," *Political Psychology* 31 (2010): 175-207.

85. John Duckitt, "A Dual-Process Cognitive-Motivational Theory of Ideology and Prejudice," in *Advances in Experimental Social Psychology* 33, ed. Mark P. Zanna (Academic Press, 2001).

86. Jan Gross, *Fear: Anti-Semitism in Poland After Auschwitz*, (Random House, 2006), 247.

87. Gross, *Fear*, 247. David G. Goodman and Masanori Miyzawa, *Jews in the Japanese Mind: The History and Uses of a Cultural Stereotype*, expanded ed. (Lexington, 2000).

88. Comments Aliza Luft about the late twentieth-century situation in Rwanda, "Hutu made choices about when to kill and when to save. Only over time did they stop perceiving their actions as murder and their neighbors as equal. This implies that a cognitive shift took place whereby Hutu individuals adapted to the action of killing and peers became dehumanized 'others.'" Aliza Luft, "Toward a Dynamic Theory of Action at the Micro Level of Genocide: Killing, Desistance, and Saving in 1994 Rwanda," *Sociological Theory* 33 (2015): 163.

89. Gross, *Fear*, 247, 260.

90. I did analyze the sources of hate by the Khmer Rouge in *The Art of Moral Protest*, chapter 16.

91. Kristen Renwick Monroe, *The Hand of Compassion: Portraits of Moral Choice during the Holocaust* (Princeton University Press, 2004), 236. Samuel and Pearl Oliner refer to this as the "extensivity" of rescuers' moral boundaries in *The Altruistic Personality* (Free Press, 1988).

92. Mary R. Jackman, *The Velvet Glove: Paternalism and Conflict in Gender, Class, and Race Relations* (University of California Press, 1994).

93. John T. Jost, Mahrazin R. Banaji, and Brian A. Nosek, "A Decade of System Justification Theory: Accumulated Evidence of Conscious and Unconscious Bolstering of the Status Quo," *Political Psychology* 25 (2004): 897, 899. This is a good summary of this literature.

94. Phillip Jenkins, *Intimate Enemies: Moral Panics in Contemporary Britain* (Hawthorne, 1992).

95. On the influence of group-based anger, see Martijn van Zomeren, Russell Spears, Agneta H. Fischer, and Colin Wayne Leach, "Put Your Money Where Your Mouth Is! Explaining Collective Action Tendencies through Group-Based Anger and Group Efficacy," *Journal of Personality and Social Psychology* 87 (2004): 649-664.

CHAPTER SIX

1. Ralph McGehee, *Deadly Deceits: My Twenty-Five Years in the CIA* (Sheridan Square, 1983), 114, 191. Melissa Everett also tells his story in *Breaking Ranks* (New Society, 1989), which contains the stories of ten former employees of the military and intelligence communities who broke ranks to contribute to the peace movement.

2. Benoît Monin, David A. Pizarro, and Jennifer S. Beer distinguish between *moral reflexes* and *moral judgments*, although the latter term downplays the felt commitments

that usually go into our judgments: "Reason and Emotion in Moral Judgment: Different Prototypes Lead to Different Theories," in Vohs, Baumeister, and Loewenstein, *Do Emotions Help or Hurt Decision Making?* (see chap. 3, n. 31).

3. T. M. Scanlon, *Moral Dimensions: Permissibility, Meaning, Blame* (Harvard University Press, 2008), 139.

4. Charles Taylor defines *hypergoods* as "goods which not only are incomparably more important than others but provide the standpoint from which these must be weighed, judged, decided about. . . . But then it would appear that we all recognize some such; that this status is just what defines the 'moral' in our culture: a set of ends or demands which not only have unique importance, but also override and allow us to judge others." Charles Taylor, *Sources of the Self: The Making of the Modern Identity* (Harvard University Press, 1989), 63. Andrew Sayer observes, "Few people can list their commitments, and they may only notice them when they are threatened. They usually emerge gradually and unintentionally through immersion in relationships and activities, and through embodiment. Although the distinction between commitments and preferences is a fuzzy one, it is not merely one of strength or attachment; there are important qualitative differences too," such as more substitutability among preferences than among moral commitments: *The Moral Significance of Class* (Cambridge University Press, 2005), 40–41.

5. Nussbaum, *Upheavals of Thought*, 1 (see intro., n. 5).

6. Dennis H. Wrong, "The Oversocialized Conception of Man in Modern Sociology," *American Sociological Review* 26 (1961): 187.

7. Antonio Damasio divides his social emotions into a similar typology. Embarrassment/shame/guilt have to do with one's own person or behavior. Sympathy and compassion are directed toward another who is suffering. He puts contempt and indignation together, however, forgetting about sources of contempt that are closer to disgust and which—as in caste settings—reflect permanent statuses. He puts pride in oneself together with recognition of others in awe and gratitude, a conflation he can make because his category is "social" rather than "moral" feelings. Damasio, *Looking for Spinoza*, 156 (see intro., n. 6).

8. Benedict de Spinoza, *Ethics* (Hafner, 1949), 279.

9. Kant scholar Ralph C. S. Walker remarks, "It is hard to resist a certain nostalgia for the time when reasonable men could think that no government could be evil enough to destroy entirely its own moral foundation; when the depths of bad government appeared to have been reached by Nero and Elgablus, and Hitler and Amin had never been thought of." Ralph C. S. Walker, *Kant* (Routledge & Kegan Paul, 1978), 162. He also observes that what Kant "actually does is tacitly to build into the conception of rationality all his substantive moral views" (158).

10. Hume, *Treatise of Human Nature* (see chap. 1, n. 53).

11. Lawrence Kohlberg, *The Philosophy of Moral Development* (Harper and Row, 1982).

12. Bernard Williams, *Problems of the Self* (Cambridge University Press, 1973), 225.

13. Carol Gilligan, *In a Different Voice* (Harvard University Press, 1982). See also G. E. M. Anscombe, "Modern Moral Philosophy," *Philosophy* 33 (1958): 1–19; Anscombe criticizes Kantian, utilitarian, and social-contract ethics for being legalistic, implying a legislator or God as the ultimate judge. They lack a sound psychology. Also see the more explicitly Aristotelian version in Alasdair MacIntrye, *After Virtue* (Notre Dame University Press, 1981); and Kristen Renwick Monroe's empirical confirmation of it in *The Hand of Compassion* (Princeton University Press, 2004), 215ff, as well as Martha Nussbaum's work.

14. Mark Johnson, *Moral Imagination: Implications of Cognitive Science for Ethics* (University of Chicago Press, 1993), 209.

15. Jonathan Haidt, *The Righteous Mind* (Pantheon, 2012), 24–25. He remarks of the Hebrew Bible that "many of the rules seem to follow a more emotional logic about avoiding disgust" (13). See also Jonathan Haidt and Jesse Graham, "When Morality Opposes Justice," *Social Justice Research* 20 (2007): 98–116; and Jonathan Haidt and Jesse Graham, "Planet of the Durkheimians, Where Community, Authority, and Sacredness are Foundations of Morality," in *Social and Psychological Bases of Ideology and System Justification*, ed. John T. Jost, Aaron C. Kay, and Hulda Thorisdottir (Oxford University Press, 2009).

16. Thomas J. Scheff, *Emotions, the Social Bond, and Human Reality* (Cambridge University Press, 1997), 74.

17. Scheff, *Emotions*. See also Jessica Tracy, Joey Chang, Richard Robins, Kali Trzesniewski, "Authentic and Hubristic Pride: The Affective Core of Self-Esteem and Narcissism," *Self and Identity* 8 (2009): 196–213.

18. Scheff, *Bloody Revenge*, 40 (see chap. 2, n. 56).

19. Geoffrey Brennan and Philip Pettit remark that esteem "involves rating a person in one or another respect," rather than in that person's entirety: *The Economy of Esteem* (Oxford University Press, 2004), 16.

20. Nussbaum, *Hiding from Humanity*, 184 (see chap. 2, n. 46).

21. Charles H. Cooley, *Human Nature and the Social Order* (1902; repr., Schocken, 1964), 184–185.

22. Jonathan Turner and Jan Stets elaborate on Parsonian values and norms, forming a continuum of evaluations: abstract values, then ideologies, then institutional norms, corporate unit norms, and finally situational norms. They insist that the more abstract end of the spectrum also demonstrates a greater "intensity of evaluative content," but it seems to me instead that it is highly concrete events in specific settings that most arouse moral emotions. See Jonathan Turner and Jan Stets, "Moral Emotions," in Stets and Turner, *Handbook of the Sociology of Emotions*, 545 (see chap. 5, n. 52).

23. Martin Buber, "Guilt and Guilt Feelings," in *The Knowledge of Man* (Harper and Row, 1965), 133.

24. Metin Başoğlu, Murat Paker, Özgün Paker, Erdoğan Özmen, Isaac Marks, Cem Incesu, Doğan Şahin, and Nuşin Sarimurat, "Psychological Effects of Torture," *American Journal of Psychiatry* 151 (1994): 76–81; Brian K. Barber, "Contrasting Portraits of War" (see chap. 3, n. 29).

25. Elster, *Alchemies of the Mind*, 150 (see intro., n. 17).

26. Arne Johan Vetlesen, *Evil and Human Agency: Understanding Collective Evildoing* (Cambridge University Press, 2005), 204; Auschwitz survivor also quoted at 204.

27. Vetlesen, *Evil and Human Agency*, 218.

28. Amélie Oksenberg Rorty, ed., *Explaining Emotions* (University of California Press, 1980), 498.

29. Derek L. Phillips, *Toward a Just Social Order* (Princeton University Press, 1986), 208ff.

30. A related feeling, *embarrassment*, more often arises from violations of social conventions than moral rules, and it sometimes arouses amusement (in others at the time, in oneself only in retrospect). Blushing, giggling, or covering the mouth with the hand are common signs.

31. Bernard Williams, *Shame and Necessity* (University of California Press, 1993), 92. Ruth Benedict contended that entire societies are either guilt- or shame-oriented,

notoriously seeing Japan as the latter without reading Japanese or doing fieldwork there: *The Chrysanthemum and the Sword* (Houghton Mifflin, 1946). She has been taken to task for her sweeping generalizations about Japanese national character, even though her book sold over a million copies there. Let's generously categorize her book as wartime propaganda. For criticism, see Takeo Doi, *The Anatomy of Dependence* (Kodansha America, 1973).

32. Gideon Kressel, "Sororicide/Filiacide: Homicide for Family Honour," *Current Anthropology* 22 (1981): 141–158.

33. On shaming, see Gay Seidman, "Naming, Shaming, and Changing the World," in *The Sage Handbook of Resistance*, ed. David Courpasson and Steven Vallas (Sage, 2016). Michael Schudson recounts the remarkable rise of transparency norms in *The Rise of the Right to Know* (Harvard University Press, 2015).

34. Cooley, *Human Nature and Social Order*.

35. Gould, *Moving Politics*, 84, 111, 91 (see chap. 4, n. 11).

36. Gould, *Moving Politics*, 89.

37. Lory Britt and David Heise, "From Shame to Pride in Identity Politics," in Stryker, Owens, and White, *Self, Identity, and Social Movements* (see chap. 4, n. 3).

38. Jasper, "Strategic Marginalizations and Emotional Marginalities," 29 (see chap. 5, n. 25).

39. Orrin E. Klapp, *Collective Search for Identity* (Holt, Rinehart, and Winston, 1969).

40. William Gamson, "The Social Psychology of Collective Action," in *Frontiers in Social Movement Theory*, ed. Aldon Morris and Carol Mueller (Yale University Press, 1992), 56.

41. Elisabeth Jean Wood, "The Emotional Benefits of Insurgency in El Salvador," in Goodwin, Jasper, and Polletta, *Passionate Politics* (see chap. 1, n. 2); and Wood, *Insurgent Collective Action* (see chap. 5, n. 25).

42. Nancy Whittier, "The Politics of Coming Out," in *Strategies for Social Change*, ed. Gregory M. Maney, Rachel V. Kutz-Flamenbaum, Deana A. Rohlinger, and Jeff Goodwin (University of Minnesota Press, 2012), 149.

43. Katherine McFarland Bruce, *Pride Parades: How a Parade Changed the World* (NYU Press, 2016).

44. Roy Mukamel, Arne D. Ekstrom, Jonas Kaplan, Marco Iacoboni, and Itzhak Fried, "Single-Neuron Responses in Humans during Execution and Observation of Actions," *Current Biology* 20 (April 27, 2010): 750–756. Primatologist Frans de Waal argues for a widespread instinct for compassion in *Good Natured: The Origins of Right and Wrong in Humans and Other Animals* (Harvard University Press, 1996) and *The Age of Empathy* (Random House, 2009).

45. Nussbaum, *Upheavals of Thought*, 330–331. She cites Heinz Kohut's insistence that "empathy is limited, fallible, and value-neutral." On the diverse definitions, see Benjamin M. P. Cuff, Sarah J. Brown, Laura Taylor, and Douglas J. Howat, "Empathy: A Review of the Concept," *Emotion Review* 8 (2016): 144–153.

46. Simon Baron-Cohen, *Zero Degrees of Empathy* (Allen Lane, 2011). He pushes his definition of *empathy* onto the terrain of sympathy so that he can make the provocative claim that sociopaths are defined by lack of empathy. But in fact they are often quite good at anticipating what another is thinking and feeling; they just do not sympathize with others. Thus the comedian Sacha Baron Cohen, Simon's cousin, uses his acute capacity for empathy to discomfit those around him (comedy being, as Aristotle suggested, a tamed form of sociopathy).

47. Sam McFarland, "Authoritarianism, Social Dominance, and Other Roots of Generalized Prejudice," *Political Psychology* 31 (2010): 453–77. Authoritarianism and social dominance increase prejudice, according to McFarland. See also Tania Singer et al., "Empathic Neural Responses Are Modulated by the Perceived Fairness of Others," *Nature* 439 (2006): 466–69.

48. As early as 1958, Herbert Blumer pointed the way toward more cognitive factors, such as collective identity, and away from "authoritarian personality" as a simple explanation of prejudice, in "Race Prejudice as a Sense of Group Position," *Pacific Sociological Review* 1 (1958): 3–7.

49. Kyle Irwin, Tucker McGrimmon, and Brent Simpson, "Trust, Sympathy, and Social Order," *Social Psychology Quarterly* 71 (2008): 379–397. They also find that interdependence increases sympathy, confirming chapter 5's argument that trust and cooperation reinforce each other.

50. Nussbaum, *Upheavals of Thought*, 302: "If there is any difference between 'sympathy' and 'compassion' in contemporary usage, it is perhaps that 'compassion' seems more intense and suggests a greater degree of suffering on the part of the afflicted person and on the part of the person having the emotion." Turner and Stets, committed to a theory of emotions in which there are primary and secondary emotions, "question whether empathy and sympathy are emotions, per se, as opposed to role-taking techniques that lead to the arousal of actual emotions": Turner and Stets, "Moral Emotions," 555. When we begin to recognize the myriad feeling-thinking components beneath our emotion labels, we can dispense with such either-or debates, along with the idea of primary and secondary emotions.

51. Nussbaum, *Upheavals of Thought*, 66. Whether we must feel what it would be like to be in that other's shoes in order to feel sympathy has been debated since the eighteenth century. Paul Hoggett criticizes Nussbaum for not recognizing identification, or a blurring of boundaries between self and other, in compassion: "Pity, Compassion, Solidarity," in Clarke, Hoggett, and Thompson, *Emotion, Politics and Society*, 147 (see chap. 2, n. 28). He is trying to preserve a range of psychoanalytic concepts along with identification. I disagree. My compassion for an elephant in the zoo is not based on any idea that, with bad luck, I might be there in its place. But it also goes beyond my pity for its physical suffering. As Nussbaum would say, it is based on my sense of the life an elephant could live in the wild, in its matriarchal family, fulfilling various capabilities normal for an elephant—an image I find inspiring. Identification may not be necessary or sufficient for compassion, but it may contribute to it.

52. On emotions and social ties, see Sieglinde Rosenberger and Jakob Winkler, "Com/Passionate Protests: Fighting the Deportation of Asylum Seekers," *Mobilization* 19 (2014): 165–184; Mark R. Warren, *Fire in the Heart: How White Activists Embrace Racial Justice* (Oxford University Press, 2010); Sharon Erickson Nepstad and Christian Smith, "The Social Structure of Moral Outrage in Recruitment to the U.S. Central American Peace Movement," in Goodwin, Jasper, and Polletta, *Passionate Politics*.

53. Chandra Russo, "Allies Forging Collective Identity: Embodiment and Emotions on the Migrant Trail," *Mobilization* 19 (2014): 489–505.

54. Jesse J. Prinz, "The Moral Emotions," in Goldie, *Oxford Handbook of Philosophy of Emotion*, 533 (see chap. 1, n. 20).

55. Norbert Elias, *The Civilizing Process* (1939; repr., Urizen, 1978), 129.

56. Elias, *Civilizing Process*, 73.

57. Michael Howard, *War and the Liberal Conscience* (Rutgers University Press, 1978).

58. Cas Wouters brings Elias's history up to date in *Informalization: Manners and Emotions since 1890* (Sage, 2007). Wouters (p. 198) mentions that in the late twentieth century, smaller families meant that "affective investments by parents in their children mounted, thus bringing family ties to higher levels of warmth, mutual trust, intimacy, and intensity." There have been parallel developments in states and personalities, where "relations came to be more equal, open, flowing, and flexible." The same pressures that once led to greater formality now lead to informality. Alan Hunt remarks that "Elias identified a contemporary trend towards informalization that requires more than the effective internalization of social norms; more important is a widely dispersed capacity that has become almost automatic by which individuals are able to select the appropriate level of formality-informality in a wide range of interaction scenarios." Alan Hunt, "The Civilizing Process and Emotional Life," in *Emotions Matter*, ed. Dale Spencer, Kevin Walby, and Alan Hunt (University of Toronto Press, 2012), 141.

59. Susan T. Fiske, *Envy Up, Scorn Down* (Russell Sage, 2011), 45.

60. Haidt, *Righteous Mind*, chap. 1.

61. Fiske, *Envy Up, Scorn Down*, 44.

62. Writing about the 1964 Democratic convention's refusal to seat the Mississippi Freedom Democrats, Francesca Polletta writes, "It was less the defeat itself than the underhanded maneuvering of Democratic Party operatives that so angered SNCC workers." Pollettta, *Freedom Is an Endless Meeting*, 92 (see chap. 3, n. 40).

63. John Rawls, *A Theory of Justice* (Harvard University Press, 1971); Brian Barry, *Theories of Justice* (University of California Press, 1989).

64. William Runciman, *Relative Deprivation and Social Justice* (Routledge and Kegan Paul, 1966); Robin M. Williams Jr., "Relative Deprivation," in *The Idea of Social Structure*, ed. Lewis A. Coser (Harcourt, Brace, Jovanovich, 1975); James C. Davies, "Toward a Theory of Revolution," *American Sociological Review* 27 (1962): 280-296.

65. Karen A. Hegtvedt, "The Effects of Relationship Structure on Emotional Responses to Inequity," *Social Psychology Quarterly* 53 (1990): 214-228; Jerald Greenberg, "Reactions to Procedural Injustice in Payment Distributions," *Journal of Applied Psychology* 72 (1987): 55-61; William A. Gamson, Bruce Fireman, and Steven Rytina, *Encounters with Unjust Authority* (Dorsey, 1982), 123.

66. See Sally Blount, "When Social Outcomes Aren't Fair: The Effect of Causal Attributions on Preferences," *Organizational Behavior & Human Decision Processes* 63 (1995): 131-144; Colin Camerer and Richard Thaler, "Ultimatums, Dictators, and Manners," *Journal of Economic Perspectives* 9 (1995): 209-219; and Ernst Fehr, Simon Gächter, and Georg Kirchsteiger, "Reciprocity as a Contract Enforcement Device: Experimental Evidence," *Econometrica* 65 (1997): 833-860. Colin Camerer, *Behavioral Game Theory*, chap. 2 (see chap. 5, n. 48), summarizes this literature. People who live in societies with well-developed markets are more attuned to fairness: Joseph Henrich, Robert Boyd, Samuel Bowles, Colin Camerer, Ernst Fehr, Herbert Gintis, and Richard McElreath, "Cooperation, Reciprocity and Punishment in Fifteen Small-scale Societies," *American Economic Review* 91 (2001): 73-78.

67. Robyn M. Dawes and Richard Thaler, "Cooperation," *Journal of Economic Perspectives* 2 (1988): 187-197.

68. Jasper, *Getting Your Way*, 149.

69. Ernst Fehr and Simon Gächter, "Cooperation and Punishment," *American Economic Review* 90 (2000): 980-994.

70. Shaul Shalvi, Ori Eldar, and Yoella Bereby-Meyer, "Honesty Requires Time (and Lack of Justifications)," *Psychological Science* 23 (2012): 1264–1270.

71. Jasper, "Constructing Indignation" (see chap. 2, n. 28).

72. See Elizabeth V. Spelman, "Anger and Insubordination," in *Women, Knowledge and Reality*, ed. Ann Garry and Marilyn Pearsall (Unwin Hyman, 1989); Sandra P. Thomas, ed., *Women and Anger* (Springer, 1993); Lyn Mikel Brown, *Raising Their Voices: The Politics of Girls' Anger* (Harvard University Press, 1998).

73. Verta Taylor, *Rock-a-by Baby: Feminism, Self-Help, and Postpartum Depression* (Routledge, 1996); Cheryl Hercus, "Identity, Emotion, Feminist Collective Action," *Gender and Society* 13 (1999): 34–55; also Verta Taylor and Leila J. Rupp, "Loving Internationalism: The Emotion Culture of Transnational Women's Organizations, 1888–1945," *Mobilization* 7 (2002): 125–144.

74. Arlie Hochschild, "The Sociology of Feeling and Emotion: Selected Possibilities," in *Another Voice*, ed. Marcia Millman and Rosabeth Moss Kanter (Anchor, 1975).

75. Brown, *Raising Their Voices*.

76. On anger in hierarchies, see Kemper, *Social Interactional Theory* (see chap. 4, n. 22).

77. V. Taylor, *Rock-a-by Baby*, 175.

78. Peter Lyman, "The Domestication of Anger," *European Journal of Social Theory* 7 (2004): 133. This was in an interesting special issue of the journal devoted to political anger.

79. Mary Holmes criticizes approaches which "assume that the political outcome of angriness is determinable in advance," but instead of recognizing the strategic dilemmas and the contingency of strategic interaction, she labels anger rather vaguely as "ambivalent": "Feeling Beyond Rules: Politicizing the Sociology of Emotion and Anger in Feminist Politics," *European Journal of Social Theory* 7 (2004): 211.

80. Hercus, "Identity, Emotion, Feminist Collective Action."

81. Daniel Blocq, Bert Klandermans, and Jacquelien van Stekelenburg find less anger among the members of movement organizations with close ties to the political establishment: "Political Embeddedness and the Management of Emotions," *Mobilization* 17 (2012): 319–334.

82. Steven J. Ross, *Workers on the Edge: Work, Leisure, and Politics in Industrializing Cincinnati, 1788–1890* (Columbia University Press, 1985), 286, 291.

83. Prinz, "Moral Emotions," 522. In *The Emotional Construction of Morals* (Oxford University Press, 2007), Prinz defends the view that morals result from our emotions.

84. Charles Tilly, *Credit and Blame* (Princeton University Press, 2008).

85. Jasper, *Art of Moral Protest*, 362ff. I called this "the power of negative thinking," but it was really based on the power of negative emotions, especially the creation of villains. I did not make this sufficiently clear. Psychologists George Bizer, Jeff Larsen, and Richard Petty found that when attitudes are framed negatively, people hold them more strongly and work harder to bring their behavior in line with the attitudes than they do for positively framed attitudes: "Exploring the Valence-Framing Effect: Negative Framing Enhances Attitude Strength," *Political Psychology* 32 (2011): 59–80.

86. This is a brief summary of the dynamics of blame, which I have written about at more length elsewhere: *Art of Moral Protest*, 118ff.; *Getting Your Way*, 48ff.

87. Jennifer S. Lerner, Julie H. Goldberg, and Phillip E. Tetlock, "Sober Second Thought: The Effects of Accountability, Anger, and Authoritarianism on Attributions

of Responsibility," *Personality and Social Psychology Bulletin* 24 (1998): 563–574. Behavioral economists have found similar effects: Ernst Fehr and Simon Gächter, "Altruistic Punishment in Humans," *Nature* 415 (2002): 137–140.

88. See James M. Jasper, Michael Young, and Elke Zuern, *Moral Characters* (forthcoming). In secular cultures, some of the divine aura of villains and heroes has diminished, but minions and especially victims have increased in rhetorical importance.

89. Prinz, "The Moral Emotions," 529.

90. In *Toward a Just Social Order* (Princeton University Press, 1986), Derek Phillips prefers the term *self-respect* for what we feel when we do the right thing, but I think he also makes this seem too normal or routine. You can feel pride in doing "well" in your moral accomplishments.

91. Tilly, *Credit and Blame*, 33. He takes an implicitly rhetorical approach, looking at the stories we tell to try to allocate credit and blame.

92. Tilly, *Credit and Blame*, 45. I borrow his summary of Neal Feigenson, *Legal Blame: How Jurors Think and Talk about Accidents* (American Psychological Association, 2000).

93. John Sabini, Brian Garvey, and Amanda L. Hall, "Shame and Embarrassment Revisited," *Personality and Social Psychology Bulletin* 27 (2001): 104–117. See also John Sabini and Maury Silver, "Why Emotion Names and Experiences Don't Neatly Pair," *Psychological Inquiry* 16 (2005): 1–10. We encountered a similar argument by Jon Elster in chapter 3.

94. Resentment, a fusion of outrage, hatred, and bitterness toward those above one in some hierarchy, used to be trotted out to explain protest movements—and to dismiss them as spiteful and ineffectual. In Friedrich Nietzsche's extreme concept of *ressentiment*, one's own sense of inferiority or failures is displaced unfairly onto external scapegoats. But as a response to genuine injustice, we may be able to revive the concept.

95. Brym, "Suicide Bombing," 298 (see chap. 4, n. 73).

96. As an introduction to what has become a vast literature, see John Torpey, *Making Whole What Has Been Smashed: On Reparations Politics* (Harvard University Press, 2006); and the special issue of *Political Psychology* 30, no. 2 (2009).

97. Martha Minow, *Between Vengeance and Forgiveness* (Beacon, 1998), 4–5. See also Hoggett, *Politics, Identity, and Emotion*, chap. 7.

98. V. Taylor, *Rock-a-by Baby*.

99. Nancy Whittier, *The Politics of Child Sexual Abuse: Emotions, Social Movements, and the State* (Oxford University Press, 2009).

100. Reported in Jasper, *Getting Your Way*, 125.

101. Whittier, *Politics of Child Sexual Abuse*, 68.

102. Sam McFarland, "The Slow Creation of Humanity," *Political Psychology* 32 (2011): 1–20.

103. Roderick Frazier Nash, *The Rights of Nature: A History of Environmental Ethics* (University of Wisconsin Press, 1989); James M. Jasper and Dorothy Nelkin, *The Animal Rights Crusade: The Growth of a Moral Protest* (Free Press, 1992); Christophe Traïni, *La Cause Animale* (Presses Universitaires de France, 2011).

104. Peter Singer, *The Expanding Circle* (New American Library, 1981), 114. Nash presents a similar idea in *The Rights of Nature*. Singer describes reason as an escalator that, once we step on, leads us to places we have not necessarily imagined. As a philosopher, Singer emphasizes this power of reason, but it often needs emotional resonance and political efforts before it can have much impact.

105. Thomas Haskell, "Capitalism and the Origins of the Humanitarian Sensibility," *American Historical Review* 90 (1985):343. See also Michael P. Young, *Bearing Witness against Sin: The Evangelical Birth of the American Social Movement* (University of Chicago Press, 2007).

106. Frederick Saunders, *Salad for the Solitary and the Social* (Thomas Whittaker, 1886), 320.

107. The indignation gap will remind older readers of relative-deprivation theories, which depended on a gap between reality and moral expectations. Raymond Tanter and Manus Midlarsky even spoke of a "revolutionary gap" in "A Theory of Revolution," *Journal of Conflict Resolution* 11 (1967): 264-280. This would seem to be a special case of an indignation gap, with the unfortunate addition that one can only know it is a revolutionary gap if a revolution results. Indignation gaps can have many outcomes or none. Even the best relative-deprivation theories (such as Ted Robert Gurr, *Why Men Rebel* [Princeton University Press, 1970]), posited a causal line from individual emotions to political mobilization, leaving themselves vulnerable to a generation of structural critics. But if we see relative deprivation as part of the arsenal by which activists and rank and file interact rhetorically, we can return it to our conceptual tool kit.

CONCLUSION

1. But see the special issue of *Group Processes and Intergroup Relations* 20 (2017), intended to bridge that gap.

2. In addition to the interactive perspective laid out in *Players and Arenas* and *Breaking Down the State*, see also Jasper et al., *Gains and Losses* (see intro., n. 1).

3. On the various definitions of mechanisms, see Peter Hedström and Peter Bearman, "What Is Analytical Sociology All About?" in *Oxford Handbook of Analytical Sociology* ed. Peter Hedström and Peter Bearman (Oxford University Press, 2009). I have been content to talk about emotions rather than the feeling-thinking processes that compose them. I am still trying to explain political action and outcomes, and emotions are mechanism enough for that. We could look at the mechanisms comprising emotions: drop down to the even lower level of neurotransmitters and chemistry and muscles to see in turn how emotions really work. I want to recognize that emotions consist of all these, in part because this approach overcomes a lot of feeling-thinking dualism. But feeling-thinking processes are a level below where we need to look for useful mechanisms in accounts of politics.

4. In *Dynamics of Contention*, Doug McAdam, Sidney Tarrow, and Charles Tilly used the term *mechanism* in this Mertonian way, with the unfortunate consequence that almost anything could be a mechanism, on a large scale as well as small. Reviewers criticized them for this kitchen-sink approach. I prefer Jon Elster's approach, in which mechanisms are found at the level of individuals and interactions among individuals, in order to explain organizational and macrolevel dynamics.

5. Elster, *Alchemies of the Mind*, 6 (see intro., n. 17).

6. Jocelyn Viterna, *Women in War: The Micro-Processes of Mobilization in El Salvador* (Oxford University Press, 2013); see also Larry W. Isaac, Jonathan S. Coley, Daniel B. Cornfield, and Dennis C. Dickerson, "Preparation Pathways and Movement Participation," *Mobilization* 21 (2016):155-176.

7. Margaret S. Archer, *Structure, Agency and the Internal Conversation* (Cambridge University Press, 2003), 141.

APPENDIX 1

1. Plato's appetites, of which hunger and thirst are his main examples, would mostly fall under my rubric of urges. Affective and moral commitments would probably be in Plato's category of reason (allowing him to focus on fear and anger). Reflex emotions and moods would mostly fit under his concept of spirit. In the modern world, "self-interest" plays some of the same role that appetites did for Plato: they are neither rational nor irrational, but often disrupt cooperative endeavors.

2. Plato was the most systematic critic of Athenian democracy, but the post-Periclean crisis reverberated throughout Greek culture, especially in rhetoric's close cousin, theater. Aristophanes ridiculed democracy in *The Knights*, and Euripides staged a sophisticated debate about it in *The Suppliants*. At the center of *Orestes* Euripides stages a public debate over Orestes's fate, which Michel Foucault brilliantly analyzed as a test of good and bad rhetorical styles in his 1983 lectures, published as *The Government of Self and Others* (Palgrave Macmillan, 2010), 163-168. "Democracy," Foucault concludes, "is in the process of being overrun by bad *parrēsia*" [roughly truth telling, but a rhetoric that can be based either on reason and truth or on flattery and tricks]. This interesting book, on *parrēsia*, is largely about Athens's post-Periclean crisis over democratic deliberation, including anxiety that demagogues appeal to the emotions rather than the reasoning power of their audiences. It shows more than any of his other work that Foucault was groping toward a strategic perspective at the end of his life. In a recent twist, Christina Tarnopolosky traces shame in Plato's *Gorgias* to argue that commentators have exaggerated the contrast between rationality and emotion in Plato: *Prudes, Perverts, and Tyrants: Plato's "Gorgias" and the Politics of Shame* (Princeton University Press, 2010).

3. The rule of the multitude, Aristotle believed, depended on the quality of deliberation—in other words, on "the rule of reason." Hence his anxiety over rhetoric. James Lindley Wilson describes his opinions in "Deliberation, Democracy, and the Rule of Reason in Aristotle's *Politics*," *American Political Science Review* 105 (2011): 259-274. Hendrik Lorenz unearths hidden parallels between Plato and Aristotle in *The Brute Within: Appetitive Desire in Plato and Aristotle* (Oxford University Press, 2006). At the end of his book (207), Lorenz finds in them both a kind of feeling-thinking that can form "motivating conditions" in a person "without reason or the intellect being active at the time in any way at all." Conscious and unconscious thinking can communicate with each other, in his reading of Aristotle.

4. Aristotle, *The Art of Rhetoric* (Penguin, 1991), 217 (pt. 3, sec. 9).

5. Quoted by Sarah B. Pomeroy, *Goddesses, Whores, Wives, and Slaves* (Schocken, 1975), 8, who argues that goddess worship does not improve women's status in a society.

6. Plato's framing of the debate between rhetoric and philosophy is the most influential, especially for the epistemological foundations of modern science. The cultural turn of the late twentieth century revived the rhetorical (or sophistic) view that truth emerges from dialogue among different points of view rather than from some objective truth that we can arrive at with proper method. Ironically, Foucault seems to defend the Platonic distinction in *Government of Self and Others*, esp. lectures 13, 17-20. See the continuation of the lecture series in Michel Foucault, *The Courage of Truth* (Picador, 2011). Philosophers seem to have escaped Foucault's well-grounded suspicion of intellectuals.

7. Harvey Yunis makes this point in one of the best sources on Athenian criticism of democracy, *Taming Democracy: Models of Political Rhetoric in Classical Athens* (Cornell University Press, 1996), chap. 3.

8. According to Foucault, in *Government of Self and Others*, "for practically eight centuries the problem of flattery as opposed to *parrēsia* was a political, a theoretical, and a practical problem, one which was undoubtedly as important during these eight centuries as the theoretical and technical problem of freedom of the press or freedom of opinion has been in our societies" (302). "What flattery reconstructs and repeats," he remarks in a later lecture, "is the passions, desires, pleasures, opinions, and everything else illusory and false" (372). Here he is reporting the ancient view, not necessarily agreeing with it.

9. Collected in any edition of Plutarch's *Moralia*. In *Therapy of Desire* (see chap. 2, n. 29), Martha Nussbaum analyzes the Stoics as well as their close Hellenistic relatives the Epicureans and the Skeptics, finding ideas that would inform her *Upheavals of Thought* (see intro., n. 5).

10. Andrew Delbanco, *The Death of Satan: How Americans Have Lost the Sense of Evil* (Farrar, Straus and Giroux, 1995), 37.

11. Quoted by Leo Strauss, *Thoughts on Machiavelli* (University of Chicago Press, 1958), 23, who emphasizes Machiavelli's multiple audiences, and the need to say certain things indirectly so as not to offend the Prince.

12. Alexander Hamilton, James Madison, and John Jay, "The Federalist Papers," in *The Federalist Papers*, ed. Ian Shapiro (Yale University Press, 2009), 320.

13. In recent years many scholars have criticized traditional crowd theory and done excellent empirical research into how crowds actually operate. A good overview by two of those scholars is Fergus G. Neville and Stephen D. Reicher, "Crowds, Social Identities and the Shaping of Everyday Social Relations," in *Political Psychology: A Social-Psychological Approach*, ed. Evanthia Lyons and Christopher J. Hewer (Wiley, forthcoming).

14. Quoted in Ehrenreich, *Dancing in the Streets*, 117 (see chap. 4, n. 20). This is an entertaining history of the repression of crowds in the modern world, and the collective joy that we are all missing as a result.

15. Charles Rosenberg and Carroll Smith-Rosenberg, "The Female Animal: Medical and Biological Views of Women," *Journal of American History* 60 (1973): 332, part of a wave of feminist research debunking portrayals of women as more emotional and less rational than men.

16. Gustave Le Bon, *The Crowd* (1895; repr., Viking Press, 1960), 50, 51.

17. Sigmund Freud, *Group Psychology and the Analysis of the Ego* (1921; repr., W. W. Norton, 1959), 15.

18. E. D. Martin, *The Behavior of Crowds* (Harper & Brothers, 1920), 35, 231. Most feeling-thinking processes are unconscious, but not in Freud's sense of The Unconscious as a thing, irrational and primitive, filled with repressed drives. Instead, "In the new view, mental processes are thought to be unconscious because there are portions of the mind that are inaccessible to consciousness due to the architecture of the brain, rather than because they have been subject to motivational forces like repression": Mlodinow, *Subliminal*, 17 (see chap. 1, n. 15).

19. See Jasper, Young, and Zuern, *Moral Characters*. These lone heroes have emotions hidden in them, of course. Romantic artists are supposed to "express" the emotions inside them—emotions are personal and subjective rather than social and interactive—while the taciturn gunslinger appears emotionless but actually harbors long-term orientations such as loyalty to the group or moral intuitions about protecting the weak.

20. An antisuffragist quoted in Aileen S. Kraditor, *The Ideas of the Woman Suffrage Movement/1890–1920* (1965; repr., W. W. Norton, 1981), 31.

21. Quoted in Kraditor, *Ideas of the Woman Suffrage Movement*, 19.

22. Quoted in Kraditor, *Ideas of the Woman Suffrage Movement*, 20.

23. Walter Lippmann, *Drift and Mastery* (1914; repr., University of Wisconsin Press, 1985).

24. Edward Bernays, *Propaganda* (H. Liveright, 1928). For an excellent history of these ideas, see Stuart Ewen, *PR! A Social History of Spin* (Basic, 1996), who points out that Theodore Roosevelt was a fan of Le Bon's, arranging a meeting with the crowd theorist in 1914.

25. Lazreg, *Torture and the Twilight of Empire*, 65 (see chap. 3, n. 29).

26. Edward Said, *Orientalism* (Pantheon, 1978), 138, 206; Jacob R. Boersema, *Afrikaner, Nevertheless* (Amsterdam University, 2013), 95.

27. Herbert Blumer, "Collective Behavior," in *Principles of Sociology*, ed. Robert E. Park (Barnes and Noble, 1939).

28. Ralph Turner and Lewis Killian, *Collective Behavior* (Prentice-Hall, 1957), 17, 58, 143; my italics.

29. McPhail's remarkable *The Myth of the Madding Crowd* (Aldine de Gruyter, 1991) represents the structural turn's devastating triumph over crowd theories, offering models of physical behavior such as clustering and locomotion but not of meaning or feeling. Historical research of the same period uncovered the informal rules that guided mobs' actions and choices of targets, such as Paul A. Gilje, *The Road to Mobocracy* (UNC Press, 1987).

30. Ted Brader, *Campaigning for Hearts and Minds: How Emotional Appeals in Political Ads Work* (University of Chicago Press, 2006), 72, 113.

31. Floyd Allport, *Social Psychology* (Houghton Mifflin, 1924).

32. Neal Miller and John Dollard, *Social Learning and Imitation* (Yale University Press, 1941).

33. Harold D. Lasswell, *Psychopathology and Politics* (University of Chicago Press, 1930).

34. Lewis S. Feuer, *The Conflict of Generations* (Basic, 1969).

35. Lasswell, *Psychopathology and Politics*; and Harold D. Lasswell, *Power and Personality* (W. W. Norton, 1948). In an uncharacteristically goofy effort, Guy E. Swanson applied Freudian personality types to participants in "Agitation through the Press: A Study of the Personalities of Publicists," *Public Opinion Quarterly* 20 (1956): 441–456; and "Agitation in Face-to-Face Contacts: A Study of the Personalities of Agitators," *Public Opinion Quarterly* 21 (1957): 288–294.

36. Eric Hoffer, *The True Believer* (Harper and Row, 1951), 98.

37. Orrin Klapp, *Collective Search for Identity* (Holt, Rinehart, and Winston, 1969), 11–13.

38. Kornhauser, *The Politics of Mass Society* (Free Press, 1959), chap. 12.

39. Classics on mass society and related personality disorders, initially a reaction to communism and especially to fascism, include Erich Fromm, *Escape from Freedom* (Farrar and Rinehart, 1941); Theodor W. Adorno, Else Frenkel-Brunswik, Daniel J. Levinson, and Nevitt Sanford, *The Authoritarian Personality* (Harper & Row, 1950); David Riesman, *The Lonely Crowd* (Yale University Press, 1950); Samuel P. Huntington, *Political Order in Changing Societies* (Yale University Press, 1968); and Edward A. Shils, "Authoritarianism: 'Right' and 'Left,'" in *Studies in the Scope and Method of the*

Authoritarian Personality ed. Richard Christie and Maria Jahoda (Free Press, 1954). It is not hard to discern an elite-driven moral panic in the United States during the 1950s having to do with protecting individualism against overconformity, at least for men. Concerns about communism, the corporate "organization man," and overly protective mothers were woven together.

40. Émile Durkheim, preface to the second edition, *The Division of Labor in Society* (Free Press, 1964), 10, 28. Inequality and a nonmeritocratic distribution of jobs (as opposed to a distribution based on "natural talents") also inspire protest, but Durkheim tended to see this as transitional and unnatural, not as an inherent part of capitalism.

41. Neil J. Smelser, *Theory of Collective Behavior* (Free Press, 1962), 11, 11, 30. Years later, Smelser pointed out to me that this book never uses the word *irrational*. In fact, he criticizes traditions that assume protest to be irrational, but he has moments in which irrationality is implied (and once he does use the word to refer to "outbursts" in contrast to organized opposition).

42. Neil J. Smelser, "Social and Psychological Dimensions of Collective Behavior," in *Essays in Sociological Explanation* (Prentice Hall, 1968), 92.

43. Smelser, "Social and Psychological Dimensions," 119–120, 121; Norman O. Brown, *Love's Body* (Random House, 1966). I compare Smelser's psychoanalytic approach with more recent cognitive and cultural approaches in "Intellectual Cycles of Social-Movement Research: From Psychoanalysis to Culture?" in *Self, Social Structure, and Beliefs: Explorations in Sociology*, ed. Jeffrey C. Alexander, Gary T. Marx, and Christine L. Williams (University of California Press, 2004).

44. Delbanco, *Death of Satan*, 182. To rely on Foucault once more, he cites Isocrates's complaint about the kind of people who get up to speak at the Assembly: they are drunk, people who have lost their good sense, or people who share out public monies among themselves. They are venal, not mortal, demagogues: Foucault, *Courage of Truth*, 36.

45. Daniel Goldhagen frontally attacked the tendency to focus all blame on Hitler for the horrors of Nazi Germany in *Hitler's Willing Executioners* (Knopf, 1996). By distinguishing long-standing affective commitments such as hatred for Jews from reflex emotions such as anger stirred up by Hitler, we can see that both contributed to the Holocaust.

46. Jasbir K. Puar, *Terrorist Assemblages: Homonationalism in Queer Times* (Duke University Press, 2007). Queer times indeed.

47. J. Craig Jenkins and Charles Perrow, "Insurgency of the Powerless: Farm Worker Movements (1946–1972)," *American Sociological Review* 42 (1977): 250.

48. John D. McCarthy and Mayer N. Zald, "Resource Mobilization and Social Movements: A Partial Theory," *American Journal of Sociology* 82 (1977): 1215. As usual, McCarthy and Zald were right on target about the work it takes to create discontent, exactly the focus of the cultural turn of the 1980s and 1990s. What is odd is their conclusion that grievances are less important as a result, rather than *more* important.

49. Karl Dieter Opp demonstrates the rational choice basis of political opportunity theory in *Theories of Political Protest and Social Movements* (Routledge, 2009), chap. 6. Christian Smith includes grievances as political opportunities in his otherwise excellent *Resisting Reagan: The U.S. Central America Peace Movement* (University of Chicago Press, 1996).

50. See the debates in Jeff Goodwin and James M. Jasper, eds., *Rethinking Social Movements* (Rowman & Littlefield, 2004) and the evidence gathered in Jeff Goodwin

and James M. Jasper, eds., *Contention in Context: Political Opportunities and the Emergence of Protest* (Stanford University Press, 2012).

51. Tilly was one of the speakers at the 1999 conference on emotions out of which my coedited volume *Passionate Politics* developed, although he later withdrew his paper to publish it elsewhere. He discussed Aristotle to show the salience of emotions to rhetoric, but it was not clear how rhetoric fit into Tilly's own political-process approach to protest. Tilly soon developed the concept of WUNC displays, by which protestors try to demonstrate their moral worth, unity, numbers, and commitment—a thoroughly rhetorical and emotional idea.

52. Herbert Kitschelt, "Political Opportunity Structures and Political Process: Anti-Nuclear Movements in Four Democracies," *British Journal of Political Science* 16 (1986): 57-85.

53. See Myra Marx Ferree's critique, "The Political Context of Rationality: Rational Choice Theory and Resource Mobilization," in Morris and McClurg Mueller, *Frontiers in Social Movement Theory*.

54. Olivier Fillieule, "Requiem pour un Concept: Vie et Mort de la Notion des Opportunités Politiques," in *La Turquie Conteste*, ed. Gilles Dorronsoro (CNRS Editions, 2005), 208-209.

55. Edward J. Walsh, "Resource Mobilization and Citizen Protest in Communities around Three Mile Island," *Social Problems* 29 (1981): 1-21.

56. For overviews, see Francesca Polletta and James M. Jasper, "Collective Identity and Social Movements." *Annual Review of Sociology* 27 (2001): 283-305; and Rawi Abdelal, Yoshiko M. Herrera, Alastair Iain Johnston, and Rose McDermott, "Identity as a Variable," *Perspectives on Politics* 4 (2006): 695-711.

57. Francesca Polletta, *It Was Like a Fever: Storytelling in Protest and Politics* (University Chicago Press, 2006).

58. Jasper, Young, and Zuern, *Moral Characters*.

59. Robert Benford makes similar observations about the framing literature in "An Insider's Critique of the Social Movement Framing Perspective," *Sociological Inquiry* 67 (1997): 409-430.

60. Amelie Rorty, "Community as the Context of Character," in *Mind in Action* (Beacon Press, 1988); E. F. Kittay and Diana T. Meyers, eds., *Women and Moral Theory* (Rowman & Littlefield, 1987); Sara Ruddick, *Maternal Thinking* (Beacon Press, 1989). Almost all modern political philosophers have taken one form or another of the liberal view, but on the ethics of care, see Carol Gilligan, *In a Different Voice* (Harvard University Press, 1982); Nel Noddings, *Caring* (University of California Press, 1984); and Virginia Held, *The Ethics of Care* (Oxford University Press, 2006). The industrious Martha Nussbaum tries to mediate with her "capabilities approach," which recommends that all humans (and other species) be allowed to develop a number of skills and capacities that are both ends and the means for other ends: Martha Nussbaum, *The Frontiers of Justice* (Harvard University Press, 2006); Martha Nussbaum, *Creating Capabilities* (Harvard University Press, 2011).

61. Martha Nussbaum, *The Fragility of Goodness* (Cambridge University Press, 1986); *Upheavals of Thought* (see intro., n. 5); *Frontiers of Justice*.

62. For a summary of the influence of feminism on theories of movement emotions, see Jo Reger and Verta Taylor, "Women's Movement Research and Social Movement Theory: A Symbiotic Relationship," *Sociological Views on Political Participation in the 21s Century* 10 (2002): 104-107.

63. Verta Taylor and Nancy Whittier, "Collective Identity in Social Movement Communities" in *Frontiers in Social Movement Theory* (see chap. 5, n. 12); Verta Taylor and Nancy Whittier, "Analytical Approaches to Social Movement Culture: The Culture of the Women's Movement," in *Social Movements and Culture*, ed. Hank Johnston and Bert Klandermans (University of Minnesota Press, 1995); Mary C. Bernstein, "Celebration and Suppression: The Strategic Uses of Identity by the Lesbian and Gay Movement," *American Journal of Sociology* 103 (1997): 531-565; Nancy Whittier, *Feminist Generations* (Temple University Press, 1995); Joshua Gamson, "Must Identity Movements Self-Destruct? A Queer Dilemma," *Social Problems* 42 (1995): 390-407; Joshua Gamson, "The Organizational Shaping of Collective Identity: The Case of Lesbian and Gay Film Festivals in New York," *Sociological Forum* 11 (1996): 231-61; Joshua Gamson, "Messages of Exclusion: Gender, Movements, and Symbolic Boundaries," *Gender and Society* 11 (1997): 178-99. Some of the other American scholars inspired by this cluster of movements include Elizabeth A. Armstrong, *Forging Gay Identities: Organizing Sexuality in San Francisco, 1950-1994* (University of Chicago Press, 2002); Tina Fetner, *How the Religious Right Shaped Lesbian and Gay Activism* (University of Minnesota Press, 2008); and Amin Ghaziani, *The Dividends of Dissent* (University of Chicago Press, 2008).

64. Gould, *Moving Politics* (see chap. 4, n. 11).

65. Sara Ahmed, *The Cultural Politics of Emotion* (Edinburgh University Press, 2004).

66. Massumi, *Parables for the Virtual*, 30 (see chap. 1, n. 44).

67. Maurice Pinard recovers the breadth of motivations, including emotions, in *Motivational Dimensions in Social Movements and Contentious Collective Action* (McGill-Queen's University Press, 2011). Although he tends to use the term *grievances*, emotions offer a more precise vocabulary about what motivates us.

68. Daniel Goleman, *Emotional Intelligence* (Bantam Books, 2006). Emotional intelligence consists of the ability to perceive emotions in oneself and others, to use them in formulating thoughts, to understand them, and finally to manage them. See the special issue of *Emotion Review* 8 (2016), October.

69. Rosabeth Moss Kanter, *Men and Women of the Corporation* (Basic Books, 1977), 22.

70. Yvonne Due Billing and Mats Alvesson, "Questioning the Notion of Feminine Leadership: A Critical Perspective on the Gender Labeling of Leadership," *Gender, Work and Organization* 7 (2000): 144-157.

71. I am pleased to have been part of that transformation, adding emotions to a cultural perspective in *The Art of Moral Protest*. I do not fully trace the new appreciation of emotions here, since it permeates this book, but I summarize it in "Emotions and Social Movements: Twenty Years of Theory and Research," *Annual Review of Sociology* 37 (2011): 285-303.

72. Hoggett, *Politics, Identity, and Emotion*, 45 (see chap. 4, n. 71).

73. L. Clarke and Chess, "Elites and Panic: More to Fear than Fear Itself" (see chap. 2, n. 16).

74. Daniel Cefaï shows the continuing relevance of this collective behavior in *Pourquoi se Mobilise-t-on?* pt. 1 (see chap. 4, n. 54).

APPENDIX 2

1. I compare psychoanalytic and cultural approaches to meaning in "Intellectual Cycles of Social-Movement Research" (see appendix 1, n. 43).

2. Francesca Polletta, "Culture Is Not Just in Your Head," in Goodwin and Jasper, *Rethinking Social Movements*, 101 (see appendix 1, n. 51).

3. Collins, *Violence*, 3–7 (see chap. 2, n. 67).

4. Jack Katz, *How Emotions Work* (see chap. 1, n. 30).

5. Thomas J. Scheff and Suzanne M. Retzinger, *Emotions and Violence: Shame and Rage in Destructive Conflicts* (Lexington Books, 1991); Irving Tallman, Peter J. Burke, and Viktor Gecas, "Socialization into Marital Roles: Testing a Contextual, Developmental Model of Marital Functioning," in *The Developmental Course of Marital Dysfunction*, ed. Thomas N. Bradbury (Cambridge University Press, 1998).

6. Scheff and Retzinger, *Emotions and Violence*.

7. On vocalization see Klaus R. Scherer, "Vocal Communication of Emotions," *Speech Communication* 40 (2003): 227–256.

8. Thomas J. Scheff, *Bloody Revenge* (see chap. 2, n. 56), 151–152. He cites Suzanne M. Retzinger, *Violent Emotions: Shame and Rage in Marital Quarrels* (Sage, 1991).

9. Erving Goffman, "Embarrassment and Social Organization," *American Journal of Sociology* 62 (1956): 264.

10. Jody Clay-Warner and Dawn T. Robinson, "Infrared Thermography as a Measure of Emotion Response," *Emotion Review* 7 (2015): 157–162.

11. Daniel Kahneman, Alan S. Krueger, David Schkade, Norbert Schwartz, and Arthur A. Stone, "Toward National Well-Being Accounts," *American Economic Review* 94 (2004): 429. The full list, from happiest to unhappiest: "intimate relations, socializing after work, dinner, relaxing, lunch, exercising, praying, socializing at work, watching TV, phone at home, napping, cooking, shopping, housework, child care, evening commute, working, morning commute." Working sucks. This is not the conclusion drawn from research that, in contrast, asks more abstractly how satisfied people are with their jobs. (Personally, I am surprised that napping is so far down the list!)

12. George Loewenstein and Peter A. Ubel point to the complexity of happiness, casting doubts on its utility in policy making in "Hedonic Adaptation to the Role of Decision and Experience Utility in Public Policy," *Journal of Public Economics* 92 (2008): 1795–1810.

13. Collins, *Interaction Ritual Chains*, 133–140 (see chap. 2, n. 36).

14. Edward J. Lawler, Shane R. Thye, and Jeongkoo Yoon, *Social Commitments in a Depersonalized World* (Russell Sage Foundation, 2009), 154–159.

15. Thomas J. Scheff, *Bloody Nationalism* (Westview, 1994), chap. 5.

16. Katherine Bischoping and Howard Schuman, "Pens and Polls in Nicaragua: An Analysis of the 1990 Preelection Surveys," *American Journal of Political Science* 36 (1992): 331–350; the classic on problems with polling for beliefs is Timur Kuran, *Private Truths, Public Lies: The Social Consequences of Preference Falsification* (Harvard University Press, 1995).

17. Bert Klandermans and Jackie Smith, eds., *Methods of Social Movement Research* (University of Minnesota Press, 2002).

18. David Heise, *Expressive Order: Confirming Sentiments in Social Action* (Springer, 2007), chap 3.

19. Camerer, *Behavioral Game Theory* (see chap. 5, n. 48).

20. Mario Diani, "Networks and Participation," in Snow, Soule, and Kriesi, *Blackwell Companion to Social Movements* (see chap. 4, n. 60).

21. Mustafa Emirbayer and Jeff Goodwin, "Network Analysis, Culture, and the Problem of Agency," *American Journal of Sociology* 99 (1994): 1411–1454; Florence Passy, "Social Networks Matter. But How?" in *Social Movements and Networks: Relational*

Approaches to Collective Action, ed. Mario Diani and Doug McAdam (Oxford University Press, 2003).

22. Ann Mische, "Cross-Talk in Movements: Rethinking the Culture-Network Link," in Diani and McAdam, *Social Movements and Networks*.

23. Elias, *Civilizing Process* (see chap. 6, n. 55).

24. Benjamin Lamb-Books, *Angry Abolitionists and the Rhetoric of Slavery* (Palgrave Macmillan, 2016).

25. Touraine's sociological interventions were designed to reproduce broader tensions and dilemmas of a movement in several small groups, the participants in which were chosen to represent distinct factions and perspectives. Participants knew very well whom they were supposed to represent, and often felt constrained by loyalty to this group, preventing them from pursuing new strategic openings or understandings. Touraine's research was designed to help movements understand their role in history, not their emotions, but the videos and transcriptions tell their own stories.

26. Jenny Kitzinger and Rosaline S. Barbour, *Developing Focus Group Research* (Sage, 1999), 5. Anna Feigenbaum, Patrick McCurdy, and Fabian Frenzel adapt focus groups, with photographic prompts, in "Towards a Method for Studying Affect in (Micro)Politics: The Campfire Chats Project and the Occupy Movement," *Parallax* 19 (2013): 21–37.

27. Robert D. Benford, "An Insider's Critique of the Social Movement Framing Perspective," *Sociological Inquiry* 67: 409–430; Hank Johnston, "Verification and Proof in Frame and Discourse Analysis," in *Methods of Social Movement Research*, ed. Bert Klandermans and Suzanne Staggenborg (University of Minnesota Press, 2002).

28. Lalich, *Bounded Choice*.

29. Kathleen M. Blee and Verta Taylor, "Semi-Structured Interviewing in Social Movement Research," in Klandermans and Staggenborg, *Methods of Social Movements Research*.

30. Mary Holmes, "Researching Emotional Reflexivity," *Emotion Review* 7 (2015): 64.

31. Swedish researchers followed judges, whose work is largely public but cannot be done by researchers: Sharyn Roach Anleu, Stina Bergman Blix, and Kathy Mack, "Researching Emotions in Courts and the Judiciary," *Emotion Review* 7 (2015): 145–150.

32. Andrea Doucet and Natasha S. Mauthner, "Emotions In/and Knowing," in Spencer, Walby, and Hunt, *Emotions Matter*, 169, discussing the "listening guide" developed by Carol Gilligan and others.

33. Catherine Theodosius, *Emotional Labour in Health Care: The Unmanaged Heart of Nursing* (Routledge, 2008), 123.

34. Sarah Maddison and Sean Scalmer, *Activist Wisdom. Practical Knowledge and Creative Tension in Social Movements* (UNSW Press, 2006); Douglas Bevington and Chris Dixon, "Movement-Relevant Theory: Rethinking Social Movement Scholarship and Activism," *Social Movement Studies* 4 (2005): 185–208.

35. Candace Clark, *Misery and Company: Sympathy in Everyday Life* (University of Chicago Press, 1997).

36. Theodosius, *Emotional Labour in Health Care*, 121.

37. Jack Katz, *How Emotions Work*, 76.

38. Gilbert, *Stumbling on Happiness*, 71 (see chap. 4, n. 40).

39. Gilbert, *Stumbling on Happiness*, 72–73.

40. Gilbert, *Stumbling on Happiness*, 77.

41. Elster, *Strong Feelings*, 13 (see intro., n. 17).

42. Kurt Danziger, *Constructing the Subject* (Cambridge University Press, 1990).

43. Pierre Bourdieu, *Science of Science and Reflexivity* (Polity Press, 2004), 39.

44. Andrew Abbott, "Against Narrative: A Preface to Lyrical Sociology," *Sociological Theory* 25 (2007): 70. Quoted in Christian Borch, "Body to Body: On the Political Anatomy of Crowds," *Sociological Theory* 27 (2009): 277.

45. Archer, *Structure, Agency and the Internal Conversation*. The private life of the individual, she says, promises nothing less than a model of how structure and agency are related.

46. Carolyn Ellis, "Sociological Introspection and Emotional Experience," *Symbolic Interaction* 14 (1991): 30; *Final Negotiations: A Story of Love, Loss, and Chronic Illness* (Temple University Press, 1995); *Evocative Authoethnography* (Routledge, 2016).

47. Kathleen M. Blee, "White-Knuckle Research: Emotional Dynamics in Fieldwork with Racist Activists," *Qualitative Sociology* 21 (1998): 381–399.

48. Sherryl Kleinman and Martha A. Copp, *Emotions and Fieldwork* (Sage, 1993); Jessica Fields, Martha Copp, and Sherryl Kleinman, "Symbolic Interactionism, Inequality, and Emotions," in Stets and Turner, *Handbook of the Sociology of Emotions*, 173–174 (see chap. 5, n. 52).

49. Natalya Godbold, "Researching Emotions in Interactions," *Emotion Review* 7 (2015): 163–168.

50. Feminists have been at the forefront of this debate, like so many others involving emotions: Doucet and Mauthner, "Emotions In/and Knowing," 162–163.

51. Blee shows how hard it is to find groups in their earliest stages, yet does a good job of it, in *Democracy in the Making: How Activist Groups Form* (Oxford University Press, 2012).

52. McPhail has published extensively on his methods of observing crowds. For starters, see David Schweingruber and Clark McPhail, "A Method for Systematic Observing and Recording of Collective Action in Temporary Gatherings," *Sociological Methodology and Research* 27 (1999): 451–498. The detailed coding could be extended to include emotional displays. Interestingly, McPhail's first published article had partly to do with emotions.

53. Richard S. Lazarus. "Toward Better Research on Stress and Coping," *American Psychologist* 55 (2000): 665–673.

INDEX

anger (*continued*)

leading to, 84, 231n21; desperation leading to, 96–97, 98; displays of, 46, 223n42; in Ekman's affect program theory, 36; good mood after protesters' expression of, 80–81, 87; in grieving, 87; information gathering discouraged by, 45; as intense rage, 43–44; Katz's phenomenological approach to, 22–23; Mao's externalizing strategy of, 96; metaphors used to express, 44, 222n35; moral impact of, 128; Nussbaum on, 42–43, 222n29; over injustice, 146, 148, 150; in panic model of emotions, xi, 44, 186; political-opportunity models not recognizing, 188; pressures for suppression of, 149–50; as reflex vs. moral commitment, 42; Scheff's markers for, 199, 200–201, 203, 208; scholars' theoretical confusion about, 186–87; shame-pride battery and, 138–39; shift away from violent public expression of, 31; social order and, 43; ties to political establishment and, 249n81; triggers for, 45; visual means of representing, 44–45; women's suppression of, 149–50. *See also* indignation; outrage

animals, extension of compassion to, 144, 156, 157

anorexia, 71, 73. *See also* hunger strikes

anti-Semitism, 122, 123–24

anxiety, 39; as affective commitment, 39, 125–26; attention and, 40, 221n18; background emotions consisting of, 39, 42; Smelser on social strain and, 183, 184; useful in mobilizing protest, 40. *See also* fear

apartheid, ix, 74–75, 155

Apostolides, Jean-Marie, 228n43

appetites, 59, 62, 172, 225n11, 252n1

appraisal theories: of Arnold, 213n9; Barrett on, 218n44; components of emotions and, 216n19; Morris's picture of moods and, 79; Nussbaum and, 6–7, 18, 19, 215n10; Prinz's version of, 215n10; Zajonc on, 214n2. *See also* Nussbaum, Martha

appropriateness of emotions, 20, 216n17

approval/disapproval, categories of, 132, 133, 135. *See also* blame; moral commitments (moral emotions); praise

Araj, Bader, 98–99

Archer, Margaret, 165, 210, 259n45

arenas: interaction chains and, 163, 165; types of, 160–61

Aristotle: on anger in social hierarchies, 150, 172; habitus and, 214n13; on moral indignation, 43; rhetoric and, 172, 252n3, 256n51. *See also* neo-Aristotelians, on moral training

Arnold, Magda B., 213n9

Art of Moral Protest, The (Jasper), 105, 128

ascetics and mystics, 70–71, 227n42, 228n43

Assad, Talal, 226n25

Asterix album, *La Zizanie*, 44–45

Athens, ancient: democracy in, 171–73, 176, 252n2; Foucault on rhetoric in, 252n2, 252n6, 253n8, 255n44

attachment theory, 104–5

Auschwitz, 69

authoritarian regimes, 55

autocracies, 173–75, 176

background emotions, 2–3; affective and moral commitments as, 19, 103, 128; anger at unfairness and, 45; long-run anxieties as, 39, 41, 42; moods as, 87, 88; reflex emotions and, 41; of research subjects not shared by researcher, 211; surveys and, 203–4. *See also* affective commitments; moral commitments (moral emotions)

band of brothers dilemma, 64, 117–18, 160; in scientific and intellectual collaborations, 241nn65–66

Bandura, Albert, 92, 233n48

Barbalet, Jack, 240n46

Barberena, Laura, 99, 236n74

Barbour, Rosaline, 205

Barker, Colin, 214n2

Baron Cohen, Sacha, 246n46

Baron-Cohen, Simon, 141, 246n46

Barrett, Lisa, 6, 21, 27–28, 213n9, 214n15, 218n44

tions in dualistic tradition and, 7-8; on signaling, 17

Freudian approaches: blaming damaged individuals for crowd dynamics, 181, 186; innate aggressive drive in, 222n33; inner conflicts in, 129; irrationality in emotions and, 215n10; Oedipal issues in, 161, 181, 184, 185; pride and honor missing in, 132

frustration: anger and, 44; crowd theorists on aggression and, 180-81; as desperate mood, 98; of Mothers of the Plaza de Mayo, 97

frustration-aggression model, 44, 222n33

Furedi, Frank, 41

Gächter, Simon, 147

game methods, 203; public goods game, 147-48; trust games, 113-14, 116, 147, 203; ultimatum game, 146-47

game theory, 31, 148, 219n50

Gamson, Josh, 192

Gamson, William, 139, 145, 146, 148

Gandhi, Mohandas K., 71

Garfinkel, Harold, 84

gay people: hate groups and, 122; moral panics directed at, 126. See also LGBTQ community, shame in; LGBTQ movements

gay pride parades, 140

gender: band of brothers dilemma and, 241n66; emotional intelligence and, 194; gestures and postures related to hierarchies and, 49; moral and political philosophy and, 191-92; patterns of lust and, 226n17; sensitivity to emotional cues and, 52; suppression of emotions and, 149-50. See also men, suppression of fear by; women

gender gap, late twentieth-century, 178

Getting Your Way (Jasper), 10

Giddens, Anthony, 41

Gigerenzer, Gerd, 16, 215nn6-7

Gilbert, Daniel, 208-9

Gilligan, Carol, 131

Gilovich, Thomas, 233n46

Giner-Sorolla, Roger, 214n11

Gitlin, Todd, 63, 64

Glassner, Barry, 40-41

global warming, 95

Glucklich, Ariel, 70, 227n42

goading, 55-56

Goebbels, Joseph, 122

Goffman, Erving: Collins's theory of emotional energy and, 82, 84; on embarrassment, 133, 199, 201; on pain cries, 68; on three types of stigma, 50

Goldhagen, Daniel, 255n45

Goodwin, Jeff, 39-40, 104, 188

Gould, Deborah, 80-81, 87, 96-97, 125, 138, 193, 235n66

government spending: symbolic racism and, 110-11; Trump supporters' attitudes toward, 167-68

Greeks, ancient: anger among, 42-43, 45, 222n29; morality among, 128; politics of emotions among, 171-73. See also Aristotle; Athens, ancient; Plato

Green, Donald, 112

Greenberg, Jerald, 146

grief, 35, 86-87, 96-98

grievances, suddenly imposed, 189-90

Griffiths, Paul, 34

Gross, Jan, 123-24

group attachments, Durkheim on, 183

group attitudes, in Sears's symbolic politics, 110

group boundaries: construction of, 107-8; in cultural approach, 190; encompassing all humankind, 124; hatred and, 123; prolongation of conflict and, 122; within protest groups, 112-13; of us and them, 111-12, 122, 124-25, 239n36. See also collective identities

group competition, hatred and, 123

group loyalties, 106-7, 116-20; morality and, 5, 128, 131, 132; unfairness and, 148. See also collective identities; solidarity

Grupo de Teatro 15 de Mayo, 24

guilt, 62, 136-37

Gulf oil spill of 2010, 152

Gusfield, Joseph, 110

habitus, 214n13, 217n26

Hackett, Edward J., 241n65

Printed and bound by CPI Group (UK) Ltd, Croydon, CR0 4YY

09/06/2025

14685712-0003